WOMEN'S RIGHTS

Selected Titles in ABC-CLIO's Perspectives in American Social History Series

African Americans in the Nineteenth Century: People and Perspectives

American Revolution: People and Perspectives

Baby Boom: People and Perspectives

British Colonial America: People and Perspectives

Civil Rights Movement: People and Perspectives

Civil War: People and Perspectives

Cold War and McCarthy Era: People and Perspectives

Colonial America: People and Perspectives

Early Republic: People and Perspectives

Great Depression: People and Perspectives

Industrial Revolution: People and Perspectives

Jacksonian and Antebellum Age: People and Perspectives

Jazz Age: People and Perspectives

Making of the American West: People and Perspectives

Reconstruction: People and Perspectives

Vietnam War Era: People and Perspectives

PERSPECTIVES IN
AMERICAN SOCIAL HISTORY

Women's Rights

People and Perspectives

Crista DeLuzio, Editor
Peter C. Mancall, Series Editor

A B C ⬤ C L I O

Santa Barbara, California • Denver, Colorado • Oxford, England

"Pre-Introductory Material," from *The Bust Guide to the New Girl Order* by Marcelle Karp and Debbie Stoller, copyright © 1999 by Bust Magazine Enterprises, Inc. Used by permission of Viking Penguin, a division of Penguin Group (USA) Inc.

Library of Congress Cataloging-in-Publication Data

Women's rights : people and perspectives / Crista DeLuzio, editor.
    p. cm. — (Perspectives in American social history)
  Includes bibliographical references and index.
  ISBN 978-1-59884-114-5 (alk. paper) — ISBN 978-1-59884-115-2 (ebook)
1. Women's rights—United States—History. 2. Feminism—United States—
History. I. DeLuzio, Crista, 1966–
  HQ1236.5.U6 W6853 2010
  305.420973—dc22   2009031359

14 13 12 11 10   1 2 3 4 5

This book is also available on the World Wide Web as an eBook.
Visit www.abc-clio.com for details.

ABC-CLIO, LLC
130 Cremona Drive, P.O. Box 1911
Santa Barbara, California 93116–1911

This book is printed on acid-free paper ∞

Manufactured in the United States of America

Contents

Series Introduction

S ocial history is, simply put, the study of past societies. More specifically, social historians attempt to describe societies in their totality, and hence often eschew analysis of politics and ideas. Though many social historians argue that it is impossible to understand how societies functioned without some consideration of the ways that politics works on a daily basis or what ideas could be found circulating at any given time, they tend to pay little attention to the formal arenas of electoral politics or intellectual currents. In the United States, social historians have been engaged in describing components of the population that had earlier often escaped formal analysis, notably women, members of ethnic or cultural minorities, or those who had fewer economic opportunities than had the elite.

Social history became a vibrant discipline in the United States after it had already gained enormous influence in Western Europe. In France, social history in its modern form emerged with the rising prominence of a group of scholars associated with the journal *Annales Economie, Societé, Civilisation* (or *Annales ESC*, as it is known). In its pages and in a series of books from historians affiliated with the École des Hautes Études en Sciences Sociale in Paris, brilliant historians such as Marc Bloch, Jacques Le Goff, and Emanuel LeRoy Ladurie described seemingly every aspect of French society. Among the masterpieces of this historical reconstruction was Fernand Braudel's monumental study, *The Mediterranean and the Mediterranean World in the Age of Philip II*, published first in Paris in 1946 and in a revised edition in English in 1972. In this work, Braudel argued that the only way to understand a place in its totality was to describe its environment, its social and economic structures, and its political systems. In Britain, the emphasis of social historians has been less on questions of environment, per se, than on a description of human communities in all their complexities. For example, social historians there have taken advantage of that nation's remarkable local archives to reconstruct the history of the family and details of its rural past. Works such as Peter Laslett's *The World We Have Lost*, first printed in 1966, and the multiauthored *Agrarian History of England and Wales*, which began to appear in print in 1967, revealed that painstaking work could reveal the lives and habits of individuals who never previously attracted the interest of biographers, demographers, or most historians.

Social history in the United States gained a large following in the second half of the 20th century, especially during the 1960s and 1970s. Its development sprang from political, technical, and intellectual impulses deeply embedded in the culture of the modern university. The politics of civil rights and social reform fueled the passions of historians who strove to tell the stories of the underclass. They benefited from historians' adoption of statistical analysis, which allowed scholars to trace where individuals lived, how often they moved, what kinds of jobs they took, and whether their economic status declined, stagnated, or improved over time. As history departments expanded, many who emerged from graduate schools focused their attention on groups previously ignored or marginalized. Women's history became a central concern among American historians, as did the history of African Americans, Native Americans, Latinos, and others. These historians pushed historical study in the United States farther away from the study of formal politics and intellectual trends. Though few Americanists could achieve the technical brilliance of some social historians in Europe, collectively they have been engaged in a vast act of description, with the goal of describing seemingly every facet of life from 1492 to the present.

The 16 volumes in this series together represent the continuing efforts of historians to describe American society. Most of the volumes focus on chronological areas, from the broad sweep of the colonial era to the more narrowly defined collections of chapters on the eras of the Cold War, the baby boom, and America in the age of the Vietnam War. The series also includes entire volumes on the epochs that defined the nation, the American Revolution, and the Civil War, as well as volumes dedicated to the process of westward expansion, women's rights, and African American history.

This social history series derives its strength from the talented editors of individual volumes. Each editor is an expert in his or her own field, and selected and organized the contents of his or her volume. Editors solicited other experienced historians to write individual chapters. Every volume contains first-rate analysis complemented by lively anecdotes designed to reveal the complex contours of specific historical moments. The many illustrations to be found in these volumes testify to the recognition that any society can be understood not only by the texts that its participants produce but also by the images that they craft. Primary source documents in each volume will allow interested readers to pursue some specific topics in greater depth, and each volume contains a chronology to provide guidance to the flow of events over time. These tools—anecdotes, images, texts, and timelines—allow readers to gauge the inner workings of America in particular periods and yet also to glimpse connections between eras.

The articles in these volumes testify to the abundant strengths of historical scholarship in the United States in the early years of the 21st century. Despite the occasional academic contest that flares into public notice, or the self-serving cant of politicians who want to manipulate the nation's past for partisan ends—for example, in debates over the Second Amendment to the U.S. Constitution and what it means about potential limits to the rights of gun ownership—the articles here all reveal the vast increase in knowledge of the American past that has taken place over the previous half-century. Social historians do not dominate history faculties in American colleges and universities, but no one could deny them a seat at the intellectual table. Without their efforts, intellectual, cultural, and political historians would be hard-pressed to understand why certain ideas circulated when they did, why some religious movements prospered or foundered, how developments in fields such as medicine and engineering reflected larger concerns, and what shaped the world we inhabit.

Fernand Braudel and his colleagues envisioned entire laboratories of historians, in which scholars working together would be able to produce *histoire totale*: total history. Historians today seek more humble goals for our collective enterprise. But as the richly textured chapters in these volumes reveal, scholarly collaboration has in fact brought us much closer to that dream. These volumes do not and cannot include every aspect of American history. However, every page reveals something interesting or valuable about how American society functioned. Together, these books suggest the crucial necessity of stepping back to view the grand complexities of the past rather than pursuing narrower prospects and lesser goals.

Peter C. Mancall
Series Editor

Introduction

In June of 1856, Elizabeth Cady Stanton wrote to her friend Susan B. Anthony, encouraging her to take the long view when charting a course for the work they had recently undertaken on behalf of women's rights. "We cannot bring about a moral revolution in a day or year," Stanton cautioned. "Now that I have two daughters, I feel fresh strength to work. It is not in vain that in myself I have experienced all the wearisome cares to which woman in her best estate is subject." Written from her home in Seneca Falls, New York, which in 1848 served as the site of the first women's rights convention in the United States, Stanton's letter presaged several themes that would remain central to subsequent generations of women's rights activists. Advising that Anthony and others needed to "rest awhile in peace and quietness and think great thoughts for the future" (DuBois 1992, 63), Stanton conceived of a necessarily dynamic relationship between thought and action in the struggle for women's rights. Her assertion that she and her comrades were fomenting a "moral revolution" suggested that securing gender equality would be as much about altering perceptions, beliefs, attitudes, and feelings as about changing laws, policies, and institutions. In reflecting that the at-times restrictive domestic and maternal duties she was compelled to perform propelled her to engage in social critique and activism, Stanton encouraged a recognition of the relationship between the private realm of home and family and larger systems of public power. In identifying that her own "wearisome cares" were common among women, Stanton saw the possibility of female solidarity, even as she alluded to likely variations in women's circumstances. Those same cares also became a source of inspiration for Stanton, and in pledging to work to better her daughters' lives, she spoke to the importance of each generation renewing and sustaining a commitment to women's rights into the future.

Stanton's insight that bringing about a "revolution" in women's rights would require the ongoing efforts of generations of women has proven to be correct. This book explores the struggle for women's rights engaged in by diverse groups of women throughout the course of the history of the United States. Broadly conceived, this struggle has encompassed women's efforts to eliminate gender hierarchy and achieve greater opportunity, autonomy, authority, and fulfillment in public and private life. First and foremost, it has entailed the organized political activity in which women have joined together self-consciously as women and as feminists (a term that did not come into regular usage until the 1910s) in order to challenge gender inequality and facilitate social change. It has also included those expressions of discontent, individual acts of resistance, changes in mind and heart, and articulations of alternative visions of social relations that have not always been immediately or directly manifested within the purview of collective social and political action.

Some feminists and historians have utilized a wave metaphor in conceptualizing and organizing the history of women's rights activism in the United States. According to this scheme, the "First Wave" of women's rights activism was inaugurated with the Seneca Falls convention of 1848 and ended with the passage of the Nineteenth Amendment in 1920, which granted women the right to vote. The "Second Wave" of feminism occurred in the 1960s and 1970s, followed by a "Third Wave" beginning in the early 1990s. The wave metaphor suggests that there have been particular moments when the energies of women's rights activists coalesced and constituted a distinctive, unified, and powerful force for social change. Other feminists and historians, however, have argued that the currents of feminism have flowed more deeply, continuously, and varyingly throughout U.S. history than the wave metaphor allows. This book draws from both approaches, giving ample attention to the major waves of women's rights activism, while also attending to the streams of feminist thought and activism that ran before, between, and within them. Each chapter focuses on a group or several groups of women whose activities and ideas played a role in the struggle for women's rights at a particular historical moment. Sidebars in each chapter tell the story of a notable or representative individual or organization from the larger group. A set of primary source documents allows readers to engage directly with the voices of women whose actions and words in some manner addressed and furthered the cause of women's rights.

Among the various groups of women involved in the struggle for women's rights, some women emerged as prominent theorists, spokeswomen, and political organizers and leaders. Even the names and contributions of such pioneers as Stanton, Anthony, Lucretia Mott, Alice Paul, Mary Church Terrell, Betty Friedan, Aileen Hernandez, and Pauli Murray (just to name a few of the women who appear in these pages) continue to be unfamiliar to many students of U.S. history. Greater numbers of ordinary women played an important role in this struggle, as well, and their words and deeds have also been largely ignored in the historical record. Many Native American women, for example, struggled to sustain the autonomy, influence, and authority they traditionally held in their tribes in the wake of the changes wrought upon their societies by colonization. Within the context of the hierarchical structures of the colonial era, women—whether free, servant, or slave—possessed almost no formal political, economic, or social power, yet many managed to assert some measure of agency in carrying out their responsibilities within the patriarchal household, while others attempted to defy the formidable social imperatives for their subordination. In the years leading up to the American Revolution, many women avidly participated in the boycotting of British goods and the manufacture of homespun clothing, drawing on their traditional activities as domestic consumers and producers to claim an enlarged political role for themselves in the colonists' struggle for independence. Likewise, black and white women in the antebellum North registered forceful protest against the slave system by forming and joining antislavery societies, refusing to use goods produced by slave labor, and conducting an ambitious petition campaign to the U.S. Congress. For some women, participation in the abolitionist cause led them to organize a movement to advocate for their own political, legal, and economic rights during the mid-19th century. During the first two decades of the 20th century, masses of women from across the social spectrum participated in the grassroots politics of local suffrage organizations. Over the course of the 20th century, as more and more women entered the paid labor force, they made increasing demands for opportunities and rights in the workplace, as well as for greater authority in marital and domestic relations at home. This book interweaves the stories of the leaders of the women's rights movement and of the ordinary women who made up its rank and file. In remarkably diverse, creative, and courageous ways—whether speaking in public, founding organizations, lobbying for legislation, participating in strikes, picketing the White House, casting ballots, circulating manifestos, marching in rallies, sharing stories of sexism in small groups, running domestic violence shelters and rape-crisis centers, creating blogs, or playing in all-girl bands—countless women have sought to assert their rights and have made indispensable contributions to furthering the cause of gender equality.

Several themes unite the chapters in this volume. The first is the attention to diversity in the history of the struggle for women's rights. The movement for women's rights was one of the first topics explored by women's historians of the 1960s and 1970s, who were part of a larger cohort of scholars dedicated to writing a history from the bottom up. These historians sought to tell the story of women's efforts to forge bonds with one another in critiquing and seeking to change their role and status in society. Over time, this story has grown to be increasingly multifaceted and complex, as historians have come to recognize that the struggle for women's rights has been marked as much by difference, conflict, and even exclusion as by unity, consensus, and sisterhood. Multiple and intersecting categories of identity—gender, race, ethnicity, class, age, sexual orientation, political inclination, and religious affiliation—shape the entire range of women's experiences, including their responses to the multiple and intersecting forms of social inequality and oppression. As several of these chapters show, at many moments in the past, white, middle-class, heterosexual women involved in the struggle for women's rights uncritically proclaimed their experience of womanhood to be the norm. In speaking for what they deemed to be women's universal needs and interests, they also replicated and reinforced existing forms of racial, class, and sexual discrimination and hierarchy. At the same time, Native American, African American, ethnic minority, working-class, and lesbian women fostered their own conceptions of womanhood and perspectives on women's rights, which were inexorably related to their priorities in achieving tribal sovereignty, racial and ethnic equality, economic justice, and sexual freedom. In the process, they called on all feminists to rethink their understanding of the category of "woman" and to broaden the scope of issues with which their movement might be concerned. Thus, the meaning of women's rights has been contested terrain over the course of U.S. history. An understanding of both the fault lines and the common ground that are the legacy of the past is vital for any effort to make sense of and continue the ongoing struggle to achieve gender equality in the present and future.

A second recurring theme in the history of the struggle for women's rights has been what is often referred to as the "equality-difference paradox." As these chapters reveal, women's rights activists and feminists have long faced the problem of whether gender equality would best be achieved by emphasizing women's sameness with or their differences from men, whether those differences were constituted by biology or culture. As historian Nancy F. Cott explains, "Feminism asks for sexual equality that includes sexual difference . . . It requires gender consciousness for its basis yet calls for the elimination of prescribed gender roles" (Cott 1987, 5). Women's rights advocates and feminists offered different conceptions of and solutions to this conundrum within historical periods and across time. For example, the problem of equality and difference was taken up during the 19th century by those engaged in the debates over the methods and purposes for female education. Were girls better served by educating them in the same manner as boys, or did the differences in their bodies and minds call for different methods of teaching and learning? Would the cause of female education be better advanced by emphasizing that its purpose was to prepare women to pursue the same opportunities as men in the public sphere or to enhance women's roles as wives and mothers? The equality-difference paradox also lay at the heart of the debates among women's rights activists over the Equal Rights Amendment (ERA) for much of the 20th century. Advocates for the ERA believed that women's rights would best be secured by ensuring women's equivalent treatment under the law, while opponents feared that such treatment would threaten sex-based labor laws that provided women with much-needed protections in the workplace.

Although often articulated in mutually exclusive terms, the relationship between equality and difference has been reconciled by women's rights activists in complex and potentially radically transformative ways. Early 20th-century suffragists, for example, simultaneously argued that they must be granted the right to vote because they were individual adult citizens in a democracy and because they would use the vote to exercise their superior moral sensibility as women in order to remake society in accordance with the maternal values of care and compassion. As historian Ruth Rosen points out, even those who have argued on behalf of women's common humanity with men have posed crucial challenges to liberal conceptions of individual rights that have forced an accounting with the realities of women's lives and of gender difference. "For liberal political culture to recast the citizen as a woman and embrace fundamental economic and social transformations in the home and the workplace," she asserts, "required nothing less than an expansion of the definition of democracy." While Rosen concedes that the realization of "a true 'gender democracy'" remains as an unfinished element of the feminist revolution, efforts to establish it continue to alter the meanings of citizenship, work, community, and family life for women *and* men alike (Rosen 2006, 77–78).

As both the theme of diversity and the theme of equality and difference suggest, the story of the history of women's rights in the United States is not marked by a straight line toward inevitable, unequivocal progress. Women have often advocated for their rights from different social positions and perspectives, with the aim of securing different interests and achieving different goals. What one group of women may have hailed as a victory for women's rights, another may have deemed a setback or failure. Certainly, this was the case in the contest over the ERA. It has also been the case for Second and Third Wave feminists as they continue to debate whether sexual harassment, anti-pornography, and anti-prostitution laws protect women from sexual violence and exploitation or infantilize and oppress them by denying them their full rights to sexual responsibility, expression, and pleasure. In addition to disagreement among feminists over what constitutes gender equality and how it might best be achieved, women's rights activists have also faced outright opposition to the advancement of their cause, which constitutes a third theme running through these chapters. Backlash against feminism has been perpetrated in many ways, including by political opposition and repression, judicial challenge, public protest, media ridicule, and individual, collective, and state-sanctioned acts of violence. Such opposition has been overwhelmingly produced and sustained by deeply rooted structures of political, economic, and social power that have created and reproduced male supremacy in its many forms throughout U.S. history. The actions of individuals and groups play a role in constituting structures of social power, of course, and it is the ideas and activities of women who have directly opposed initiatives on behalf of women's rights that is perhaps one of the most surprising aspects of this history. For example, in addition to the potent hostility to woman suffrage by owners and operators of liquor and textile businesses, who feared that women would use the vote to regulate their industries, women formed their own organizations to try to defeat suffrage during the late 19th and early 20th centuries. Likewise, politically conservative women in the 1920s, 1950s, 1970s, and 1980s associated feminism with radical left-wing politics, and organized to thwart the advancement of a range of feminist initiatives, including those on behalf of women's and children's health, international peace, the ERA, and reproductive freedom. More recently, some women have received widespread media attention for writing books bemoaning the betrayals of feminism and extolling the virtues of traditional femininity, thereby joining what Ruth Rosen calls "a long and dishonorable American tradition in which women made careers out of telling other women to stay home with their families" (Rosen 2006, 365). While such women should not be considered feminists, it is worth noting the irony that their ability to claim a public voice for their particular political interests owed much to the legacy of women's rights activism and to feminists' longstanding insistence that women have a vital role to play in the political and intellectual life of the nation.

A fourth theme explored in this volume is the relationship between women's reform activities and women's rights. As noted above, not all of women's politics is feminist politics. Likewise, women's reform activities should not be conflated with women's rights activism. Nonetheless, as several of these chapters show, a vital relationship has long existed between women's participation in movements for social reform and the creation and perpetuation of a movement on behalf of their own rights. During the antebellum period, women's involvement in benevolent organizations; temperance, education, and moral reform efforts; labor organizing; and especially abolitionism enabled them to foster crucial organizational, political, and public speaking skills, as well as encouraged them toward new ways of thinking about social problems and articulating visions of social change. Women reformers also experienced limits in their capacities to achieve their goals because of their subordinate political and legal status, as well as by deliberate efforts of some male reformers to contain their activities within the bounds of the conventional norms of female behavior. These experiences prompted some women to join together to form a movement to secure their own rights, thereby launching the first organized effort for women's rights in U.S. history. A similar pattern abided in the years leading up to the emergence of the Second Wave of feminism in the 1960s. During the two decades following World War II, women from different generations and varying social backgrounds gained political skills, honed modes of social analysis and critique, and experienced painful discrimination through their ongoing involvement in mainstream women's organizations, the labor movement, the Civil Rights movement, the student movements of the New Left, and the antiwar movement. Out of the possibilities and the limits they encountered in these contexts, women again came together to organize a movement focused on the advancement of women's rights and the realization of women's liberation. At other moments, as well, women's involvement in women's rights and other reform efforts was marked by a symbiotic relationship. During the Gilded Age and Progressive Era, many women came to realize that their attempts to establish Prohibition, end child labor, clean up urban neighborhoods, win shorter hours and safer conditions in the industrial workforce, and outlaw lynching were tied to their securing the right to vote. At the same time, during this and other time periods, women involved in a variety of social movements broadened conceptions of what counted as women's issues. They encouraged an expansion of the feminist agenda—beyond the securing of individual economic opportunity and political and legal equality for women—to encompass more far-reaching claims for social transformation and social justice.

A fifth theme developed in these chapters is encapsulated in the famous phrase coined by Second Wave feminists: "the personal is political." The notion that realms of life conventionally considered private and naturally ordained (including sexuality, marriage, reproduction, housework, and motherhood) are shaped by larger structures of social power that can be changed had roots in some variants of 19th-century women's rights activism and early 20th-century feminism. Challenging the boundary between the personal and the political was further advanced by Second Wave feminists, who sought to make women aware of the ways in which sexism shaped all aspects of their lives and to encourage them to act individually and collectively to uproot it. The premise that the personal is political remains fundamental to feminist thinking and politics today. Even so, some contemporary feminists claim that misinterpretations of this idea have undermined feminist unity and progress, especially in the tendency of some feminists to rely on personal lifestyle choices as a litmus test for true feminism, and in the proclivity of other feminists to claim individual acts of self-expression as a substitute for collective political action. These chapters reveal the longevity of the notion that there are political dimensions to private life, as well as the variety of ways in which the relationship between the public and the private has been conceptualized by women's rights activists and feminists over time.

A sixth theme explored in this volume is the role of education in furthering the advancement of women's rights. A sustained debate about female education began in the United States in the post–Revolutionary War period. In this and in subsequent eras, not all those arguing for expanded educational opportunity for girls and women supported the full political, legal, economic, and social equality of women. Indeed, many made the case that girls and women should be educated primarily to better fulfill their domestic roles and responsibilities in the private sphere. All women's rights activists and feminists, however, have been avid advocates of female education. They have insisted that girls and women have the same capacity as boys and men for intellectual and moral development, and thereby have an equal right to cultivate their minds as far as and in whatever directions their individual abilities and inclinations can take them. In addition to claiming for girls and women equal opportunity to master conventional academic subjects, feminists have also embraced education about women's lives and women's history as a vital tool for developing gender consciousness and fostering women's rights activism. Women need knowledge about women's experiences in their own time, feminists have contended, so that they can situate the individual challenges they face in relation to larger patterns of gender hierarchy, and glean possibilities for collectively mobilizing against them. Women need knowledge of women's lives in the past, as well, so that they can see that women's roles and status are not natural or inevitable, but are the products of social and historical conditions that can be changed. Furthermore, any education about women's history must include knowledge about the history of the struggle for women's rights, for that has been one of the primary agents of change in women's lives across time.

The dangers of forgetting this history are great. As Stanton predicted, and as is revealed in a final theme that connects the chapters in this volume, the revolution in women's rights has been perpetuated and recreated over the course of U.S. history, and is, as yet, incomplete and ongoing. As this history attests, women have experienced significant gains since the 16th century, especially in the securing of their political and legal rights. But many inequalities and injustices remain. Women in contemporary society wrestle with such problems as job discrimination, unequal pay, poverty, sexual objectification, sexual harassment, domestic violence, racism, homophobia, and limits on their reproductive freedom, as well as threats to their health and to the well-being of their families and communities from environmental destruction. They also face enduring cultural expectations that they will be the primary caretakers of home and family life, even as their public roles and responsibilities continue to expand. The tenacity and prevalence of these and other challenges mean that women must persist in joining together to fight for their rights into the future. This collective mobilization will continue to be made possible, in part, by women's awareness and understanding of the long history, both inspirational and disconcerting, of women's efforts to achieve gender equality. Indeed, many Second Wave feminists have expressed anger and regret that they were required to undertake their activism in the 1960s and 1970s with little knowledge about the attempts to secure women's rights that had been carried out by generations of women before them (Evans 2003, 5). Some of them sought to rectify this by devoting themselves to the creation of the scholarly field of women's history. This book is a beneficiary of those efforts and, in some small way, hopes to make a contribution to them, for it begins with the assumption that in knowing about their past, women will be better prepared to comprehend the challenges of the present and to envision their way into a more equitable and just future.

References and Further Reading

Cott, Nancy F. *The Grounding of Modern Feminism*. New Haven, CT: Yale University Press, 1987.

Dubois, Ellen Carol, ed. *Elizabeth Cady Stanton & Susan B. Anthony: Correspondence, Writings, Speeches*. Rev. ed. Boston: Northeastern University Press, 1992.

Evans, Sara M. *Tidal Wave: How Women Changed America at Century's End*. New York: Free Press, 2003.

Rosen, Ruth. *The World Split Open: How the Modern Women's Movement Changed America*. Rev. ed. New York: Penguin Books, 2006.

About the Editor and Contributors

Crista DeLuzio is Associate Professor in the William P. Clements Department of History at Southern Methodist University, where she teaches courses on the history of women, children, and families in the Unites States, including a seminar on the history of women's rights. DeLuzio received her PhD from the Department of American Civilization at Brown University. She is the author of *Female Adolescence in American Scientific Thought, 1830–1930*, which was published by the Johns Hopkins University Press in 2007. Her current research focuses on the history of sibling relationships in American thought and culture at the turn of the 20th century.

Susan Goodier was awarded a PhD in history from the University at Albany, NY in May 2007. She teaches Women's History, U.S. History, and World History at the State University of New York Institute of Technology in Utica. An article, "'To Establish the Liberty of Conscience and the Legal Status of Women': Rebecca Shelley and her Struggle for U.S. Citizenship," is forthcoming from the *Michigan Historical Review*. A recent Margaret Storrs Grierson Scholar-in-Residence Fellowship at the Sophia Smith Collection, Smith College, Northampton, MA facilitated her newest project, "Reward or Punishment? Suffrage and Women's Work during the Great War, 1914–1918."

Andrea Hamilton received an MA from Indiana University and a PhD in History from Tulane University. Her research has focused on the history of American education and women's history in the 19th and 20th centuries. She is the author of *A Vision for Girls: Gender, Education, and the Bryn Mawr School*, published by the Johns Hopkins University Press. She currently lectures at Southern Methodist University in Dallas, Texas.

Julie Holcomb is a Lecturer in Museum Studies at Baylor University. Prior to her appointment at Baylor, Ms. Holcomb served as Director of the Pearce Civil War and Western Art Museums at Navarro College. A doctoral candidate in history at the University of Texas at Arlington, her dissertation research focuses on the role of women in the transatlantic free produce and antislavery movements. In 2009, Ms. Holcomb was selected for Baylor University's Summer Faculty Institute and was named a finalist for a Woodrow

Wilson Dissertation Fellowship in Women's Studies. Her publications include *Southern Sons, Northern Soldiers: The Civil War Letters of the Remley Brothers, 22nd Iowa Infantry* (Northern Illinois University Press, 2004), numerous encyclopedia entries and book reviews, and an essay "'Tell It Like It Was': Texas, the Civil War, and Public History," which was published in *The Fate of Texas: The Civil War and the Lone Star State* (University of Arkansas Press, 2008).

Pia Katarina Jakobsson received her PhD in the History of Ideas from the University of Texas at Dallas in 2009. Her current research includes a project on gender performance in British satirical prints in the 18th century, and tracing the publication history of a satire on vanity over two continents and three centuries. She currently works as a Lecturer at the University of Texas at Dallas.

Kathleen A. Laughlin is professor of history at Metropolitan State University, St. Paul, MN. She received her PhD in history from Ohio State University in 1993. She specializes in U.S. public policy and women's political activism after World War II. Her book on the history of the Women's Bureau, U.S. Department of Labor, was published by Northeastern University Press in 2000. She is coeditor of a forthcoming anthology, *Breaking the Wave: Women, Their Organizations, and Feminism, 1945–1982,* to be published by Routledge.

Gillian Nichols-Smith received her JD from Chicago-Kent College of Law, with a Certificate in International and Comparative Law. She holds a BA in Gender and Women's Studies from the University of Illinois at Urbana-Champaign, where she wrote her thesis on sexual violence as a weapon of war. Her research and writing contributions can be found in a variety of academic journals. She is currently working as an attorney in Chicago, IL.

Janice Okoomian holds a PhD in American Civilization from Brown University and teaches Women's Studies and Cultural Studies at Bryant University and Rhode Island College. She has published in Armenian American women's literature, racial identity, and the body. As a ritual artist, Ms. Okoomian creates and conducts ceremonies that draw upon practices from diverse cultural traditions. She is currently at work on a book about creative ritual practice for contemporary times.

Alison M. Parker is Associate Professor and Chair of the History Department at SUNY, College at Brockport. She received her PhD and MA from the Johns Hopkins University, and her BA from the University of California, Berkeley. Parker is the author of *Purifying America: Women, Cultural Reform, and Pro-Censorship Activism, 1873–1933* (University of Illinois Press, 1997). Her new book is entitled *Articulating Rights: Nineteenth-Century Women on Race, Reform and the State* (Northern Illinois University Press, 2010). She is also coeditor of the Gender and Race in American History series, University of Rochester Press.

Amy Meschke Porter is an assistant professor of history at Texas A & M University, San Antonio. She recently published "The Women of San Esteban do Nueva Tlaxcala: Cultural Adaptation and Persistence in Their Last Will and Testaments, 1750–1828" in the April 2008 issue of *The Journal of South*

Texas. Porter earned her PhD from Southern Methodist University in 2004 and is currently working on a manuscript that examines women and inheritance in the Spanish and Mexican borderlands.

Jessica O'Brien Pursell received her MA in History from the University of Southern Illinois, where she began researching the changing role of women in the 20th century. She is currently teaching history at a rural high school before pursuing her PhD.

Jeffrey M. Schulze received his PhD from Southern Methodist University in 2008, and is currently a Senior Lecturer at the University of Texas at Dallas. He is the author of "The Rediscovery of the Tiguas: Federal Recognition and Indianness in the Twentieth Century," published in the *Southwestern Historical Quarterly* in 2001, as well as "'The Year of the Yaqui': Texas Tech's Sonoran Expeditions, 1934–1984," which will appear in a forthcoming issue of the *Journal of the West.* He is currently revising his dissertation, entitled *Trans-Nations: Indians, Imagined Communities, and Border Realities in the Twentieth Century,* for publication.

Natasha Zaretsky is an associate professor of history at Southern Illinois University at Carbondale. She received her PhD from the Department of American Civilization at Brown University in 2003. Her essays have appeared in *The World the Sixties Made: Culture and Politics in Recent America* (Temple University Press, 2003) and *Race, Nation, and Empire in American History* (University of North Carolina Press, 2007). Her book, *No Direction Home: The American Family and the Fear of National Decline, 1968–1980,* was published by the University of North Carolina Press in 2007.

Chronology

12,000 BCE   Evidence indicates human habitation of the Americas.

c. 1450 CE   Iroquois Confederacy is founded.

1492–1504   Christopher Columbus voyages to the New World.

1520   Epidemics of Old World diseases break out in the Americas.

1565   The Spanish found Saint Augustine, Florida.

c. 1595   Pocahontas is born.

1598   The Spanish found New Mexico.

c. 1600   The Powhatan confederacy is established.

1607   The English found Jamestown, Virginia.

1608   The French found Quebec.

1617   Pocahontas dies in England after a failed attempt to incorporate the English into the Powhatan Confederacy through her "diplomatic marriage" to John Rolfe.

1619   The first African slaves arrive in Virginia.

1620   The Pilgrims establish Plymouth, Massachusetts.

1624   The Dutch establish the colony of New Netherland.

1629   The Puritans establish Massachusetts Bay Colony.

1636   Roger Williams establishes Rhode Island.

1636–1638   Anne Hutchinson leads Bible discussions in her Boston home and challenges the Massachusetts authorities who put her on trial. She is excommunicated and expelled from Massachusetts Bay colony.

1643   Virginia colonists pass a law requiring household heads to pay a tax on "Negro women," thereby defining these women as workers. This law ignores the fact that many white women perform similar labor and lowers the status of black women.

1650 Anne Bradstreet's first collection of poetry, *The Tenth Muse Lately Sprung Up in America, By a Gentlewoman of Those Parts*, is published.

1662 Virginia passes a law that dictates that children born to slave mothers are slaves. The same law doubles the fines for fornication between an African and a white person, making interracial sex illegal.

1664 The English invade New Netherland and rename the colony New York.

1670 The English found the colony of South Carolina.

1675–1676 New England Algonquians under the leadership of Metacom, known by the English as King Philip, join together to fight the English settlers in New England in King Philip's War.

1676 Nathanial Bacon leads a rebellion consisting primarily of formerly indentured servants in Virginia. Bacon's group attacks Indians and then burns Jamestown.

1682 Mary Rowlandson publishes *Sovereignty and Goodness of God*, which chronicles her capture and imprisonment among Narragansett Indians in Massachusetts during King Philip's War.

1692 The Salem witch trials begin because several young women accuse some women and men of practicing witchcraft. The colonial governor of Massachusetts halts the trials in 1693.

1702 Pierre Le Moyne d'Iberville founds Mobile (in present-day Alabama), giving the French a strong claim to the Louisiana area.

1727 Ursuline nuns open a convent in New Orleans.

1730s–1770s The Great Awakening occurs in the British colonies of the present-day United States as ministers from different Protestant denominations lead religious revivals. The revivals begin in the Middle and New England Colonies and spread to the South by the 1750s.

1738 At age 15, Eliza Lucas (Pickney) moves with her family to South Carolina, where she soon begins to experiment with growing the indigo plant.

1742 Bethlehem Female Seminary (now coed Moravian College) is founded in Pennsylvania, the first American boarding school for young women.

1754–1763 The French and Indian War, also known as the Seven Years' War, is fought between the French and the English and their Indian allies in the Americas and spreads to Europe. Many colonial men die in the war, leaving women widowed and children orphaned. The war also highlights differences between English and American culture.

1763 The French cede Louisiana to the Spanish.

1764 The British impose the Sugar Act on the American colonies, which enforces duties on non-British imports of molasses and refined sugar.

1765   The British Parliament passes the highly unpopular Stamp Act, which imposes a tax on printed paper and documents such as wills, newspapers, and playing cards.

       Colonists begin boycotting British goods.

1767   The British Parliament passes the Townshend Duties, which taxes ordinary items imported into the American colonies, including tea.

1769   The Spanish begin settlements in California.

1772   Mercy Otis Warren publishes *The Adulateur,* a satirical play directed against the British Governor of Massachusetts, Thomas Hutchinson.

       The Little Girls' School (now Salem College) is founded. It is one of the first schools to accept non-white students.

1773   Colonists organize the Boston Tea Party. In protest against the Tea Act, which gave the East India Company a monopoly over the importing of tea to America, a group of men dressed in Native American clothing walk aboard the company's three tea ships in Boston Harbor and throw all the tea overboard.

1774   The women of Edenton, North Carolina sign a nonconsumption agreement, solemnly declaring that they would not drink tea.

1775   The first armed confrontations of the American Revolution take place at Lexington and Concord.

1776   Abigail Adams writes to her husband, John, asking him and his colleagues in the Continental Congress to "remember the ladies" as they undertake the task of forming a new government.

       The Declaration of Independence is signed by the representatives of all 13 states.

       New Jersey adopts a state constitution that allows women to vote, a measure that remains in place until 1807.

1777   Printer and postmaster of Baltimore, Mary Katherine Goddard, prints the first copies of the Declaration of Independence with all the signatures affixed.

       The Articles of Confederation, America's first constitution, are adopted by the Continental Congress. The Articles are ratified in 1781.

1778   Mary Hays McCauley, mythologized as "Molly Pitcher," takes over her husband's cannon when he is wounded in the battle of Monmouth, NJ.

1780   Esther DeBerdt Reed, wife of the governor of Pennsylvania, and Sarah Franklin Bache, daughter of Benjamin Franklin, organize women's fundraising on behalf of the Patriot cause, under the name of the Ladies Association of Philadelphia.

1781   The British surrender at Yorktown.

1782   Deborah Sampson enlists in the Continental Army.

1783   The Treaty of Paris is signed, officially ending the American Revolution.

1787   Benjamin Rush's *Thoughts upon Female Education* is published.

1788   The U.S. Constitution is adopted.

1790s The Second Great Awakening begins.

1790   Judith Sargent Murray publishes "On the Equality of the Sexes."

Catharine Macaulay publishes *Letters on Education,* arguing that women should be educated the same as men in order for women to be useful members of society, as well as good wives and mothers.

1792   British author Mary Wollstonecraft's *A Vindication of the Rights of Woman,* which asserts the equality of women, is published.

The Litchfield Female Academy is founded.

1797   The New York Society for the Relief of Poor Women with Small Children is established.

1800   The Boston Female Asylum is organized.

1807   England bans the international slave trade.

1808   The United States bans the international slave trade.

1814   The Association for the Relief of Respectable, Aged, and Indigent Females is formed.

1817   The American Colonization Society organizes, which pledges to return freed slaves and free blacks to Africa.

1819   An economic crisis, known as the Panic of 1819, ensues, causing business failures, unemployment, and widespread human suffering.

1820   Congress passes the Missouri Compromise, admitting Missouri as a slave state and Maine as a free state. Moreover, Congress limits slavery in Louisiana Purchase lands to areas south of latitude 36° 30'.

1821   Mexico becomes independent of Spain.

Emma Willard opens the Troy Female Seminary in New York, a school that offers serious academic study to young women at a time when no colleges or universities will admit them.

Catharine Beecher, an outspoken advocate for better-quality female education and a female teaching force, opens her school in Hartford, Connecticut.

1824   The American Sunday School Union is organized.

Women in Boston organize a ladies auxiliary for the Boston Penitent Females' Refuge, which was established in 1819.

British Quaker Elizabeth Heyrick publishes *Immediate, Not Gradual Abolition.*

1826   The American Temperance Society is formed.

The American Home Missionary Society is established.

1828   Scottish-born Frances Wright is the first woman to address a "promiscuous," or mixed-gender, American audience.

American Quakers divide over doctrinal and secular issues, including abolitionism, and go on to form Orthodox and Hicksite meetings.

1829   The Female Association for Promoting the Manufacture and Use of Free Cotton organizes in Philadelphia.

1830   Congress passes the Indian Removal Act, which targets Indian groups living in the present-day Southeast, including the Cherokees.

1831   The Colored Female Free Produce Society organizes in Philadelphia.

William Lloyd Garrison begins publication of *The Liberator.*

1832   African American women found the first female antislavery society in Salem, Massachusetts.

1833   Oberlin College, founded by abolitionists, admits women and African Americans, and becomes the first coeducational college in the United States.

Prudence Crandall opens a school for African American girls in Connecticut but soon closes it in the face of legal action and threats against her and her students.

The American Anti-Slavery Society is organized. Lucretia Mott helps write the Declaration of Sentiments.

The Philadelphia Female Anti-Slavery Society is organized.

The Female Society of Lynn (Massachusetts) is organized for the protection and promotion of female workers.

1834   Women operators in Lowell, Massachusetts "turn out," or strike, in protest against a proposed wage reduction.

The New York Female Moral Reform Society is organized.

1836   Sarah and Angelina Grimké begin their antislavery speaking career.

Congress passes a gag rule requiring the tabling of antislavery petitions.

1837   Economic panic begins major depression.

Horace Mann becomes Secretary of Education for Massachusetts, and uses his position to promote the spread and improvement of common schools for girls and boys.

Mary Lyon's Mount Holyoke Seminary opens in South Hadley, Massachusetts, promising to provide girls from modest backgrounds with education and preparation for teaching.

The first Anti-Slavery Convention of Women meets in New York.

Abolitionists Sarah and Angelina Grimké are rebuked by the Congregational General Association of Massachusetts for speaking in public before audiences of men and women.

1838   The second Anti-Slavery Convention of Women meets at Pennsylvania Hall in Philadelphia. The meeting is disrupted when an anti-abolitionist mob burns the hall.

After many failed attempts to challenge removal legislation, a sizeable contingent of Cherokee Indians is removed to present-day Oklahoma via the Trail of Tears.

1839   Mississippi passes the first Married Woman's Property Act.

The third and final Anti-Slavery Convention of Women meets in Philadelphia.

1840   Abby Kelley is appointed to the Business Committee of the American Anti-Slavery Society. Led by Lewis Tappan, opponents of Kelley's appointment and of women's abolitionist activism separate and form the American and Foreign Anti-Slavery Society.

The first World's Anti-Slavery Convention is held in London. British organizers refuse to seat the American female delegates. William Lloyd Garrison chooses to sit with the women in the balcony rather than be recognized as a delegate to the convention. As a result of their treatment at the convention, Lucretia Mott and Elizabeth Cady Stanton resolve to call a convention to advocate for women's rights upon their return to the United States.

1843   Dorothea Dix exposes treatment of the insane in Memorial to the Legislature of Massachusetts.

1848   The New York state legislature passes the Married Woman's Property Act, which becomes a model for similar legislation in other states.

Radical Hicksite Quakers leave the Genesee Yearly Meeting and form the Congregational, or Progressive, Friends.

The first women's rights convention is held in Seneca Falls, New York. The Declaration of Sentiments is signed by 100 of the participants. This marks the birth of an organized movement for women's rights.

1849   Elizabeth Blackwell receives the first medical degree awarded to a woman, and goes on to found a medical school for women.

1850   The Fugitive Slave Act is passed. It imposes stiff penalties for aiding fugitive slaves.

The first National Women's Rights Convention is held in Worcester, Massachusetts.

1851   Sojourner Truth draws on her experiences as a black woman to deliver a speech in favor of women's rights in Akron, Ohio.

Elizabeth Cady Stanton and Susan B. Anthony meet, beginning their friendship and collaboration in the cause for women's rights.

1852   Harriet Beecher Stowe publishes *Uncle Tom's Cabin*.

The New York State Women's Temperance Society is formed.

1855   Martha Coffin Wright, sister of Lucretia Mott, chairs the Woman's Rights Convention in Saratoga, New York.

1860   The New York State Legislature passes a second Married Woman's Property Act, which is more comprehensive than the 1848 law.

         Southern states begin to secede from the Union.

1861–1865   The United States is embroiled in civil war.

1863   Lincoln issues the Emancipation Proclamation.

         Elizabeth Cady Stanton and Susan B. Anthony organize the Woman's National Loyal League, which petitions Congress to pass an amendment abolishing slavery.

1865   Vassar College opens, followed by other Seven Sister colleges in the 1870s and 1880s.

         The Thirteenth Amendment is adopted, abolishing slavery.

1866   The American Equal Rights Association is formed.

1868   The Fourteenth Amendment to the United States Constitution is ratified, granting all rights and privileges of the Constitution to men regardless of race. This is the first time the word "male" appears in the Constitution.

         The Hampton Normal and Agricultural Institute opens to educate African American women and men. The school sets a model for industrial education as a means of raising African Americans out of poverty.

         The first secular women's clubs—Sorosis, and the New England Woman's Club—are formed.

1869   The American Equal Rights Association splits to form the National Woman Suffrage Association and the American Woman Suffrage Association.

         Wyoming Territory grants women the right to vote on equal terms with men. When Wyoming is admitted to the Union in 1890, it becomes the first state with woman suffrage.

1870   The Fifteenth Amendment to the United States Constitution is ratified, guaranteeing the voting rights of African American men.

         Women in Utah Territory are enfranchised. The right is revoked in 1887.

1872   Susan B. Anthony is arrested for attempting to vote based on her interpretation of the Fourteenth and Fifteenth Amendments.

1873   Dr. Edward H. Clarke's *Sex in Education; Or, A Fair Chance for the Girls* is published and makes nominally scientific arguments about the dangers that pursuit of higher education pose for young women's health.

1874   The National Woman's Christian Temperance Union (WCTU) is founded, following an evangelical Women's Crusade against alcohol in the Midwest.

1875   The U.S. Supreme Court issues its decision in the *Minor v. Happersett* case. The Court declares that voting is not a right of citizenship. Woman suffrage advocates realize they will not be granted voting rights on the basis of the Fourteenth and Fifteenth Amendments, and that a separate constitutional amendment is needed to guarantee women's equal political rights.

1879   Frances E. Willard becomes president of the Woman's Christian Temperance Union, a position she holds until her death in 1898.

1881–1922   The *History of Woman Suffrage* is published (6 volumes).

1883   *Life among the Paiutes: Their Wrongs and Claims* by Sarah Winnemucca is published. It is the first book published in English by a Native American woman.

1885   Bryn Mawr College opens, with M. Carey Thomas vowing to offer an academic education as rigorous as that of the best colleges open to men.

The extermination of the Plains' buffalo herds is completed.

1886   In the Haymarket Tragedy, a bombing at a rally for striking workers kills seven police officers. Leading anarchists are wrongly blamed for the bombing and are given death sentences.

1887   Congress passes the Dawes Severalty Act, an assimilationist policy that carves up many reservations into private allotments in an attempt to undercut communal landholding patterns in Indian country.

1889   Hull House, the first settlement house in the United States, is founded in Chicago, Illinois, by Jane Addams and Ellen Gates Starr.

1890   The National American Woman Suffrage Association (NAWSA) is formed, reuniting the two factions of the suffrage movement.

The General Federation of Women's Clubs is formed by Jane Cunningham Croly.

The Wounded Knee Massacre in South Dakota marks the symbolic end of Plains Indian resistance.

1891   Ida B. Wells-Barnett begins her anti-lynching campaign.

1892   A new national political party, the People's or Populist Party, is the first to formally endorse a constitutional amendment to secure women's right to vote.

1893   Colorado women are enfranchised.

Settlement house resident, lawyer, and labor activist Florence Kelley successfully promotes protective labor laws for women and children in Illinois.

1895   Elizabeth Cady Stanton publishes *The Woman's Bible* and is ostracized by many in the NAWSA.

Utah women are enfranchised (again). The right is retained when Utah becomes a state in 1896.

1896   Idaho enfranchises women.

The U.S. Supreme Court decides *Plessy v. Ferguson,* giving federal sanction to segregation laws, on the basis that facilities and transportation can be "separate and equal."

Black clubwomen form the National Association of Colored Women, and elect Mary Church Terrell as their first president.

1900 Carrie Chapman Catt replaces Susan B. Anthony as president of the NAWSA.

Zitkala-Sa publishes *The School Days of an Indian Girl,* which recollects the experiences of a young girl in an Indian boarding school.

1903 The National Women's Trade Union League, an alliance of elite and laboring women, works on behalf of better wages, conditions, and hours for working women.

1904 Mary McCloud Bethune opens the Daytona School for Negro Girls, based on the industrial education model, and becomes a national figure promoting the rights of African American women.

1908 The U.S. Supreme Court decides *Muller v. Oregon,* allowing for protective labor laws for women, based on their ostensible physical weakness and status as mothers and potential mothers.

1909 In what is known as "the Uprising of the Twenty Thousand," a Jewish immigrant, Clara Lemlich, inspires between twenty thousand and thirty thousand mostly female garment workers in New York City to walk off their jobs to protest cuts in wages and bad working conditions.

1910 The women of Washington State are enfranchised.

1911 California women are enfranchised.

The Triangle Shirtwaist Factory fire raises awareness of the need for safety regulations.

1912 The Progressive Party endorses woman suffrage.

Kansas, Oregon, and Arizona enfranchise women.

The Bread and Roses strike in Lawrence, Massachusetts unites textile workers from over 30 countries under the leadership of the International Workers of the World (IWW).

The Federal Children's Bureau is created in the Department of Labor.

1913 Alice Paul and Lucy Burns form the Congressional Union.

The first national suffrage parade is held in Washington, D.C.

1914 The General Federation of Women's Clubs formally endorses woman suffrage.

Margaret Sanger publishes the *Woman Rebel,* and is charged with violating the 1873 Comstock Act for distributing birth control information.

Montana and Nevada enfranchise women.

1915 Woman suffrage referenda campaigns fail in Massachusetts, New York, New Jersey, and Pennsylvania.

The Woman's Peace Party is formed, with Jane Addams as its first chair.

Jane Addams helps establish the International Committee of Women for Permanent Peace (ICWPP) (renamed the Women's International League for Peace and Freedom in 1919).

1916   NAWSA president Carrie Chapman Catt introduces what she calls her "winning plan" in the campaign for suffrage.

Jeannette Rankin of Montana is elected as the first female member of Congress.

The National Woman's Party is formed.

Margaret Sanger opens the first birth control clinic in Brooklyn, New York, for mostly Jewish and Italian immigrant wives and mothers. Over 400 patients are assisted before police close the clinic nine days later for violating "obscenity" laws.

1917   The National Woman's Party begins picketing the White House to protest President Wilson's and the Democratic Party's failure to support woman suffrage.

The United States Congress declares war on Germany, and the United States enters the Great War.

New York women are enfranchised.

1918   Oklahoma, South Dakota, and Michigan women are enfranchised.

The Armistice ending World War I is signed in November.

1919   The Eighteenth Amendment (Prohibition) is ratified.

The International Committee of Women for Permanent Peace is reorganized as the Women's International League for Peace and Freedom (WILPF).

1920   The Federal Women's Bureau is established.

The Nineteenth Amendment, guaranteeing women the right to vote, is added to the U.S. Constitution on August 26.

The National American Woman Suffrage Association becomes the League of Women Voters (LWV).

The Women's Joint Congressional Committee (WJCC) is founded.

The Council for Interracial Cooperation (CIC) is founded.

Crystal Eastman co-founds the American Civil Liberties Union.

Women comprise almost half of the college student population and receive almost one-third of all graduate degrees.

1921   The Sheppard-Towner Maternity and Infancy Protection Act provides funds for health information for mothers.

Congress establishes first immigration quotas.

Amelia Earhart takes her first flying lesson from Neta Snook.

The Women Pioneers statue is dedicated in the U.S. Capitol crypt.

The first Miss America Pageant is held in Atlantic City, New Jersey.

Margaret Sanger founds the American Birth Control League (eventually the Planned Parenthood Federation of America).

Josephine Baker's career is launched with her appearance in the traveling musical *Shuffle Along*.

Edith Wharton becomes the first woman to win a Pulitzer Prize for literature for her novel, *The Age of Innocence*.

Zona Gale becomes the first woman to win a Pulitzer Prize for drama, for her play, *Miss Lulu Bett*.

1922 Mary B. Talbert organizes an executive committee of 15 black women to supervise women all over the country in an Anti-Lynching Crusade.

The National Council of Women, representing 13 million women, endorses the Anti-Lynching Crusade.

1923 The National Woman's Party proposes an Equal Rights Amendment to the Constitution.

Bessie Smith records "Down Hearted Blues" for Columbia Records.

Edna St. Vincent Millay is the first woman to be awarded the Pulitzer Prize for poetry.

Margaret Sanger opens the Birth Control Clinical Research Bureau.

1924 The federal government grants citizenship to all Indians.

The Johnson-Reed Immigration Act further limits immigration.

Evangelist Aimee Semple McPherson opens the Angelus Temple in Los Angeles.

1925 Florence Sabin becomes the first female member of the National Academy of Sciences.

Mary Breckinridge organizes the Frontier Nursing Service in Kentucky.

Zora Neale Hurston registers her play, *Meet the Mama*, for copyright.

Striptease dancing is invented when a dancer's shoulder strap breaks during a police raid at Minsky's Burlesque House in New York City.

F. Scott Fitzgerald's *The Great Gatsby* is published.

1926 Bertha K. Landes is elected mayor of Seattle, the first woman to lead a major American city.

1928 Margaret Mead publishes *Coming of Age in Samoa*.

1929 The stock market crashes.

Under the pseudonym, Carolyn Keene, Mildred Augustine Wirt Benson contracts to write the first three Nancy Drew mysteries, including *The Secret of the Old Clock*.

Gerty and Carl Cori develop the Cori Cycle theory to explain movement of energy in the body. In 1947, Gerty Cori becomes the first American woman to win a Noble Prize in Science.

1931   Jane Addams wins a Nobel Peace Prize for her work for international peace and arbitration.

1932   Section 213 of the National Economy Act is passed, requiring that only one family member be employed by the federal government.

Molly W. Dewson becomes director of the Women's Division of the Democratic National Committee.

1933   Eleanor Roosevelt becomes First Lady when Franklin D. Roosevelt is sworn in as president of the United States.

Frances Perkins becomes Secretary of Labor and the first woman cabinet member.

Ellen S. Woodward becomes director of the Women's Division of the Federal Emergency Relief Administration (FERA).

Prohibition is repealed.

1934   Congress passes the Indian Reorganization Act, which overturns the Dawes Act and attempts to shore up reservation economies and revitalize tribal cultures.

1935   The Social Security Act is passed.

The Congress of Industrial Organizations (CIO) is founded.

1936   *United States v. One Package of Japanese Pessaries* holds that contraception information is not obscene and can be sent through the U.S. mail.

Mary McLeod Bethune becomes the head of Negro Affairs of the National Youth Administration (NYA).

1937   Women organize the Women's Emergency Brigade and carry out militant activities in support of the autoworkers' sit-down strike in Flint, Michigan.

1938   The Fair Labor Standards Act is passed.

1939   World War II begins in Europe.

1941   Pearl Harbor is bombed and the United States enters World War II.

The War Advertising Council (WAC) is established.

1942   Women are recruited into defense jobs and the military.

The Office of War Information (OWI) is established.

President Roosevelt orders that people of Japanese heritage on the West Coast be confined to relocation camps.

1944   Congress passes the GI Bill of Rights.

1945   The United States drops atomic bombs on Hiroshima and Nagasaki.

World War II ends when Japan surrenders.

The Cold War era begins.

Reconversion of women war workers begins, and many are fired.

The United Nations is founded by 58 nations, which sign the Charter of the United Nations to mediate conflicts among members.

1946   The baby boom begins.

Seventy-five percent of women who worked during the war are employed, most at lower wages.

The United Automobile Workers Conference is held, at which the Women's Bureau is made a part of the Fair Practices and Anti-Discrimination Department.

1950   Congress passes the Internal Security Act (McCarran Act), requiring communist organizations to register with the federal government.

1953   The Democratic National Committee disbands the Women's Division.

Congress passes House Concurrent Resolution 108, commonly referred to as the "termination policy," which attempts to sever the trust relationship between the federal government and the nation's reservation-based Indians.

1957   The National Manpower Commission publishes the influential report, *Womanpower*.

1956   Congress passes the Federal-Aid Highway Act, also known as the National Interstate and Defense Highway Act. The act provides federal appropriations for an interstate highway system.

1961   President John F. Kennedy establishes the President's Commission on the Status of Women.

The birth control pill, approved a year earlier, is made available.

1962   Helen Gurley Brown publishes her best selling *Sex and the Single Girl*.

1963   The President's Commission on the Status of Women publishes its findings in a report entitled *The American Woman*.

Betty Friedan publishes *The Feminine Mystique*.

Congress passes the Equal Pay Act.

1964   Congress passes the Civil Rights Act. Title VII of the act prohibits discrimination in employment.

1965   President Lyndon Johnson signs an Executive Order requiring that federal contractors undertake affirmative action in hiring racial minorities.

Women activists in Students for a Democratic Society (SDS), a New Left organization, meet alone for the first time to discuss sexism.

1966   The Third Annual Conference on the Status of Women is held, where a group of women create the National Organization for Women (NOW).

NOW demands that the Equal Employment Opportunities Commission (EEOC) end job classifications that are segregated by sex.

1967   President Johnson extends affirmative action policy to women.

The Chicago Women's Liberation Group and New York Radical Women are formed.

1968   Members of New York Radical Women begin forming consciousness-raising groups.

Shirley Chisholm is the first African American woman to be elected to Congress.

Women who oppose NOW's enforcement of legalized abortion form the Women's Equity Action League (WEAL).

Radical feminists in New York publish *Notes from the First Year.*

New York women's liberation activists stage a protest against the Miss America pageant in Atlantic City.

The American Indian Movement (AIM) is founded.

1969   Members of the Redstockings demand the repeal of abortion laws at the New York State Legislature.

1970   Bella Abzug is elected to Congress.

Shulamith Firestone publishes *The Dialectic of Sex;* Kate Millet publishes *Sexual Politics;* and Robin Morgan publishes *Sisterhood is Powerful.*

In August in New York City, fifty thousand march to commemorate the 50th anniversary of woman suffrage in the Women's Strike for Equality.

1971   New York Radical Women holds it first "Speak Out on Rape."

The National Women's Political Caucus is founded.

The first feminist women's health center is founded in Los Angeles.

President Richard Nixon vetoes the Comprehensive Child Development Bill.

1972   The Equal Rights Amendment (ERA) passes both houses of Congress.

Congress passes Title IX of the 1972 Educational Amendment of the Civil Rights Act, requiring sex equality in education.

Congress passes the Equal Employment Opportunity Act, prohibiting sex discrimination in the workplace.

The first issue of *Ms. Magazine* is published.

1973   In *Roe v. Wade,* the Supreme Court rules that women have a constitutional right to an abortion.

AT&T settles an EEOC class action lawsuit, agreeing to reform sexist policies.

The National Black Feminist Organization is formed.

Women office workers form Women Employed in Chicago and Nine to Five in Boston.

The first battered women's shelters in the United States are opened.

The Supreme Court rules that sexually-segregated classified ads are illegal.

The AFL-CIO endorses the Equal Rights Amendment.

The first edition of *Our Bodies, Ourselves* is published.

1974   Congress passes the Equal Credit Opportunity Act, enabling married women to get credit in their own name.

Domestic workers win coverage under the minimum wage law.

The Coalition of Labor Union Women is formed in Chicago.

Women of All Red Nations (WARN) is founded.

1975   The UN sponsors its first International Conference on Women.

The first National Women's Health Conference is held in Cambridge, Massachusetts.

1976   ERAmerica begins to promote state ratification of the ERA.

The National Alliance of Black Feminists is organized in Chicago.

1977   Twenty thousand women gather in Houston for the first National Women's Conference.

The National Coalition Against Domestic Violence is formed.

1978   Congress passes the Pregnancy Discrimination Act, which prohibits job discrimination against pregnant women.

Feminists in San Francisco organize the first "Take Back the Night" march to call attention to violence against women.

Poststructuralist philosopher Michel Foucault's *History of Sexuality: An Introduction* is first translated into English.

1979   The Moral Majority, a conservative group dedicated to overturning *Roe v. Wade* and other conservative causes, is formed by the Reverend Jerry Falwell and five other men.

1980   The U.S. Census no longer defines the head of the household as the husband.

1981   Sandra Day O'Connor becomes the first woman to be appointed to the U.S. Supreme Court.

1982   The Equal Rights Amendment (ERA) is defeated.

1983   Sally Ride becomes the first woman astronaut to go into space.

1984   Walter Mondale asks Geraldine Ferraro to be his running mate on the Democratic ticket for the presidency. Ferraro is the first woman to run on a major party ticket, but Mondale/Ferraro lose the election.

Madonna releases the album *Like a Virgin*.

1985   Wilma Mankiller becomes the Cherokee Nation's first female principal chief.

1987   Operation Rescue, an anti-abortion activist group, is founded; it uses methods such as blockading the entrances to family clinics.

1989   In *Webster v. Reproductive Health Services,* the Supreme Court declines to overturn *Roe v. Wade*. but upholds the right of states to ban the use of public funds or facilities for abortions.

1990   Ani DiFranco launches independent music label, Righteous Babe Records.

Judith Butler publishes *Gender Trouble: Feminism and the Subversion of Identity.*

1991   *Hues,* a self-published multi-culti indie magazine, begins five-year run.

Susan Faludi's *Backlash* and Naomi Wolf's *The Beauty Myth* are published.

At the Senate Confirmation Hearings of Clarence Thomas, law professor Anita Hill testifies that Thomas sexually harassed her. The Senate goes on to confirm Thomas' appointment to the Supreme Court.

In *Rust v. Sullivan,* the Supreme Court supports a Congressional ban on federal funds for organizations that provide abortion counseling.

1992   The *Ms.* Foundation launches Take Our Daughters to Work Day.

In *Ms.,* Rebecca Walker writes, "I am not a postfeminist feminist, I am the Third Wave."

The Riot Grrrl convention is held in Washington, D.C.

In *Planned Parenthood v. Casey,* the Supreme Court initially has a majority to overturn *Roe v. Wade,* until Justice Anthony Kennedy changes his mind during deliberations. However, the court narrows the window of time in which a fetus is considered nonviable, and upholds parental notification and mandatory 24-hour waiting period restrictions.

1993   The first (zine) edition of *BUST* is published.

Congress passes the Family and Medical Leave Act, guaranteeing unpaid leave for employees needing to care for family members.

1994   Congress passes the Violence Against Women Act, allowing women to seek civil rights remedies for gender-related crimes, as well as funding victim services, prevention, and prosecution programs.

1995   *Bitch* begins publication as a zine.

The UN Fourth World Conference on Women in Beijing addresses gender inequality as a global issue.

1996   U.S. women win 19 gold, 10 silver, and 9 bronze medals at the Summer Olympics.

1997   First tour of Lilith Fair, a women's music festival, is organized by Sarah McLachlan and others.

Buffy the Vampire Slayer and *Ally McBeal* are launched on television. Both series center on young women whose value as feminist role models is much debated among feminists.

1998   V-Day is inaugurated with a New York benefit performance of Eve Ensler's *The Vagina Monologues.*

Sex and the City, a TV series about four women seeking sexual liberation, begins six-year run.

1999   The Women's World Cup is won by the U.S. Women's soccer team, watched by 130 million people.

2000   Jennifer Baumgardner and Amy Richards's *Manifesta* is published.

2001   Condoleezza Rice becomes the first female U.S. National Security Advisor.

2002   Halle Berry becomes the first African American woman to win an Academy Award for Best Actress.

2003   The Partial Birth Abortion Ban Act, the first law to ban a specific type of abortion procedure, is signed into law by President George W. Bush.

2004   Jessica Valenti launches Feministing, a blog.

2005   Shark-fu launches Angry Black Bitch, a blog; Natalie Bennet launches The Carnival of Feminists, a semi-monthly showcase of feminist blogs.

2006   The U.S. Supreme Court upholds the Partial-Birth Abortion Ban Act.

2007   Senator and former First Lady Hillary Clinton launches a campaign for the U.S. Presidency.

Nancy Pelosi becomes the first female Speaker of the U.S. House of Representatives.

2008   Hillary Clinton loses the Democratic presidential primary campaign to Barack Obama, who is the first African American to win the nomination.

Republican John McCain names Alaska Governor Sarah Palin as his running mate in the 2008 presidential election. Palin is the first woman to be nominated for vice president by the Republican Party.

2009   Sonia Sotomayor is appointed to the Supreme Court, becoming the first Hispanic and the third woman to serve on the nation's highest court.

Native American Women | 1

Jeffrey M. Schulze

As one historian of the Native peoples of North America recently argued, "American history without Indians is mythology—it never happened" (Calloway 2004, 9). In recent decades, scholars have gradually begun highlighting the contributions American Indians have made in influencing, and often determining, the trajectory of U.S. history. The Indian perspective appears with far more regularity in the literature than it did only a couple of decades ago, and our understanding of America's past is far richer for it. We have also witnessed a shift from Indian histories that dwell on Indians' victimization and cultural decline to narratives that more thoughtfully explore relationships between Indians and Euro-Americans, relationships in which it is not always easy to discern who was *really* dictating the terms of accommodation and coexistence. But one problem persists: the absence of Native women's voices. Although scholars have done an admirable job of correcting the imbalance between Indian and non-Indian voices in their stories of America's past, their efforts have often yielded a portrait of American history in which a substantial portion of the equation remains unaccounted for.

By exploring a variety of Native American women's historical and contemporary experiences, this chapter attempts to account for the other half of that equation. The picture that emerges, though still incomplete, contrasts sharply with the experiences of non-Indian women, since for Indian women the challenge has been not so much the pursuit of new and expanded rights, but rather the maintenance of existing rights. In other words, Indian women enter the American historical stage primarily as equals to their male counterparts, or at least enjoying a similar degree of authority and agency within their respective societies. The infiltration of Euro-American cultural values and prerogatives, however, threatened this arrangement, ultimately giving rise to ever more inventive strategies on the part of Native women to prevent their marginalization to the same social and cultural peripheries occupied by Euro-American women for much of American history. Although their efforts remain ongoing, a look at the historical record reveals a long and notable string of successes, some literally centuries in the making.

Recovering Native Women's Voices

The recovery of Native American women's voices from the American past remains one of the most difficult tasks a historian can undertake. European and, later, American men were often solely responsible for chronicling Indian-white relations. Thus, Indian historians have little more to work with than accounts of a postconquest world produced by individuals who were not always receptive to the Indian viewpoint. Further, since these men were most often interested solely in trade, war, and land acquisition, they had little incentive to document the experiences of Native women. And further still, because of the strict division of labor between men and women in most Native societies, non-Indian men rarely had sustained access to Indian women, leaving them with little opportunity to assess these women's contributions to their communities. Thus, Euro-American men's encounters with Native women most often went unnoted, either because they were so superficial or, as was sometimes the case, because they were merely sexual in nature.

Biographies of notable Indian leaders line library shelves, from Powhatan to Pontiac, from Cochise to Crazy Horse. Conspicuously scarce, however, are substantive accounts of Native women. Although Indian women were grandmothers, mothers, daughters, sisters, and wives, and although they produced foodstuffs, processed hides, traded goods they themselves often produced, and served as clan mothers, medicine women, and even warriors and chiefs, they have mostly been rendered silent by the passage of time. Instead, only a handful of Native American women have entered our national mythology, and most of these have done so as caricatures—as Indian princesses, "squaws," or one-dimensional symbols of cross-cultural cooperation and accommodation—but rarely as flesh-and-blood human beings with their own agendas and agency.

In confronting this methodological problem, scholars have increasingly resorted to a creative reading of available sources in order to locate even passing glimpses of Native women's perspectives in American history, a process that often entails an unusual degree of speculation. Scholars are also discovering the value of less traditional sources, including winter counts (painted representations of tribal history), calendars, and, perhaps most significantly, oral testimony. As writer-scholar and Oklahoma Choctaw Devon Mihesuah has argued, "If writers want to find out what Native women think, they should ask them. If they want to know about past events and cultures, they should do the same" (2003, 4). Once upon a time, scholars of Native America got their information almost solely from written source material, including government documents, tribal records, and the like, and would approach Native oral accounts skeptically, if at all. That pattern is gradually changing, and, again, our understanding of the American past is far richer for it. However, Mihesuah cautions that scholars who approach Indian women with the expectation of fashioning a homogenous Native women's perspective will likely

Sarah Winnemucca (Thocmetony)

Born in 1844, Sarah Winnemucca, or Thocmetony ("Shell Flower"), lived during a period of transition for Native Americans. Best known for her popular lecture tours, during which she highlighted abuses being heaped upon her people, the Northern Paiutes, by the U.S. government, Winnemucca was an aggressive advocate for Native American rights and for peace between Indians and whites, until her death in 1891.

As of 1844, the Paiutes controlled vast tracts of land in present-day Nevada, California, and Oregon. In the late 1840s, however, whites began arriving in the region, and contact between the Paiutes and their new neighbors became commonplace. The Paiutes proved remarkably accommodating, at least initially. Winnemucca even picked up both English and Spanish, and, while in her teens, assumed the name "Sarah" and converted to Christianity. Relations between the Paiutes and their non-Indian neighbors deteriorated dramatically from the 1850s on, however, and the government ultimately confined the Paiutes to a reservation near Pyramid Lake, north of Reno. Facing starvation, many Paiutes joined the Bannock Indians in present-day Idaho, ultimately participating in the dramatic 1878 Bannock War. Winnemucca, meanwhile, signed on as an interpreter with the U.S. army, a controversial decision, but one that she believed would help to secure peace between the warring factions. When hostilities ceased in 1879, the government forcibly relocated the Paiutes to the Yakima reservation in present-day Washington State, where they again faced starvation.

These developments catalyzed Winnemucca's activism. She organized a lecture tour of San Francisco, happily playing the part of a stereotypical, buckskin-clad Indian Princess in order to attract attention and advance her political agenda. Winnemucca then took her grievances all the way to Washington, D.C. In 1880, she met with President Rutherford B. Hayes and Secretary of the Interior Carl Schurz. While she secured their promise to allow the Paiutes to return to their former reservation, it was not to be. Pyramid Lake had already been opened up to white settlement.

Distraught but not defeated, Winnemucca accepted a teaching position at an Indian school in present-day Washington state, using her earnings to fund an East Coast lecture tour. She also completed her autobiography, entitled *Life among the Paiutes: Their Wrongs and Claims,* in 1883, which became the first book published in English by a Native American woman. Although she helped educate the public, Winnemucca was unable to force officials to right the wrongs done to her people. She ultimately returned to Nevada, taught school for several years before retiring, and on October 16, 1891, succumbed to tuberculosis.

Winnemucca lived with each foot in a different world. Her own people often questioned her loyalty, particularly given her participation in the U.S. army's campaigns against them. White America, meanwhile, admired her courage and eloquence, but often viewed her as a curious relic of a vanishing race. Still, Winnemucca made white America reexamine their treatment of Indian peoples. After her death, the *New York Times* memorialized Winnemucca, and one of her contemporaries, in a short biographical sketch, argued that she "should have a place beside the name of Pocahontas in the history of our country" (Canfield 1983, 259). And her legacy remains strong. In 2005, Nevada officials added a statue of Winnemucca to the U.S. Capitol's National Statuary Hall Collection. Because of her determination to expose the hypocrisy of those who, as she put it, "cry out Liberty" while "driving [Indians] from place to place as if [they] were beasts," she has entered America's pantheon of minority rights activists (Hopkins 1994, 243–44).

be disappointed. For example, during an interview with an elderly descendant of a prominent Cherokee leader, Mihesuah asked whether or not she spoke Cherokee and attended stomp dances. "Hell no, I'm no heathen," she replied (Mihesuah 1998, 40). Not surprisingly, Native women do not speak with one voice.

Any discussion of Native American women must begin, then, with an acknowledgment that generalizations will only get one so far. Tribal values, gender roles and relations, physical appearances, and definitions of "Indianness" have constantly evolved, and continue to do so. Furthermore, cultural differences from tribe to tribe exist, particularly when it comes to religions, social systems, and economies. But although historical generalizations rarely stand up to the variety of human experience, one can nevertheless identify general patterns across Native societies that can help us better understand women's rights and roles within them.

Gender Roles and Relations in Native Societies

Prior to colonization, Native American women lived in societies that were far less hierarchical than were those of Europeans. European society placed women somewhere between children and men in a kind of status hierarchy, a hierarchy that demanded women's unwavering obedience, stipulated their dependence, and often relied on coercion for its maintenance. Native American women exercised far more autonomy and authority within their societies, enjoying more respect and prestige than did their Western counterparts. They also enjoyed specific domains in which to assert their authority. For example, Iroquois women were responsible for the control and distribution of foodstuffs within the community. If they disagreed with a decision to go to war, they simply withheld these supplies, thereby forcing men to reconsider their decision.

Although most, if not all, Native societies were organized along gender lines, gender roles could be quite flexible. These societies looked to gender to determine the nature of one's participation in economic, political, and ceremonial activities. In general, men handled hunting and warfare, while typically serving as intermediaries between the tribal community and the outside world. Women, meanwhile, generally tended to the household, produced non-animal foodstuffs, and handled the distribution of food. They also bore and raised children, an undertaking that commanded a great deal of respect and reverence. Thus, women and men both had important, and often complementary, roles within their societies, with equal levels of power and prestige.

Although the gender divide was quite distinct, not all Indians felt pressured to strictly conform to it. In fact, many Native societies institutionalized what was in essence a third gender, often referred to as "berdache." Indian societies knew that gender was a social construction that was not always dictated by one's biological makeup. Instead, one's gender depended on the type of work one did. Those Indian men who chose to eschew the kinds of work typically reserved for male tribal members simply adopted the symbols of femininity, including style of dress, while also taking on women's work-related responsibilities. They were respected members of the community, and were often even taken as wives. And although the word "berdache" is typically used by scholars to refer to Indian men who did women's work, it could go the other way. Although rare, some historical accounts discuss female chiefs, warriors, and even entire tribal councils.

Native American author Paula Gunn Allen has gone so far as to describe American Indian societies as "woman-centered." As such, they have often been characterized by a kind of "free and easy sexuality," a trait that early Euro-American visitors found troubling, but one that Allen argues helped produce "self-defining, assertive, decisive women," which ultimately benefited the group as a whole by adding another level of social stability (Allen 1992, 2). For example, unmarried Cherokee women could enter into a sexual relationship with whomever they chose so long as they obeyed incest taboos and avoided intercourse with a member of their own clan or the clan of their fathers. As for married women, female infidelity was far less problematic and disruptive than male infidelity, since women had more of what one scholar called a "proprietary interest" in men than men had in women (Perdue 1998, 57). Thus, wayward husbands created more community disharmony than did wayward wives. In the case of female infidelity, then, Cherokee males most often ignored it and, in some cases, simply took another wife.

Aside from this surprising degree of social power, Native women were also believed to possess a great deal of spiritual power. For example, many Native societies secluded women during menstruation as another means of imposing social stability. The spilling of blood from the body was thought to have a polluting effect that could threaten the community's spiritual and sexual equilibrium. Some groups also believed that menstruating women could jeopardize access to food sources, as was the case with Columbia Plateau peoples, who feared that women's blood could potentially offend salmon and preclude their annual return. Thus, during menstruation, Native women often retired to menstrual huts placed at a considerable distance from their residences. Non-menstruating women would provide these women with food and, if necessary, perform their chores until the cycle was complete. "Any breach of the rules," one scholar explained, "was an extremely serious offense" (Perdue 1998, 29). Although non-Indian visitors often mistakenly assumed that the community considered these women unclean, in reality they were believed to be particularly powerful and potentially dangerous while menstruating.

Native women consistently and diligently worked to enhance their status not only within their own societies, but also, with the advent of colonization, within Euro-American society. For example, Native women were not above using their role as mothers and caretakers to exert influence over politics and diplomacy. Writing to Benjamin Franklin in 1787, a Cherokee woman named Katteuha called for an end to conflict between their two nations, stating, "I am in hopes if you Rightly consider it that woman is the mother of All—and that woman Does not pull Children out of Trees or Stumps nor out of old Logs, but out of their Bodies, so that they ought to mind what a woman says . . . I am in hopes you have a beloved woman amongst you who will help to put her Children Right if they do wrong, as I will do the same" (Shoemaker 1995, 9). By highlighting her reproductive capacity, a primary source of authority within *her* society, Katteuha hoped to establish credibility in the diplomatic arena. Thus, although Native women's roles within their society were often carefully proscribed, they retained the right to behave in ways that ran counter to gender-related expectations.

Myths and Realities of Contact and Conquest

Despite the centrality of women in Native societies, however, early European accounts of Indian women typically characterize them as either drudges, laboring under the thumb of male oppressors, or as voluptuous and promiscuous sex objects, who exist solely for men's pleasure. In the absence of substantive source material from the colonial period, a great deal of mythologizing has filled the vacuum, resulting in a skewed understanding of Native women's historical experiences in early American history. The story of Pocahontas, for example, is one of many popular and persistent, though notoriously misleading, myths involving colonial-era Native women. Despite owing its genesis to scanty documentary evidence that reveals more about the Euro-American male perspective than it does anything else, the myth has nonetheless proven stubbornly durable. Recent scholars, however, have taken these shreds of evidence and tried to creatively fashion a more meaningful interpretation of Pocahontas's life, one that offers deeper insight into Native women's oft-overlooked contributions to colonial American history, their responses to European contact, and the predicaments they faced, as the Euro-American presence threatened not only Native gender roles, but also Native survival.

Pocahontas has long been cast as the "sexy savior" of the Jamestown settlement, an Indian "princess" who befriended and ultimately saved the lives of the earliest colonists (Richter 2001, 76). The most resilient version of her story imagines Pocahontas as the favorite daughter of the powerful chief Powhatan. Just as she is developing a romantic attachment to the Englishman Captain John Smith, her people attempt to take Smith's life in an inexplicable act of aggression. Pocahontas, however, intercedes at the last moment, throwing herself across a prostrate Smith, begging her father to spare his life. The romance between Pocahontas and Smith blooms from there, until Smith is injured and forced to return to England to seek medical care. In his absence, a devastated Pocahontas gradually learns to love again. The target of her affection this time is the tobacco-growing Englishman John Rolfe. Pocahontas eventually marries Rolfe, converts to Christianity, adopts the name "Rebecca," bears Rolfe a child, then accompanies him, with child in tow, to England, whereupon she contracts a mysterious illness and dies. Pocahontas, then, is cast as a kind of hapless romantic with a seemingly insatiable interest in, and attraction to, her non-Indian neighbors. By submitting to intermarriage, the myth tells us, she acknowledged the lure of English society and ultimately forsook her own people for the promise of a better life.

The more realistic story of Pocahontas's life, however, contains much less romantic intrigue but says a lot more about Native politics and diplomacy, along with women's roles within them. To begin with, her name was not Pocahontas. She, in fact, had two names. Her public name was Amonute, while her real name, which would have been known solely by her kin, was Matoaka. "Pocahontas," meanwhile, was most likely either a nickname or a simple descriptive term that meant "playful one" or "mischievous girl." As for the romance between Pocahontas and Smith, Pocahontas was a child of about 10 at the time of Jamestown's founding in 1607 and, thus, her feelings for Smith likely amounted to either a detached curiosity or, at most, a vague fondness. As for the attempt on Smith's life, Smith was almost certainly an unwitting bit player in a native drama of ancient vintage, one in which Powhatan demonstrated his authority over Smith and, by extension, the English, in order to ensure their incorporation into his realm as *subordinates*. As for Pocahontas's relationship with Rolfe, she had actually chosen a husband from among her own people in the years following Smith's departure. In 1613, however, the English took her captive. Although Rolfe was evidently genuinely smitten with Pocahontas, whether or not Pocahontas, then only about 15 years of age, requited his love is simply unknowable. She likely viewed a union with Rolfe as a way out of captivity.

Nonetheless, by marrying Rolfe, Pocahontas was fulfilling a traditional function within Native society, forging kinship ties in order to seal an alliance between her people and his. It was a diplomatic marriage into which Pocahontas likely entered out of a sense of duty. It did not take her long to realize that the English either misunderstood the terms of the union, or decided not to adhere to them, because relations between them and Pocahontas's people deteriorated rapidly in the ensuing years, particularly following her death in exile in 1617. By 1646, in fact, the English had executed Powhatan's successor, Opechancanough, and her people had been forced to flee to the perimeters of the ever-expanding English settlements due to nearly constant conflict. Thus, despite Pocahontas's best intentions, the English refused to play by native rules. It was a lesson Indians would learn again and again as non-Indian invaders expanded into lands to the west.

Native Women in a Euro-American World

Contact and colonization, then, dramatically affected Native women's lives, forcing them to devise new strategies to prevent their marginalization in the ever-evolving social, economic, and political order. Although it is tempting to approach Native women's history as the story of Western concepts of gender winning out over Native ones, there are simply too many exceptions to this trend to do so. Native women sometimes gained as much as they lost, in terms of authority and agency. Although no two Native women experienced colonization the same way, one can locate broader patterns in Native women's responses to their changing circumstances as Euro-America encroached.

Perhaps surprisingly, many Native women fared quite well, at least initially. For example, Native women were key players in the early fur trade, an enterprise that helped drive the North American economy, especially in the Great Lakes region, from the late 17th century until the mid-19th century. They took the lead in processing hides, they manufactured and sold pemmican (a kind of buffalo and berry jerky eaten by the traders), and they sometimes

Women from England were brought to Jamestown, Virginia to marry the settlers and ensure the growth of the colony. (Library of Congress)

served as bilingual intermediaries between Indians and their European trading partners. In some cases, their role as intermediaries involved the bonds of marriage. Traders often welcomed these unions, since Native women were well versed in not only cooking, sewing, and shoemaking, but in canoeing and trapping, as well. This arrangement did not last long, however. First of all, by the early 1800s, the population of the furbearing animals that were central to cross-cultural trade had been decimated. Secondly, the practice of taking Native wives fell by the wayside as European traders gradually gained access to white ones. Incoming white women, in fact, were often appalled by the degree of racial intermingling in frontier settlements, with one recent arrival insisting on relocating to an area where there were not so many "jet black eyes and high cheek bones" (Van Kirk 1983, 240). Thus, gender and racial biases on the part of Europeans gradually rendered Native women's participation in the fur trade a thing of the past.

The Cherokees offer another example of the complicated ways in which the lives of Native American women changed in the wake of colonization. Until the 1830s, the Cherokees inhabited lands in the present-day Southeast, primarily in the state of Georgia. Although gender roles within Cherokee society were often carefully and firmly proscribed before their disruption by whites, the system was far from hierarchical. Women were charged with tasks that were of paramount importance to the group's survival. Not only did they care for the household, tend to communal crops, and process and produce trade goods, but they also took charge of war captives. Women alone decided who would be adopted to replace relatives lost in battle, and they also decided who would be executed to avenge those same deaths. Women were further used to determine tribal membership. A child of a Cherokee mother,

A marriage between a trapper and a Native woman is romanticized in American painter Alfred Jacob Miller's *The Trapper's Bride.* (MPI/Getty Images)

for example, would always be a Cherokee, no matter the ethnicity of his or her father. The reverse, at least according to tradition, was not true. Thus, women were responsible for the clan's perpetuation.

The first Euro-American traders began arriving in Cherokee country in the late 17th century, and the most sweeping changes to Cherokee culture and society occurred over the course of the 18th. Incoming whites failed to grasp the importance of *both* genders to the group's maintenance. As white men increasingly pursued relations with Cherokee men around matters of warfare and trade, Cherokee men assumed greater importance within Cherokee society, as well as in the broader regional, colonial, and global economies. Men's roles as warriors took on heightened significance in Cherokee society as the Cherokees were drawn into wars involving rival European nations. At the same time, European trade introduced a range of European-produced goods into Cherokee society, including iron hoes, brass kettles, and European-style clothing, goods for which Cherokee men traded slaves and deerskins. Since Cherokee women came to rely on these goods to keep their households functioning, they also came to depend on Cherokee men as intermediaries between themselves and non-Indian traders. Thus, Cherokee men became disproportionately responsible for the group's maintenance, to the detriment of Cherokee women.

The delicate gender balance within Cherokee society was also offset by changes in how men conducted both the hunt and warfare. As for the hunt, the act once held a great deal of spiritual significance. The Cherokees would, through ceremony, announce their intentions to kill their game, but promised to do so in a way that would prepare the animal's spirit for the afterlife. Once the exchange of hides and skins with outsiders became an *economic* imperative, however, the goal of the hunt became killing as much game as possible. The change that this brought on was subtle, but significant: once divested of its spiritual significance, the hunt became a way for Cherokee men to establish their dominion over the animal world. A hierarchy of sorts was thus taking shape, and the balance between men and women within Cherokee society was increasingly offset. Similarly, warfare was not a facet of Cherokee life that owed its impetus to the arrival of whites. Still, warfare had once amounted to little more than small-scale coordinated raids on enemies, conducted by war parties of two or three Indians, with the intention of exacting vengeance for previous deaths, and often of taking captives. Very rarely would casualties result from these raids. By the mid-18th century, however, war parties had grown to contain as many as one hundred members, while what once were small raids became violent, destructive paramilitary operations that could result in numerous casualties. The English presence was at the root of these changes, since they often pressured or even bribed Cherokee men to attack neighboring tribes. Meanwhile, the act of going to battle lost its spiritual significance as the ritual complex associated with battle fell by the wayside. Since it was often conducted at the whim of outsiders on short notice, warfare no longer required preparatory ceremonies. While women had once figured prominently in these preparatory ceremonies, now their participation was no longer required.

Following the American Revolution, Cherokee society was again transformed, this time by U.S. government efforts to assimilate the Cherokees into Euro-American culture. With the formation of the Cherokee republic, some Cherokees, men mostly, embraced the federal government's civilization program, recognizing value in adopting the Euro-American political system, in converting to evangelical Protestantism, and in turning to, as one scholar has phrased it, "the acquisitive individualism of nascent capitalism" (Perdue 1998, 185). Even given these sweeping changes, however, certain aspects of Cherokee culture remained intact, and Cherokee women, by and large, continued to enjoy a great deal more prestige, authority, and agency than their Euro-American counterparts. This was because U.S. officials failed to supplant one of the cornerstones of Cherokee culture: the maintenance of a communal land ethic, which had long been the responsibility of women. The Cherokees' insistence on holding tribal lands in common, as opposed to dividing them into privately held plots, ensured that women would remain central to the Cherokee republic. Thus, while some amount of cultural modification seemed inevitable, the Cherokees refused to wholeheartedly embrace Euro-Americans' concept of civilization. In the end, however, the Cherokees' refusal to fully conform to Euro-American expectations led U.S. officials to conclude that the group was failing to submit to their authority. In the 1820s, the Cherokees became the targets of a new federal policy that called for their removal to lands to the west. From this point forward, U.S. federal Indian policy would dramatically shape the lives of Indian peoples as it wavered between an emphasis on segregation and assimilation, and Native women would emerge as key players who adjusted to, coped with, and resisted these currents.

Native Women and U.S. Federal Indian Policy

As the 19th century progressed, many Native women found their rights and prerogatives increasingly impinged upon by U.S. federal Indian policy. The earliest policy currents hammered out by the new nation often focused on assimilation, or the integration of Indians into the Euro-American mainstream. Government officials, missionaries, and reformers attempted to minimize differences between Indians and non-Indians through education, conversion to Christianity, and participation in the regional economy. Proponents of assimilation drew directly from 18th-century Enlightenment ideals that stressed the environment in explaining Indians' seeming backwardness. Assimilation advocates believed that Indians and whites were essentially equal, but that Indians had not enjoyed the benefit of a Western-style education, nor had they been given the opportunity to learn from the example of whites.

In implementing their assimilationist policies, 19th-century reformers often targeted gender relations first. They attempted to restructure the Native American family according to the ideology of separate gender spheres, which relegated women to a submissive, dependent role as domestic caretakers of the private home. Reformers working amongst the Cherokees, for example, leveled an attack on polygamous and serial marriages, common practices within many Native communities, and insisted on Anglo-style domestic unions. They enjoyed a remarkable degree of cooperation from Indian women on many fronts, particularly when it came to entrusting missionaries with their children's education, but Cherokee women often failed to meet the missionaries' expectations when it came to domestic relations. In some cases, polygamous and/or serial marriages proved hard habits to break, their most vocal proponents often being the Cherokee political elite (who were most likely to have multiple wives); in other cases, the missionaries' insistence on ending polygamy meant that many women and children were abandoned, as Cherokee males attempted to conform to the outsiders' expectations. "In the war on 'savagery,'" one scholar deftly observed, "women and children suffered collateral damage" (Perdue 1998, 177).

The U.S. government's emphasis on assimilation was by no means sustained, however. Instead, for much of the 19th century, federal Indian policy teetered between two seemingly contradictory currents: removal on the one hand and assimilation on the other. When the project of assimilating Indians did not produce immediate results, as in the Cherokee case, policymakers developed the reservation system as a way to remove Indians from the perimeters of white settlement, thereby freeing up Indian lands for whites. By 1850, thousands of Indians, mostly from the Southeast and Midwest, had been relocated, either peacefully or otherwise, to small reserves west of the Mississippi River, the most infamous example being the Cherokees' Trail of Tears ordeal. Women might have actually fared better than men in making this transition to the reservation system. Men's roles, such as hunting and conducting warfare, required mobility. Confinement to the reservation meant that they could no longer participate in these activities. Women, however, could continue in their roles as mothers and caregivers. Thus, their contributions to the community's maintenance remained a source of authority and prestige, even as their male counterparts underwent a painful period of adjustment. Still, the transition was not entirely painless for Native women. Attacks on their position within their respective societies began early, as Indian agents made a habit of distributing sorely needed provisions only to male heads of household. Many also had to contend with the sudden presence of Euro-American female reformers, whom the U.S. government employed to educate Native women in what it considered to be women's domestic responsibilities. Thus, the reservation experience could be just as demeaning for women as it could be for men.

Among the most significant federal policy developments, and among the most detrimental to the status of Indian women, was the 1887 Dawes Act. The act was another in a long line of assimilation-minded policies. Its primary goal was to supplant the communal style of land ownership that had long characterized Native American societies and to convert Indians into yeomen farmers. The new policy ultimately proved destructive, however, resulting in the loss of millions of acres of Indian land to whites. Reflecting the gender bias of policymakers, the Dawes Act placed the interests of Indian men above all others', granting them sole title to allotted lands. Thus, Indian women who lost their husbands or male heads of households, who decided to divorce, or who simply lived alone, were ignored when officials assigned allotments, and thus often remained landless and dependent on others.

The federal government supplemented the Dawes Act with a renewed push toward assimilation through education. During the latter years of the 19th century, reformers established both on- and off-reservation boarding schools, and often left Indian parents with little choice but to send their children to these schools. Indian children were then transformed physically, a process that included cutting their hair and dressing them in Anglo-style clothing. Then the task of enforcing a rigid sexual division of labor began: Indian boys learned potential occupations like carpentry and farming, while girls learned domestic skills, such as sewing, cooking, and cleaning. They were forbidden to speak their native language, and many lost touch with both their tribal families and their Indian identities. Not surprisingly, however, some students and their families resisted reformers' efforts. It was not unusual, for instance, for parents to encourage their children to run away, which was evidently a frequent occurrence, and reports from some schools are peppered with references to "mysterious" fires on school grounds, fires likely set by disgruntled students. In private, students also engaged in what one scholar called "clandestine acts of cultural preservation," sharing legends, folktales, and stories taught to them by elders (Adams 1995, 233). Indians also commonly worked to maintain Native religious traditions, as was the case with a group of Ponca girls who continued holding midnight peyote meetings at their boarding school. Federal Indian policies, however, would con-

Native American students participate in a mathematics class at the Carlisle Indian School in Carlisle, Pennsylvania, c. 1903. The use of textbooks and a structured academic routine added to the rigid atmosphere at the boarding school. (Library of Congress)

tinue to dramatically affect the lives of Native American women well into the 20th century, serving as one of many factors that catalyzed their political mobilization and inspired their creative expression.

Native Women in the 20th Century

Over the course of the 20th century, Native American women became more visible than ever in American culture and politics, sometimes in their more traditional capacity as caretakers and repositories of tribal history and culture, and sometimes as nationally recognized and path-breaking writers, artists, political activists, and tribal leaders. As Native American women increasingly acquired literacy, they began committing their thoughts and their life stories to paper more frequently, ultimately producing a vital literary tradition. Anna Moore Shaw's *A Pima Past* (1974), Beverly Hungry Wolf's *The Ways of My Grandmothers* (1980), and Maria Campbell's *Halfbreed* (1973) shed light on Native women's roles within their societies. Seminal works such as Gretchen Bataille's *American Indian Women* (1987) and Paula Gunn Allen's *The Sacred Hoop* (1986) supplemented these earlier efforts, along with a host of works by authors like Leslie Marmon Silko, Louise Erdrich, Linda Hogan, and Joy Harjo, among many others. Writings like these, as Paula Gunn Allen has said about her own work, have helped Native women "affirm [their] identity and [their] heritage and to make peace with the tortures of an Indian woman's life in the first three quarters of the twentieth century" (Allen 1992, ix).

Women increasingly entered tribal politics during the second half of the 20th century, as well, serving on councils, working as administrators within on-reservation Indian programs, and communicating directly with U.S. policymakers in their efforts to change the exploitative tenor of U.S.-Indian relations. Native women also began capitalizing on their more traditional role as caregivers within their societies to tackle challenges facing their communities, such as poverty, unemployment, alcoholism, and infant mortality, entering institutions of higher education to specialize in fields like education, health care, and social welfare.

As for political activism, the largest and most visible Indian rights organization during the second half of the 20th century was the American Indian Movement, or AIM. Founded in 1968, AIM worked to address problems plaguing both urban- and reservation-based Indians, including police brutality, alcoholism, unemployment, poverty, and political apathy, by mobilizing public opinion through protest and maintaining a positive presence within reservation communities. Many Native women, however, felt that AIM was failing to adequately represent *their* interests. In the mid-1970s, Native women organized WARN, or Women of All Red Nations. An influential organization, WARN was most concerned with issues like domestic violence and forced sterilization of Native women, a shocking but very real Indian policy initiative carried out by the Indian Health Service. These women also worked to shore up Native cultures and protect Native rights more generally, supplementing the efforts of AIM. As WARN cofounder Madonna Thunderhawk, a Hunkpapa Lakota, explained, "Indian women have had to be strong because of what the colonialist system has done to our men. I mean, alcohol, suicides, car wrecks, the whole thing. And after [AIM's 1973 siege of Wounded Knee village at Pine Ridge, South Dakota], while all that persecution of men was going on, the women had to keep things going" (Josephy, Nagel, and Johnson 1999, 52).

Although deeply concerned with issues affecting Native women's lives, many Indian women responded to the late-20th-century women's liberation movement with ambivalence. Indian women were already powerful members of their respective societies, and many viewed feminists' new emphasis on women's rights as irrelevant, and even potentially damaging to cultures that emphasized gender balance. Instead, they often preferred the labels "tribalist" or "activist" to the label "feminist." As Pima-Maricopa Vivian Jones explained, "I have no personal interest in feminism or 'women's issues.' It's more important to be part of the community" (Shoemaker 1995, 230).

Native women have also worked toward reservations' economic development, the protection of treaty rights, and the strengthening of tribal sovereignty, while also serving as more general social and environmental activists. Wilma Mankiller, the first female principal chief of the Cherokee Nation, and Ada Deer, who famously led Wisconsin's Menominee Indians in opposition to the federal government's efforts, via the termination policies of the 1950s and 1960s, to sever the trust relationship between itself and reservation Indians, are prime examples. As Devon Mihesuah concluded, "Native women to-

Police arrest an American Indian Movement activist for blocking the route of a Columbus Day Parade in Denver, Colorado on October 7, 2000. (AP/Wide World Photos)

day are a far cry from the stereotypical images of the 'princess' and the 'squaw drudge'" (Mihesuah 2003, xix).

Yet challenges remain. The gradual loss of status among Native American women in the centuries following contact has ultimately manifested itself in subtle but significant ways. For example, among Florida's Seminoles and New Mexico's Santa Domingo Pueblos, custom dictates that those women who marry white men forfeit their right to live on the reservation. The same rules, however, do not apply to Native men who marry white women. Thus, gender inequality is no longer a foreign concept to some Indian women. Native women also still contend with the legacy of stereotypes. Particularly troubling for many is the term "squaw," which still appears in popular vernacular and on maps. It is a term many Native women find insensitive and demeaning.

Among the more pressing problems throughout Native America, however, remains the steady social and economic deterioration of many reservation communities. As Standing Rock Sioux and scholar Flo Wiger stated, "Let's face it, on our reservations, we haven't had jobs, we haven't had choices. We will do whatever we have to do to survive" (Katz 1995, 3). On the Navajo reservation, for example, the effects of alcohol and drugs have been devastating, the breakup of multigenerational families has left Indian youth isolated and disillusioned, and the lack of educational opportunities, coupled with the lack of opportunities to *apply* an education, has produced an apathetic, uninspired younger generation. Native women have and still are capitalizing on their roles as mothers and caretakers within their societies to address these problems, however, while also stepping outside of these roles to formulate wholly new approaches in nontraditional arenas. Thus, Native women have consistently played central roles within their communities, despite centuries of painful cultural adjustments and both the erosion and evolution of their rights. As the artist Emmi Whitehorse recently revealed after reflecting upon her childhood on the Navajo reservation, "The female owned everything, the woman ran everything." Another Navajo woman added to that, "For the most part, they still do" (Katz 1995, 11).

References and Further Reading

Adams, David Wallace. *Education for Extinction: American Indians and the Boarding School Experience, 1875–1928.* Lawrence: University Press of Kansas, 1995.

Allen, Paula Gunn. *The Sacred Hoop: Recovering the Feminine in American Indian Traditions.* Boston: Beacon Press, 1992.

Bataille, Gretchen M., ed. *Native American Women: A Biographical Dictionary.* New York: Garland, 1993.

Bataille, Gretchen M. and Kathleen Mullen Sands, eds. *American Indian Women: Telling Their Lives.* Lincoln: University of Nebraska Press, 1984.

Calloway, Colin G. *First Peoples: A Documentary Survey of American Indian History.* Boston: Bedford/St. Martin's, 2004.

Campbell, Maria. *Halfbreed.* Toronto, Canada: McClelland and Stewart, 1973.

Canfield, Gae Whitney. *Sarah Winnemucca of the Northern Paiutes.* Norman: University of Oklahoma Press, 1983.

Devens, Carol. *Countering Colonization: Native Women and Great Lakes Missions, 1630–1900.* Berkeley: University of California Press, 1992.

Garceau-Hagen, Dee, ed. *Portraits of Women in the American West.* New York: Routledge, 2005.

Hopkins, Sarah Winnemucca. *Life among the Paiutes: Their Wrongs and Claims.* Reno: University of Nevada Press, 1994.

Hungry Wolf, Beverly. *The Ways of My Grandmothers.* New York: Morrow, 1980.

Josephy, Alvin M., Joane Nagel, and Troy Johnson, eds. *Red Power: The American Indians' Fight for Freedom.* Lincoln: University of Nebraska Press, 1999.

Katz, Jane, ed. *Messengers of the Wind: Native American Women Tell Their Life Stories.* New York: Ballantine Books, 1995.

Klein, Laura F. and Lillian A. Ackerman, eds. *Women and Power in Native North America.* Norman: University of Oklahoma Press, 1995.

Mankiller, Wilma, ed. *Every Day is a Good Day: Reflections by Contemporary Indigenous Women.* Golden, CO: Fulcrum Publishing, 2004.

Mihesuah, Devon Abbott. *Indigenous American Women: Decolonization, Empowerment, Activism.* Lincoln: University of Nebraska Press, 2003.

Mihesuah, Devon Abbott, ed. *Natives and Academics: Researching and Writing about American Indians.* Lincoln: University of Nebraska Press, 1998.

Perdue, Theda. *Cherokee Women: Gender and Culture Change, 1700–1835.* Lincoln: University of Nebraska Press, 1998.

Perdue, Theda, ed. *Sifters: Native American Women's Lives.* New York: Oxford University Press, 2001.

Richter, Daniel K. *Facing East from Indian Country: A Native History of Early America.* Cambridge, MA: Harvard University Press, 2001.

Senier, Siobhan. *Voices of American Indian Assimilation and Resistance: Helen Hunt Jackson, Sarah Winnemucca, and Victoria Howard.* Norman: University of Oklahoma Press, 2001.

Shaw, Anna Moore. *A Pima Past.* Tucson: University of Arizona Press, 1974.

Shoemaker, Nancy, ed. *Negotiators of Change: Historical Perspectives on Native American Women.* New York: Routledge, 1995.

Van Kirk, Sylvia. *Many Tender Ties: Women in Fur-Trade Society, 1670–1870.* Norman: University of Oklahoma Press, 1983.

Women of the Colonial Period | 2

Amy Meschke Porter

From the late 16th century to the late 18th century, women came to the present-day United States from England, Spain, France, the Netherlands, other European countries, and Africa. Women's experiences in colonial America differed, depending on their social and cultural backgrounds, their place of settlement, the historical moment in which they lived, and the laws of the colonial powers that governed them. Across the colonies, women faced legal, economic, and political subordination, as well as religious beliefs and social organization that placed them as inferiors to men. Despite these constraints, women took care of their families, sometimes sought to protect their own interests, and in some cases, challenged authority and the established order.

Women in the Spanish Colonies

Women first settled in the Spanish colonies in the present-day United States in 1565, in Saint Augustine, Florida. Women would continue to settle in the Spanish colonies of Florida, New Mexico, Texas, Arizona, and California. In the Spanish colonies, women enjoyed property rights that women in other colonies did not have. Under Spanish law, all children inherited fairly equally, so that sons did not inherit most of their parents' estates. Women maintained property when they married. Women did have dowries, but husbands could not sell a dowry without the consent of the wife. Finally, the Spanish colonies had community property laws, meaning that men and women shared all property that they earned while married. All of these laws meant that women had opportunities to own land and businesses, and to pass these on to their children. For example, when a San Antonio woman had a notary write her will, she noted, "When I married the said Mariano Lopez, my second husband . . . I only contributed my household goods, jewelry and slaves" (Luisa Gertrudis de La Rua, 1820). This notation is important because under Spanish law this woman would continue to own what she brought into the marriage, while her new husband would own what he brought into the marriage.

The Spanish colonial frontier could be a rough place to live. There were high mortality rates as men and women died in Indian attacks and several smallpox epidemics. Thus, life expectancy was not high. In the southwestern areas of the present-day United States, especially New Mexico, Indians took captive other Indian women and children, and ransomed them to the Spanish settlers. The Spanish colonists would take these women and children, known as *criados,* into their homes as servants. The *criados* were educated in the Spanish language and the Catholic religion. These women *criadas* bridged the gap between two worlds, Indian and Spanish. They often faced discrimination in both worlds because they did not fit clearly into one or the other. Nonetheless, these women made lives for themselves and contributed greatly to Spanish culture. An important contribution occurred in the kitchen, where the *criadas* introduced Indian foods and food preparation techniques to Spanish families. They passed on medical and herbal knowledge as well. Spanish households incorporated these servants to different degrees, meaning that some *criados* were treated like family and some were mistreated.

For Spanish colonial elites, marriage was essential in retaining their elite status. Parents often arranged or maneuvered good matches for their children. Fathers carefully guarded the chastity of their daughters as an important step in arranging a good marriage. Despite these efforts, there were high rates of premarital pregnancies in the Spanish colonies. While men considered it honorable to protect their wives and daughters, they also sought sexual conquests of other women, contributing to the high rates of premarital and extramarital pregnancies. Adultery was illegal, but this law was widely violated. The lack of priests in the colonies to perform marriage ceremonies also contributed to the high rates of premarital pregnancies. Thus, some couples lived as though married, until a priest could validate their marriage in the Church. Not all of these relationships resulted in marriage. Numerous court cases involved women suing men who had promised to marry them. The courts often decided on monetary payment from the man to the woman to restore her honor. When women spoke out, the courts often moved to protect them.

The lack of church supervision showed itself in other areas as well. In some church records, people were able to change their racial status. Race was a vital part of status in the Spanish colonies, as the *castas* defined and ranked every possible racial combination. On the northern frontier of the Spanish colonies, especially in Texas, children might be baptized as *mestizos,* persons of Spanish and Indian parentage, but later in life be recorded as Spaniards. Thus, race might have been slightly less important in the colonies on the northern frontier of the Spanish empire than in the central areas such as Mexico City. Women in the Spanish colonies had some similarities, especially related to the legal system, to women in another European settlement, New Netherland.

María Calvillo

Ranching was an important business in Spanish colonial Texas, and while most of the ranchers were men, some were women. María del Carmen Calvillo became one of the largest ranch owners in the San Antonio area. She inherited the Rancho de Las Cabras from her father, Ignacio Calvillo, in April of 1814, when he was killed in an attack on the ranch. Spanish officials thoroughly investigated this raid, and the official in charge interviewed numerous witnesses, finding that the ranch was attacked by a group of Lípan Apaches and some Spaniards, including Calvillo's grandson, Ignacio Casanova. After these tragic events, María Calvillo inherited the ranch and operated it independently because her husband, Juan Trinidad Delgado, had left in the 1810s when he joined the losing side of a revolt against the Spanish government. María continued to run the ranch until her death on January 15, 1856, and she left the ranch to two of her adopted children. Calvillo's experiences were not necessarily typical of women in the Spanish colonies of the present-day United States, but they show how women could own property under the Spanish legal system and potentially become successful businesswomen in their communities, competing with the wealthiest men.

Women in the Dutch Colony of New Netherland

The Dutch colony of New Netherland began in 1624. Women in the Dutch colonies enjoyed property rights similar to those of Spanish women. Dutch women could own property when they married, and they had community property rights as well. One common practice was for spouses to write joint wills. Marten and Maeycke Cornelissen wrote their will together, which read, in part, "They, the testators, out of mutual and particular love, which during their marriage estate they have steadily borne and do now bear toward each other, declare that they have reciprocally nominated and instituted, as by these presents they do, the survivor of the two their sole and universal heir to all the property" (Cornelissen and Cornelis 1916–1919, 359–61). In the event that one of the spouses died before the other, the living spouse would receive all of the property. Women's strong property protections were short-lived in New Netherland, because English colonists invaded and incorporated New Netherland into the English colony of New York in 1664. While at first the English did not force the Dutch to use English legal practices and customs, by the 1720s, the Dutch had adopted these laws. As English law became more prominent, women began to lose their property protections.

Women in the French Colonies

France's first attempts to establish colonies in the present-day United States were not successful. French Huguenots tried to establish Fort Caroline around the present-day Georgia–South Carolina border, but the Spanish led by Pedro Menéndez de Áviles destroyed the settlement and killed the settlers. The first successful French settlements were in Canada, the Great Lakes region, and

Louisiana. While Protestants had tried to found the first French colonies, the early successes brought Catholics to the Americas. Women helped to settle the French colonies in the upper Mississippi area, as well as Louisiana, and to develop their economies based upon fur trading and farming. Men were generally fur traders, and often went out hunting for long periods of time. Many of these fur traders married Native American women, and their children were called *metís,* similar to the Spanish term *mestizo.*

In Louisiana, New Orleans became an important settlement, as its location at the mouth of the Mississippi River made it a prosperous port. A few women were offered an opportunity in New Orleans that was not present in the Spanish and Dutch colonies. In 1727, a group of Ursuline nuns from France came to New Orleans and opened a convent. The Ursulines were an order of Catholic nuns that began in northern Italy in 1535. The nuns in New Orleans opened their convent with the purpose of educating young girls, housing orphans, and acting as a hospital for the sick. Traditionally, convents acquired money for operations from young women's dowries. When a woman married, her family was obligated to provide money and material goods to her husband under French law. If a woman did not marry, but entered a convent, the dowry went to the convent. The New Orleans convent deviated from this norm. The New Orleans nuns made their money from teaching students, taking in orphans (the government gave them money to do so), selling agricultural products, and conducting other small business endeavors. As a result, the nuns began to accept Creole Cuban women without dowries into the convent. Thus, they made their convent more independent of male control than were convents in France, because the New Orleans convent did not depend upon the dowries coming from fathers for its operation. The presence of this convent offered some young girls the rare opportunity of a formal education. The convent also allowed women to devote their lives to God if they chose, and gave some a chance to avoid marriage if they desired. The New Orleans convent did not house a large number of women, but it is remarkable that the convent accepted poor women when convents in France only allowed the wealthy to enter.

Women in the English Colonies

Women came to the British colonies for a variety of reasons. Whether they settled in New England, the Chesapeake, or the South, free white women enjoyed privileges over unfree women. British women had fewer property rights than did Spanish and Dutch colonial women. Under British common law, married women lost their separate legal status; this was known as *coverture.* Any property or money a woman brought into marriage, as well as any wages she earned during marriage, belonged to her husband. A married woman could not execute a contract, make out a will, sue, or be sued. In the rare case of divorce, she was denied custody of her children. British common law dictated that a widow receive one-third of her husband's estate, but this property was not hers to sell or bequeath. She only retained use rights to it until she died. In this system, men were the preferred heirs. There were some loopholes that allowed wealthy women to maintain property, but these loopholes were not available to all women.

The Chesapeake

Throughout the British colonies, women's experiences varied based upon region and social position. The Chesapeake region saw the first successful settlements of English colonists with the founding of Jamestown in 1607. The sex ratio in early Jamestown was uneven, as there were more men than women. Many of the women who came to the Chesapeake region were indentured servants; these were people who signed a contract to work for another person, who in return would pay their passage to America. The English colonists did not use African slaves as often as indentured servants, in the early years of the Chesapeake colonies. Indentured women faced both opportunities and problems as a result of the uneven sex ratio. Women had more choices in marriage because of the abundance of men. At the same time, indentured women were punished if they became pregnant while indentured, and some were raped by their masters or other men. Immigrating without their families offered women some freedom, but also meant that they had less protection and supervision. Few of these women could read, and even fewer could write, so they did not leave behind many letters. One indentured woman in Maryland wrote to her parents and described her difficult experiences in the following manner:

> What we unfortunate English People suffer here is beyond the probability of you in England to Conceive, let it suffice that I one of the unhappy Number, am toiling almost Day and Night, and very often in the Horses druggery, with only this comfort that you Bitch you do not halfe enough, and then tied up and whipped to the Degree that you'd not serve an Annimal, scarce any thing but Indian Corn and Salt to eat and that even begrudged nay many Negroes are better used, almost naked no shoes nor stockings to wear, and the comfort after slaveing during Masters pleasure, what rest we can get is to rap ourselves up in a Blanket and ly upon the Ground, this is the deplorable Condition your poor Betty endures, and now I beg if you have any Bowels of Compassion left show it by sending me some Relief, C[l]othing is the principal thing wanting. (Sprigs 1935, 151–52)

This woman illustrates the difficult life of indentured servants, who suffered from inadequate food and clothing, isolation from family, loneliness, and long hours of hard work. As a result of these conditions and of high rates of disease, many indentured servants died young. The average life expectancy for men in the early years of the Chesapeake colonies was 43, and it was even younger for women. If indentured women lived long enough to finish their terms of service, they usually married. This meant that they had children late in life. Also, if they survived childbirth, many women outlived their husbands, so there were many widows in the Chesapeake. As a result of the high rates of widowhood and the scarcity of women in the Chesapeake, men in these colonies tended to leave widows more property than the typical one-third of the estate given to widows elsewhere, especially in New England. In fact, many Chesapeake men left their full estates in the power of their wives.

The Chesapeake colonies moved away from using indentured servants and turned towards using slaves from Africa, partly as a result of Bacon's Rebellion in 1676. Nathaniel Bacon led a group of former indentured servants and slaves, first in attacking Indians, and later in attacking Jamestown and burning down the town. The rebellion ended quickly when Bacon died of dysentery. Many women participated on both sides of the rebellion. On Bacon's side, women helped to spread information about Bacon and his efforts; on the side of the government of colonial Virginia, the Governor's wife, Lady Berkeley, often spoke out against the rebellion. As Bacon tried to legitimize his authority, he began to use formal institutions of power, such as political conventions, that excluded women. So, while Bacon's rebellion brought women some opportunities for political participation, these opportunities were limited. The increase in the use of slavery in the Chesapeake would affect women for many years to come.

New England

In contrast to settlers who came to the Chesapeake, women who came to New England generally came with their families. The largest colony, Massachusetts Bay, was a Puritan colony. This Puritan colony organized itself based upon the principles of hierarchy, patriarchy, and order. God was at the top of this hierarchy, and men were above women. The Massachusetts poet, Anne Bradstreet, describes her relationship with her husband, writing:

> If ever two were one, then surely we;
> If ever man were loved by wife, then thee;
> If ever wife was happy in a man,
> Compare with me ye women if you can.
>
> (Bradstreet 1897, 270)

Bradstreet reveals the ideal Puritan relationship between husband and wife. While the relationship was hierarchical, husbands and wives were expected to love one another. In a poem entitled "An Epitaph," Bradstreet describes the ideal Puritan goodwife:

> Here lies
> A worthy matron of unspotted life,
> A loving mother, and obedient wife,
> A friendly neighbor, pitiful to poor,
> Whom oft she fed and clothed with her store;
> To servants, wisely aweful, but yet kind,
> And as they did so they reward did find;
> A true instructor of her family,
> The which she ordered with dexterity;
> The public meetings ever did frequent,
> And in her closet constant hours she spent;
> Religious in all her words and ways . . .
>
> (Bradstreet 1897, 248)

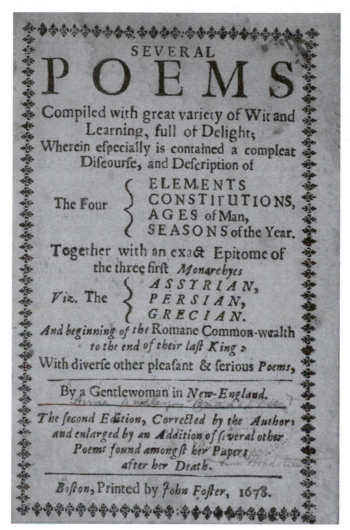

Title page of the first American printing of writer Anne Bradstreet's *Several Poems Compiled with Great Variety of Wit and Learning.* Bradstreet was the first woman poet to be published in colonial America. Her widely praised poems were published in London in 1650 and posthumously published in an expanded version in Boston in 1678. (Library of Congress)

Bradstreet describes the characteristics and roles of an ideal Puritan woman. She is pure, a good mother, an obedient wife, helpful to others, a kind but stern mistress to servants, and religious. This remarkable poet depicted the ideal woman as one who followed society's expectations and did not challenge authority. Ironically, Bradstreet was challenging conventional standards for Puritan womanhood by writing.

Not all women, however, embodied Bradstreet's ideal of the Puritan goodwife. New Englanders viewed some women as deviant and problematic. Anne Hutchinson offers one example. Hutchinson challenged the authority of the clergy when she held Bible discussions in her Boston home. Her challenges led to a trial and excommunication. Other women who fell into this category sometimes faced witchcraft accusations. Accused witches in New England were usually women, although some men were accused of practicing witchcraft, as well. The most famous of the colonial witchcraft incidents

Anne Hutchinson

In the 1630s, a woman named Anne Hutchinson presented a challenge to authorities in Massachusetts. Hutchinson led discussions of the Bible and religion in her home in Boston. At first, primarily women attended the sessions, although, later, men began to attend as well. Hutchinson argued that salvation was not achieved through visible acts or good works, but rather from faith, which was internal. This belief challenged Puritan ministers because it implied that an individual's personal relationship with God was more important than the role of the minister, and Hutchinson specifically criticized some ministers. The colonial authorities put Hutchinson on trial, at which she argued effectively with such leaders as Governor John Winthrop. Winthrop accused Hutchinson of being "one of those that have troubled the peace of the commonwealth and the churches here." He continued, "You are known to be a woman that hath had a great share in the promoting and divulging of those opinions that are the cause of this trouble" (The Examination of Mrs. Anne Hutchinson 1637, 312). When asked why she held such meetings, Hutchinson responded using the Bible arguing, "I conceive there lyes a clear rule in Titus that the elder women should instruct the younger; and then I must have a time wherein I must do it" (315). Hutchinson's ideas challenged the leaders of the colony, but the fact that she was a woman publicly speaking out about religion was a challenge as well. In the end, Hutchinson was excommunicated and exiled from the colony; she took her family to Rhode Island and then to New Netherland, where she died in an Indian attack in 1643.

took place in Salem, Massachusetts, in 1692. Scholars have debated the causes of the Salem witch accusations, but gender was a factor. During the last decades of the 17th century, many demographic changes took place that affected women's lives. There were more women than men in the population, as women were living longer than men. King Phillip's War (1675–1676) killed large numbers of men, and many young men continued moving west to acquire land. As a result, more women faced diminished marriage prospects and widowhood. The age of marriage also rose for women and, consequently, they gave birth to fewer children in general and to sons in particular. Economic changes occurred as well. Salem was an old community, with much of the land occupied by the older generation. As children found themselves less well-off than their parents, anxieties and tensions arose over inheritance within families and the larger community.

Within this context, a group of young women, many between the ages of 16 and 25, accused various men and women of witchcraft. Most of the women who were accused of witchcraft were 40 years of age or older, and past their childbearing and child-rearing years. Puritans viewed these roles as the most important for women, implying that these women no longer played vital roles in the community. The majority of the accused were women who lived alone without men. When a married woman was accused of practicing witchcraft, her husband defended her, which indicates that unmarried women were more vulnerable to witchcraft accusations. Others among the accused included women without male heirs, and the daughters of these women. This pattern indicates that Puritans considered these women a threat because they had found ways around the legal system that kept most property out of the control of women. One scholar, Carol Karlsen, argues that the accusers were worried about their inheritance, or lack of inheritance, and this was the major reason for the witchcraft accusations. These young women were not married, and many of them had lost one or both parents in Indian attacks. As a result, most of these young women were servants and did not have dowries, which would have offered them a good chance of marriage, and the subsequent improvement of their social status. These young women expressed their discontent through demonic possession, and by accusing other women of witchcraft. Throughout the course of the trials, 185 people were accused of witchcraft, 59 were tried, 31 were convicted, and 19 were executed. The colonial Governor stopped the trials in 1693. Once the trials had ended, several of the accused who had eventually confessed to practicing witchcraft took back their confessions. The Reverend Increase Mather met with Mary Osgood, who told him that "the confession that she made upon her examination for witchcraft, was wholly false, and that she was brought to the said confession by the violent urging and unreasonable pressings that were used toward her" (Recantation of Confessors of Witchcraft 1815, 221–25). Other women also explained that they had confessed because they had been pressured to do so.

The witch trials reveal women's vulnerability in a social order premised on their subordination. Other women played major roles in religion in ways that gave them more moral authority within their families and communities. The Great Awakening was a Protestant revival movement that began in the middle colonies and New England in the 1730s. Prior to this period, women tended to belong to churches, in which they participated more than did men, so this religious revival at first brought men into churches who had female relatives already attending. Later, many new women began to attend the revivals as well. In the South especially, many slave women participated in the revivals and became Christians. The emphasis by revivalist ministers on the emotional nature of religious experience was especially appealing to women. Although few churches allowed women to preach publicly, women claimed an equal right to testify before others about their religious faith. The Great Awakening also offered women some new opportunities to take part in church governance, through participation in business meetings, and sometimes through voting. Finally, because of their religious participation and devotion, women assumed expanded roles as spiritual leaders within their families.

The Middle Colonies

The middle colonies of New Jersey, New York, and Pennsylvania were characterized by national and religious diversity. Immigrants came from Holland, Sweden, Germany, Scotland, Ireland, France, Switzerland, and Africa, as well as England. In New Jersey and Pennsylvania, many of the original European settlers were Quakers seeking to escape religious persecution. In contrast to the Puritans, Quakers allowed women an important place in their religion. Women could lead church services, and women decided whether the church would

Anne Hutchinson mounted a major challenge to the male-dominated Puritan religious establishment. Banished from the Massachusetts Bay Colony for her independent views, she has been hailed as one of America's earliest feminists. Illustration from *Harper's Monthly*, vol. 102, 1901. (Library of Congress)

approve a marriage between a man and woman. Although Quaker women were bound by the laws of coverture, their religious values promoted egalitarianism between husbands and wives, and afforded women a measure of authority in the public life of their community. Besides Quakers, French Protestants, known as Huguenots, and Mennonite women traveled to the middle colonies. In the early days of these colonies, settlers lived mostly in farming communities, where men, women, and children labored inside and outside of the home.

The Deep South

In the southern colonies of the Carolinas and Georgia, mortality rates were high for men and women in the early years. For women, making food and clothing were important tasks. Many women lived in agricultural areas, and some were the mistresses of large plantations. Some of these women and their husbands owned slaves. Women in the southern colonies had stronger property rights than women in the other British colonies, as the life of Eliza Lucas Pinckney of South Carolina demonstrates. Pinckney left behind a collection of letters that provides insight into the life of a privileged colonial woman. Pinckney's father left his daughter in charge of the family plantation in South Carolina while he was out of the country. Pinckney notes, "I have the business of 3 plantations to transact, which requires more business and fatigue of other sorts than you can imagine" (Pinckney 1972, 7). Pinckney is most famous for her experimentation with the indigo plant. She wrote to her father, "I make no doubt Indigo will prove a very valuable Commodity in time if we could have the seed from the West Indias [in] time enough to plant the latter end of March, that the seed might be dry enough to gather before our frost" (16). Here, Pinckney shows her knowledge of the seed and the growing season, as well as of the South Carolina climate. She experimented with other plants as well. "I have planted a large figg orchard with design to dry and export them," says Pinckney, once again revealing her plant knowledge and business sense (35). Elizabeth Lucas Pinckney might not have been a typical South Carolina woman, but she shows that some women were able to exercise power within their families and businesses.

As the economy developed in the South and wealthy colonists turned almost exclusively to the labor of slaves, southern elites began to push for the education of their daughters to teach them to be good hostesses. While these women would not receive the same education as men, they did receive some schooling. In the 1700s, women in the southern colonies had more opportunities for work outside of the home. Some women owned shops or helped out with their husbands' shops. Others ran taverns, inns, took in boarders, educated children, or were milliners. Wealthy women did not engage in these types of work.

Women in Slavery

African women were brought to all of the English colonies as slaves, but colonists depended upon slave labor the most in the Chesapeake and the South. Slaves were kidnapped in Africa and bought by Europeans, who transferred them to the Americas across the Atlantic Ocean. The slaves made the transatlantic voyage on overcrowded ships with inadequate food. Diseases spread rapidly in the crowded conditions. As many as one in five slaves died on the journey. Life expectancy in the Americas was not much better. Slaves came from different parts of Africa, which meant that they spoke different languages and had trouble communicating with other slaves.

The British colonists first imported slaves to Virginia in the early 1600s, but since there were few slaves in the colony, their status was in flux. Slaves in early colonial Virginia had some opportunities to gain their freedom, but colonists slowly began to define white and black womanhood differently, to guarantee privilege for whites in the colony. The Virginia colonists passed a law in 1643 requiring heads of households to pay a tax on "negro women," because these women were agricultural workers. This created an artificial

Four children and a woman carrying wooden bucket on her head in foreground on a Georgia plantation, c. 1823. (Library of Congress)

distinction, since many white women also worked in the fields; but this distinction provided white women with higher status (Brown 1996, 118). In 1662, Virginia passed a law that further entrenched slavery. The first part of the law said that children born to slave women would be slaves. The second part of the law doubled the fines that whites who committed the crime of fornication had to pay when their sexual partner was a person of African descent. These laws defined slaves as being lower in status than all white colonists, even if the colonists were unfree laborers, such as indentured servants.

While colonists did not at first import slaves in large numbers to the Chesapeake region, the Carolinas and, later, Georgia did import large numbers of slaves early in the development of the colonies. At first, more male than female slaves were brought to the colonies. Most slave owners in the colonies wanted male slaves to perform difficult agricultural labor, despite the fact that women in West Africa were the agricultural laborers. In fact, so many slaves died at first that owners did not try to buy women to reproduce the slave population naturally until the 18th century. Slave women faced many hardships and short life expectancies. Some slave women did marry slave men, but these relationships were difficult because of the circumstances of slavery, especially the possibility of being separated through sale. Slave men had a difficult time finding spouses, as there were many more slave men than women. On large plantations, the ratio was even more imbalanced in favor of men. Also, children could be sold and separated from their mothers, and sons were at the highest risk of separation. Despite the difficulties, women did create and maintain families. Family and communal relationships were a fundamental source of meaning, purpose, and endurance for enslaved women.

Faced with the hardships of separation from family, forced labor, physical punishments, and vulnerability to sexual abuse by their masters, many slave women challenged authority through different means of resistance. Women resisted slavery in their everyday lives by pretending to be ill or pregnant, breaking or hiding tools, as well as by other means. Some women resorted to more extreme measures to escape slavery, by participating in rebellions or running away from their owners. Whatever the form of resistance, slave women tried to find ways to survive and cope with slavery, and in some cases to escape it.

Sexuality, Marriage, and Divorce

Women in all of the colonies faced rigid social expectations about sexuality and marriage. Women were expected to remain chaste until marriage, or if a woman did engage in a sexual relationship with a man, the woman was expected to marry the man. This was true in the Dutch, English, French, and Spanish colonies. These societal norms did not apply to slave women, as slave women often lived on different plantations than their spouses or partners, or could be separated by sale. Some flexibility was allowed in the Spanish colonies; as previously mentioned, a couple could live together as though they were married, and once a priest came to their town, the Catholic Church would validate their marriage. In all of these colonies, if women openly defied expectations and committed adultery or participated in premarital sex, they were likely to face charges. During the first generations of settlement in the English colonies, men and women were treated fairly equally after committing adultery or other sexual crimes. By the 18th century, though, women faced harsher penalties for these acts, and bore much of the responsibility for them. Despite this change, divorce was possible for women in the New England colonies because Puritans understood marriage to be a civil contract that could be broken; however, divorces remained rare. Women in the southern colonies had fewer opportunities for divorce. In the Spanish colonies, the Catholic Church did not allow couples to divorce and remarry. If one spouse harshly mistreated or neglected the other and the couple could not be reconciled, the couple could separate, but neither party could remarry unless their spouse died. In cases of adultery or premarital sex being openly flaunted, Spanish colonial authorities prosecuted women, and often the penalty was to send them to a household where the woman could be monitored. Women were not sent to jail in the Spanish colonies. Thus, in general, the settlers in the colonies of the present-day United States expected women to follow strict guidelines concerning their sexuality. When women challenged these strictures, they were punished.

Women's Work

In all of the colonies, women's work was similar, and was based upon gendered divisions of labor. Men and women had different jobs, but all of these jobs were vital in the functioning of the household. Women labored inside and outside of their homes. They cooked, cleaned, cared for animals, procured and prepared food, and made clothing. Many women, especially indentured servants and slaves, performed grueling agricultural labor. Women bore, cared for, and raised children. They acted as midwives. Sometimes they ran businesses or helped out with their husbands' businesses. An example of women's work is illustrated in a book published in colonial Virginia, called *The Compleat Housewife*. In this work, Eliza Smith explains how to prepare a pigeon pie and how to prepare eel. She also tells how to prevent miscarriages. She writes: "Take of Dragon's blood the Weight of a silver Two-pence, and a Drachm of red Coral, the Weight of two Barley-corns of Ambergrease, the Weight of three Barley-corns of *East India* Bezoar; make all this into a very fine powder, and mix them well together, and keep them close in a Box; and if you are frighted or need it, take as much at a Time as will lie on a Penny, and keep very still and quiet" (Smith 1742,191). Colonial women had to know how to prepare meals, as well as know medical information that could save their lives or the lives of family members. Wealthier women often had the help of servants or slaves, and this allowed elite women free time in which they could read, write, do needlework, and entertain; in other words, servant and slave labor allowed elite women the time and opportunity to create an elite culture. Also, as colonial economies became more developed and complex, wealthier women began to buy some of the things they needed, rather than producing them at home. Because it was essential for the survival of the household, women's domestic work was respected and valued in colonial society. In addition, the work women sometimes performed outside of the household enabled them to move into public areas and challenge accepted gender roles, or at least to increase their authority within their accepted roles.

Conclusion

Colonial women had different experiences, but whether of Spanish, Dutch, French, English, or African descent, women were expected to conform to their societies' expectations for proper gender roles, which emphasized female dependence and subordination. Most women followed these guidelines. Some women challenged them, however, in ways both dramatic and quiet. Such challenges caused social disruption and were met with a punitive response. They also enabled women to carve out some new opportunities for autonomy, influence, and authority in the household, and in the world beyond it.

References and Further Reading

Berkin, Carol. *First Generations: Women in Colonial America*. New York: Hill & Wang, 1996.

Bradstreet, Anne. *The Poems of Mrs. Anne Bradstreet: Together with Her Prose Remains.* Introduction by Charles Eliot Norton. New York: Duodecimos, 1897.

Brooks, James F. *Captives and Cousins: Slavery, Kinship, and Community in the Southwest Borderlands.* Chapel Hill: University of North Carolina Press, 2002.

Brown, Kathleen M. *Good Wives, Nasty Wenches, and Anxious Patriarchs: Gender, Race, and Power in Colonial Virginia.* Chapel Hill: University of North Carolina Press, 1996.

Chipman, Donald E., and Harriet Denise Joseph. *Notable Men and Women of Spanish Texas.* Austin: University of Texas Press, 1999.

Clark, Emily. "Patrimony without Pater: The New Orleans Ursuline Community and the Creation of a Material Culture." In *French Colonial Louisiana and the Atlantic World,* ed. Bradley G. Bond, 95–133. Baton Rouge: Louisiana State University Press, 2005.

Cornelissen, Marten, and Maeycke Cornelis. "The Will of Marten Cornelissen and Maeycke Cornelis, 1676–1677." In *Early Records of the Colony and County of Albany and the Colony of Rensselaerswyck,* ed. A. J. F. Van Laer and trans. Jonathan Pearson, 359–61. Albany: State University of New York Press, 1916–1919.

Cummins, Light T. "Church Courts, Marriage Breakdown, and Separation in Spanish Louisiana, West Florida, and Texas." *Journal of Texas Catholic History and Culture* 4 (1993): 97–114.

Dunn, Mary Maples. "Saints and Sinners: Congregational and Quaker Women in the Early Colonial Period." *American Quarterly* 30 (1978): 582–601.

Evans, Sara M. *Born for Liberty: A History of Women in America.* New York: Free Press Paperbacks, 1997.

"The Examination of Mrs. Anne Hutchinson at the Court at Newtown." In *The Antinomian Controversy, 1636–1638: A Documentary History,* ed. David D. Hall, 311–48. Middletown, CT: Wesleyan University Press, 1968.

Gutiérrez, Ramón. *When Jesus Came the Corn Mothers Went Away: Marriage, Sexuality, and Power in New Mexico, 1500–1846.* Palo Alto, CA: Stanford University Press, 1991.

Luisa Gertrudis de La Rua, Bexar County Archives. WE 98, June 25, 1820.

Karlsen, Carol F. *The Devil in the Shape of a Woman: Witchcraft in Colonial New England.* New York: W. W. Norton & Company, 1987.

Kierner, Cynthia A. *Beyond the Household: Women's Place in the Early South, 1700–1835.* Ithaca, NY: Cornell University Press, 1998.

Lindley, Susan Hill. *"You Have Stept Out of Your Place": A History of Women and Religion in America.* Louisville, KY: Westminster John Knox Press, 1996.

McDonald, Dedra S. "Negotiated Conquests: Domestic Servants and Gender in the Spanish and Mexican Borderlands, 1598–1860." PhD diss., Albuquerque: University of New Mexico, 2000.

Narrett, David E. *Inheritance and Family Life in Colonial New York City.* Ithaca, NY: Cornell University Press, 1992.

Norton, Mary Beth. *Founding Mothers and Fathers: Gendered Power and the Forming of American* Society. New York: Vintage Books, 1996.

Pinckney, Eliza Lucas. *The Letterbook of Eliza Lucas Pinckney, 1739–1762,* ed. Elise Pinckney. Columbia, SC: University of South Carolina Press, 1972.

"Recantations of Confessors of Witchcraft." In *Collections of the Massachusetts Historical Society,* 2nd ser., 3 (1815): 221–25.

Salmon, Marylynn. *Gender and the Law of Property in Early America.* Chapel Hill: University of North Carolina Press, 1986.

Shammas, Carole, Marylynn Salmon, and Michel Dahlin. *Inheritance in America from Colonial Times to the Present.* New Brunswick, NJ: Rutgers University Press, 1987.

Smith, E. *The Compleat Housewife, or Accomplished Gentlewoman's Companion,* 5th ed. Williamsburg, VA: William Parks, 1742.

Sprigs, Elizabeth. "Elizabeth Sprigs to John Sprigs." In *Colonial Captivities, Marches, and Journeys,* ed. Isabel Calder, 151–52. New York: MacMillan, 1935.

Stuntz, Jean A. *HERS, His, & Theirs: Community Property Law in Spain and Early Texas.* Lubbock: Texas Tech University Press, 2005.

Sumaria against Residents of Calvillo Ranch for his Murder, Bexar Archives. Roll 053:713–14, 728, April 15, 1814.

Tjarks, Alicia V. "Comparative Demographic Analysis of Texas, 1777–1793." In *New Spain's Far Northern Frontier: Essays on Spain in the American West, 1540–1821,* ed. David J. Weber, 135–69. Dallas, TX: Southern Methodist University Press, 1979.

Tjarks, Alicia V. "Demographics, Ethnic, and Occupational Structure of New Mexico, 1790." *The Americas* 35 no. 1 (July 1978): 45–88.

Ulrich, Laurel Thatcher. *Goodwives: Image and Reality in the Lives of Women in Northern New England, 1650–1750.* New York: Vintage Books, 1980.

Weber, David J. *The Spanish Frontier in North America.* New Haven, CT: Yale University Press, 1992.

Daughters of Liberty: Women and the American Revolution

3

Pia Katarina Jakobsson

The 18th century was a period of both dramatic change and surprising stability. The Revolutionary War created an independent nation, yet the new American republic retained many of the elements of the older colonial order. Similarly, women made important contributions to the war effort both leading up to and during the Revolutionary War, sometimes dramatically challenging traditional gender roles, yet the overall changes in the status and roles of women, as a group, in the early Republic were surprisingly limited.

Women's Status and Roles in Colonial America

Gender roles and relations in the colonies at the beginning of the 18th century resembled those in earlier periods, although the increase in native-born colonists had diminished the early imbalance between men and women. Society continued to be organized as a hierarchical, interdependent network, in which individual members had limited flexibility of movement and were bound to others in the family, community, and state by a system of mutual obligation. Men were expected to take on leadership positions, both within the family and in society. Women, servants, and children were seen as dependents, represented by the head of household because it was assumed that their interests were the same. Younger men deferred to older men, and women deferred to their husbands. Formal education was, with few exceptions, only available to the elite, and then mostly to men, but Protestant women were sometimes taught to read the Bible, and on occasion, daughters were educated as a symbol of the wealth of the family.

Traditionally, women had been seen as lesser men, with their capacities for physical strength, rationality, and morality inferior in degree, but not different in kind, from men's capacities. Somewhat like children or feeble-minded people, women were thought to be less responsible and capable than men. The Bible said God created woman from Adam's rib as the helpmeet of man. The bodies of men and women were thought to be similar enough that illustrations in medical books showed a male body representing both the male and the female, since, apart from the minor matter of women carrying the fetus and the position of the genitals, women's bodies were simply less developed versions of male bodies.

Over the course of the 18th century, society changed in numerous ways, as a result of the Great Awakening, the Enlightenment, the growth of commercialization, the expansion of the public sphere, and the American Revolution. These changes profoundly affected the relationship between the individual and society, and also altered conceptions of gender difference and gender roles in the new American republic.

Gender and Religion

In the 16th century, the Protestant Reformation had shifted the balance between society and the individual by making one's personal relationship to God more important than the clerical hierarchy that was so powerful in the Catholic Church. Protestant women no longer had access to the monastic life, which had been an acceptable alternative to marriage, but they secured other advantages. Protestants held that salvation came out of faith and God's love, rather than out of good works and participation in church-sanctioned sacraments, thus making the external hierarchies less important. To Protestants, the Bible, not the church fathers, was the ultimate source of authority. People were encouraged to learn to read so they could know God's words themselves. According to the Moravian Bishop John Amos Comenius, girls and women too should learn to read, since "they too are formed in the image of God, and share in his grace and in the kingdom of the world to come" (Comenius 1967, 68). Accordingly, in 1742, the Moravians founded the first educational institution for young women in the present-day United States, Bethlehem Female Seminary in Pennsylvania.

The understanding of salvation as individual and internal grew even stronger with the Great Awakening, the religious revival movement that came from England and swept across the colonies during the 1730s and 1740s. Women played active roles in this movement, empowered by the call to conversion from the heart rather than the head, and by the challenge against established church structures. A religious appeal based on emotion, rather than tradition, scriptures, or theological sources in Latin was a lot more accessible to women. Although only Quakers officially accepted female ministers, women in sectarian groups remained active as itinerant preachers even after the revival ebbed out. These women gave witness to their conversion experiences and shared their faith at informal meetings, sometimes even baptizing newcomers. Women also supported religious movements by fundraising for local churches, providing hospitality for visiting preachers, and by encouraging their husbands and sons to attend services. By the end of the 18th century,

An emotional meeting of the United Society of Believers in Christ's Second Coming, a utopian community in New York state founded by Anne Lee in 1774. Known as the Shakers for their vigorous dancing, the group favored communal work over specialized duties of men and women. Both sexes participated in domestic labor, and profits from sales of canned goods and furniture were shared by all. During the Second Great Awakening, 19 major Shaker communities were established in New England, New York, Kentucky, Ohio, and Indiana. Because of the requirement for absolute chastity, however, the group's numbers declined from a high of over 5,000 to virtual extinction by 1988. (Library of Congress)

the Shakers emerged. They believed that Jesus would return in the form of a woman, and each congregation was led by a man and a woman together.

Revolutions in Science and Philosophy

The religious revivals were, at least in part, a response to the scientific revolution and the Enlightenment, intellectual movements originating in Europe in the 17th and 18th centuries that shook the established order and questioned conventional authority. Rooted in the educational changes coming out of the Reformation and the Renaissance, new ways to think about the world developed in the 17th century. A number of people, such as Francis Bacon, Rene Descartes, and Isaac Newton, explored new approaches to the study of nature. They shared a desire to develop reliable methods to explore the natural world by experiment and reason, relying on mechanical explanations rather than resorting to divine intervention. They believed nature was governed by natural laws that could be understood and used to manipulate the environment. Earlier, religious study had been the major focus of scholarly effort, and study of the world a potential diversion. To these intellectuals, science was not a distraction, and did not take time and effort away from the contemplation of God. In particular, Newton thought that, by studying nature, he was studying God's work. In the 18th century, this focus on scientific reasoning and practical experiment led to a steady flow of discoveries, technical inventions, and improved mechanical processes.

French philosopher Rene Descartes saw the mind as an abstract, rational entity that was separate from the body and the physical world, a disembodied entity that was, for all intents and purposes, classless and sexless. This led some writers to argue that if the mind had no sex, perhaps there was no difference between the intellectual capacity of men and women. As Mary Astell put it, "Sense is a portion that God himself has been pleas'd to distribute to both Sexes with an impartial Hand, but learning is what Men have engross'd to themselves" (Springborg 1996, 21). Although not always framed in Cartesian terms, the idea that the main intellectual differences between men and women stemmed from differences in education was to be taken up by numerous writers over the 18th century.

British philosopher John Locke took the idea of an independent reasoning subject even further. He suggested the mind at birth "to be, as we say, white paper, void of all characters, without any ideas" until it was furnished with them "from Experience" (Locke 1995, Bk. 2, Ch. 1, sec. 2). This position had radical implications for the understanding of the individual and his or her relationship with society. If the individual is the sum total of his or her experience, then all are the same at birth; there is no innate hierarchy and there are no essential gender differences. From this it follows that changing the kinds of experience a person has will change who they are. Thus, education is not just a means of acquiring specific information or the development of learning. Rather, a person can re-create himself through education. In the 18th century, this translated into the concept of the self-made man. The narrative of the self-made Benjamin Franklin became hugely popular as an example of the empty slate written on through a lifetime of education and deliberately created experiences. The notion of the mind as an empty slate only written on by experience would also strengthen the argument in favor of education for women. This did not necessarily translate into a demand for changing gender roles; the stated goal was usually to make women more useful as helpmeets and mothers.

For women, the Enlightenment presented both an opportunity and a challenge. It was an opportunity because theoretically women could claim participation in society as rational, disembodied, unsexed minds. At the same time, Enlightenment scientists and philosophers made new distinctions between women and men that justified women's exclusion from the public sphere. Women were increasingly portrayed as emotional and frivolous and lacking in the rational capacity necessary to participate in political and economic life. The new science, in the form of autopsies and other empirical investigation, was used to show that women really were physically different from men. Women's physical pleasure was no longer seen as a prerequisite for conception to take place, and the female body began to be portrayed as different in kind (rather than degree) from the male body. Women came to be considered as constituting a group in their own right, but that also meant they were seen as completely other than the norm, which was male. Likewise, a newfound focus on racial distinctions made it clear that slaves (blacks) were different from free people (whites). By the end of the 18th century, the rational individual subject was marked as a white, public, professional male, with the colored, domestic, emotional, and female designated as something other than—and decidedly inferior to—the Enlightenment ideal.

Another radical idea proposed by John Locke was that marriage, and political institutions, were built on contractual relationships rather than being divinely ordained. In the state of nature, Locke claimed, all people had perfect freedom and perfect equality. From that came the first society, the "conjugal society" between husband and wife, created by "a voluntary compact between man and woman" (Locke 1998, Bk. 2, Ch. 6, sec. 77). When husband and wife disagree, as must happen, one of them has to make the final decision and this "naturally falls to the man's share, as the abler and stronger." This only goes for the things they share, however, leaving "the wife in the full and free possession of what by contract is her peculiar right" (Locke 1998, Bk. 2, Ch. 6, sec. 82). In other words, Locke believed that people did not have power over others by divine proclamation, but because, in a structured society, some division of responsibilities was desirable.

The notion that social relations were founded on a voluntary compact between people who were equals in a state of nature became very important to the founders of the American republic. A contract is an agreement between two or more parties in which each party agrees to give something to receive something else. If one party breaks the contract by not contributing what they have agreed, the other party is no longer bound by the agreement, and the contract is null and void. In the American colonies, political thinkers such as Thomas Jefferson, Thomas Paine, and James Otis took from Locke the idea that this is how social relations between a ruler and the people work as well, and if the king or government does not live up to the contract, the governed could withdraw their consent to be governed by that person or entity. Other, traditionally disenfranchised groups, including women, poor people, and African Americans, picked up on the voluntary and reciprocal aspects of a contract, suggesting that they too might be parties to a contract, and had the right to give consent and to withdraw consent in the governments of both the family and the state.

The American version of Enlightenment thought was less averse to religion than some European interpretations, and was more influenced by republican political ideals as developed by thinkers such as Montesquieu and later Thomas Paine. Republican principles—especially rejecting inherited rule by a monarch and supporting rule by the consent of the governed, sovereignty of the people, and rule of law—became increasingly important to the American colonists as tensions with England grew in the second half of the 18th century.

Social and Economic Changes

Social and material conditions changed as dramatically as did the worlds of science and philosophy. Understanding of the world greatly increased, and the ability to produce both greater quantities and better quality food and other goods increased as well, making it possible to provide for more people. During the first half of the 18th century, the size of the population in the English colonies exploded, growing from less than 300,000 in 1700 to four times that number (over 1 million) in 1750. By 1800, the population had quadrupled again, and stood at 5.3 million people. The economy grew as well, but the growth was not even. Those with the resources to invest in commercial ventures, including shipping, fishing, and commercial farming enterprises, became rich very quickly. Those people who had once been farmhands and now moved to the cities to work for weekly wages improved their fortunes only to some extent, and they were increasingly vulnerable to being replaced by cheaper labor. Thus, social inequality increased, and the number of landless poor grew significantly at the same time as commerce and general wealth grew. Also, as wage labor outside the home became the norm, the work women did within the domestic sphere became increasingly invisible as work, a development that would grow much more pronounced in the 19th century.

Not only labor moved out of the home. People met in coffee houses, taverns, and other public places to discuss news, politics, and ideas; and they increasingly thought of themselves as members of a public with opinions to express and share. The demand for information about political ideas, new technology, business transactions, and consumer goods was strong, and new media struggled to keep up. Early in the 18th century, the press had been a mouthpiece for the colonial administration, but by the middle of the century, there were around twenty publications in circulation published by independent printers, which represented a variety of interests and political affiliations. It is difficult to say exactly how widespread literacy was, or how many people would have read any particular text, since people shared reading materials, and newspapers and pamphlets could circulate for a long time after their initial publication. There were large differences in literacy rates between white men and other groups, and between rural and urban areas; but in the second half of the 18th century, literacy rates are estimated to have been 75 to 90 percent among white men in New England, and about half that among white women.

Although women were not welcome in taverns (although they sometimes worked in them as waitresses), they read newspapers at home and found ways to express their views about the changing world around them. It is clear from diaries and letters that many women kept up with current events and debated their positions with both male and female friends and family. Women from well-to-do families were expected to read, although there were regular debates in the press as to what specifically they should read, and some forms of writing were acceptable for women to participate in, even professionally. Women did not hold political office and did not have the right to vote, but elite women sat at the dinner table with, and intimately knew, the men in power. Much of political life and debate was taking place in people's homes, and women were actively involved in at least some of those debates. On rare occasions, women would contribute articles or poems to newspapers or pamphlets (such as those written by Mercy Warren), the author usually only identified as "a Lady."

Mercy Otis Warren—First Lady of the Revolution

Mercy Otis Warren (1728–1814) lived all of her life in Massachusetts. She came from one of Boston's first families, both socially and politically: her brother James Otis and her husband James Warren were both involved in the Revolution and the establishment of the American republic. She was a staunch republican and patriot, who believed that men and women were intellectual equals, although she thought men and women had different responsibilities. In a letter to an anonymous young female, she wrote, "My dear, it may be necessary for you to *seem* inferior . . . but you need not be so. Let them have their little game, since it may have been so willed. It won't hurt you; it will amuse them" (Warren n.d.).

Warren's first published work, *The Adulateur,* was printed in 1772. Like the next four of her publications, it was ostensibly a play, but clearly one that was not intended to be acted on a stage. All of the plays were political allegories, with the villains clearly identifiable as members of the British administration. Despite publishing anonymously, Warren was not secretive about her work. She corresponded extensively with family and with a circle of friends that included John and Abigail Adams and a group of elite Massachusetts women.

One of Warren's most influential works was a pamphlet outlining her reaction to the proposed new constitution put together by the Constitutional Convention held in Philadelphia in 1787. She attacked the proposal as a many-headed monster that would create a "Republican *form* of government, founded on the principles of monarchy" because it centralized power far too much (Warren 1888). She listed 18 points of contention and pushed for a Bill of Rights that, among other things, included liberty of the press, limits of the judiciary power, rotation of terms, or term limits, for political office, and increased state powers. Warren's clear statement of what became the anti-Federalist position was widely distributed. For the debates preceding ratification of the Constitution, 1600 copies of her *Observations* were printed up in New York alone. It did not succeed in stopping ratification, but Warren's pamphlet contributed to the immediate passing of the Bill of Rights.

In 1805, Warren's magnum opus was published, under her own name, entitled *History of the Rise, Progress and Termination of the American Revolution.* She died in 1814.

Trouble Brewing

As the colonists developed their own customs and culture, and built communities far away from England, they found it increasingly difficult to be dependent on the mother country. This became particularly obvious during the French and Indian War, a conflict fought between the English and the French, and the Native American allies of both countries, which began on the North American continent and spread to Europe. In North America, the war lasted from 1754 to 1763, and effectively ended French colonial power on the continent. During the conflict, the colonists had opportunities to notice differences between American and English culture, particularly within the respective military forces, since there were thousands of British troops involved. The British officers, in charge of a conscripted army, did not hide their

contempt for the American volunteer forces, which were based on cooperation rather than hierarchy. The colonists in turn thought the British officers
were arrogant. Men from different colonies fighting together far away from
home also helped build a sense of community among the Americans. Those
on the home front followed developments in the growing number of newspapers, and felt as if they were part of a common struggle.

When the French and Indian War ended, 10,000 British troops remained
in North America, creating a constant source of tension between the soldiers
and the colonists. Additionally, the war had left Britain seriously in debt, and
it took steps to increase revenue from duties and tariffs in America, claiming
it only right for the colonists to help pay for the defense of the empire. The
British Parliament passed the Sugar Act in 1764, and set up a series of Admi-
ralty courts to quell the expected challenges to the act. This was followed by
the Stamp Act in 1765, the first act to impose a direct tax on domestic consumption in the colonies, rather than merely assigning tariffs on trade. From
this point, there was a constant tug-of-war between the British Crown and
the American colonists. The colonists increasingly felt that their interests were
different than those of the British, and resented being taxed with no direct
representation in Parliament. The British saw the colonists as disloyal and
dangerously unruly; colonies were part of the motherland and should not
have an independent agenda.

In 1770, the Boston Massacre angered and frustrated the population of
Boston. As illustrated by a classic engraving by Paul Revere, Bostonians felt
that British soldiers had shot, unprovoked, into a crowd of innocent people,
including women and children. The British soldiers claimed the crowd had
been throwing things at them and had acted threateningly. In 1773, colonists
dumped tons of tea into Boston Harbor to protest the Tea Act, an event known
as the Boston Tea Party. In response, the British Parliament introduced a
number of Coercive Acts in 1774. The colonists referred to them as the Intol-
erable Acts, furious that their rights as free men were infringed upon. The
acts did nothing to suppress opposition, and in fact were the impetus for the
first collective colonial assembly, the First Continental Congress, which was
organized to coordinate the response and step up resistance. Colonists were
still hoping for a peaceful resolution, but as the situation deteriorated, people
started planning for alternatives. In 1775, armed conflict began with the events
in Lexington and Concord, but it was only in 1776, when Thomas Paine's
Common Sense was published, that the call for independence overcame colonists' fears of separating from England. Even so, only about a third of the
colonists were active Patriots. One-third remained loyal to the British, and
about one-third were more or less neutral. In July of 1776, the American
colonies declared independence, but the fighting would go on for another
seven years.

Women and the Road to War

During the period leading up to the war, women participated in the patriotic
cause in several different ways. They organized and participated in boycotts,

they produced boycotted goods at home, and they helped shape public opinion by writing about political events and their own activities. In doing so, they regularly challenged conventional notions of gender roles, but their activities were largely framed in terms of traditional female concerns about family and virtue.

Women were actively involved in making decisions about household purchases and consumption. That made them a powerful force in boycotts of imports such as tea and textiles, which was an important way to protest tariffs and trade limitations imposed by the British. Women also acted as a peer pressure group toward each other and toward their male family members. On some occasions, women even made and signed their own petitions. On October 25, 1774, one of the most well-known petitions was signed by 51 women of Edenton, North Carolina, who promised they would abide by the nonimportation resolutions passed by the First Continental Congress and proudly pledged that they would not drink tea.

Not only did women refrain from buying boycotted products, they organized spinning bees where women got together, each bringing their own spinning wheels and spending the day together producing homespun cloth and encouraging each other to keep up a patriotic spirit. In Boston, the Daughters of Liberty was formed to organize home manufacture. In the southern colonies, it took longer for home manufacture to spread. Plantation owners raised cash crops and used the money to buy the things they needed, which made it a bigger adjustment to set up the facilities and teach slave women to spin and weave. In boycotting goods and engaging in home manufacture, and in linking these activities to the larger civic good, women imbued their domestic activities with political meaning, drawing on their conventional duties to claim a role for themselves in the events unfolding in the public sphere.

Often, women supported men's activities from home. When the Boston Tea Party took place in 1773, women were not part of the group that boarded British ships. However, the event was planned at the house of Sarah Bradlee Fulton, and it was to her home the men returned to change out of their Native American disguises. Such private involvement is very difficult to trace unless mentioned in diaries or letters, and it is impossible to know how widespread women's participation in this kind of activity was. Such acts appear to have been common enough not to be shocking, but uncommon enough not to be expected.

Contemporary writers emphasized both the real and the symbolic importance of female patriotic activity, and used women's efforts to help create enthusiasm for the Patriot cause. Initially, although many pamphlets, articles, poems, and letters were apparently aimed at women, this was as much to shame men into action as it was to engage women in active participation. In 1768, a poem entitled "The 20 Daughters of Liberty" was published in the *Pennsylvania Gazette*. The anonymous author says, "Since the men . . . Are kept by a sugar-plum quietly down . . . Let the Daughters of Liberty nobly arise." Women were asked to do their patriotic duty, not because their actions would make a direct difference, but because when women acted they "pointed out their duty to men." If even women were prepared to make sacrifices for the Patriot cause, this author chastises, men, who possessed political agency and

A British cartoon ridicules a group of women from North Carolina who, on October 25, 1774, boldly declared in the Edenton Proclamation that they would not drink tea or use English-made goods "untill [*sic*] such time that all Acts which tend to Enslave this our Native Country shall be repealed." (Library of Congress)

responsibility, should be ashamed at not doing their part (Kerber 1980, 38). Later appeals were wholeheartedly positive toward female patriotism. In 1776, Anne Terrell wrote in the *Virginia Gazette,* urging soldiers' wives to support the war effort with boycotts and prayers, while their husbands provided armed support for the "glorious cause of liberty" (Terrell 1776). The political theorist and historian Mercy Otis Warren expressed her patriotism in a number of pamphlets, plays, and poems. She and other female writers and activists justified their transgression of gender boundaries in two main ways, by claiming that they were simply defending the domestic sphere, since "every domestic enjoyment depends on the unimpaired possession of civil and religious liberty," and by framing themselves as patriots first and women second (Warren 1805, iv).

Among the Patriots, appropriate female behavior was, at least for the time being, defined to include active participation in political activities on behalf of the colonists. The British saw it differently. They specifically used gender roles to criticize the protests against them. Women such as the ladies of Edenton were portrayed as bad mothers and neglectful wives. In numerous satirical prints and texts, the British warned that women's participation in political activities would rob them of their femininity and make them un-suitable for domestic life, upend the natural hierarchy between men and women, and inevitably lead to family dissolution and social chaos.

Women at War

As the boycotts and protests escalated into armed conflict in the spring of 1775, women remained involved in the war effort in numerous ways, which both conformed to and challenged conventional gender expectations. They raised funds, collected materials (including saltpeter for gunpowder), knitted stockings, manufactured cartridges, engaged in public protests, and acted as deputy heads of household in the absence of their husbands and fathers; some even went along to the battlefield. The kinds of activities women participated in during the Revolution were shaped in part by their status, with upper-class women more involved in writing and fundraising activities, and lower-class women more involved in street protests and going along to the battlefield.

In 1780, Esther DeBerdt Reed, wife of the governor of Pennsylvania, and Sarah Franklin Bache, daughter of Benjamin Franklin, organized a women's fundraising organization for the cause, The Ladies Association of Philadel-phia. Reed published a call for support entitled "Sentiments of an American Woman," in which she gave historical examples of women patriots, and ar-gued that women were as willing to sacrifice for their nation as were men. DeBerdt framed women's effort in terms of support and gratitude for the men who were fighting. She clearly envisioned women's involvement in public affairs as ancillary, not independent, although as vitally important.

The women who joined the Ladies Association solicited funds in person, knocking on doors. Mary Frazier of Chester County, Pennsylvania and her neighbors participated by "day after day collecting from neighbors and friends far and near, whatever they could spare for the comfort of the destitute soldiers" ("A Reminiscence" 1922, 55). Reed and Bache wanted to give the money they had collected directly to individual soldiers, but their idea was vetoed by George Washington. After some negotiation, Washington agreed with the association that they would use the money to make shirts that could be given directly to individual soldiers. By the end of 1780, over 2,000 linen shirts had been donated, each with the name of the woman who made it sewn into the fabric. This group of elite women thus claimed the right to publicly express their patriotism, while still remaining limited by conventional expectations as to the domestic nature of women's contributions to the politi-cal sphere.

Women, mostly those of lower status, were important participants in group protests. On more than 30 occasions, between 1776 and 1779, colo-nists gathered to protest food prices. This was a traditional form of female activism, both in the colonies and in Europe, perhaps because concern over food supplies was seen as an extension of the domestic sphere. Still, oppo-nents sometimes ridiculed female involvement in food riots as inappropri-ate, claiming that the artisans' and tradesmen's wives who participated were abandoning their familial duties and roles. Sometimes women acted together with men, and sometimes they acted by themselves. Some of the protests were peaceful, but some of them became violent, as mobs challenged merchants who were hoarding or overcharging for food.

Women also contributed to the war effort by taking over men's labor at home. Farmwives like Abigail Adams (wife of Johns Adams) managed farms, and the wives of artisans and shop owners ran businesses, sometimes with the help of a trusted apprentice or son, sometimes by themselves. They settled accounts, paid taxes, maintained production and sales, and in other ways acted as deputy husbands. The war touched them in other ways too. Women left behind were forced to support large families with limited means, and were at risk of rape by looting soldiers who had, by choice or accident, been separated from their unit. They had to function independently to survive, and there is no way their fathers, husbands, and sons could have been successful at the front without the contributions of women at the home front. Some women responded to the challenges brought on by the war with anxiety. For others, taking on unconventional responsibilities instilled in them a newfound confidence in their abilities, and a new sense of possibility for their roles as women in the American nation.

Women at the Front

Not all women stayed at home. Some went to the front lines and were actively involved in the war effort, as camp followers, and sometimes by serving as soldiers. Although some camp followers were prostitutes, many of the women who traveled with the Continental Army were married to soldiers and performed important support functions for the troops, such as cooking, doing laundry, and nursing the sick and wounded. Wives both of officers and enlisted men accompanied the troops, although most camp followers were poor women who had no other way of supporting themselves and their children while their husbands were away at war. There were so many women going along with the troops, and doing such important work, that George Washington unofficially set a quota of 1 woman for every 15 soldiers in Continental Army regiments. Such women drew regular rations and were tolerated, since they left the men free to fight, but they were not encouraged, and they were subjected to strict rules and regulations. Camp followers were allowed to remain with the troops only if they were married and if they charged only minimal fees for laundry and other services, but they were not allowed to be visible when the army marched. Although they performed critical services for the army, camp followers traveled, lived, and worked under highly stressful conditions that put their own and their children's health and lives at risk.

A very small group of women saw military action themselves, and they were sometimes honored for their soldierly contributions to the war effort. Usually they were wives who had gone along with their husbands, and who took over when their husbands were wounded or killed. For instance, Margaret "Captain Molly" Corbin fought alongside her husband John in Fort Washington, New York in 1776 when the fort was attacked. John had been assisting a gunner until the gunner was killed; then John took charge of the cannon, and Margaret assisted him until he, too, was killed. Margaret continued loading and firing the cannon by herself until she was wounded. She never fully recovered from her wounds, and she became the first woman to receive a pension from the United States government as a disabled soldier. She was buried at West Point beneath a statue dedicated to her memory.

Very unusual, but not unique, was Deborah Sampson, who enlisted on her own. Disguised as a man, Sampson served in the Continental Army under the name of Robert Shurtleff. Deborah grew up as an indentured servant in a family with ten sons, and then worked as a schoolteacher before enlisting in 1782. She posed as a man too young to have to shave, and the loose-fitting clothes and minimal attention to hygiene in the army made her masquerade successful for more than a year. The first time she was wounded, she cared for herself to avoid detection. Her sex was finally detected when she was wounded again and examined by a doctor, who realized that she was a woman. He quietly informed her superiors, and she was discharged. For years after the war, Sampson traveled the country and gave lecture tours in which she wore her uniform, told of her exploits, and executed the manual of arms. After a long struggle, she was finally granted a pension for her services (including two years of back pay) in 1805.

A number of more or less mythological narratives of brave women have also become part of Revolutionary lore. Molly (Hays) Pitcher is one of the more famous woman soldiers of the Revolutionary War, but we know very little about her. According to legend, Hays traveled with her soldier husband, and earned her nickname by carrying pitchers of water for the soldiers at the Battle of Monmouth, New Jersey in 1778. During the battle, her husband was wounded, and Hays took over his gun. There is no actual evidence for any of this. The only thing known about the historical woman, Mary Ludwig Hays McCauley, is that she was awarded a pension by the State of Pennsylvania for her service during the war, which does seem to indicate her having done something out of the ordinary. Another legendary Revolutionary era woman, Nancy Hart, is known as the Amazon Warrior. Hart supposedly killed several British soldiers when they stopped at her family's farm. She also purportedly fought Indians and acted as a spy on several occasions, wandering into a British camp dressed up as a simpleminded man, and gathering information by listening to people talk around her. As with the story of Molly Pitcher, there is very little historical detail to back up the tall tales about Hart. However, the myths themselves served an important function. On the one hand, they highlighted how unusual the exploits of Hays and Hart were, revealing the limited opportunities most women had to participate in the American Revolution. On the other hand, the myths of these brave women emphasized the seriousness of the conflict and the importance of unity in the new nation by valorizing female participation in battle. Desperate times call for desperate measures, and these were times when everybody was called to serve.

African Americans, too, were involved in the Revolutionary War in several ways. Many black people sided with the British in the hope that slavery would be forbidden by them, or at least that individuals who had served would be freed. Some slave men served in the Continental Army under their

Deborah Sampson Gannett—Continental Soldier

Deborah Sampson (1760–1827) served in the Continental Army under the name of Robert Shurtleff. She was born in Plympton, Massachusetts, where she spent the first few years of her life. After her father abandoned the family, her mother sent her and several of her siblings off to live with relatives. At the age of ten, Deborah became an indentured servant in the household of Mr. and Mrs. Thomas in Middleborough. She stayed there for about ten years and learned spinning and weaving, cooking, the handling of farm equipment, as well as how to handle a musket. During the winters, she was able to attend school. When she left the Thomas family, she stayed in Middleborough and worked as a weaver and as a schoolteacher for about three years.

After two of the Thomas's sons died in the Revolutionary War, she enlisted in the Continental Army. She was accepted by her fellow soldiers, who, although they made fun of her lack of facial hair, appear to have simply believed she was too young to shave. At 5 foot 7 inches, she was tall enough to fit in, and she bound her breasts tightly to look like a man. When she was wounded, she came down with a fever that put her under medical care, and her physician discovered her gender. She was discharged discreetly, but honorably, in October of 1783, after over a year in service.

After her stint in the military, Sampson moved to Sharon, Massachusetts, married Benjamin Gannett, and had three children. In 1792, she successfully petitioned the state of Massachusetts for back pay and was granted 34 dollars. Newspaper reports said that she "had done her duty without a stain on her virtue or honour," and were generally supportive and surprisingly accepting of her transgression (*Argus* 1792, 3).

Together with Herman Mann, she wrote a memoir, *Female Review*, which was published in 1797, and went on several lecture tours publicizing her past. She also petitioned the U.S. Congress for a pension, this time enlisting the help of nationally known poet and editor Philip Freneau, but this petition was not successful until 1805.

owners. Some free black men served because they believed in the revolutionary cause. All in all, it is estimated that around 5,000 African Americans served on the Patriot side, and around 20,000 on the side of the Loyalists. There is limited knowledge about how the war affected African American women, partly because so very few of them were literate and left a written record. Most of them were slaves, and remained at the home front, subject to the same risks and problems faced by the white women serving as deputy husbands; but slave women were even more vulnerable, since they had no legal recourse if assaulted or raped.

Some Native American tribes tried to remain neutral, thinking this was not their fight, but sometimes they were attacked anyway. Many of them sided with the British, hoping to get a better deal from a ruler who was far away than they could from a group of people who were directly competing for the use of the land, and who they expected to expand westward if given any opportunity. The effect on Native American women was mostly indirect. As a result of the war, tribes lost many men or were displaced, and crops were harder to maintain with fewer people. It was also difficult to maintain traditional Native American gender roles with women doing most of the agricultural work. The Americans wanted Indians to adopt Euro-American conventions, having the men perform agricultural labor and the women carry out the domestic responsibilities customary for white women—spinning, weaving, and cooking. Adapting to a social structure imposed from without came at a high price for Native women.

Loyalist Women

Roughly one-third of the American colonists remained loyal to the British, some of them because they were either dependent on trade with the British or were paid by them, and some because they genuinely believed it was better for the country to remain part of the British nation. Traditional gender relations put the wives of men loyal to the British—the Tories, as they were called—at a particular disadvantage, since they were at risk of losing their property through choices made by their spouses. Some state legislatures passed laws to strip Loyalists of their property and, generally, in accordance with the laws of coverture, it was simply assumed that a wife sided with her husband. If the wife remained behind on the estate, she might persuade the local authorities to let her keep her "widow's third," the part of the property that would fall to her as inheritance. This way, the community did not have to support a penniless woman and her children, and it sometimes encouraged women to side with the Patriots. Some women stayed behind, claiming neutrality or adherence to the Patriots, while they were secretly helping the Loyalists by collecting information for the British, or hiding and helping spies.

Sometimes, declared loyalist women were excused for their sympathies, since it was taken for granted that they had no choice but to follow their husbands' allegiance; but some women were deemed to be traitors solely on the basis of their husbands' position, whether the woman had expressed any opinion or not. Both legally and in practice, there appears to have been some ambiguity. For example, Grace Galloway was openly loyalist, but stayed behind in Philadelphia, when her husband and daughter sailed for England in 1778, in order to retain control of the family's property. When their property was confiscated, Grace took steps to protect for her daughter the part of the property she had previously inherited from her father. She claimed it as her private possession and argued that it should therefore be exempt from the confiscation of her husband's assets. The court found that the property might be hers, but as long as her husband was alive, he controlled it, under coverture laws. Only after his death would she be able to claim it back. In the end, after both Grace and her husband had died, the assets Grace had claimed as her separate property were returned to the family and passed on to Grace's daughter.

Other women were not so lucky. Some women were suspected of being spies or smugglers and were kept under house arrest or some other sort of detention, since letting them go might have improved enemy morale and allowed dangerous information and supplies to fall into the wrong hands. However, only a very small group of women were directly charged with treason.

In most of those cases, it appears that the women's names were attached to those of their husbands in order to make sure that the confiscation of property that came with a writ of treason would encompass all of the property these families owned. It is notable that there were *any* cases of married women accused of treason in the Revolutionary era. The implication of such an accusation was that married women could be seen as independent decision makers in certain circumstances, and when it served the interests of the court, this is what happened. As circumscribed as the lives of women were, according to prescriptive documents, pragmatic considerations regularly trumped the general rules.

The Early Republic

When the war ended in 1783, with the Treaty of Paris, the colonists had won independence, and the British troops and the Loyalists left for England or Canada. Yet there was much work left to do. The country was organized by the vague and limited Articles of Confederation. They had served during the war (ratified in 1781), but did not even provide for the federal government to issue taxes or regulate commerce. Individual states set about developing state constitutions and it slowly became evident that a federal Constitution was needed as well. It took until 1787 for a new constitution to be written, debated, voted on, and finally ratified. Although the principles on which the new republican government was based—liberty and equality—were broadly recognized and embraced, questions about the nature of government and the meaning of citizenship were still very much up for debate in the post-Revolution years. There were a number of contentious issues to be decided—how closely tied to each other the states should be, what the role of the federal government should be, and who should have the right to vote in what elections. Another unsettled issue was the role and status of women in the new nation.

Women had valiantly supported the war efforts in various ways, and had helped secure the survival of the new republic. Often, their contributions were framed as an extension of traditionally female concerns, but at times they had emphasized patriotic duty over gender expectations. Some women were hoping that their participation in the fight for freedom and the spread of Enlightenment ideas about rational individuals would translate into active participation in the political life of the republic, but in the end the legacies of the Revolution for women and women's rights were mixed. Abigail Adams famously wrote her husband John in March 1776, when he was serving as the Massachusetts representative to the Second Continental Congress in Philadelphia, asking him to "remember the ladies." She threatened, "If particular care and attention is not paid to the Ladies, we are determined to foment a Rebellion and will not hold ourselves bound by any Laws in which we have no voice or Representation." John responded by saying that he and other men knew better than "to repeal our masculine systems," continuing by saying that since men really only had the name of masters, they would cling to the illusion of control as long as they could (Butterfield, 1963–1993, 370–71).

His tone was chivalrous, which let him be nice without having to seriously engage with the issue. Adams was willing to discuss politics with his wife and women like Mercy Warren, but he saw no reason to change the political structure or established gender roles.

Although the laws of coverture persisted, in some ways women's roles and status broadened and improved. One of the concrete legal changes was that divorce was made more available in several states, particularly in New England. There had to be a compelling reason cited as the cause (adultery was common), and since it was difficult for single women to provide for themselves, divorce was uncommon. However, the fact that divorce became more permissible indicates a clear shift in the direction of viewing marriage as a reciprocal contract.

The discussions about equality and representation put questions about women on the national agenda, even if it was for a limited time. The two decades following the American Revolution witnessed an outpouring of political debate over the role and status of women in society. The writings of women such as American author Judith Sargent Murray and British writer Mary Wollstonecraft were widely read and even more widely discussed. In 1790, Murray published a series of essays, including such titles as "On the Equality of the Sexes." A collection of her essays were also published under a male pen name, "the Gleaner," in 1798. Murray believed most differences between men and women were the result of differences in education. She contended that if women were educated, they would be better equipped to become efficient administrators of their households and proficient teachers of their children. She questioned women's status more than she questioned women's roles, and she argued in favor of companionable marriages based on mutual love and respect. She even thought that for some women it was better to remain single. Wollstonecraft, in *A Vindication of the Rights of Woman* (1792) advanced similar ideas about women's intellectual equality, arguing that all the negative traits and behavior women were charged with were a result of their inferior education. As long as men encouraged women to focus on superficial things such as their beauty, and discouraged reading and higher pursuits, women would remain vapid and useless creatures. Her book was highly controversial, but aroused a lot of interest, and within a few months, a second edition was published in England. Both an American edition and a French translation came out soon after.

Writers such as Judith Sargent Murray espoused the notion that women needed to be educated in order to raise and support virtuous, active citizens in a republic based on consent by the people, an idea that historian Linda Kerber has called the ideology of "Republican Motherhood" (1980). Widely endorsed in the decades following the Revolution, Republican Motherhood afforded women respect for their domestic role, and gave them an accepted, although circumscribed, means of engaging in political life.

The most immediate effect of these ideas was the establishment of schools for young women. Educational opportunities for middle- and upper-class girls had started to expand before the war and grew significantly in the first decades of the new republic, as female academies opened in Philadelphia, Litchfield, Boston, and other places. By the census of 1852, almost all white women in New

Mercy Otis Warren was a historian, as well as a poet and playwright, of the Revolutionary War era. She became well acquainted with many of the well-known figures of the American Revolution. Her three-volume history of the revolution, written in 1805 and titled *History of the Rise, Progress, and Termination of the American Revolution*, provides insightful commentary on public affairs and personalities of the time. (Cirker, Hayward and Blanche Cirker, eds. *Dictionary of American Portraits,* 1967)

England were literate, and the numbers in other parts of the country had also improved. The Young Ladies' Academy of Philadelphia, although founded about a decade earlier, received its official charter in 1792. More than 100 women studied subjects such as grammar, arithmetic, history, and geography, as well as musical instruments and other skills. The school had support from the highest levels. In 1787, Benjamin Rush, a prominent physician and one of the signers of the Declaration of Independence, gave a speech at the school that outlined his "Thoughts upon Female Education." He believed young women needed education to prepare them for their roles as mothers and to equip them to raise good citizens, but he believed they had to do more than that. Women needed training to handle the management of servants, and to know how to be good companions to, and helpmates for, their husbands. This included learning how to figure accounts and how to write neatly, in order to help with business records and correspondence. Students spoke eloquently about what their education at the academy offered them. Ann Harker viewed it as a way to free women from the "shackles, with which we have been so long fettered," and Priscilla Mason saw education as a way to open the door to the professions—the church, the bar, and the Senate—that had been closed to women because the contemptible Saint Paul had "declared war on the whole sex" (Nash 1997, 187). It is difficult to know how representative these views were, but the trustees of the Ladies' Academy let both Harker's and Mason's speeches be published in a book that was used to market the academy.

In 1797, the novelist, playwright and actress Susanna Rowson retired from the stage to form the Young Ladies Academy in Boston. In 1792, Sara Pierce founded the Litchfield Female Academy in Litchfield, Connecticut. The school educated over 3,000 women during the 40 years of its existence. Pierce regularly reorganized her schedules, but among the topics on her students' curricula were subjects such as logic, chemistry, botany, and mathematics. Students were also instructed in what were known as the "ornamental" subjects.

While daughters in well-to-do white families began to take advantage of new educational opportunities, other groups of women did not fare as well. African American women in the North experienced some expanded opportunities for freedom, as gradual emancipation took hold. However, they continued to battle racial discrimination, barriers to schooling and economic advancement, and limits on their civil rights. In the South, slavery became more firmly established, and spread more widely, spurred by the invention of the cotton gin in 1793. For Native American women, the legacy of the Revolution was almost uniformly bad. The disruption of Native American customs and traditions in favor of European social structures entailed severe restrictions on the lives of most Native American women.

Even white women, although they did better than other groups, faced serious challenges and limitations after the Revolution. Although Republican Motherhood gave women a platform for political engagement, the ideology could also be used to limit that engagement to the domestic sphere. Women were denied full citizenship rights in the new republic—the laws of coverture continued to abide and, with the brief exception in New Jersey, where women had had suffrage since the Revolution, they were denied the right to vote. The New Jersey laws were changed in 1807 to specify that only men were eligible for suffrage, and no other state in the country let women vote until almost a century later. As the franchise was broadened over time to include all white men, whether property owners or not, and as citizenship became more closely tied to voting rights, women were explicitly marginalized from political life.

Conclusion

From the women who engaged in political debate with men and those who refused to drink tea and began making their own cloth, to the women who acted as deputy husbands while their men were fighting and those who fought on the battlefield, women were vital participants in the intellectual and practical creation of the American republic. Some of them were praised for their contributions, while others were criticized for their lack of femininity.

Many were simply forgotten. Women themselves did not forget their contributions to the war effort. Though they did not at this time secure for themselves the independence they had helped to win for their country, by the middle of the 19th century, a new generation of American women would be ready to take up the call of Abigail Adams to foment a new rebellion, until the Revolution's promise of equality for all would also encompass women.

References and Further Reading

Anthony, Katherine. *First Lady of the Revolution: The Life of Mercy Otis Warren.* New York: Doubleday, 1958.

Applewhite, Harriet B., and Darline G. Levy, eds. *Women and Politics in the Age of Democratic Revolutions.* Ann Arbor: University of Michigan Press, 1990.

Argus, January 20, 1792, 3.

Basch, Norma. *Framing American Divorce: From the Revolutionary Generation to the Victorians.* Berkeley: University of California Press, 1999.

Brekus, Catherine A. *Strangers and Pilgrims: Female Preaching in America 1740–1845.* Chapel Hill: University of North Carolina Press, 1998.

Butterfield, L. H., ed. *Adams Family Correspondence.* Cambridge, MA: Belknap Press of Harvard University Press, 1963–1993.

Comenius, John. *The Great Didactic.* 1632. Ed. M. W. Keating. New York: Russell & Russell, 1967.

Cott, Nancy. *The Bonds of Womanhood: "Woman's Sphere" in New England. 1780–1835.* New Haven, CT: Yale University Press, 1997.

DePauw, Linda Grant. *The Eleventh Pillar: New York State and the Federal Constitution.* Ithaca, NY: Cornell University Press, 1966.

Elliot, J. H. *Empires of the Atlantic: Britain and Spain in America 1492–1830.* New Haven, CT: Yale University Press, 2007.

Fries Ellet, and Elizabeth Lincoln Diamant, eds. *Revolutionary Women in the War for American Independence.* Westport, CT: Greenwood, 1998.

Galloway, Grace. *Diary of Grace Growden Galloway,* ed. Raymond C. Werner. New York: New York Times, 1971.

Gannett, Deborah, and Herman Mann. *Female Review or Memoirs of a Young American Lady.* Dedham, MA: Printed by Nathaniel and Benjamin Heathom, 1797.

Green, Harry Clinton, and Mary Wolcott Green. *The Pioneer Mothers of America: A Record of the More Notable Women of the Early Days of the Country, and Particularly of the Colonial and Revolutionary Periods.* New York: Putnam, 1912.

Gunderson, Joan. *To be Useful to the World: Women in Revolutionary America, 1740–1790.* Chapel Hill: University of North Carolina Press, 2006.

Haines, Michael R., and Richard Hall Steckel. *A Population History of North America*. Cambridge: Cambridge University Press, 2000.

Kann, Mark E. *The Gendering of American Politics: Founding Mothers, Founding Fathers, and Political Patriarchy*. Westport, CT: Praeger, 1999.

Kelley, Mary. *Learning to Stand and Speak: Women, Education, and Public Life in America's Republic*. Chapel Hill: University of North Carolina Press, 2006.

Kerber, Linda. *Toward an Intellectual History of Women*. Chapel Hill: University of North Carolina Press, 1997.

Kerber, Linda. *Women of the Republic: Intellect and Ideology in Revolutionary America*. Chapel Hill: University of North Carolina Press, 1980.

Locke, John. *An Essay Concerning Human Understanding*. 1690. Amherst, NY: Prometheus Books, 1995.

Locke, John. *Two Treatises of Government*. 1690. Cambridge: Cambridge University Press, 1998.

Lockridge, Kenneth E. *Literacy in Colonial New England: An Enquiry into the Social Context of Literacy in the Early Modern West*. New York: Norton, 1974.

Murray, Judith Sargent. *The Gleaner: A Miscellaneous Production in Three Volumes*. 3 vols. Boston: L. Thomas and E. T. Andrews, 1798.

Murray, Judith Sargent. "On the Equality of the Sexes." *Massachusetts Magazine* (March 1790): 132–35, (April 1790): 223–26.

Nash, Margaret. "Rethinking Republican Motherhood: Benjamin Rush and the Young Ladies' Academy of Philadelphia." *Journal of the Early Republic* 17, no. 2 (Summer 1997): 171–91.

Nash, Margaret. *Women's Education in the United States, 1780–1840*. New York: Palgrave Macmillan, 2005.

Norton, Mary Beth. *Liberty's Daughters: The Revolutionary Experience of American Women 1750–1800*. Ithaca, NY: Cornell University Press, 1996.

Perkins, Edwin. "The Entrepreneurial Spirit in Colonial America: The Foundations of Modern Business History." *The Business History Review* 63 (1989): 160–86.

Perlmann, Joel, and Dennis Shirley. "When Did New England Women Acquire Literacy?" *William and Mary Quarterly* 48, no. 1 (January 1991): 50–67.

"A Reminiscence," *Pennsylvania Magazine of History and Biography* 46 (1922): 55

The Rise and Progress of the Young Ladies' Academy of Philadelphia. Philadelphia: Stewart & Cochran, 1794.

Rush, Benjamin. *Thoughts upon Female Education*. Philadelphia: Pritchard and Hall, 1787.

Smith, Barbara Clark. "Food Rioters and the American Revolution." *The William and Mary Quarterly* 51 (1994): 3–38.

Springborg, Patricia, ed. *Astell: Political Writings*. Cambridge: Cambridge University Press, 1996.

Terrell, Anne. "To the Ladies whose husbands are in the continental army." *Virginia Gazette*. September 21, 1776, 2. http://research.history.org/Digital Library/VirginiaGazette/VGIssueThumbs.cfm?IssueIDNo=76.DH.41.

Warren, Mercy Otis. *The Adulateur—as It Is Now Acted in Upper Servia*. Boston: 1773.

Warren, Mercy Otis. *History of the Rise, Progress and Termination of the American Revolution*. Boston: Manning and Loring, 1805.

Warren, Mercy Otis. Mercy Otis Warren Papers, Massachusetts Historical Society, n.d.

Warren, Mercy Otis. "Observations On the New Constitution, and on the Federal and State Conventions." 1788. In *Pamphlets on the Constitution of the United States,* ed. Paul Leicester Ford. Brooklyn: 1888, 1–54.

Wiesner, Merry E. *Women and Gender in Early Modern Europe*. New York: Cambridge University Press, 2000.

Wollstonecraft, Mary. *A Vindication of the Rights of Woman*. Philadelphia, 1792.

Wulf, Karin. *Not All Wives: Women of Colonial Philadelphia*. Ithaca, NY: Cornell University Press, 2000.

Young, Alfred F. *Masquerade: The Life and Times of Deborah Sampson, Continental Soldier*. New York: Alfred A. Knopf, 2004.

Zagarri, Rosemarie. *Revolutionary Backlash: Women and Politics in the Early American Republic*. Philadelphia: University of Pennsylvania Press, 2007.

Women Reformers and Radicals in Antebellum America

4

Julie Holcomb

In July 1848, as many as 300 men and women gathered in Seneca Falls, New York to discuss the civil, social, religious, and political rights of women. At the conclusion of the two-day meeting, 100 people signed the Declaration of Sentiments and Resolutions, which claimed "that all men and women are created equal; that they are endowed by their Creator with certain inalienable rights; that among these are life, liberty, and the pursuit of happiness." Moreover, the signers asserted, "The history of mankind is a history of repeated injuries and usurpations on the part of man toward woman, having in direct object the establishment of an absolute tyranny over her" (Stanton, Anthony, and Gage 1887, 70). In a conscious parallel to the Declaration of Independence, women's rights advocates outlined male offenses and demanded redress for a system that legitimized male authority at the expense of female rights.

In the *History of Woman Suffrage,* women's rights leader Elizabeth Cady Stanton attributed the inspiration for the Seneca Falls convention to the exclusion of female delegates from the first World's Anti-Slavery Convention in London in 1840. In the spring of that year, the American antislavery movement had split over the relationship between women's rights and the antislavery movement. Conservative abolitionists Lewis and Arthur Tappan worried that the controversy over women's rights would hinder the antislavery movement. Radical abolitionist William Lloyd Garrison believed otherwise. In May 1840, at the annual meeting of the American Anti-Slavery Society (AASS), the Tappans and their supporters left the AASS and formed the American and Foreign Anti-Slavery Society (AFASS). Garrison, in the meantime, assumed leadership of the AASS. The AASS welcomed women into the association as equals, while the AFASS emphasized the fundamental differences between men and women. Both organizations sent representatives to the Convention in London in June. The AASS sent both male

Lucretia Mott

Lucretia Coffin Mott was born in 1793 on the island of Nantucket, Massachusetts. A birthright Quaker, she remained a lifelong member of the Society of Friends, despite painful schisms in the sect in the 1820s and again in the 1840s that placed her at odds with some family and friends. At the age of 13, her parents sent her to Nine Partners, a coeducational Quaker boarding school in Dutchess County, New York. While at Nine Partners, Mott came under the influence of school superintendent James Mott, Sr. and Quaker farmer and reformer Elias Hicks. Both men were ardent abolitionists and free produce activists. Mott, Sr. used maple sugar instead of cane sugar, refused to write on cotton paper, and dressed in linen rather than cotton. Hicks believed consumer demand drove the need for slave labor; thus, to maintain a consistent antislavery testimony, abolitionists needed to abstain from slave produce. Around this same time, young Lucretia read British abolitionist Thomas Clarkson's *An Essay on Slavery*, which described the horrors that took place aboard slave ships crossing the Atlantic Ocean. The early influence of Clarkson,

Mott, Sr., and Hicks shaped her view that consistency in behavior and in word was the most effective testimony against social evils. In 1811, she married James Mott. When Mott converted to free produce principles in the early 1820s, she noted that it was "like parting with the right hand, or the right eye." Yet, for the next 40 years, she remained convinced "that it was wrong to partake of the products of slave labor" (Hallowell 1884, 87).

A tireless reformer, Mott was an abolitionist, women's rights advocate, and peace activist. She helped write the American Anti-Slavery Society's Declaration of Sentiments, and she helped form the racially integrated Philadelphia Female Anti-Slavery Society in 1833, serving as president of the association. In 1840, Mott was selected as a delegate to the World's Anti-Slavery Convention in London. When she and other female delegates were refused recognition, Mott used every opportunity outside the convention to advocate for women's equality. Mott and Elizabeth Cady Stanton also discussed plans to hold a women's rights convention when they returned to the United

and female delegates, including Quaker abolitionist Lucretia Mott, while the AFASS sent an all-male delegation. Not surprisingly, the conservative British organizers refused to seat the female delegates of the AASS. When Garrison learned that the women delegates had not been recognized, he refused to enter the convention and instead watched the proceedings with the women in the balcony. While women delegates were not allowed to participate in the convention, the event did bring together Mott and Stanton, who was attending the convention with her new husband, the abolitionist Henry Stanton. Stanton later recalled, "As Mrs. Mott and I walked home, arm in arm, commenting on the incidents of the day, we resolved to hold a convention as soon as we returned home, and form a society to advocate the rights of women" (Penney and Livingston 2004, 69).

Was the origin of the 19th-century women's rights movement as straightforward as Stanton claimed? Certainly the meeting of Stanton and Mott marked a watershed moment in the history of women's rights. Still, women's activism already had a lengthy history at the time of the Stanton-Mott meet-

States. Mott's speech, "Discourse on Women," delivered in 1849, reflected the influence on her thinking of Mary Wollstonecraft, author of *A Vindication of the Rights of Woman*. Like the 18th-century British author, Mott believed women's social roles were a reflection of their limited education rather than innate inferiority. Mott also credited her Nantucket heritage, especially the female independence fostered among islanders due to the often long absences of husbands and fathers working in the fishing industry, as well as her Quaker upbringing, for shaping her views on women's rights: "I grew up so thoroughly imbued with women's rights that it was the most important question of my life from a very early day" (Cromwell 1958, 125). Women as well as men were responsible for the injustices women faced, Mott believed: "Women should train themselves to take a dignified place in the world, to be rational companions, to share the responsibilities of life" (126).

After the Civil War, Mott distinguished herself from other abolitionists. William Lloyd Garrison and many other abolitionists believed their work was done with the passage of the Thirteenth Amendment, which abolished slavery. True to her belief in social justice, Mott became active in fighting for black civil and political rights, as well as aid for freed people. She also continued to fight for women's rights after the Civil War. In 1866, despite her age and poor health, Mott was elected as the first president of the American Equal Rights Association (AERA), which advocated for universal adult suffrage. In the late 1860s, a rift developed among women's rights advocates over the Fourteenth and Fifteenth Amendments, which secured political rights for black men but failed to extend suffrage to women. Mott tried unsuccessfully to heal the divide between those who supported the amendments and those who did not.

In addition to her work on rights for women and blacks after the Civil War, Mott was involved in the establishment of Swarthmore College in Pennsylvania, one of the first coeducational colleges in the United States, founded by the Society of Friends in 1864. She died in 1880.

ing in 1840. The women's rights movement evolved from women's participation in other activities, including charity work, movements for temperance, education, prison, and moral reform, labor activism, and, particularly, antislavery. Participation in these movements enabled some women to envision a new form of citizenship based on the concept of women as morally and legally autonomous individuals who participated directly in democratic politics and civil society, rather than through the institution of the family.

Women's reform work, including women's rights, was based on a comprehensive critique of antebellum American society. As abolitionist Lydia Maria Child wrote in 1842, "Great political changes may be forced by the pressure of external circumstances, without a corresponding change in the moral sentiment of a nation, but in all such cases, the change is worse than useless; the evil reappears, and usually in a more exaggerated form" (DuBois 1998, 62). Women's rights activists, in particular, sought more than suffrage. In order to achieve gender equality, women needed to alter not only legal and political institutions but also change the heart of the country.

A Quaker minister, abolitionist, and women's right advocate, Lucretia Mott played a major role in the transformative movements for social reform in 19th-century America. (Library of Congress)

Women and the Market Revolution

The change of heart women activists sought was rooted in the dramatic social transformations of the antebellum period (1820–1860), which fundamentally altered Americans' understandings and experiences of gender, the family, politics, freedom, and the individual. During the early 19th century, a new economic order took shape (albeit gradually and unevenly) based on large-scale manufacturing and trade, competition, consumption, and cash exchange. This market revolution was made possible in part by advances in transportation, which in less than 100 years had evolved from the river and trail routes of the Indians to turnpikes, canals, and finally, by the mid-19th century, railroads. Improved transportation aided the development of the factory system by making the movement of people, raw materials, and finished products easier and more efficient. Across the Northeast in particular, factories replaced the home-based artisan workshop. In this newly industrializing market economy, people no longer produced items solely for family sustenance or for their local communities; instead, workers used industrial technology to manufacture goods for unseen consumers in distant markets.

The rise of industrial capitalism set off a wave of social changes, including the development of an urban working class, the formation of a new urban middle class, and experiences of and anxieties about economic instability across the social spectrum. Increasingly, men and women worked in factories, offices, or as domestics in middle- and upper-class homes. The personal relationship that had once existed between a master or mistress, on the one hand, and his or her servant or apprentice, on the other, was replaced by an impersonal, commodity-based relationship that often pitted the two groups against each other. Moreover, industrialization created distinct divisions between the working and middle classes. For example, industrialization increased leisure time for middle-class men and women while working-class men and women often struggled to survive in the new economy. The urban-based economy also meant workers were increasingly dependent on cash wages, rather than living off the land as men and women did in an agricultural society. For workers, this meant their financial well-being ebbed and flowed with shifts in the economy. This vulnerability was particularly evident in the events leading up to and during the Panic of 1819, an economic crisis that occurred in the United States after Britain and France ended years of warfare. The economy slowed precipitously as demand for American products declined. The Bank of the United States, as well as state and private banks, recalled loans. Many farmers, unable to pay their loans, lost everything. Money also became scarce, making it even more difficult for people to pay off their debts, or even to purchase the goods they needed to survive. During this period, an estimated half-million workers were unemployed as businesses failed, foreclosures increased, and bank notes depreciated.

The market revolution also transformed the relationship between the family and society, and gave rise to a new paradigm in gender relations. In this development, the urban middle class led the way. During the colonial period, work, domestic life, and leisure were all centered in the patriarchal household. Women were decidedly subordinate to men in law and custom, but there was no strict dividing line between work and home, or between public and private life. With the rise of industrial capitalism, more and more men left their homes to go to work in shops, offices, or factories, as many as six days a week. In exchange, they received a cash salary based on their individual labor, which could be used to purchase goods for their own and their family's needs. As husbands spent more time away from home, they surrendered responsibility for the functioning of the household to their wives.

This division between home and work was explained, justified, and enabled by a set of ideas about gender and society that historians have termed the "ideology of separate spheres." According to this ideology, men and women were endowed by God and nature with opposite, complementary traits, which dictated that men occupy the public realms of economic and political activity, and women occupy the private realm of the home and family. The ideology of separate spheres was premised on the assumption that men earned enough money to support their non-laboring wives and children at home. It thus did not accurately describe the reality of enslaved, immigrant, working-class, and female-headed families, in which—by force or necessity—all members were required to make an economic contribution to the household. Middle-class men and women were the greatest proponents and propagators of separate spheres, yet even they were not always able to fully live up to its idealizations. Nonetheless, separate spheres constituted a powerful set of prescriptions in antebellum America, to which many men and women aspired, and against which all men and women were assessed and measured.

The ideology of separate spheres deemed men to be rational, competitive, aggressive, and independent, qualities that perfectly suited them to take on the role of breadwinner in an industrializing capitalist economy. The extension of suffrage to all adult white men reinforced the association between men and the public domain. After 1815, state after state revoked property qualifications for voting and holding elected office. Thomas Jefferson's view that "every man who fights and pays" should be granted the ballot asserted that the right to vote should be based on the ability to serve the nation (Isenberg 1998, 7). Basing voting rights on military service and the payment of taxes signaled an allegiance between the individual white male and the state. White men from across the social spectrum eagerly embraced the expanding opportunities for political participation, joining political parties, participating in campaigns, and turning out to vote in record numbers. By 1840, nearly 80 percent of eligible voters participated at the ballot box. At the same time, most black men and all women were excluded from participating in electoral politics. As the perceived dependents of white men, they were viewed as incapable of service to the nation, and therefore were not eligible to vote.

The ideology of separate spheres also contributed to a new ideal of womanhood. While men were ascribed power and influence in the public sphere, women maintained primary importance in the private sphere. The ideal of true womanhood was based on four traits: piety, purity, submissiveness, and domesticity. Piety served as the core of woman's virtue, and reflected a common belief that women were naturally drawn to religion. Like piety, the absence of sexual purity in women was deemed unnatural and unfeminine. Purity was woman's greatest treasure, to be saved as a gift for her husband on their wedding night. Submissiveness was considered the most feminine of virtues. Men were actors; women were reactors. Domesticity reinforced the idea that "the domestic fireside is the great guardian of society against the excesses of human passions" (Welter 1966, 162). In the home, woman created a haven from the rough and tumble public world of work and politics in which men participated. Because she possessed these characteristics, the true woman was deemed to be morally superior to man and was expected to wield virtuous influence over her husband, brothers, and sons through her guidance and example.

Historians initially interpreted women's confinement to the domestic sphere and the rise of the ideal of true womanhood "as signs of woman's defeat at the hands of the Jacksonian era's 'true man,' who was aggressive, virile, competitive, and domineering" (Hewitt 1984, 18). Certainly, the ideology of separate spheres limited women's participation in the political, economic, and social life of the nation. Separate spheres justified women's ongoing exclusion from the elective franchise. The central tenet of the ideology that women were not workers contributed to at least two effects. When women did enter into the wage workforce, they found themselves in a gender-stratified economy, relegated to a low-paying, low-status female job sector. At same time, the economic contributions of women's domestic labor went unrecognized and uncompensated. Separate spheres also reinforced the legal subordination of women, since it easily coexisted with existing laws of domestic relations that were based on the doctrine of *coverture*.

However limiting the ideology of separate spheres and the ideal of true womanhood may have been, they also accrued some advantages to women. According to these sets of beliefs, the wife and mother served as the moral authority for the family and, by association, for society. In 1832, the New York Maternal Association noted that because mothers were primarily responsible for the cultivation of Christian values in their children, they would play a critical role in bringing about a "third moral revolution . . . When every nursery shall become a little sanctuary, and not before, will the earth be filled with the knowledge and glory of the Lord" (Meckel 1982, 412). Women were thus to be lauded for their domestic roles, and recognized for the vital contributions they made to ensuring the moral progress of the American nation.

The ideology of separate spheres also provided women with an intense network of relationships from which they could draw emotional and practical support. Women visited one another; cared for one another's babies; cleaned, sewed, and shopped for one another; and exchanged frequent letters. Bonds between women were often maintained for a lifetime. In a letter to her daughter Anne about her own half-sister Phoebe, Quaker matron Martha Jefferis wrote: "In sister Phoebe I have a real friend—she studies my comfort and waits on me like a child . . . She is exceedingly kind and this to all other homes (set aside yours) I would prefer—it is next to being with a daughter." Phoebe expressed similar feelings in a letter to Martha: "Thou knowest my dear sister, there is not one . . . that exactly feels [for] thee as I do, for I think without boasting I can truly say that my desire is for thee" (Smith-Rosenberg 1985, 62–63).

Antebellum women drew on the tenets of true womanhood, as well as their female friendships and communal networks, to form benevolent and social reform organizations intended to ameliorate the myriad ills plaguing antebellum society. Of paramount importance in leading women out of the home to serve the needs of the wider world was the growing influence of evangelical Christianity. The revivals of the Second Great Awakening in the 1820s and 1830s, led by ministers such as Lyman Beecher and Charles Finney, gave followers a sense of order in a chaotic world. Finney and other ministers repudiated traditional Calvinist ideas about innate depravity, predestination, and everlasting punishment, and exhorted followers to seek a personal relationship with a loving and merciful God. Since sin was the result of selfish choices, men and women could determine their own eternal fate. Moreover, if individuals used their innate free will to make better choices, Finney and other revivalist ministers promised, the collective effect would mitigate social evils such as poverty, intemperance, and prostitution, and lead to the perfection of American society. Evangelical ministers promulgated the view that women held "a unique responsibility to disseminate Christian virtues and counter the materialism and greed of the nineteenth-century male" (Ginzburg 1990, 14). Women eagerly embraced this message and quickly outnumbered men among the converts. Inspired by their sense of moral superiority and encouraged by the evangelicalism of the Second Great Awakening, they ventured into the public sphere, paradoxically both bolstering and challenging the dictates of separate spheres and true womanhood as they took up the mantle of benevolence and social reform.

Benevolence and Reform

Women's reform work thus developed within a context of major social, economic, and religious ferment. Beginning in the 1790s, women organized benevolent associations to care for widows and orphans, as well as to provide aid for the elderly and medical care to pregnant women. Generally, these associations were organized along class and racial lines. For example, in Boston and New York, women from upper- and middle-class families organized groups such as the New York Society for the Relief of Poor Women with Small Children (1797) and the Boston Female Asylum (1800). Women's benevolent organizations were often organized within churches or local communities, further reinforcing class and racial divisions, and were established to take care of people—generally women and children—overlooked by existing social programs. These organizations relied upon traditional networks of influence for financial and political support, and rarely made broad appeals to the public or published reports of their activities. For example, the Boston Female Asylum listed Sarah Bowdoin as its manager. Bowdoin was the daughter-in-law of a former governor and the wife of a prominent state politician. The organization drew on Bowdoin's social standing and political connections to obtain financial support from private and public organizations, as well as political support, when the group sought passage of a legislative bill to incorporate the association.

The women participating in these early benevolent organizations did not seek sweeping changes in society or transformations of the existing racial, class, or gender order. Rather, they simply sought to provide material and spiritual aid to those in unfortunate circumstances. Benevolent women believed it was their duty as privileged Christian women to provide relief to the less fortunate members of their community. The ideology of separate spheres, with its emphasis on women's superior morality, encouraged women to venture into the public sphere, yet their public role as benevolent women reinforced their self-identification as moral mothers, rather than challenged traditional gender ideals.

By the late 1820s, an important development in women's public activities occurred as the economic, political, and religious changes of the period intensified. New women's organizations emerged, devoted not only to charitable assistance for the downtrodden, but to social reform. Unlike benevo-

Dorothea Dix was world-renowned for her work on behalf of the mentally ill and for her services as a nurse during the Civil War. (Library of Congress)

lent organizations, reform groups wanted to restructure society rather than just to ameliorate its evils. Drawing directly from the religious revivals of the period, which emphasized individual action, perfectibility, and female morality, women reformers went further than benevolent did women in pushing against the boundaries of separate spheres, even as they continued to espouse the ideal of domesticity. Women reformers sometimes organized associations across lines of race and class and, occasionally, gender. Some white middle-class women claimed to identify with women who were poor, enslaved, or in other dismal circumstances. Women reformers thus cultivated a "gender consciousness," the notion that all women embodied common characteristics, faced similar hardships, and shared a sisterly obligation to relieve one another's suffering.

The temperance movement was the largest and most sustained reform movement of the 19th century. Concerned about the increasing popularity of alcohol, northern Whig evangelicals established temperance organizations, including the American Temperance Society, which was formed in 1826.

Temperance reformers linked alcohol consumption with a variety of social evils, including poverty, crime, family violence, and poor child rearing. Because of the impact of alcohol consumption on the family, temperance drew a significant number of women into the ranks of the movement. Temperance advocates used lectures, pamphlets, and rallies to persuade men to pledge abstinence from alcohol. As legal writer Henry Folsom Page wrote in 1850, intemperance "blunted" men's morals and rendered them unable to fulfill their "relations" as spouse, father, and citizen (Isenberg 1998, 159). As historian Nancy Isenberg summarizes, Page believed chronic intemperance violated "the most basic conjugal right of fidelity . . . the wife was forced to share her bed with a virtual stranger—a man devoid of any understanding of his duty as a husband because he lacked affection for her" (159). In the 1830s, working-class men's participation in the movement grew, as concerns over the effects of alcohol on job performance increased. By 1835, more than 5,000 temperance societies had been established throughout the United States. By the 1840s, temperance reformers had significantly reduced the consumption of alcohol and, by the 1850s, many states either limited or prohibited the sale of alcohol and allowed drunkenness as grounds for divorce.

Women were also involved in education reform, which focused in part on establishing tax-supported schools. Calvin Stowe, Horace Mann, and other education reformers worried about the effects of an illiterate electorate on democratic institutions and principles. State-supported schools would provide education to the masses and help build individual character, which in turn would create informed voters and responsible citizens. Moreover, the state of women's education came under scrutiny as reformers emphasized women's role as the moral core of the family. During the 1820s and 1830s, education pioneers Emma Willard, Catharine Beecher, and Mary Lyon founded several notable seminaries for girls. The primary function of these schools was to train girls in the proper fulfillment of their maternal roles and to enable them to exercise their moral guardianship more broadly by preparing them to become teachers. Maintaining that female students could meet the highest standards for intellectual rigor, education reformers nonetheless also emphasized women's distinct role as moral protectors of the family and society. They thus reiterated expectations for separate spheres, even as they made available the tools that would enable some women to think critically about traditional gender conventions and to act to move beyond them.

Crime and vice were also the focus of several reform movements. Advocating reform of the individual rather than physical punishment, incarceration, or execution, prison reformers called for programs that emphasized instruction and personal discipline. Crime resulted from childhood neglect, which was better addressed by rehabilitation than punishment. Prison reform also influenced changes in the treatment of the mentally ill. Often the mentally ill were confined to prisons or poor houses. In the 1840s, reformers like Dorothea Dix led a movement to establish insane asylums to aid the mentally ill.

Moral reformers focused on the crime of female prostitution. The New York Female Moral Reform Society, organized in 1834, was followed by the American Female Moral Reform Society, which boasted more than 500 local chapters by 1840. Drawing on evangelical ideas about women's innate sexual purity, moral reformers placed blame for prostitution on men rather than women. Sympathizing with their fallen sisters, they decried a sexual double standard that punished all women more harshly than men for sexual indiscretions, and criticized a male-dominated economic system that rendered all women vulnerable to poverty. To further their cause, moral reformers engaged in such bold, and unfeminine, public acts as visiting prostitutes, publishing the names of their male clients, and campaigning for anti-seduction laws. As with other reform efforts of the period, moral reform drew from and perpetuated the ideology of separate spheres. It also helped to pave the way for the women's rights movement by developing women's gender consciousness and heightening their recognition of the need for women to act collectively to improve society and their own condition within it.

While much of early 19th-century reform was spearheaded by women of the white middle class, other groups of women also acted to improve their lives and create a more just and egalitarian society. White working-class women engaged in a number of protests against reduced wages, increased hours, and undesirable working conditions during the antebellum period. In 1824, Pawtucket, Rhode Island's female weavers voted to abandon their looms after employers announced a reduction in piece rates. In 1828, Dover, New Hampshire textile workers walked off the job protesting low wages and long hours. In February 1834, the women textile mill operatives of Lowell, Massachusetts "turned out" (went on strike) when employers proposed a wage reduction. While many of these protests or strikes were unsuccessful, as was the Lowell turnout, they nonetheless signaled a growing activism among women workers.

The sporadic strikes of the 1820s and early 1830s were followed by more-concerted efforts at labor organizing. In 1836, mill hands in Lowell came together to form the Factory Girls Association; other textile workers around New England followed suit by establishing local organizations devoted to furthering working women's interests. In the 1840s, women workers joined with men in the labor movement in agitating for the 10-hour day. In a courageous move that countered conventional imperatives for female silence and submissiveness, a group of Lowell workers testified before the Massachusetts legislature about poor working conditions in the mills. While this effort was also unsuccessful, it signaled the development of a growing class and gender consciousness among working women, who recognized that they shared common struggles, and, accordingly, could and should join together to advocate for their interests and secure their rights. When opportunities first opened up for them in the textile industry in the 1820s, many mill workers proclaimed an allegiance to the ideals of true womanhood, and defended their respectability as ladies, even as they ventured away from the confines of the patriarchal family. With the protests of the 1830s and 1840s, some working women more deliberately questioned and pushed beyond the boundaries of women's sphere and joined other antebellum reformers in claiming a broader role for women in speaking and acting in public life.

Like working- and middle-class white women, African American women worked to reform society and improve their lives. Significantly, African American women's benevolent and reform work also emphasized racial uplift.

For example, when the Colored Female Religious and Moral Society of Salem (Massachusetts) organized in 1818, the society pledged "to be charitably watchful over each other" and "to advise caution and admonish where we judge there is an occasion, and that it may be useful; and we promise not to resent but kindly receive such friendly advise [*sic*] from our members" (Cott 2000, 219). The constitution of the Afric-Female Intelligence Society of America, established in Boston in 1831, emphasized "the welfare of our friends" as well as the abolition of slavery (Yee, 1992, 63). This pledge of mutual aid and improvement was an integral part of African American women's groups because racism affected the black elite and the black poor in similar ways. To promote racial betterment, African American women also formed literary societies. Philadelphia, for example, had 106 African American literary societies by 1849, with membership of more than one-half of Philadelphia's African American population. Some African American clubs also raised funds to build schools and libraries for the African American community. One such club, the Ohio Ladies Educational Society, had opened, by the 1840s, more African American schools than any other American organization, black or white. However, of all the reform causes African American women worked in, none was more important than abolitionism.

Abolitionism

Of the antebellum reform movements, abolitionism was the best known and most controversial. The abolitionist movement that developed in the late 1820s and 1830s came from earlier attempts in the United States and England to abolish the slave trade and slavery. In the Revolutionary period, antislavery societies were generally organized by white elite males, usually Quakers, who sought the gradual abolition of slavery. When the international slave trade was abolished in England in 1807 and in the United States in 1808, abolitionists hailed the events as a great victory. In 1817, American abolitionists organized the American Colonization Society (ACS), which focused on establishing an American colony in Africa for freed slaves and free blacks. Supporters of the ACS believed that removing the free black population from the United States would speed the abolition of slavery. However, many black abolitionists feared forced emigration to Africa and opposed the antiblack sentiment of the ACS. Black abolitionists organized black and white supporters to discredit the ACS.

The movement for the immediate abolition of slavery in the United States evolved from black and white abolitionists' fight against colonization. The fight for the immediate abolition of slavery in the United States also benefited from the British antislavery movement. In 1824, British Quaker Elizabeth Heyrick published *Immediate, Not Gradual Abolition*, the most influential antislavery tract of the day. Heyrick challenged the gradualist stance of the British antislavery leadership. Moreover, she staked a claim for grassroots participation in abolitionism by calling on men, women, and even children to abstain from the products of slave labor, most notably sugar from the West Indies. In England, Heyrick's pamphlet influenced a shift in national antislavery strategy, which by 1831 emphasized the immediate abolition of slavery. In the United States, Heyrick's tract inspired numerous women to abstain from the products of slave labor.

Heyrick also influenced William Lloyd Garrison. In 1831, Garrison published the first edition of *The Liberator*. While Garrison's newspaper is credited with creating a new, radical abolitionist movement based on the immediate abolition of slavery and racial equality, Garrison's views drew directly from the early activism of women and black abolitionists. Moreover, Garrison was deeply influenced by the religious revivals of the 1820s. Like many reformers, Garrison believed that slavery prevented blacks from exercising their innate free will, and that slavery corrupted the slaveholder by sanctioning force against an entire group of people. In 1832, Garrison helped organize the New England Anti-Slavery Society, and in 1833, he helped form the American Anti-Slavery Society. By the 1840s, men and women had formed more than 1,500 local and regional antislavery groups.

Abolitionists were clearly in the minority even in the North; thus, women's support was crucial to the movement. In the 1820s, inspired by Heyrick and the activism of British women in the abolitionist movement, American women organized "free produce societies" to encourage abstention from the products of slave labor. In the 1830s, many of those same women organized antislavery societies. In addition to forming groups that were auxiliary to men's organizations, women also participated in local, state, and national antislavery organizations. In 1832, African American women formed the Female Anti-Slavery Society of Salem, the first female antislavery organization in the United States. One year later, women aided the formation of the American Anti-Slavery Society. Lucretia Mott helped write the organization's Declaration of Sentiments. Mott also played a key role in organizing the Philadelphia Female Anti-Slavery Society (PFASS) in 1833, the most radical and most influential of female antislavery societies. That same year, Boston women formed their own Female Anti-Slavery Society. African American women played an important role in establishing both societies. Abolitionism held particular appeal for women activists, regardless of race, who saw in slavery the violation of traditional ideas of family and gender. Significantly for women abolitionists, slavery encouraged the sexual abuse of slave women and violated the mother-child bond by masters who held absolute power over slaves and their families. The misuse of the female body under slavery paralleled the misuse of free female bodies. Still, tensions did exist between white and black female abolitionists. White women generally focused on moral suasion in their fight against slavery, while African American women focused on a broader agenda, including racial uplift, with abolitionism. Moreover, white women frequently held conservative views of racial equality.

To promote their cause, abolitionists used a number of tactics. In 1835, abolitionists organized a postal campaign targeting ministers, politicians, and newspaper editors throughout the South. Reformers flooded the South with thousands of pieces of abolitionist literature, believing that once convinced of the hostility of world opinion against slavery, slaveholders would voluntarily end slavery. Instead, the abolitionists' postal campaign sparked a wave of mob violence. Throughout the North and the South, anti-abolitionist mobs formed, destroying property and threatening the lives of reformers.

The mid-1830s also saw the beginnings of an intensive national petition campaign against slavery. The campaign emphasized local organizing, as volunteers went door-to-door, gathering signatures on petitions to send to Congress. Like the free produce movement, the petition campaign appealed to women and to others who found signing a petition a safe way to voice their support for the abolitionist cause. Signing a petition did not require facing down an angry mob. The American Anti-Slavery Society estimated that, between 1835 and 1838, more than 415,000 petitions had been sent to Congress; significantly, more than half of those petitions bore the signatures of women. Still, no Congressional action was taken as a result of the petitions, because they were automatically tabled. The Gag Rule, adopted in 1836 in the wake of anti-abolitionist rioting, remained in force until 1844. Rather than easing sectional tensions, as intended, the Gag Rule contributed to the growing sectionalist divide in American politics, helped politicize the American abolitionist movement, and, for women, underscored the corrupt nature of politics and the need for women to take an active role in abolishing slavery and in reforming the American political system.

Petitioning and abstention from slave-labor produce were antislavery tactics particularly suited to women because they did not require a dramatic, public statement of antislavery sentiment. However, by the mid-1830s, some of the more radical antislavery women consciously sought an equal and public role for abolitionist women. In 1836, Garrison hired Angelina and Sarah Grimké as lecturers for the American Anti-Slavery Society. The Grimké sisters were members of a well-known South Carolina slave-holding family. Recent converts to the Society of Friends and to antislavery, the Grimké sisters were powerful and popular spokespersons for the antislavery cause. Their lectures soon drew mixed-sex audiences, which challenged traditional views of appropriate female behavior. The Congregational clergy of Massachusetts publicly rebuked the sisters in 1837, declaring that when women like the Grimkés assumed the public role of men, they risked shame and dishonor: "[W]hen [woman] assumes the place and tone of man as a public reformer, our care and protection of her seem unnecessary, we put ourselves in self-defense against her, she yields the power which God has given her for protection, and her character becomes unnatural" (Melder 1977, 83).

Even more disturbing were Angelina Grimké's claims for an equal role for women in the fight against slavery. In *Letters to Catharine E. Beecher, in Reply to an Essay on Slavery and Abolitionism,* Grimké asserted, "The rights of all men, from the king to the slave are built upon their moral nature; and as all men have this moral nature so all men have essentially the same rights." Thus, if these rights were "founded in moral being . . . then the circumstances of sex could not give to man higher rights and responsibilities, than to woman" (Sklar 2000, 36–37). In other words, Grimké saw women's historically and socially constricted position as similar to that of the slave. At its most radical, then, the antislavery movement claimed absolute human equality, regardless of race or gender. The Grimkés' actions and their words emphasized women's ascribed morality, which other women reformers had also relied on to stake out a more public role in reform and in politics. However, the Grimkés defined women as autonomous individuals rather than as subordinate members of the family.

From Abolitionism to Women's Rights

Between 1837 and 1840, reformers continued to debate the proper role for women in the abolitionist movement. In 1837, women organized the Anti-Slavery Convention of Women, which drew more than 200 women. A second convention was held in 1838, bringing 300 women to Pennsylvania Hall in Philadelphia; however, the convention was interrupted and then forced to move when anti-abolitionist mobs burned down the hall. In 1839, attendance was significantly less than the previous year. At each of the conventions, women gave speeches and passed resolutions, including a call to women to claim a more public role in the antislavery movement. However, many men and women opposed a public presence for women. In May 1840, when Abby Kelley was nominated to the business committee of the American Anti-Slavery Society (AASS), Lewis Tappan and 300 supporters (including the entire executive committee) left the society. In June, male and female delegates from the AASS arrived in London to participate in the first World's Anti-Slavery Convention organized by the British and Foreign Anti-Slavery Society. However, the conservative British abolitionists refused to recognize the women delegates.

While the exclusion of women delegates from the London convention had a decided impact on events leading to the first women's rights convention in Seneca Falls eight years later, other developments helped shape the debate about women's rights and gender equality. In 1848, Liberty Party men and antislavery Whigs and Democrats organized the Free-Soil Party after Democrats denied the presidential nomination to Martin van Buren, a nominally antislavery candidate. Not all Free-Soil supporters joined the party because of antislavery principles. Still, many did, and many took seriously the idea of rights for blacks and women. Also in 1848, the Society of Friends in New York experienced a division among its members over the relationship between antislavery activism and Quaker doctrinal issues. Of particular significance was the debate about the structure of Quaker meetings. The Congregational Friends, which formed from the split, adopted a new style of organization. Congregational Friends rejected creeds, rituals, and ministers, and embraced cooperation with non-Quaker abolitionists. Moreover, they rejected any hierarchical organization of Quaker meetings.

Debates about women's economic vulnerability also influenced the Seneca Falls convention. The instability of the rising market economy exacerbated women's vulnerable economic status. Prior to 1828, wealthy New Yorkers could protect the property rights of their wives and daughters through trusts administered through equity courts. However, in 1828, the law was revised and the equity courts abolished, which ended protection for married women's property rights. Despite this setback, support for married women's property rights in New York and other states grew throughout the 1830s. After the financial panic of 1837, federal and state governments began passing laws to protect the assets of debtors. The first married women's property act, passed in Mississippi in 1839, exempted a married woman's real and personal property from the debts of her husband. In New York, a new state constitutional convention was organized in 1846. Two years later, after several petitions from women and much public pressure, New York finally passed a married women's property law. Similar laws were passed in other states. Still, married women's property laws did little to alter women's subordinate position in marriage. Moreover, married women's property laws often did not extend protection to women's earnings. The women's rights movement would expand the issue of economic rights to include women's legal status in marriage.

Elizabeth Cady Stanton believed the passage of the Married Woman's Property Act in New York created a favorable environment for a women's rights convention. As she later noted in the *History of Woman Suffrage,* "Discussion in the constitutional convention and the Legislature, heralded by the press to every school district culminated at last in a woman's rights convention" (Wellman 2004, 172). After the Anti-Slavery convention, Stanton balanced reform work with her growing family and with husband Henry's developing legal and political career. In 1847, she moved to Seneca Falls. Henry joined her a year later, a year described by historian Judith Wellman as a period "of emotional and physical stresses more severe than she had ever known, testing both her religious values and her reform commitments" (Wellman 2004, 165). In July 1848, a tea party hosted by Quaker Jane Hunt brought Stanton and Mott together again. Joined by Mott's sister, Martha Wright, and by Quaker Mary Ann McClintock, the women decided to "do and dare anything," as Stanton later recalled (Bacon 1980, 126).

Just 10 days later, 300 men and women gathered at the first women's rights convention. The two-day meeting focused on the writing and signing of the movement's founding document, called the Declaration of Sentiments, so named after the founding document of the American Anti-Slavery Society. The Declaration of Sentiments outlined women's civil and political grievances, namely the failure of men to grant women the elective franchise; legal discrimination against women, especially married women; the limitations on women's rights in relationship to work, education, and participation in the church; the sexual double standard; and the exclusion of women from the public sphere. The Declaration of Sentiments proffered a comprehensive critique of women's social role in the antebellum period. In a significant omission, the Declaration of Sentiments did not address whether these rights were intended for all women, regardless of race. Once convention delegates agreed to the wording of the Declaration, the document was offered for signature. Sixty-eight women signed the document and 32 men signed a separate document, representing a compromise that allowed women to make their own demands, yet still gave men a voice on the issue.

Reaction to the Seneca Falls Convention and the Declaration of Sentiments was decidedly mixed. The *Lowell Courier* in Massachusetts worried that the Declaration was nothing more than a reversal of gender roles. Another paper called convention participants "erratic, addle-pated comeouters," and

Cartoon representation of a speaker at the Woman's Rights Convention at Seneca Falls, New York on July 19–20, 1848. The Seneca Falls Convention marked the birth of an organized women's rights movement in the United States. (Library of Congress)

another called the convention itself "a most insane and ludicrous farce" (Wellman 2004, 209). Other newspapers were more positive, or at least neutral, in their assessment of the convention. The New York *Herkimer Freeman* extolled the "success to the cause in which they have enlisted! A railroad speed to the end they would accomplish! . . . I look forward to woman's emancipation with the most intense anxiety; I hail it as a great jubilee of the nation." The *Daily Centre-State American* in Tennessee noted the presence of "a respectable audience" at the convention. The ensuing public debate, often vehement, over women's rights led more cautious women to retreat from the cause, while more-radical women affirmed their activism (Wellman 2004, 210).

Throughout the 1850s, the Declaration of Sentiments served as a touchstone for women's rights reformers. In contrast to the antislavery movement, women's rights activists prior to the Civil War formed no national or regional associations to lead the movement. Organization was left to a core group of dedicated activists such as Susan B. Anthony, Amy Post, Paulina Wright Davis, Sojourner Truth, and Frances Watkins Harper, as well as Lucretia Mott and Elizabeth Cady Stanton. What formal structure existed actually came through the movement's association with the American Anti-Slavery Society. The close relationship between the two reform movements, according to historian Ellen Carol DuBois, provided a significant source of support, while at the same time limiting the growth of the women's rights movement. Women's rights activism was often secondary to abolitionism. Moreover, because antislavery provided women's rights activists with a constituency, activists did not seek out new members, especially conservative women who embraced traditional ideas about family and gender roles.

Nevertheless, activists kept the issue of women's equality before the public throughout the 1850s, through a series of annual women's rights conventions, as well as a broad range of reform activities. Conventions in Massachusetts, Ohio, Indiana, Pennsylvania, and New York asserted the need for women's full political, civil, and economic rights, including control of wages, property and legal rights, educational and employment opportunities, and the right to vote. Women's rights activists also spoke and wrote about the importance of securing women's personal freedoms, including women's right to self-determination (the right to define goals and ambitions outside women's traditional sphere) and the right of voluntary motherhood (the right of married women to choose when to have sexual relations with their husbands). They advocated for more liberal divorce laws and for women's rights to custody of their children in cases of marital dissolution. The convention movement strengthened women's reform activities in the 1850s and aided the establishment of national women's suffrage associations after the Civil War.

Contrary to their critics' opinions, women's rights advocates did not seek to abolish marriage or the family; rather, they sought to protect women's rights within the family and to assure women the right to pursue activities outside the structure of the family. Separate spheres proponent and suffrage opponent Catharine Beecher advocated clothing reform, water cures, exercise, and healthy diets for women. Likewise, more-radical reformers like Paulina Wright Davis and Elizabeth Cady Stanton called for more-comfortable forms of dress and greater reproductive knowledge for women. Women from a variety of perspectives on women's rights shared the view that women were born with the same capacity as men's for vigor and vitality. Women who cultivated healthy habits would be better able to perform their responsibilities as wives and mothers, as well as assume more-active roles in the wider world.

Women's rights activists suspended their efforts during the Civil War (1861–1865). Instead, women turned their attention to the monumental task of providing food, clothing, and medical care to northern and southern soldiers. In 1861 in New York City, women formed the Women's Central Association of Relief, which became the largest women's organization dedicated to soldiers' relief work. African American women in the North also formed organizations to aid freed slaves and, beginning in 1863, black soldiers. At the same time, women's rights activists continued to draft petitions for the freedom of black slaves.

Conclusion

During the first half of the 19th century, Americans experienced significant social, economic, and cultural changes that fundamentally altered how they lived and worked, and that transformed their conceptions of the individual, the family, and society. New gender ideologies relegated women to the private domestic sphere, and justified their ongoing exclusion from the provinces of economic, political, and social power. However, the bonds women forged in their separate female sphere, and women's adherence to the tenets of true womanhood, also helped to create an activist female community engaged in the work of benevolence and social reform. Through their involvement in charity work; temperance, education, prison, and moral reform; labor activism; and abolitionism, women claimed a more active role in public life. In the process, they cultivated political, social, and organizational skills, and developed ways of thinking and talking about human oppression, rights, and freedoms that would be essential once they began to agitate on behalf of their own interests. Participation in the abolitionist movement, especially, encouraged women toward an awareness of their shared grievances and of the necessity of organizing an autonomous movement for women's rights.

Such a movement was launched at Seneca Falls in 1848, with the accompanying Declaration of Sentiments laying the foundation for women's rights activism for generations to come. Although they did not abandon separate spheres and true womanhood altogether, women's rights activists of the late 1840s and 1850s issued the most far-reaching and multifaceted critique of conventional gender roles of the antebellum period. For their efforts, women's rights activists were soundly criticized, ridiculed, and ostracized, but they were not easily deterred. Although they temporarily suspended their efforts during wartime, women's rights activists of the antebellum period inaugurated a social movement that, in one form or another, has endured to the present day.

References and Further Reading

Bacon, Margaret Hope. *Mothers of Feminism: The Story of Quaker Women in America*. San Francisco: Harper and Row Publishers, 1986.

Bacon, Margaret Hope. *Valiant Friend: The Life of Lucretia Mott*. New York: Walker and Company, 1980.

Boylan, Anne. *The Origins of Women's Activism: New York and Boston, 1797–1840*. Chapel Hill: University of North Carolina Press, 2002.

Burin, Eric. *Slavery and the Peculiar Solution: A History of the American Colonization Society*. Gainesville: University of Florida Press, 2005.

Cott, Nancy, ed. *No Small Courage: A History of Women in the United States*. New York: Oxford University Press, 2000.

Cromwell, Otelia. *Lucretia Mott*. Cambridge, MA: Harvard University Press, 1958.

Douglas, Ann. *The Feminization of American Culture*. New York: Avon Books, 1977.

DuBois, Ellen Carol, ed. *Elizabeth Cady Stanton, Susan B. Anthony Reader, Correspondence, Writings, Speeches*. New York: Schocken Books, 1981.

DuBois, Ellen Carol, ed. *Woman Suffrage and Women's Rights*. New York: New York University Press, 1998.

Fladeland, Betty. *Men and Brothers: Anglo-American Antislavery Cooperation*. Urbana: University of Illinois Press, 1972.

Ginzberg, Lori D. *Untidy Origins: A Story of Woman's Rights in Antebellum New York*. Chapel Hill: University of North Carolina Press, 2005.

Ginzberg, Lori D. *Women and the Work of Benevolence: Morality, Politics, and Class in the Nineteenth-Century United States*. New Haven, CT: Yale University Press, 1990.

Griffith, Elisabeth. *In Her Own Right: The Life of Elizabeth Cady Stanton*. New York: Oxford University Press, 1984.

Hallowell, Anna Davis, ed. *James and Lucretia Mott: Life and Letters*. New York: Houghton, Mifflin, and Co., 1884.

Hansen, Debra Gold. *Strained Sisterhood: Gender and Class in the Boston Female Anti-Slavery Society*. Amherst: University of Massachusetts Press, 1993.

Hewitt, Nancy A. *Women's Activism and Social Change: Rochester, New York, 1822–1872*. Ithaca, NY: Cornell University Press, 1984.

Heyrick, Elizabeth. *Immediate, Not Gradual Abolition; Or, An Inquiry into the Shortest, Safest, and Most Effectual Means of Getting Rid of West Indian Slavery*. London: Hatchard & Son, 1824.

Isenberg, Nancy. *Sex and Citizenship in Antebellum America*. Chapel Hill: University of North Carolina Press, 1998.

Jeffrey, Julie Roy. *The Great Silent Army of Abolitionism: Ordinary Women in the Antislavery Movement*. Chapel Hill: University of North Carolina Press, 1998.

Johnson, Paul E. *A Shopkeeper's Millennium: Society and Revivals in Rochester, New York, 1815–1837*. New York: Hill and Wang, 1978.

Kennon, Donald R. "'An Apple of Discord': The Woman Question at the World's Anti-Slavery Convention of 1840." *Slavery and Abolition* 5 (1984): 244–66.

Kessler-Harris, Alice. *Out to Work: A History of Wage-Earning Women in the United States*. New York: Oxford University Press, 1982.

Lerner, Gerda. *The Grimké Sisters from South Carolina: Pioneers for Women's Rights and Abolition*. New York: Schocken Books, 1967.

Lutz, Alma. *Crusade for Freedom: Women in the Antislavery Movement*. Boston: Beacon Press, 1968.

Lutz, Alma. *Susan B. Anthony: Rebel, Crusader, Humanitarian*. Boston: Beacon Press, 1959.

Mayer, Henry. *All on Fire: William Lloyd Garrison and the Abolition of Slavery*. New York: St. Martin's Press, 1998.

Maynard, Douglas H. "The World's Anti-Slavery Convention of 1840." *Mississippi Valley Historical Review* 47 (1960): 452–71.

Meckel, Richard. "Educating a Ministry of Mothers: Evangelical Maternal Associations, 1815–1860." *Journal of the Early Republic* 2 (1982), 403–23.

Melder, Keith E. *Beginnings of Sisterhood: The American Woman's Rights Movement, 1800–1850.* New York: Schocken Books, 1977.

Midgley, Clare. *Women Against Slavery: The British Campaigns, 1780–1870.* London and New York: Routledge, 1992.

Mott, Lucretia. "Discourse on Woman." Reprinted in *Lucretia Mott: Her Complete Speeches and Sermons*, ed. Dana Greene, 143–62. New York: Edwin Mellen Press, 1980.

Nuermberger, Ruth Ketring. *The Free Produce Movement: A Quaker Protest against Slavery.* New York: AMS Press, 1942.

Penney, Sherry H., and James D. Livingston. *A Very Dangerous Woman: Martha Wright and Women's Rights.* Amherst: University of Massachusetts Press, 2004.

Richards, Leonard L. *Gentlemen of Property and Standing: Anti-Abolition Mobs in Jacksonian America.* New York: Oxford University Press, 1970.

Ryan, Mary P. *Women in Public: Between Banners and Ballots, 1825–1880.* Baltimore and London: Johns Hopkins University Press, 1990.

Salerno, Beth. *Sister Societies: Women's Antislavery Organizations in Antebellum America.* DeKalb: Northern Illinois University Press, 2005.

Sellers, Charles. *The Market Revolution: Jacksonian America, 1815–1846.* New York: Oxford University Press, 1991.

Sklar, Kathryn Kish. *Women's Rights Emerges within the Antislavery Movement, 1830–1870: A Brief History with Documents.* Boston: Bedford/St. Martin's, 2000.

Sklar, Kathryn Kish. "'Women Who Speak for an Entire Nation': American and British Women at the World Anti-Slavery Convention, London, 1840." In *The Abolitionist Sisterhood: Women's Political Culture in America*, ed. Jean Fagan Yellin and John C. Van Horne, 301–33. Ithaca, NY: Cornell University Press, 1994.

Smith-Rosenberg, Carroll. *Disorderly Conduct: Visions of Gender in Victorian America.* New York: Oxford University Press, 1985.

Soderlund, Jean. "Priorities and Power: The Philadelphia Female Anti-Slavery Society." In *The Abolitionist Sisterhood: Women's Political Culture in America*, ed. Jean Fagan Yellin and John C. Van Horne, 67–88. Ithaca, NY: Cornell University Press, 1994.

Stanton, Elizabeth Cady, Susan B. Anthony, and Matilda Joslyn Gage, eds. *History of Woman Suffrage*, vol. 1. 1881. Rochester, NY: Charles Mann, 1887.

Stokes, Melvin, and Stephen Conway. *The Market Revolution in America: Social, Political, and Religious Expressions, 1800–1880.* Charlottesville: University of Virginia Press, 1996.

Wellman, Judith. *The Road to Seneca Falls: Elizabeth Cady Stanton and the First Woman's Rights Convention.* Urbana: University of Illinois Press, 2004.

Welter, Barbara J. "The Cult of True Womanhood, 1820–1860." *American Quarterly* 18 (Summer 1966): 151–74.

White, Deborah Gray. *Ar'n't I A Woman?: Female Slaves in the Plantation South.* New York: W. W. Norton & Company, 1985.

Winch, Julie. *Philadelphia's Black Elite: Activism, Accommodation, and the Struggle for Autonomy, 1787–1848.* Philadelphia: Temple University Press, 1988.

Wollstonecraft, Mary. *A Vindication of the Rights of Woman.* Philadelphia, 1792.

Yee, Shirley J. *Black Women Abolitionists: A Study in Activism, 1828–1860.* Knoxville: University of Tennessee Press, 1992.

Yellin, Jean Fagan, and John C. Van Horne, eds. *The Abolitionist Sisterhood: Women's Political Culture in Antebellum America.* Ithaca, NY: Cornell University Press, 1994.

School Girls and College Women: Female Education in the 19th and Early 20th Centuries

5

Andrea Hamilton

Many Americans enjoyed new educational possibilities in the 19th and early 20th centuries, and girls and women shared in the growing opportunities for basic and advanced study. Advances in female education supported the knowledge, skills, confidence, and relationships that women would need to broaden their participation in American public life. Yet the story of schoolgirls and college women cannot be oversimplified as a straightforward stepping-stone in the fight for women's rights. Sometimes, education empowered women to challenge the status quo. At other times, female education reinforced persistent notions about women's roles in the family and society.

Why Educate Girls and Women?

By the close of the 18th century, a growing number of Americans had come to agree that some education for girls and women was desirable. Their understandings of how and for what girls and women should be educated differed, however, and were shaped by a variety of influences.

Enlightenment philosophers of the 18th century had emphasized the capacity for reason in *all* human beings, and they believed that education should be used to cultivate the minds of *both* women and men. Many elite families encouraged their daughters to pursue education. As Americans struggled to secure the future of their new country, some thought that educating girls could help strengthen the health of the young republic. Educated girls would become educated mothers—or "Republican Mothers"—who could raise their sons to be responsible and virtuous citizens. Linking women's childrearing duties to the quality of civic life provided a powerful rationale for educating girls and young women.

Such secular theories combined with religious impulses, which also stressed the importance of women's roles in society. Religious revivalism in the 1820s and 1830s (known as the "Second Great Awakening") encouraged evangelical Christians to act on their faith in shaping society. Women's roles as wives, mothers, and teachers came to be viewed as key to spreading Christian virtues in homes, schoolrooms, and communities across America. Many Americans were worried that forces like increasing numbers of immigrants, the growth of cities and industry, and westward expansion threatened the nation. They hoped that education for girls and women might help safeguard Christian civilization against these forces. Women were thus encouraged to use their influence over children and men, even if these same women were formally excluded from politics and much of public life.

Formation of the middle class in the early 19th century likewise promoted the growth of female education. Many middle-class parents sought education for their sons to help prepare them for future employment, and they believed that education would help their daughters in their future roles as wives and mothers. A few families also sought education to train their daughters as teachers. Education was a mark of social distinction. Working-class parents often could not afford education for either their sons or their daughters. Social class, therefore, was generally a better indicator than gender of whether or not a child would be formally educated.

Another factor in the growth of educational opportunities for girls at all levels was the common school movement in the first half of the 19th century. Reformers like Horace Mann (often referred to as the "father of American education") worked to establish schools that, in theory, would provide *all* Americans with a common education that would give them the skills and moral foundation necessary for citizenship and participation in society. Under the guidance of Mann and other reformers, Americans would embark upon what would become the largest experiment in universal public education ever undertaken in history. From their beginnings, most common schools included girls. With little controversy, much of America accepted the common school ideal that the nation's daughters, as well as its sons, deserved basic education. Although common schools did not reach most children until the late 19th and early 20th centuries, the foundations had been laid for what became a nationwide coeducational public school system.

Educating Young Ladies in the 19th Century: Female Academies and Separate Spheres

In the first half of the 19th century, the vast majority of colleges were open only to men. At this time, several notable women established female academies to provide more-advanced education to elite young women. Most of these founders were shaped by the "separate spheres" ideology, which dictated that men belonged in the public realm of politics and business, while women belonged in the private sphere of the home. Although this understanding of gender roles in many ways limited women's opportunities, it also encouraged women to develop an expanded understanding of domesticity that championed the value of female education.

Emma Hart Willard founded the Troy Seminary in New York in 1821. The school boasted a curriculum similar to that of leading male colleges, and also trained girls in female accomplishments such as needlework. Willard authored numerous successful textbooks, and she argued for equal funding for female education to the New York state legislature. In stating her case for women's advanced education, Willard argued that the health of the state rested on mothers' influences. Although she believed women to be as capable of learning as men, she also argued that women should not seek power in the public sphere. Willard called fathers, brothers, and husbands the "natural guardians" and "rulers" of women (Willard 1819, 31).

Catharine Beecher established female academies in the Midwest and wrote a number of influential manuals for American women, which instructed them on managing their homes and families. Beecher believed that women belonged in the domestic or home sphere, whereas men operated in the public sphere of work and politics. Beecher opposed suffrage for women but argued that women had vitally important roles as the moral guardians of society. "The proper education of a man decides the welfare of an individual," Beecher wrote in *A Treatise on Domestic Economy for the Use of Young Women* in 1841. "But educate a woman, and the interests of a whole family are secured" (Beecher 1843, 37). Beecher helped transform teaching into a female profession. She believed women made ideal teachers because they could shape the morals of the schoolchildren who would one day run the country. Teaching also could provide unmarried women with respectable means of employment. Beecher won over some school boards that were skeptical about hiring women by arguing that female teachers could be paid much less than male teachers.

Mary Lyon opened Holyoke Seminary in Massachusetts in 1837. Holyoke was to be "an institution of the highest opportunities for improvement, and of very moderate expense" that would train "self-denying teachers." Lyon hoped these teachers would help Christianize, as well as educate, the nation. As Lyon noted in a fund-raising pamphlet to other women, "This work of supplying teachers is a great work, and it must be done, or our country is lost, and the world will remain unconverted" (Hitchcock 1852, 232–38). Holyoke students followed strict schedules of study, exercise, and worship, and they performed all their own cooking and domestic chores. At least 70 percent of Holyoke graduates became teachers, and many of Holyoke's graduates established seminaries for other young women. After the Civil War, Mount Holyoke served as a model for many of the nation's first colleges for women and trained many of their early female leaders.

In the antebellum South, educating girls and young ladies of the planter class was an established tradition. Female seminaries offered both serious academic study and training in female accomplishments. Unlike schools in other parts of the country, southern schools never offered teacher training or encouraged women to use their education to expand their influence in the public sphere. Education was intended to reinforce elite white women's place in the southern social order and to help buttress a patriarchal society. For the South's African

An aerial view of the Emma Willard School in Troy, New York. Originally the Troy Female Seminary, headed by Emma Willard, the school pioneered the teaching of math, science, and social studies to female students. The academy, renamed the Emma Willard School in 1895, remains a prestigious educational facility today. (Emma Willard School)

American slaves and for the majority of its nonelite white women (as well as for most nonelite men), formal education was almost nonexistent.

Willard, Beecher, and Lyon illustrate how female education grounded in the separate spheres ideology opened new opportunities for girls and young women in the 19th century, while also denying them full access to the opportunities men enjoyed in the public realm. In contrast, a few reformers, like Elizabeth Cady Stanton (educated at Willard's academy) and Susan B. Anthony, emphasized women's likeness to men, and argued that they deserved equal education and opportunities because of their rights as human beings, instead of because of their different female natures.

These two strains of thought coexisted uneasily in the 19th century. Supporters of female education drew on both—and not always consistently—to argue for educational opportunities for girls and women. The separate spheres ideology predominated in the 19th century, but tensions between different ways of thinking about female education would escalate in later decades.

Educating the Masses

Attendance at private academies was a privilege few could afford, but the growing number of public schools gradually spread rudimentary education across the country. Girls from a variety of backgrounds in both cities and rural areas reaped the benefits. In 1790, about half as many women as men were literate. But by 1870, girls comprised 49 percent of pupils in public schools, and girls ages 10–14 actually had higher literacy rates than their male counterparts.

Although private academies and colleges were overwhelmingly single sex, the large majority of children attended coeducational schools. Most educators and most American families seemed to view schools as institutions similar to the family and the church, where the sexes mixed without threatening the distinct roles of either. Expediency no doubt encouraged coeducation as well. Maintaining separate schools for girls and boys was expensive and impractical in most parts of America, and only a few cities could afford it.

Traditionally, school leaders and parents had preferred male teachers. But cultural shifts, as well as expediency, made female teachers increasingly popular. Changing views of childhood that emphasized the innocence of young children and the importance of maternal nurture made women attractive candidates. A shortage of male teachers for the growing number of classrooms in cities and on the frontier encouraged school districts to tap a new and less expensive labor force: single women.

Teaching rapidly evolved into a sex-segregated profession in the late 19th and early 20th centuries. By 1890, in cities with populations over 10,000, women comprised 92 percent of all teachers. Women filled the bottom ranks of the bureaucracy as classroom teachers, particularly in lower grades, and were usually placed under the supervision of men, who served as principals, administrators, and sometimes high-school teachers. Schools paid female teachers less than men were paid, as a matter of policy. Once again, the situation was paradoxical in regards to women's rights. As teaching became a feminized field, women gained important new opportunities for more advanced education, for respectable employment, and for means of self-support. Women garnered these new opportunities, however, under an institutionalized system of sex segregation, limited opportunities for advancement, and unequal pay.

Building the public-school system went hand-in-hand with growth in women's education. Common schools spread education to more girls and, in turn, more girls became teachers to staff the growing number of schools. By the late 19th and early 20th centuries, new institutions known as high schools were gaining popularity among the middle classes. Girls flocked to high schools in far greater numbers than boys, and, once there, outperformed them. In 1889, approximately three-fourths of high school students in the nation's largest cities were female. In 1890, girls comprised 65 percent of high school graduates. While middle-class males were more likely to enter the workforce or to attend private colleges and preparatory schools than they were to attend public high schools, girls and their families seemed to view high school as a respectable interim place between girlhood and marriage. High school could provide training for respectable employment (such as teaching or, later, clerical work), and girls reported enjoying the social aspects of high school.

By the first decade of the 20th century, many educators were actually beginning to worry that the feminization of high school was driving away boys. They perceived girls' success in high school as a problem. In order to combat

Native American Girls' shorthand class, Haskell Institute, Lawrence, Kansas, 1910. (National Archives and Records Administration)

it, schools introduced measures such as competitive athletics, in an attempt to attract male students. The early 20th century also saw the introduction of some gender-specific courses, such as home economics for girls. But despite some sex segregation in electives, most female and male students enrolled in the same basic academic curriculum.

America's education system opened opportunities for many first- and second-generation immigrant women who came to the United States in the late 19th and early 20th centuries. In her semi-autobiographical novel *Bread Givers,* Anzia Yezierska (2003) portrayed the struggles of a Jewish girl to escape from poverty and traditional beliefs about women's place in family and society. Schools taught young Sara Smolinsky how to read and write, and they also acculturated her by teaching her the manners and customs of middle-class Americans. After graduating from college, she returned to her childhood neighborhood as a teacher dedicated to helping other children. In contrast, some immigrant children found that schools denigrated their religious and ethnic customs and did little to help them escape from poverty.

Despite the American ideal of universal education, not all children enjoyed equal access to public schooling. In particular, African Americans had long been denied educational opportunities. In the antebellum North, some African Americans attended public schools, but were routinely segregated into inferior schools. Members of the free black community in some Northern cities fought to open and equalize public education for their children, but they faced harsh resistance. Others turned to private schooling. Some white philanthropists supported their efforts. When Quaker Prudence Crandall admitted an African American student to her female academy, white parents withdrew their daughters in protest. In response, Crandall established a school for African American girls in Connecticut in 1833. The state then passed a law making it illegal to provide a free education for African Americans, and Crandall was arrested and tried. Although the case against her was dismissed, a white mob attacked her school, threatening her and her students, and the school closed after only two years. The story of Crandall's school illustrates the real hardships and dangers that accompanied pursuit of education for African Americans.

Under the slave system of the Old South, many whites feared education would encourage African Americans to question their status and agitate for freedom. Laws, such as an 1819 Virginia law declaring a gathering of slaves in schools for the purpose of teaching reading and writing an "unlawful assembly" punishable by not more than twenty lashes, sought to prevent the spread of literacy among slaves (Goodell 1853, 320). Despite such efforts, evidence suggests that the slave community valued learning and, in the wake of the Civil War, the African American community went to heroic efforts to obtain education, seeing it as a crucial step in obtaining equality. Some African Americans attended schools taught by white female missionaries (women who themselves had benefited from the increased education available to white, middle-class women). Some of these teachers were selflessly devoted to their students, while others condescended to African Americans as inferiors.

The educational and social goals of blacks and whites in regards to African American education often varied significantly. African Americans struggled to establish primary schools for their communities when public school systems failed to do so. Schools funded by northern white philanthropists in the late 19th and early 20th centuries emphasized manual training or industrial education, which many whites and some African Americans saw as a means of lifting former slaves and their descendents out of poverty. Industrial education for African American women often meant training for jobs as cooks, housekeepers, and seamstresses.

Founded in 1904, Mary McLeod Bethune's Daytona Educational and Industrial School for Negro Girls followed trends of the time in teaching girls domestic skills. Bethune herself became a national figure fighting for the rights of African Americans. Some schools for African Americans ran large normal departments (teacher training programs), and for African American women, teaching in the nation's segregated schools became an important and respected source of employment. For some African American women, schools opened new avenues of opportunity and inspiration from their fellow students and teachers. Other African American women resented education designed to train them as domestic servants for white families. From their perspective, white Americans supported education designed to keep African Americans in a distinct and inferior position in the social order.

By the 1890s, virtually all Native Americans had lost their lands to white settlers moving westward, and had been confined to reservations. The US government began creating boarding schools for Native American children as a means of assimilating them. For young females, that meant abandoning many of their traditional cultural practices and learning English, adopting European-style dress, and undertaking training in domestic skills. As in the case of African Americans, education for Native Americans all too frequently meant training for an inferior social position. At the Hampton Normal and Agricultural

Institute in Virginia, for example, Native American girls served as domestic servants for European-American families as part of their education.

Opening the Doors of Higher Education

The number of girls and young women attending primary and secondary schools throughout the country rose steadily in the 19th and early-20th centuries. But colleges and universities proved more resistant to admitting women. In 1833, Oberlin College was the first college to open its doors to women (and to African Americans). Women also gained admission to some state universities (such as those of Iowa in 1844, Wisconsin in 1867, and Kansas, Indiana, and Minnesota in 1869) and to newly founded private research universities (such as Cornell University in 1868, Boston University in 1873, and The University of Chicago in 1892). While women at coeducational institutions enjoyed new opportunities, not all doors were open to them. Many coeducational colleges and universities restricted female students to certain courses of study, limited women's access to facilities, and prohibited their participation in many extracurricular activities.

Colleges founded specifically for women in the late 19th century trained generations of influential women. Because all the students were female, women at those colleges participated fully in academic and campus life. Vassar, which was modeled on older female academies and initially struggled to find adequately prepared students, opened in 1865 with the mission of educating better teachers. In 1884, Bryn Mawr College offered an academically rigorous course equal to that of the best men's colleges. Radcliffe began in 1879 as the Annex to Harvard University, where females could study with Harvard professors, even though the university denied women admission. These colleges—among the northeastern Seven Sister colleges—were influential models for women's schools elsewhere.

Although female academies had flourished in the antebellum South, higher education for women lagged behind that of other regions in the post-Civil War South. Devotion to romanticized notions of the southern lady, as well as poverty, worked against increasing standards. Only a few of the southern female colleges in the late 19th century maintained serious academic standards. Southern female colleges were open only to a select few white women who could afford to attend. Education open to black women in the South largely focused on manual training, although some institutions, such as Spellman College, founded in 1881, would evolve into liberal arts colleges in the early 20th century.

From 1870 to 1900, the number of women in higher education increased about eight times, from around 11,000 to 85,000. These significant inroads into higher education provoked worry that young women were entering an improper and potentially harmful realm. Some experts, like Dr. Edward Clarke, claimed that too much study for young women was dangerous, and would damage their health. Some colleges responded by arguing that the education they were extending to women would enhance, not threaten, women's tradi-

Dr. Edward Clarke and the Science against Too Much Education for Women

In the 1870s, new, purportedly scientific, findings roused old fears that too much mental exertion could harm a young woman's physical and mental well-being. Former Harvard Medical School professor Dr. Edward H. Clarke's *Sex in Education; Or, A Fair Chance for the Girls* (1873) studied a group of Vassar students and warned of the risks inherent in higher education for women. Clarke explained that when an adolescent girl studied too much, "the stream of vital and constructive force evolved within her was turned steadily to the brain, and away from the ovaries and their accessories." The result could be a nervous breakdown or sterility. Clarke did not deny that women were capable of higher education, but he sent the clear message that women who pursued higher education were putting themselves at risk. M. Carey Thomas recalled, "We did not know when we began whether women's health could stand the strain of education. We were haunted in those days by the clanging chains of that gloomy specter, Dr. Edward H. Clarke's *Sex in Education*" (Rosenberg 1982, 10, 12).

Thomas and other women rejected the notion that their biology constrained them, and their success in higher education disproved Clarke's claims. M. Carey Thomas attended the newly opened coeducational Cornell University, and then enrolled at Johns Hopkins University for graduate study. Thomas left Hopkins because, although the school admitted her, it refused to let her attend classes with male students. Thomas then traveled to Europe to complete her studies and earn a doctoral degree. When Quakers opened a new college for women in Pennsylvania in 1884, Thomas became first its Dean and then its President. At Bryn Mawr College, Thomas was an outspoken advocate for women's rights, including their access to education and the professions.

---

tional roles as wives, mothers, and moral guardians of society. But college (and, to some extent, high-school) experiences often had unexpectedly profound effects on young women. They were exposed to new ideas, were inspired by female teachers, and bonded with fellow female students. Many completed their college course inspired to *use* their education. As a group, college-educated women were more likely to remain single (half of all college-educated women in the late 19th century never married). If they did marry, they did so later and had fewer children.

By 1900, women comprised about 35 percent of the total higher education student population. These new college women challenged older ideas about women's possibilities. Some fought for admissions to more advanced study and became professors at women's colleges (coeducational institutions often refused to hire female professors). They, in turn, served as mentors to future generations of women. Many college graduates became teachers—the primary profession open to educated women. Settlement houses (the most famous of which was Jane Addams's Hull House, founded in 1889) attracted educated women who sought to use their education for social good, and also provided them with places of friendship and support. Other women fought for access to the traditionally male professions. A few law schools admitted women in the latter decades of the 19th century, although many states refused to license women to practice. In 1849, Elizabeth Blackwell was the first woman to earn a medical degree. By the 1880s and 1890s, female students made up as much as 10 percent of their medical school classes.

Undoubtedly, women faced significant barriers within academia and within the professions, and they still struggled to gain full access to public life. But education increased women's options, and it opened possibilities for independence and choices about family and career. Although many college women followed traditional paths of marriage and motherhood, they were more likely to be active in voluntary organizations outside the home than were their non–college-educated peers. As education afforded women more opportunities to gain knowledge, experience, and confidence, it could also encourage them to resist when they felt they were unfairly denied the rights and opportunities men enjoyed. Women lobbied for expanded rights so they could *use* their education. Some focused on increased access to careers. Others demanded that women be allowed to use their skills to help the less fortunate and to clean up the public realm. Many came to focus on political rights—particularly woman suffrage—as key to raising women's status within American society.

Women's advances in education by the early 20th century were impressive. By 1920, women made up almost half of the college student population and

Elizabeth Blackwell was the first woman to receive a medical degree in the United States. (Library of Congress)

received about one-third of all graduate degrees. But such educational advances did not always correlate directly with increased rights. Notably, for instance, women's employment, and particularly their access to the professions, did not keep pace with their gains in education. The greatest increases in female employment were among immigrants and African American women who worked in factories and domestic service. Educated women continued to have great difficulty gaining access to traditionally male professions. Percentages of women in graduate schools actually dropped in the early 20th century, sometimes in the face of quotas that restricted access. (Medical schools, for instance, formalized a 5 percent female quota in 1925, and the number of female physicians subsequently dropped). At colleges and universities, female professors and students were often clustered into female colleges, and in fields such as education, home economics, nursing, or social work.

By the 1920s, going to college did not mean the same thing for many young women and their families that it had for first-generation college women. Women who had undertaken what was commonly perceived as the masculine pursuit of higher education in the 1870s and 1880s had defied traditional expectations about women's nature and place in society. Going to college, by the 1920s, was more commonplace for well-to-do young women. (Although, significantly, attending college was still a luxury that most Americans—either male or female—could not afford.) Pursuit of a college education had become a safe and socially desirable option for middle-class women and their families. Women's college attendance no longer signified defiance of traditional expectations about women's nature and place in society.

Conclusion

The growth of education for girls and women in the late 19th and early 20th centuries was phenomenal. More girls than ever were receiving rudimentary education in public schools. Growing numbers of young women had the options of attending high schools, colleges and universities, and even professional and graduate schools. Increases in women's education had encouraged women to move beyond traditional female roles in the home, and had spurred them to engage in fights for access to rights in the public realm traditionally reserved for men.

The increasing visibility of women at all levels of the education system, however, did not signify that all barriers for girls and women in the educational world had been surpassed. Many of the country's most elite schools denied women admission. Graduate and professional schools established quotas to restrict women's access. Some high schools and colleges channeled women into special (and often less-than-equal) female tracks. The traditional expectations of families, teachers, and the girls themselves exerted powerful influences in schools and on students, and education could function to limit the options girls and women perceived to be open to them. Minority women faced even greater obstacles. Too often, they were restricted to schools designed to serve the purposes of the whites who funded them, rather than to increase the rights of the young women who attended them. In addition to racism, poverty severely limited access to educational opportunities.

Margaret Haley: Fighting for Teachers' Rights

Margaret Haley (1861–1939) was the daughter of Irish immigrants. Like many young women in the late 19th and early 20th centuries who wanted a respectable means of earning a living, she decided to become a teacher. She attended normal school—a school designed to establish teaching norms (hence the name) and train teachers—and began teaching sixth-grade students in a very poor neighborhood in Chicago. She was discouraged by the conditions in her school—her classes had 50 to 60 students—and by the way the school treated its teachers. Most female teachers not only were paid less than male teachers were, but were paid less than were unskilled male and female workers, as well. In 1905, a National Education Association survey showed that in 44 out of 48 cities, street and sewer workers earned more than female elementary-school teachers.

Haley became a paid organizer for the Chicago Teachers Federation (CTF). Haley believed teachers needed to organize to fight for issues such as better pay, improved working conditions, and pensions for retired teachers. She also wanted to improve teacher training and give classroom teachers, rather than school bureaucrats, more power. Haley fought to advance women's positions in the National Education Association (NEA), which, like most education and teachers' associations, was dominated by male school administrators. In 1904, Haley became the first woman and teacher to deliver an address—"Why Teachers Should Organize"—at a National Education Association meeting. She decried what she saw as the trend to "factoryizing education"—treating teachers like mere factory hands who were to follow orders rather than engage with and truly educate children for a democratic society (Tyack 1974, 257).

Haley believed that school reform and the fight for teachers' rights was critical to all kinds of social reform. Under her leadership, her teachers' union allied with the labor movement. She also mobilized teachers to fight for progressive causes such as woman suffrage and legislation against child labor.

And yet the liberating effects of education on schoolgirls and college women in American history cannot be underestimated. Schools and education—even with all their imperfections—often raised expectations. They encouraged female students to think beyond their existing circumstances and to imagine the possibilities the future could hold. That sense of possibility was surely a necessity for the women who fought for their own rights and for those of their fellow citizens.

References and Further Reading

Almeida, Deirdre A. "The Hidden Half: A History of Native American Women's Education." *Harvard Educational Review* 67.4 (Winter 1997): 757–71.

Anderson, James D. *The Education of Blacks in the South, 1865–1935.* Chapel Hill: University of North Carolina Press, 1988.

Banner, Lois. *Elizabeth Cady Stanton: A Radical for Women's Rights.* New York: Longman, 1997.

Beecher, Catharine E. *A Treatise on Domestic Economy for the Use of Young Ladies at Home and at School.* Rev. ed. Boston: Thomas H. Webb, and Co., 1843.

Clarke, Edward H. *Sex in Education; Or, A Fair Chance for the Girls.* 1873. Reprint, New York: Arno Press, 1972.

Cott, Nancy F. *The Bonds of Womanhood: "Woman's Sphere" in New England, 1780–1835.* New Haven, CT: Yale University Press, 1977.

Farnham, Christie Ann. *Education of the Southern Bell: Higher Education and Student Socialization in the Antebellum South.* New York: New York University Press, 1995.

Goodell, William. *The American Slave Code in Theory and Practice: Its Distinctive Features Shown by Its Statutes, Judicial Decisions, and Illustrative Facts.* New York: American & Foreign Anti-Slavery Society, 1853.

Goodsell, Willystine. *Pioneers of Women's Education in the United States.* New York: Macmillan, 1931.

Haley, Margaret A. *Battleground: The Autobiography of Margaret A. Haley.* Ed. Robert L. Reid. Urbana: University of Illinois Press, 1982.

Harris, Barbara J. *Beyond Her Sphere: Women and the Professions in American History.* Westport, CT: Greenwood Press, 1978.

Hitchcock, Edward. *The Power of Christian Benevolence Illustrated in the Life and Labors of Mary Lyon.* Northampton, MA: Hopkins, Bridgman, and Company, 1852.

Hoffman, Nancy. *Woman's True Profession: Voices from the History of Teaching.* 2nd edition. Cambridge, MA: Harvard Education Press, 2003.

Horowitz, Helen Lefkowitz. *The Power and Passion of M. Carey Thomas.* New York: Alfred A. Knopf, 1994.

Jurmain, Suzanne. *The Forbidden Schoolhouse: The True and Dramatic Story of Prudence Crandall and Her Students.* New York: Houghton Mifflin, 2005.

Kaestle, Carl F. *Pillars of the Republic: Common Schools and American Society, 1780–1860.* New York: Hill and Wang, 1983.

Kantor, Harvey, and David B. Tyack, eds. *Work, Youth, and Schooling: Historical Perspectives on Vocationalism in American Education.* Palo Alto, CA: Stanford University Press, 1982.

Kerber, Linda K. *Women of the Republic: Intellect and Ideology in Revolutionary America.* Chapel Hill: University of North Carolina Press, 1980.

Matthaei, Julie. *An Economic History of Women in America: Women's Work, the Sexual Division of Labor, and the Development of Capitalism.* New York: Schocken Books, 1982.

Morrison, Anne Henry. *Women and Their Careers: A Study of 306 Women in Business and the Professions.* New York: National Federation of Business and Professional Women's Clubs, 1934.

Nash, Margaret A. *Women's Education in the United States, 1780–1840*. New York: Palgrave Macmillan, 2005.

Rosenberg, Rosalind. *Beyond Separate Spheres: Intellectual Roots of Modern Feminism*. New Haven, CT: Yale University Press, 1982.

Ryan, Mary P. *The Cradle of the Middle Class: The Family in Oneida County, New York, 1790–1865*. Cambridge, MA: Cambridge University Press, 1981.

Sklar, Kathryn Kish. *Catharine Beecher: A Study in Domesticity*. New Haven, CT: Yale University Press, 1973.

Solomon, Barbara Miller. *In the Company of Educated Women: A History of Women and Higher Education in America*. New Haven, CT: Yale University Press, 1985.

Strane, Susan. *A Whole-Souled Woman: Prudence Crandall and the Education of Black Women*. New York: W. W. Norton & Company, 1990.

Thomas, M. Carey. "Present Tendencies in Women's College and University Education." *Educational Review* 35 (January 1908): 64–85.

Tyack, David B. *The One Best System: A History of American Urban Education*. Cambridge, MA: Harvard University Press, 1974.

Tyack, David, and Elisabeth Hansot. *Learning Together: A History of Coeducation in American Public Schools*. New York: Russell Sage Foundation, 1992.

Willard, Emma. *An Address to the Public; Particularly to the Members of the Legislature of New-York, Proposing a Plan for Improving Female Education*. Middlebury: S. W. Copeland, 1819.

Woody, Thomas. *A History of Women's Education in the United States*. 2 vols. New York: Science Press, 1929.

Yezierska, Anzia. *Bread Givers*. 1925. New York: Persia Books, 2003.

Suffragists | 6

Jessica O'Brien Pursell

The Nineteenth—or Susan B. Anthony—Amendment was officially added to the U.S. Constitution on August 26, 1920. The text of the amendment is straightforward: "The right of citizens of the United States to vote shall not be denied or abridged by the United States or by any State on account of sex. Congress shall have the power to enforce this article by appropriate legislation." This marked the culmination of 72 years of organized struggle. Women fought and even gave their lives for these 40 words. The passage of the Nineteenth Amendment was an undisputed victory for women's rights and was essential for forging the United States into a more democratic nation. Unfortunately, the fight for full gender and social equality was far from over.

Inspiring national activists such as Susan B. Anthony, Elizabeth Cady Stanton, Carrie Chapman Catt, and Alice Paul led the struggle for the vote, but focusing solely on these women leaves much of the story untold. Many women worked for suffrage on the local level, and the women of several western states won the vote with little help from the foremost national suffrage group, the National American Woman Suffrage Association (NAWSA). Women in many communities also lobbied successfully for partial voting rights that allowed them to vote in certain types of elections, such as school-board selection, before the Nineteenth Amendment enfranchised all women. African American women also formed local suffrage groups and built coalitions within their communities. Despite the racism that was endemic in turn-of-the-century American society and prevalent in the suffrage movement, some African American women played important roles in the national suffrage organizations. Working-class women also supported the suffrage movement, sometimes risking their livelihoods to do so. Although the visible leadership of the national movement was predominantly white and middle class, by 1920 women from every walk of life were working for the vote. Women argued for the vote on the basis of their common humanity with men, asserting that they had an equal right to suffrage as adult citizens in a democracy; they also argued for the vote on the basis of their gender difference, claiming that as morally superior beings they would use the vote to improve society. Whatever their arguments and backgrounds, all suffrage advocates saw the vote as a vital tool for bettering their own lives and ensuring the progress of the American nation.

The Organized Struggle Begins: Seneca Falls and the Birth of a Women's Rights Movement

Women of the early and mid-19th century were bound by the legal principle of coverture. In most states, they could not sign contracts or hold property after marriage. Single women who were independent and worked made only a fraction of what men earned in the industrial economy. In 1807, New Jersey, the only state in which women could vote, passed a law revoking that right, and all women in the United States were excluded from the elective franchise. Many people believed that women were morally superior to men, but were biologically ill suited to participate in the activities of public life. Some women, however, drew on assumptions about their moral superiority and became involved in various reform efforts in the antebellum period (1820–1860), including moral reform, temperance, and the abolitionist movement.

As more women became active in social reform, they began thwarting customs by speaking in public, holding executive offices, and even managing the affairs of large organizations. Women's participation in the reform movements of the antebellum period not only helped women hone their leadership and organizational skills, it brought their subordinate position in society into sharp focus. An example of this was the 1840 World's Anti-Slavery Convention held in London. Some American abolitionist societies sent women as their delegates to the London convention. One such delegate was Lucretia Mott, a Quaker activist. Although these women were elected by their home societies and traveled across the Atlantic, they were not allowed to participate or vote in the affairs of the convention. Outraged, Mott and fellow abolitionist Elizabeth Cady Stanton discussed the need for a convention that would focus solely on women's issues.

The first women's rights convention convened eight years later in Seneca Falls, New York. This marked the birth of an organized women's rights movement in the United States. Stanton drafted the convention's Declaration of Sentiments and Resolutions, which, like the Declaration of Independence, called for a repressed people to rise up against an oppressive government and demand their "inalienable" rights. In the first part of the Declaration, Stanton specified the many ways in which men oppressed women by both law and custom. Women were denied voting rights, legal and property rights in marriage, rights to child custody in cases of divorce, and educational and economic opportunity. They were subjected to a sexual double standard, which punished them for "moral delinquencies" that men were allowed to commit with impunity. Women who did own property were taxed by a government in which they had no voice and no representation. By subjecting woman to all of these travesties, man relegated her to a separate and narrow "sphere of action," and worked hard "to destroy her confidence in her own powers" so as to convince her that her subordination was ordained by God and nature. In the Declaration, Stanton stated that some women were no longer willing to accept the inferior position to which men had assigned them. "[B]ecause women do feel themselves aggrieved, oppressed, and fraudulently deprived of their most sacred rights," she declared, "we insist that they have immediate admission to all the rights and privileges which belong to them as citizens of the United States." Stanton then went on to enumerate a list of resolutions that proclaimed woman to be identical to man in "capabilities and responsibilities" and that claimed for her the equal right to determine the course of her own life and to participate fully in the public life of the nation, including in the realm of electoral politics (Stanton, Anthony, and Gage 1887, 70–72).

Although many of the participants at Seneca Falls agreed that women should have more rights in society, Stanton's resolution calling for the vote was too radical for some. Of all of her demands, this was the one that posed the greatest threat to women's dependence on and subordination to men. Following debate on the suffrage issue, it was ratified and included in the Declaration. At the close of the convention, 68 women and 32 men signed the Declaration of Sentiments, with all of its resolutions approved, including the controversial one demanding the right to vote.

The Seneca Falls Convention inspired many local conventions and a yearly national convention. These became the main vehicle for women's rights activism until the Civil War. Two women quickly rose to respected positions within the fledgling movement, Susan B. Anthony and Elizabeth Cady Stanton. Susan B. Anthony began her career as a speaker and leader in the temperance movement, but like Mott and Stanton, she soon felt the need to address women's causes. Stanton, a mother of seven, remained active in the women's movement by sending letters and written statements to various conventions and officials, but like many women, she would be unable to attend most events due to her familial responsibilities. Anthony and Stanton met in 1851 and developed a close and productive friendship devoted to one another and to the cause of women's rights. When Stanton was unable to attend conventions, it was Anthony who delivered her inspiring speeches. Anthony's own skills were strongest in organizing and planning, although she also became a popular speaker on suffrage and women's issues.

Throughout the 1850s, women's rights activists wrote and spoke about the range of grievances and demands articulated in the Declaration of Sentiments. They advocated for equal legal rights in marriage, educational opportunity, equal wages, and access to jobs and the professions. Some, most notably Stanton, boldly pushed for more radical reforms, such as married women's control over their own reproduction, dress reform, and divorce reform. Stanton also repeatedly emphasized that the most essential tool for realizing any fundamental and lasting improvements in women's status and condition was the elective franchise. "Think you, if woman had a vote in this government, that all those laws affecting her interests would so entirely violate every principle of right and justice?" she pointedly asked at Seneca Falls. "Had woman a vote to give, might not the office-holders and seekers propose some change in her condition?" (DuBois 1992, 32) Other women's rights activists quickly embraced Stanton's reasoning. Following the nation's terrible Civil War, the vote would decisively come to dominate the women's rights agenda for more than 50 years.

Mobilizing for and against Suffrage after the Civil War

During the upheaval of the Civil War (1861–1865), the conventions and agitation for women's rights were put aside. The destruction and chaos caused by the war necessitated the full attention of the nation. In the North and South, women and men suffered from the terrible loss of life and the destruction of homes and communities. Women also played active roles in the war effort, by running homes, farms, plantations, and businesses when men were called away to fight, and by serving the Union and Confederate armies as cooks, laundresses, nurses, and spies. Some women disguised themselves as men and served as soldiers. Northern women drew on their decades of experience in social reform movements and formed the U.S. Sanitary Commission, which proved to be highly successful in improving sanitary conditions in hospitals, raising money, organizing relief supplies, and coordinating nursing efforts for the Union army. Women volunteers won high praise for their work with the Sanitary Commission; they also honed the organizational skills and sense of self-confidence that helped to prepare them for involvement in a new round of social reform efforts in the years following the Civil War. Led by Anthony and Stanton, some northern women also participated in the Woman's National Loyal League, which organized a petition campaign to pressure members of Congress to pass an amendment to the constitution abolishing slavery. In part due to these efforts, the Thirteenth Amendment was passed and ratified in 1865. For many women's rights activists, it seemed that their ardent work in the abolitionist movement was finally paying off.

The Civil War was followed by a period of Reconstruction (1865–1877), during which Americans engaged in crucial struggles over the terms of national reunification and the meaning of U.S. citizenship. At war's end, women's rights advocates resumed their activities, hopeful that this was the moment when full citizenship rights for African Americans and women would at last be achieved. In 1866, Anthony and Stanton, along with other women's rights activists, founded the American Equal Rights Association (AERA) to fight for universal suffrage, or voting rights for both African Americans and women. That same year, Radical Republicans in Congress passed the Fourteenth Amendment, with the intent to grant former slaves citizenship. The wording of the first paragraph gave women hope as well. The amendment began with the guarantee that "[a]ll persons born or naturalized in the United States, and subject to the jurisdiction thereof, are citizens of the United States and of the State wherein they reside." The second section of the Fourteenth Amendment, however, encouraged states to grant voting rights exclusively to their adult male citizens. This marked the first mention of gender in the federal constitution. Some women's rights activists were dismayed by the wording and petitioned members of Congress to change it. In response, they were told by their former abolitionist male allies that this was the "negro's hour" and that black male suffrage was to take priority over woman suffrage (Dubois 1978, 61). Following the ratification of the Fourteenth Amendment in 1868, Congress more vigorously sought to secure black male voting rights when it passed the Fifteenth Amendment, which declared that the right of U.S. citizens to vote could not be denied on the basis of "race, color, or previous condition of servitude." Ratified in 1870, the Fifteenth Amendment explicitly excluded voting rights protections on the basis of gender.

Women's rights activists disagreed over the Fourteenth and Fifteenth Amendments. Some, such as Anthony, Stanton, and Sojourner Truth, opposed the amendments, and once they were ratified, called for the passage of a sixteenth amendment, one that would clearly grant women the right to vote. Others, such as Fredrick Douglass, Lucy Stone, and her husband Henry Blackwell, supported the amendments. They thought that the rights of black men had to be secured before rejoining the struggle for woman suffrage. The American Equal Rights Association disintegrated over the controversy. In its wake, two rival organizations emerged: The National Woman Suffrage Association (NWSA) and the American Woman Suffrage Association (AWSA). Both founded in 1869, these organizations pursued different visions of gender equality and utilized different tactics for achieving their goals. Together, they marked the establishment of an independent movement on behalf of woman suffrage in the United States.

The National Woman Suffrage Association was formed by Anthony and Stanton. Anthony and Stanton continued to agitate for the wide range of women's issues mapped out in the Declaration of Sentiments, and leaned toward more-radical strategies in working toward their goals. The NWSA's main publication, *The Revolution,* addressed such controversial issues as abortion, marriage reform, divorce, and prostitution. Anthony and Stanton also sought to win working-class women's support by advocating for equal pay for equal work and access to male-dominated jobs. Women needed political power, they argued, in order to achieve opportunity, justice, and equality in all areas of their lives.

Even as it reached out to working women, the NWSA turned its back on the issue of racial equality and came to associate women's rights exclusively with white women. Stanton's "Address to the New York Legislature on Women's Rights" in 1854 foreshadowed the racist arguments that would surface during the post-Civil War debates over universal suffrage. "We [white educated women] are moral, virtuous, and intelligent, and in all respects quite equal to the proud white man himself," she declared, "and yet by your laws we are classed with idiots, lunatics, and Negroes" (DuBois 1992, 45). This argument, that the vote should be limited to educated persons regardless of sex, was a chilling forerunner of the language used in the laws passed in southern states in the aftermath of Reconstruction to prevent African

Americans from voting. Some such laws required a man to prove that his grandfather had voted before he himself could vote, or required a potential African American voter to take a literacy test that was impossible to pass. African Americans were also required to pay poll taxes to register to vote, which most could not afford. Sanctioned by the U.S. Supreme Court, these laws effectively ignored the intent of the Fourteenth and Fifteenth Amendments, and kept many African Americans, both men and women, from voting until the Civil Rights Movement of the 1950s and 1960s.

Several months after the founding of the NWSA, Lucy Stone and Henry Blackwell organized the American Woman Suffrage Association. Stone and Blackwell, who were married to each other, were ardent suffrage workers. Stone even retained her maiden name after their marriage. Maintaining ties with former abolitionists and the Republican Party, the AWSA supported the passage of the Fourteenth and Fifteenth Amendments, but also worked for the passage of woman suffrage on the local and state levels. Unlike the radical NWSA, the more conservative AWSA focused almost completely on the vote and avoided controversial issues such as divorce and women's reproductive rights. Stone served as the chief editor of the AWSA's newspaper, *The Woman's Journal,* which exclusively reported on suffrage news. While its rival *The Revolution* survived for only two years, *The Woman's Journal* would be published continually for the next half-century, and became the primary organ of the suffrage movement.

While the AWSA devoted its energies to local and state campaigns, the NWSA pursued a strategy that entailed a creative interpretation of the Fourteenth and Fifteenth Amendments known as the "New Departure." This argument asserted that women were persons, and therefore entitled to the full rights of national citizenship, as provided by the Fourteenth Amendment. Furthermore, voting was one of the privileges and immunities guaranteed to citizens under that same amendment. Among the women arriving at polling places armed with this constitutional argument was Susan B. Anthony, who cast her vote for the Republican ticket in Rochester, New York in 1872. "No barriers whatever stand today between women and the exercise of their right to vote," Anthony contended, "save those of precedent and prejudice, which refuse to expunge the word 'male' from the constitution" (DuBois, 1992, 155–56). For her act, Anthony was arrested, tried, and found guilty by order of the judge. She was fined $100 plus court costs, which she adamantly refused to pay. The New Departure ended when the Supreme Court ruled in *Minor v. Happersett* (1875) that suffrage was not an inherent right of citizenship. "It is clear," Chief Justice Morrison Waite wrote in the unanimous opinion of the Court, "that the Constitution has not added the right of suffrage to the privileges and immunities of citizenship as they existed at the time it was adopted" (Waite 1875). The Supreme Court affirmed that women were undoubtedly citizens, but being a citizen did not automatically guarantee suffrage. NWSA leaders now knew they would need to work for a separate constitutional amendment in order to secure woman suffrage as a right of national citizenship.

As the NWSA and the AWSA pursued their various strategies for winning women the vote, they encountered opponents trying to thwart their efforts. In the same year that these organizations were founded, another group related to woman suffrage was born: the Woman's Anti-Suffrage Association of Washington City. There were many reasons why a woman might not wish to see women enfranchised. Some believed that politics was too corrupt and would taint and degrade women. Others firmly believed that a woman's main duty was to her family and that involvement in politics would hinder her in that duty. When a pro-suffrage proposal was introduced in the Massachusetts State Legislature in 1869, close to 200 women signed a petition arguing that suffrage would "diminish the purity, the dignity and the moral influence of woman, and bring into the family circle a dangerous element of discord" (Robinson 1881, 101). The members of the Legislature agreed with the petitioners, and no action was taken on the matter of suffrage during that session. Cartoonists of the era never grew tired of imagining the disarray of homes where women were too busy with politics to fulfill their domestic duties. Still others argued that although some women were entirely capable of undertaking civic duties, the majority of women were not. This argument often included concerns about lower-class, immigrant, Native American, and African American women voting.

Despite the discouraging influence of the anti-suffragists, in 1869, Wyoming became the first territory to grant women the right to vote. When the decidedly anti-suffragist United States Congress balked at conferring statehood on the territory in 1890, Wyoming did not even consider denying women the vote in order to appease those in Washington. Nevertheless, in 1890, "The Equality State" was admitted to the union. The second territory where women could vote equally with men was the Utah territory, where women began voting in 1870. In addition to these victories in the West, the suffrage movement received a great boost in the 1880s, when leader of the Woman's Christian Temperance Union (WCTU), Frances Willard, endorsed the suffrage cause. Founded in 1874, the WCTU was one of a growing number of women's clubs during the Gilded Age (1870–1900) devoted to women's self-improvement and to social reform. Under Willard's leadership, the WCTU became the largest and most important women's organization in the late 19th century. Willard reasserted a link between temperance and women's rights. She argued that because women were morally superior beings, God called on them to advocate for the right to vote so that they could one day use their political power to protect the Christian home. "Women will bless and brighten every place she enters," Willard asserted, "and she will enter every place" (Gifford 1995, 119). Willard's appeal for what she called the "Home Protection Ballot" won over many evangelical women to the suffrage cause. It also advanced what would become the most prominent argument for suffrage during the Progressive Era (1900–1920). Whereas the Declaration of Sentiments asserted that the vote was a natural right that belonged to every individual citizen in a democracy, regardless of gender, Willard and other women reformers at the turn of the century would proclaim that women needed the vote so that they could bring their unique female moral and emotional qualities to bear on efforts to improve public life.

The argument by WCTU members and other women reformers that women would use the vote to clean up society generated determined opposition from several business interests. Most notable was the liquor industry.

Women of Washington State

All of the western states, except New Mexico, adopted woman suffrage before the Nineteenth Amendment enfranchised women nationwide. There are many theories as to why the women in the West won the vote so universally and so early. One possible explanation is that the chronic shortage of women in the West led men to give women the vote in order to attract more women to the area. Another supposition is that some men believed women voters would help curb the wildness and lawlessness of western frontier society. Whether or not these explanations are correct, in most cases women won the vote because they worked hard to convince both men and women that women not only deserved to vote, but had a right to vote as American citizens. The women of Washington state were an example of a group of local women who were able to organize a successful campaign to gain the vote.

The struggle for suffrage in Washington was long and rocky. Women began organizing suffrage groups in the Washington territory in the 1870s. In 1883, the Washington territorial government voted for woman suffrage, and the courts backed a law ensuring that women would have the right to sit on juries. The women of Washington voted until 1887, when the Territorial Supreme Court ruled against woman suffrage. In 1889, Washington was admitted as the 42nd state in the Union.

By the turn of the century, a new generation of leaders was preparing for battle. Women organized the state more thoroughly than ever before, forming crucial coalitions with other groups to ensure women's voting rights. Working women became the link between the suffrage movement and the labor movement in Washington. Other political groups in the state, such as the Progressives, were also in favor of women voting. In addition to forming political coalitions, suffragists used their influence as wives, mothers, daughters, and sisters to influence male voters. Their political savvy soon paid off. In 1910, the women of Washington won the unconditional right to vote by a nearly two-to-one margin. Although women won the vote, many minorities still faced prejudices and obstacles at the ballot box.

The women voters of Washington quickly united around issues that affected women. Some, including one magazine writer, still believed that women had to prove that they deserved the vote. In one of the first votes after women were enfranchised, over 20,000 women from Seattle were instrumental in recalling a mayor many believed to be corrupt. Women voters also united in nonpartisan efforts to ensure an eight-hour day and a minimum wage for women. Not only were the women of Washington being tested; they were on display for the rest of the nation. States where women had not yet won the vote looked to western states like Washington to see what the effects of woman suffrage would be on society. Washington served as a model for suffragists in other states, which showed that when women voted, they made a difference.

Saloonkeepers, brewers, and distillers all feared that women would use the vote to support national prohibition. They also predicted that even without the passage of anti-liquor laws, the industry would lose business because men would avoid their customary pre-voting saloon trip if they expected to encounter women at the polls. Other industries joined liquor proponents in organizing against woman suffrage, especially those, such as the textile indus-

AN

ACCOUNT OF THE PROCEEDINGS

ON THE

TRIAL OF

SUSAN B. ANTHONY,

ON THE

Charge of Illegal Voting,

AT THE

PRESIDENTIAL ELECTION IN NOV., 1872,

AND ON THE

TRIAL OF

BEVERLY W. JONES, EDWIN T. MARSH
AND WILLIAM B. HALL,

THE INSPECTORS OF ELECTION BY WHOM HER VOTE WAS RECEIVED.

ROCHESTER, N. Y.:
DAILY DEMOCRAT AND CHRONICLE BOOK PRINT, 3 WEST MAIN ST.
1874.

Title page from the trial proceedings against Susan B. Anthony for voting in the 1872 presidential election. (Library of Congress)

try, that employed large numbers of women and children to work in deplorable conditions for low wages. They, too, feared that women would use the vote to force industry regulations that would undermine their autonomy and threaten their profits.

In the 25 years following the Civil War, suffragists faced formidable obstacles from federal and state governments and big business, as well as from ordinary men and women. Suffrage victories in these years were few. Nonetheless, suffragists mobilized two national organizations on behalf of their cause, whose varying goals and approaches generated some interest and participation in the movement at the grassroots level. In the broader terrain of women's rights, women made important strides in these years in gaining access to higher education. They also increasingly found their way into the public sphere by becoming involved in organizations dedicated to social reform, by taking jobs in the burgeoning postwar industrial workforce, and by entering into some professions. All of these developments would have important consequences as women persisted in their struggle for the vote and the suffrage movement entered a new phase as the 19th century drew to a close.

Building a Mass Movement: Unity and Diversity in the Suffrage Movement after 1890

During the first two decades of the 20th century, millions of American women from a range of social backgrounds were drawn into support for the suffrage cause. The development of suffrage into a mass movement was no easy achievement. Suffragists continued to face resistance from external opponents. They also wrestled with divisions within the movement over issues related to race, ethnicity, and class, as well as over strategies and tactics. The turn-of-the-century suffrage movement was thus characterized by unity and diversity, cooperation and disagreement. The mix proved to be both volatile and vitalizing as suffragists continued with the hard work of securing women's political equality.

The first step toward the development of suffrage as a mass movement occurred in 1890, when the American Woman Suffrage Association merged with the National Woman Suffrage Association to form the National American Woman Suffrage Association . During the previous 20 years, women had become more comfortable in asserting themselves in the public sphere as they took part in the expanding and increasingly civic-minded women's club movement. Clubwomen justified their activities outside the home on the basis of their maternal qualities and responsibilities, and as a result, received growing public acceptance for their efforts. Many women concluded that they needed the vote in order to achieve the social reforms they desired, and were eager to join an organization that would help them achieve this goal. Susan B. Anthony saw this as a great opportunity for the suffrage movement and envisioned the NAWSA as a broad-based organization focused exclusively on the issue of the vote.

Elizabeth Cady Stanton served as the NAWSA's first president. Now that Stanton's children were older, she had more time and energy to devote to the causes dearest to her. Stanton disagreed with Anthony's focus on the vote, and still had broad reform in mind. Stanton's radical views, including her assertion that Christianity was misogynistic, caused so much turmoil that she left the NAWSA in 1892. Anthony then presided over the organization until her resignation in 1900. The NAWSA's strategy was to work for suffrage on the state level. Despite the newfound interest by clubwomen in the vote as a tool for social reform, the organization was slow to grow, claiming only 17,000 members in 1905. In the early 1890s, three western

Suffragists march down Pennsylvania Avenue in Washington D.C., March 3, 1913. George Grantham Bain Collection, Item in LOT 11052-2. (Library of Congress Prints and Photographs Division, Washington, D.C.)

states—Colorado, Utah, and Idaho—awarded women full voting rights, and some Midwestern states granted them the right to vote in local elections. Between 1896 and 1910, however, the NAWSA's state campaigns met only with discouraging defeat.

The earliest histories of the suffrage movement, including the monumental six-volume *History of Woman Suffrage* (1881–1922), edited by Elizabeth Cady Stanton, Susan B. Anthony, Matilda Joslyn Gage, and Ida Husted Harper, told the story of the white middle-class leaders of the movement. Most of the women in local suffrage organizations had no one to write their histories, and the stories of working-class and minority suffragists went largely untold. In recent years, historians have begun to piece together the many other facets of the suffrage effort. They have discovered a complex suffrage movement that was at times compromised by struggles over issues related to race, class, and ethnicity, but that was also energized by the many contributions of diverse groups of women devoted to the cause.

Women across the country, from Florida to Washington, organized local suffrage clubs in order to work for the vote. The NAWSA courted local southern women to join the movement by holding conventions in Atlanta, New Orleans, and Baltimore. By 1903, every southern state had at least one NAWSA affiliate, and strong state leaders such as Laura Clay and Kate Gordon were advocating southern issues to the NAWSA leadership. In the North, where suffrage groups had a longer history, Ida B. Wells-Barnett organized a Chicago suffrage club for African American women, called the Alpha Suffrage Club. Local organizations elected officers, held meetings, and even lobbied local governments for increased voting rights in local, state, and national elections.

Ida B. Wells-Barnett

Ida B. Wells-Barnett was a leader of the African American community. She was born to slave parents in 1862 and became the head of her family at the age of 16, when a yellow fever epidemic killed her parents. Wells-Barnett valued education and supported her younger siblings with her wages as a teacher. She also fought for democracy and justice throughout her life. Wells-Barnett became famous by writing against lynching, and as one of the founding members of the National Association for the Advancement of Colored People (NAACP) in 1909.

Although Wells-Barnett is best known for her anti-lynching crusade, she was also an active suffragist. Many suffrage leaders did not actively seek African American women to join local or national groups. In some areas, racism was the reason for the lack of African American participation. Leaders feared that if there were too much activity by African American women, the southern states would not support female voting rights. One national suffrage leader even assured a southern politician that African American women could be kept from voting the same way that African American men were kept from voting, by using poll taxes, grandparent laws, and bogus literacy tests. Wells-Barnett challenged these suffrage organizations to fully include African American women.

During the planning stage of the 1913 Washington, D.C. suffrage parade, organizers feared that southern women would not participate if African American women marched. Alice Paul, who was organizing the parade, compromised by suggesting that the African American women be placed after the other marchers. Wells-Barnett and others thought that this was insulting. The National American Woman Suffrage Association was flooded with protests from African American women, including Wells-Barnett. Her fight for equality paid off. African American women marched according to their trade or home state, not according to the color of their skin. Wells-Barnett marched with the Illinois delegation.

Wells-Barnett also formed the first African American suffrage club that same year, the Alpha Suffrage Club. The Alpha Suffrage Club not only helped educate African American women on the mechanics of voting, but also allowed women a chance to influence politics. Wells-Barnett organized women to canvass for an independent African American candidate in Chicago. Although the candidate did not win the election, local Republicans noticed the power of the African American women and asked them to canvass for their candidates in the next election.

Throughout her life, Wells-Barnett never wavered from the principle that all people, regardless of race or sex, were created equal. This conviction, reinforced by her experiences of oppression in the South, allowed her to become a leader in the African American community, as well as a role model to all women.

After 1890, these local suffrage groups could chose to affiliate themselves with the NAWSA. This relationship worked both ways. The NAWSA benefited from the increased membership, from the efforts of local suffragists working on its behalf , and from additional funds that were raised by local groups. Local and state groups, in turn, received training materials and news of the national suffrage movement from the NAWSA. The NAWSA also sent its lecturers and organizers to its affiliates to help in local and state struggles, as it did for Colorado.

Colorado was the first state to approve woman suffrage in a general election. The liquor industry, fearing women's votes would hurt their business, campaigned against the suffrage measure. Their opposition, however, did not daunt local and national suffrage workers. Future NAWSA president Carrie Chapman Catt represented the NAWSA in Colorado and organized tirelessly. Catt, however, was not the only woman working for suffrage in Colorado. The local Colorado Non-Partisan Equal Suffrage Association united women's organizations, churches, political parties, charity groups, unions, and farmers' alliances in the battle for suffrage. Elizabeth Ensley was one such local leader, who helped to mobilize the African American community. Ensley and her peers were convinced that women voters could help bring about much needed reforms in Colorado. The concentrated efforts of both local and national organizers in Colorado paid off when the measure passed by a healthy margin in 1893.

Ensley was far from alone as an African American woman fighting for the vote. In the beginning of the 20th century, racism was rampant in the United States. In the South, African Americans were legally denied their civil and political rights. This system of racial apartheid was endorsed by the federal government and maintained by brutal racial violence. In the North, African Americans faced discrimination in employment, housing, and education. Despite the hostile atmosphere, many African American women organized to gain the vote. While white women hoped that their votes would counterbalance white men, African American women hoped that their votes might work in tandem with African American men in order to combat racism. Unlike their white counterparts, African American men never organized formally against woman suffrage. Clubs for African American women grew and thrived during the last decade of the 19th century and in the first decade of the 20th. In 1896, the National Association of Colored Women (NACW) was formed as an umbrella organization for the many local organizations, representing a multitude of causes, including suffrage. By 1900, there were approximately 400 local clubs, with somewhere between 150,000 and 200,000 members, aligned with the NACW. The NACW's first president, Mary Church Terrell, wrote and spoke widely about woman suffrage.

Terrell and other African American women faced pronounced racism within the suffrage movement. Southern delegates to the NAWSA, in particular, refused to participate on an equal footing with African American women. The NAWSA accepted segregated affiliates and held many segregated events, fearing that if they supported full integration they would lose support in the South. Some southern leaders, such as Kate Gordon and Laura Clay, insisted that a whites-only clause be added to any suffrage proposal, but the NAWSA continued to advocate suffrage for all women. Despite this position, the leadership of the NAWSA, and later the National Woman's Party (NWP), alienated and discriminated against African American women. In a 1918 letter to a congressman, Carrie Chapman Catt used a racist argument to solicit the congressman's support for woman suffrage. "The women of New York are now the political equals of the men of New York, but the white women of the South are the political inferiors of the negroes" (Terborg-Penn 1998, 127). In 1919, the NAACP attempted to get Alice Paul, leader of the NWP, to repudiate her statement that she was only organizing white women, and "that all this talk of Negro women voting in South Carolina was nonsense" (130).

Despite the racism in the suffrage movement and the country at large, African American women played a vital role in the fight for woman suffrage. Mary Church Terrell worked for suffrage and equality among the races her whole life, both in the NACW and in the NAWSA. In her address to a 1900 NAWSA convention, Terrell attacked the injustices of sex and race:

> The elective franchise is withheld from one half of its citizens, many of whom are intelligent, cultured, and virtuous, while it is unstintingly bestowed upon the other, some of whom are illiterate, debauched and vicious, because the word "people," by an unparalleled exhibition of lexicographical acrobatics, has been turned and twisted to mean all who were shrewd and wise enough to have themselves born boys instead of girls, or who took the trouble to be born white instead of black. (Terborg-Penn 1998, 66)

Like Terrell, Ida B. Wells-Barnett fought against both racism and sexism throughout her life. Wells not only organized the Alpha Suffrage Club, but helped to integrate the famous Washington D.C. suffrage parade of 1913. When she was asked to march at the back of the parade, Wells told her critics, "If the Illinois women do not take a stand now in this great democratic parade then the colored women are lost" (122). African American women formed local organizations, sometimes allying themselves with national organizations that cared little for their problems. Throughout the struggle for woman suffrage, African American women were on the front lines, whether white women wanted them there or not.

Women from diverse backgrounds shared the common goal of winning the vote, but there were class as well as racial tensions in the movement. Although Anthony courted working-class women when she and Stanton formed the NWSA, she ignored the plight of working women, many of them immigrants, during her tenure as the NAWSA's president. Anthony had come to believe that the struggle for suffrage had no room for other concerns, either race- or labor-related. Other middle-class suffragists, however, actively sought to bring working women into the movement. In 1907, Harriot Stanton Blatch, Elizabeth Cady Stanton's daughter, founded the Equality League of Self-Supporting Women, later called the Women's Political Union (WPU). Blatch strove to make ties between college-educated professional women and working women. Professional and working-class women both desired the vote to improve their conditions. Members of the Equality League spoke to the New York State Legislature on suffrage in 1907. "To be left out by the State just sets up a prejudice against us," argued Clara Silver. "Bosses think and women come to think themselves that they don't count for so much as men" (DuBois 1998, 194).

Working-class women saw the vote as an essential tool for achieving higher wages and better working and living conditions, and eagerly embraced the suffrage cause. Following the models of the labor movement and the British Suffrage movement, which Blatch admired, working-class women brought a new enthusiasm to the cause. Although working-class women participated in all aspects of the suffrage movement, they did not always feel that their interests were represented within the NAWSA. Not only was the typical NAWSA member wealthy and white, the NAWSA leadership focused solely on the vote. Neither the NAWSA nor the WPU were concerned about equal work for equal pay, the eight-hour day, or factory safety.

Along with working-class women, wealthy women also joined the suffrage movement in the early 20th century. Women such as Alva Belmont, wife first of millionaire William Vanderbilt and then of millionaire August Belmont, committed their money and respectability to the cause. However, elite women also sometimes brought with them class prejudices and a sense of entitlement that undermined prospects for cross-class sisterhood, especially with working women.

After the deaths of Elizabeth Cady Stanton in 1902 and Susan B. Anthony in 1906, new leaders emerged who also helped to facilitate the development of suffrage into a mass movement. Carrie Chapman Catt, who had been involved in the Colorado campaign, followed Anthony as president of the NAWSA. This signified a new era in the character of the organization. The NAWSA began to use strategies imported from the younger English movement, as well as from the labor movement. NAWSA members spoke in street meetings, held parades, and courted the media heavily. In 1904, Catt was succeeded as NAWSA president by the Reverend Anna Howard Shaw, who served until 1915. During her presidency, the NAWSA grew from 17,000 members to 200,000 members. Although they pursued a broad constituency for their cause and experimented with some more-modern methods of advocating and advertising, Catt and Shaw clung to the NAWSA's state-by-state approach. Some suffragists, however, were coming to the conclusion that the NAWSA's strategy would never be able to achieve suffrage for all women, and revived ideas about working for a federal amendment to the constitution.

Alice Paul and Lucy Burns led the renewed battle for a federal amendment. Paul and Burns were leaders of a younger and more radical faction in the suffrage movement. These young women benefited from the work of the old guard: they had had increased opportunity for advanced education and greater freedom to move into the public sphere, and some had even grown up around women voters in the West. They were eager to try new methods, and sought out new sources of inspiration for their activism. Paul and Burns met in England during a 1909 prison stay, resulting from their work in the English suffrage movement. British "suffragettes," as they proudly called themselves, led by Emmeline Pankhurst and her daughter Christabelle, began to seek media attention with their increasingly militant tactics. Many of the British suffrage activists were jailed for their actions, which included parades, demonstrations, and even vandalism and destruction of property. Alice Paul and Lucy Burns were influenced greatly by their work in England with the Pankhursts, which included jail time, hunger strikes, and forced feedings.

Paul returned to the United States and joined the NAWSA in 1912. She and Burns convinced NAWSA leaders to let them direct a drive for a new federal amendment. In 1913, Paul became the chair of NAWSA's Congressional Committee and subsequently formed the Congressional Union. Paul was eager to apply her experiences in England to suffrage efforts in the United States. One of her earliest suggestions was a suffrage parade that would coincide with President-elect Woodrow Wilson's inauguration in March 1913. The timing of the parade would guarantee publicity for the suffrage cause. The NAWSA leadership accepted her proposal on the condition that Paul would raise the funds for the parade herself. Accompanied by Burns, she organized the first national American suffrage parade.

The parade showcased a wide variety of women who worked for suffrage. The final product was an elaborate production costing almost $15,000. A female lawyer, Inez Milholland Boissevain, led the parade from a white horse. The parade included sections for women from enfranchised countries, suffrage pioneers, working women in professional dress, college women in academic gowns, state delegations, and male supporters, as well as floats and bands. African American women were originally excluded from the parade, but after protests by Mary Church Terrell and others, African American women were allotted a place in the rear of the parade. Ida B. Wells-Barnett, however, took it upon herself to fully integrate the affair by refusing to march at the rear. Although the parade started without incident, military intervention was needed in order to quell riots of protest by the conclusion. Despite the violence, the marchers completed their parade and formed a dramatic tableau at the Treasury Building.

The parade and subsequent mob violence produced all the publicity Paul could have wanted. A few weeks later, the suffrage amendment was reintroduced in Congress. It was not long, however, before Paul began to argue with the NAWSA's leadership over money and, more importantly, tactics. Paul and Burns adopted the British method of holding the political party in power responsible for its failure to pass measures ensuring women's suffrage. Therefore, they campaigned against any Democratic candidate, even if that specific candidate had supported suffrage. Their strategy was to punish the Democrats because they had failed to pass the federal amendment. The NAWSA, on the other hand, remained nonpartisan, and courted any politician who would support woman suffrage.

A split between the two groups seemed inevitable. Paul left the NAWSA in 1914 and founded the National Woman's Party in 1916 to pursue a federal constitutional amendment, using her own methods. Far from defeated, Paul founded the National Woman's Party (NWP) in 1916 to pursue a federal constitutional amendment, using her own methods. It would take the energy and vision of both the NAWSA and the NWP, exercised over the course of several more years of determined effort, before these organizations' shared goal of woman suffrage would at last be achieved.

National Woman's Party

From the beginning, the National Woman's Party had a single goal: the passage of a federal constitutional amendment. In the 1916 elections, the NWP urged western women voters to use their votes to oust any Democrats, because the Democrats had refused to use their majority in the federal government to pass the amendment. Although in 1916 no major political party endorsed the suffrage amendment and Wilson won reelection, the NWP succeeded in winning national publicity for its cause.

In January of 1917, the NWP began a new strategy: they would picket the White House until the amendment passed. At the gates to the White House, women dressed in the NWP colors of purple, white, and gold, and carried signs with slogans such as "Mr. President, how long must women wait for liberty?" or "Mr. President, what will you do for woman suffrage?" (Library of Congress, American Memory Web site, "Women of Protest"). President Wilson nodded to the women and treated the picketers cordially at first. When the United States entered World War I in April 1917, however, the picketers became more of a nuisance. The NWP made banners bearing quotes from Wilson's war messages, hoping to embarrass the administration with the contradictions. One such banner read, "We shall fight for the things which we have always held nearest our hearts—for democracy, for the right of those who submit to authority to have a voice in their own governments.—President Wilson's War Message, April 2, 1917" (Lunardini 1986, 114). The president wished to present a united American front to the world, and increasingly the banners of the NWP pointed out the hypocrisies of the administration. No matter how embarrassed the president may have been privately, he still took no action against the NWP publicly. Paul and other NWP leaders decided to challenge the President in a more direct way.

After an embarrassing banner drew the attention of a visiting Russian delegation, Paul was warned that any further picketers would be arrested, despite the complete legality of the picketing of the White House. NWP members informed Paul that they were willing to take that risk. In June, picketers began to be arrested and charged with obstructing traffic. At first, NWP picketers were released, or received very light sentences. When these light sentences also failed to stop the NWP, harsher penalties were administered. Picketers were soon sentenced to from 30 to 60 days at the Occoquan Workhouse. The arrested women maintained that the traffic violation charges were nothing more than a pretext, and tried to claim rights as political prisoners. In her first person narrative of her involvement with the NWP, *Jailed for Freedom*, Doris Stevens recounted the experiences of the NWP women who were arrested. The conditions at the workhouse were harsh. After agitation by the NWP and its allies, the District Commissioners held an investigation of conditions at Occoquan. An affidavit made by prison matron Mrs. Bovee addressed the substandard food as well as the violence of Superintendent Whittaker. "The beans, hominy, rice, cornmeal, and cereal have all had worms in them . . . I know of one girl who has been kept seventeen days on only water this month . . . I know of one girl beaten until the blood had to be scrubbed from her clothing and from the floor (Stevens 1995, 96).

Despite the conditions in the workhouse, the pickets and arrests continued. According to Stevens, 500 women picketed, 200 were arrested, and 168 spent time in jail. Both Paul and Burns served time. Many of the imprisoned suffragists went on hunger strikes. Rose Winslow of New York was able to smuggle letters out to her husband and friends during her hunger strike in Occoquan. The following excerpt is from the letter Winslow wrote after being force fed by prison officials:

> I had a nervous time of it, gasping a long time afterward, and my stomach rejecting during the process . . . I heard myself making the most hideous sounds . . . One feels so forsaken when one lies prone and people shove a pipe down one's stomach . . . I am waiting to see what happens when the President realizes that brutal bullying isn't quite a statesmanlike method for settling a demand for justice at home. (118–19)

While its members were being jailed, the rest of the NWP used the arrests, prison conditions, and hunger strikes to drum up more publicity and support for their cause. Although the NWP continued to picket until January 1919, the extent of the arrests and punishments dramatically decreased in November 1917, apparently due to the publicity the NWP had created. One of the most significant effects of the NWP's activism in 1916 and 1917 was to push the NAWSA to revise its suffrage strategy, which included emphasis on securing a federal amendment.

The Winning Plan

Although Carrie Chapman Catt's first presidency of the NAWSA was cut short by other obligations, she returned to the NAWSA's highest office in 1915. By 1915, there were 11 states where women had full suffrage rights, all in the West: Wyoming (1890), Colorado (1893), Utah (1896), Idaho (1896), Washington (1910), California (1911), Oregon (1912), Kansas (1912), Arizona (1912), Montana (1914), and Nevada (1914). In 1913, Illinois granted women the right to vote in presidential elections. In 1914, the conservative General Federation of Women's Clubs at last endorsed woman suffrage, indicating that the movement had reached far into the mainstream of American life. In 1915, however, campaigns for the vote in the eastern states of Massachusetts, New York, New Jersey, and Pennsylvania all failed. Motivated by the recent victories in the western states, sobered but undaunted by the eastern defeats, and prodded by the militant activism of the NWP, Catt developed a new plan to bring about woman suffrage nationwide, dubbed the "Winning Plan." Unveiled in 1916, Catt's plan had five distinct parts: a leader who would inspire as well as organize the massive suffrage movement, a strict hierarchy within the organization, effective and extensive publicity, attention to practical matters, and the unshakable belief that woman suffrage would win and would be an asset to America. Under Catt's plan, the NAWSA would continue to conduct state campaigns at the same time that it would pressure Congress to pass the federal amendment.

When the United States entered World War I in 1917, Catt urged women to support the war, even though she was a member of the Woman's Peace Party. Catt served on the Woman's Committee of the Council of National Defense, but throughout the war, her active support of woman suffrage never faltered. She carefully brought attention to women's war work, and fervently suggested that women's role in the war should be recognized with the passage of the federal amendment.

Although Congress declared that they would vote only on war-related measures during 1917, many states had suffrage on the ballots. At least partial suffrage was granted in North Dakota, Ohio, Indiana, Arkansas, Nebraska, Michigan, Nebraska, Rhode Island, and New York. The NAWSA campaigned heavily in New York, committing huge amounts of money and resources to the cause. Following a crucial 1917 victory in New York, the NAWSA and Catt committed all of their resources to securing the federal amendment. Catt also developed a relationship between Wilson and the NAWSA. Despite the picketing by the NWP, Wilson personally supported a national amendment. He wrote letters of support and encouragement to Catt and other leaders of the NAWSA, although he did little publicly at first.

In the 11th hour of the 11th day of the 11th month of 1918, the combatants declared an armistice ending World War I. In the mid-term congressional elections of 1918, so many suffrage supporters were elected that the passage of the Susan B. Anthony Amendment at last seemed certain, even though the amendment had failed to pass the Senate the previous year. Before Congress even convened in 1919, the NAWSA began to reconstitute itself into the League of Women Voters. The House of Representatives passed the amendment again as their first piece of business in the new session. The Senate passed the amendment in the first week of June. Thirty-six states now needed to ratify the amendment to add it to the constitution. The NAWSA and the NWP again mobilized their forces to lobby for support at the state level, especially where the vote was expected to be close.

Within four months, Illinois, Wisconsin, Michigan, Kansas, New York, Ohio, Pennsylvania, Massachusetts, Texas, Iowa, Missouri, Arkansas, Nebraska, Montana, Minnesota, New Hampshire, and Utah voted for ratification. One by one, subsequent ratifications trickled in. With time running out and 35 states secured, Tennessee prepared to vote on the Susan B. Anthony Amendment in August 1920. Suffrage activists organized for the last fight of their long struggle. Suffrage workers poured into Nashville to secure the state, against heavy opposition. On August 18, the Tennessee state legislators filed in to vote on the amendment. The vote was tied 48 to 48 when Harry T. Burn shocked the audience by switching his vote. At the last minute, the young senator had received a telegram from his mother requesting that he vote to support woman suffrage. Burn's dramatic reversal broke the tie, and the Susan B. Anthony Amendment became the Nineteenth Amendment to the United States Constitution.

Historians have debated whether it was Catt's winning plan or the NWP's protests that finally pushed lawmakers to pass the Susan B. Anthony Amendment. Most agree that it was a combination of the two. As the NAWSA secured more support on the state level, the federal government could not help but notice that public opinion favored votes for women. On the other hand, the international attention and pressure the NWP's tactics provoked were also influential in persuading the federal government to act. Although Wilson never communicated directly with the NWP, he was able to respond to their tactics by supporting women's suffrage though the more respectable

Three suffragists casting votes in New York City, c. 1917. (Library of Congress Prints and Photographs Division, Washington, D.C.)

NAWSA. In the end, it was the combined efforts of diverse women who ensured that women would have a voice in the government.

Conclusion

In 1920, only one signer of the 1848 Declaration of Sentiments, Charlotte Woodward, was still alive to vote. Many history books state simply that after World War I women were given the vote because of their participation in the war effort. This ignores the years of strategic planning and organizing by suffragists to win the right for women to participate fully as United States citizens by voting. Although enfranchisement was a major victory, it did not affect all women equally. In the South, African Americans of both sexes were prevented from voting by poll taxes, outrageous literacy tests, and grandparent clauses. Some immigrants found their access to the vote similarly barred, and many Native American women and men were denied both citizenship and the vote. Furthermore, gaining the right to vote was only one of many women's rights goals outlined in the Declaration of Sentiments. Suffragists from many backgrounds rejoiced in the passage of the Susan B. Anthony

Amendment because of the increased rights and responsibilities it promised, but for many women those promises remained unfilled. The Nineteenth Amendment did not institute full gender equality in the United States. Nonetheless, through the long struggle for the vote, women demonstrated and cultivated their capacity to organize to achieve their goals. The suffragists' achievement in 1920 enabled women individually and collectively to claim an expanded voice in their government. Women have used that voice to continue the struggle to realize the fullness of their nation's promises for liberty, equality, and justice—for themselves and for others—up to the present day.

References and Further Reading

Attie, Jeanie. *Patriotic Toil: Northern Women and the American Civil War.* Ithaca, NY: Cornell University Press, 1998.

Baker, Jean H. *Sisters: The Lives of America's Suffragists.* New York: Hill and Wang, 2005.

Buhle, Mari Jo, and Paul Buhle. *The Concise History of Woman Suffrage: Selections from History of Woman Suffrage.* Urbana: University of Illinois Press, 2005.

DuBois, Ellen Carol. *Feminism and Suffrage: The Emergence of an Independent Women's Movement in America, 1848–1869.* Ithaca, NY: Cornell University Press, 1978.

DuBois, Ellen Carol. *Woman Suffrage and Women's Rights.* New York: New York University Press, 1998.

DuBois, Ellen Carol, ed. *The Elizabeth Cady Stanton-Susan B. Anthony Reader: Correspondence, Writings, Speeches.* Rev. ed. Boston: Northeastern University Press, 1992.

Fowler, Robert Booth, and Spencer Jones. "Carrie Chapman Catt and the Last Years of the Struggle for Woman Suffrage: 'The Winning Plan.'" In *Votes for Women: The Struggle for Suffrage Revisited,* ed. Jean H. Baker, 130–42. Oxford: Oxford University Press, 2002.

Gifford, Carolyn De Swarte. "Frances Willard and the Woman's Christian Temperance Union's Conversion to Woman Suffrage." In *One Woman, One Vote: Rediscovering the Woman Suffrage Movement,* ed. Marjorie Spruill Wheeler, 117–33. Troutdale, OR: NewSage Press, 1995.

Ginzberg, Lori D. *Women in Antebellum Reform.* Wheeling, IL: Harlan Davidson, 2000.

Green, Elna C. *Southern Strategies: Southern Women and the Woman Suffrage Question.* Chapel Hill, NC: University of North Carolina Press, 1997.

Griffith, Elizabeth. *In Her Own Right: The Life of Elizabeth Cady Stanton.* New York: Oxford University Press, 1984.

Jablonsky, Thomas. "The Anti-Suffrage Campaign." In *Votes for Women: The Struggle for Suffrage Revisited,* ed. Jean H. Baker, 118–29. Oxford: Oxford University Press, 2002.

Kerber, Linda K. "'Ourselves and Our Daughters Forever': Women and the Constitution, 1787–1876." In *One Woman, One Vote: Rediscovering the Woman Suffrage Movement,* ed. Marjorie Spruill Wheeler, 21–36. Troutdale, OR: NewSage Press, 1995.

Kraditor, Aileen S. *The Ideas of the Woman Suffrage Movement, 1890–1920.* New York, Columbia University Press, 1965.

Leonard, Elizabeth. *All the Daring of the Soldier: Women of the Civil War Armies.* New York: W. W. Norton & Co, 1999.

Library of Congress, American Memory Web site. "Votes for Women: Selections from the National American Woman Suffrage Collection, 1848–1921." Rare Books and Special Collections Division. http://www.memory.loc.gov/ammem/naw/nawshome.html.

Library of Congress, American Memory Web site. "Women of Protest: Photographs from the Records of the National Woman's Party." http://memory.loc.gov/ammem/collections/suffrage/nwp/.

Lunardini, Christine A. *From Equal Suffrage to Equal Rights: Alice Paul and the National Woman's Party 1910–1928.* New York: New York University Press, 1986.

Newman, Louise Michele. *White Women's Rights: The Racial Origins of Feminism in the United States.* New York: Oxford University Press, 1999.

Painter, Nell Irvin. *Sojourner Truth: A Life, a Symbol.* New York: W. W. Norton & Company, 1996.

Parker, Alison M. "The Case for Reform Antecedents for the Woman's Rights Movement." In *Votes for Women: The Struggle for Suffrage Revisited,* ed. Jean H. Baker, 21–41. Oxford: Oxford University Press, 2002.

Robinson, Harriet. *Massachusetts in the Woman Suffrage Movement.* Boston: Roberts Brothers, 1881.

Stanton, Elizabeth Cady, Susan B. Anthony, Matilda Joslyn Gage, and Iola Husted Harper, eds. *History of Woman Suffrage.* 6 vols. New York: Fowler & Wells, 1881–1922.

Stanton, Elizabeth Cady, Susan B. Anthony, and Matilda Joslyn Gage, eds. *History of Woman Suffrage,* vol. 1. 1881. Rochester, NY: Charles Mann, 1887.

Stevens, Doris. *Jailed for Freedom: American Women Win the Vote.* 1920. Ed. Carol O'Hare. Troutdale, OR: NewSage Press, 1995.

Stuart, Amanda Mackenzie. *Consuelo and Alva Vanderbilt: The Story of a Daughter and a Mother in the Gilded Age.* New York: HarperCollins, 2005.

Terborg-Penn, Rosalyn. *African American Women in the Struggle for the Vote 1850–1920.* Bloomington, IN: Indiana University Press, 1998.

Van Voris, Jacqueline. *Carrie Chapman Catt: A Public Life.* New York: The Feminist Press, 1987.

Waite, Morrison. "Opinion of the Court 88 U.S. 162 Minor V. Happersett, 1875." Cornell University Law School Supreme Court Collection. http://www.law.cornell.edu/supct/html/historics/USSC_CR_0088_0162_ZO.html.

Ward, Geoffrey C. Ward, and Ken Burns. *Not for Ourselves Alone: The Story of Elizabeth Cady Stanton and Susan B. Anthony.* New York: Alfred Knopf, 1999.

Weatherford, Doris. *A History of the American Suffragist Movement.* Santa Barbara, CA: ABC-CLIO, 1998.

Wells-Barnett. *Crusade for Justice: The Autobiography of Ida B. Wells.* Ed. Alfreda M. Duster. Chicago: University of Chicago Press, 1970.

Clubwomen, Reformers, Workers, and Feminists of the Gilded Age and Progressive Era

7

Alison M. Parker

Northern black and white women reformers entered the Civil War with high hopes that slavery would be abolished and that all women and men would achieve the right to vote, universal suffrage, at the end of the conflict. During the war, some women participated in the Woman's National Loyal League, organized by Elizabeth Cady Stanton and Susan B. Anthony, which collected 400 thousand signatures on petitions to Congress, demanding that it pass the Thirteenth Amendment to end slavery. Others joined the U.S. Sanitary Commission, a volunteer women's organization that achieved official sanction from the government; it raised tens of millions of dollars for the war effort, improved sanitary conditions at hospitals, and organized relief supplies, lodgings, and nursing for Union soldiers. Southern white women did not create similarly sophisticated organizations to help the Confederate cause, but did volunteer as nurses and donate supplies to the troops. A few women broke gender boundaries by dressing as men, in order to fight in the war. Slave women, especially those who lived in areas occupied by the Union army, often ran away with their families to the Union lines, where they worked as laundresses and cooks. Overall, women's wartime voluntary efforts increased their organizing skills, self-confidence, and determination to play an expanded role in politics.

In the decades after the Civil War, women engaged in maternalist politics—arguing that their roles as mothers and potential mothers justified their participation in the political arena. This chapter focuses on clubwomen, reformers, workers, and feminists during the Gilded Age and Progressive Era, from about 1870 through the 1910s, as they fought for increased social, legal, and political rights for women.

The Gilded Age refers to approximately the last three decades of the 19th century, when the U.S. government's policy of *laissez-faire* capitalism allowed industrialists and corporate leaders to amass huge fortunes. The industrial revolution produced the wealth that allowed leisured women opportunities to participate in club work and reform, even as it also produced poverty and terrible working conditions among wage-earning women and men. During the last two decades of the 19th century, immigrants, from eastern and southern Europe in particular, arrived in a huge influx of almost nine million per decade. Living in crowded tenements and working in dangerous factories, their health and safety suffered. Determined to improve their working conditions, wage-earning women and men participated in strikes and work stoppages, and joined unions.

Concerned that their cities and even their own children might be harmed by the problems of increasing industrialization and immigration, middle-class and elite women began to work for reform during the Progressive Era, from approximately 1890 through the 1910s. Progressives tried to expand the role of government and reign in the worst aspects of industrial capitalism by passing state and federal legislation, such as child labor laws, laws mandating school attendance, and laws stipulating maximum hours and minimum wages for factory work. By the 1910s, some women refused to rely on the ideology of separate spheres, or true womanhood, upon which most clubwomen's and reformers' maternalist politics were based. Pushing beyond conventional expectations of women's roles and status in society, they identified themselves as feminists and strove for economic, personal, and sexual independence for women. Whatever their differences, clubwomen, reformers, workers, and feminists supported woman suffrage by the start of World War I, and viewed the passage of the Nineteenth Amendment in 1920 as a milestone achievement for women's rights.

Clubwomen in the Gilded Age and Progressive Era

The first secular women's club formed after the Civil War, Sorosis, was organized in 1868 by the journalist Jane Cunningham Croly, who found herself and other female journalists excluded from a press dinner hosted by the Press Club of New York. Croly decided to provide a venue for educated women interested in literature, music, drama, and art to meet, network, and develop themselves and their professional careers. Sorosis, its constitution proclaimed, "aims to establish a kind of freemasonry among women of similar pursuits, to render them helpful to each other" (Croly 1975, 8–9). The creation of a women-only club for professionals provoked considerable ridicule in the press, especially when its members chose to meet in what had been considered men's domain, such as restaurants and banquet rooms at the best hotels. To broaden their appeal, Sorosis members chose not to support the seemingly radical demand for woman suffrage.

The New England Woman's Club was also formed in 1868, by Caroline Severance of Boston. Fewer of these clubwomen had professional careers than did the members of Sorosis; more of them had participated in antebellum causes such as women's rights, temperance, abolitionism, and transcendentalism. Because of their reform backgrounds, members of the New England Woman's Club supported higher education for women, dress reform, and, especially, woman suffrage.

During the Gilded Age, other middle-class women across the country took advantage of their increased leisure to educate themselves and increase their cultural refinement and class status. Middle-class women formed clubs to study art, history, and literature. Most of these women had not been able to attend college, so self-education was important to them. In 1890, Sorosis founder Jane Cunningham Croly established the General Federation of Women's Clubs (GFWC) to unite the vast array of disparate white women's clubs. The GFWC's national structure allowed for greater communication and coordination among clubwomen, who were expanding beyond their original focus on self-improvement, to what settlement house leader Jane Addams termed "Civic Housekeeping" (Joslin 2004, 45). Some clubs pursued plans for community uplift, to solve problems such as intemperance and children's health and safety. Municipal reform projects that promoted responsible government and legislation to help working families captured the interests of clubwomen. The GFWC formally endorsed woman suffrage in 1914; by that point, clubwomen and suffragists shared the view that women could best achieve their reform goals through the vote.

Middle-class black women were not accepted into white women's clubs, and so formed their own clubs, most of which also had self-improvement as their goal. Middle-class black clubwomen hoped to further their educations and establish themselves as respectable, refined ladies—a status that middle-class white women often claimed for themselves alone. This assertion of true womanhood on the part of black women was subversive because it challenged the dominant stereotype of white women as the only pure women. In the context of increased segregation and violence against African Americans, the black women's club movement was a form of resistance against racist stereotypes that wrongly categorized black women as either "Jezebels" or "Mammies" (Hale 1998, 32).

Reformers of the Gilded Age and Progressive Era

The Woman's Christian Temperance Union (WCTU), founded in 1874, was the largest 19th-century women's organization. Its members cannot be narrowly defined as clubwomen because from the start they worked as reformers for political and legislative change. Frances Willard, WCTU president from 1879 to 1898, had been educated at a Methodist female seminary, North Western Female College. She became the first dean of the new Woman's College at Northwestern University in 1871, and moved on to her work with the WCTU after Northwestern University's president (her former fiancé) tried to diminish her power and autonomy.

Embracing her role as WCTU president, Willard successfully mobilized tens of thousands of women around two central concepts: a "Do Everything" policy and the "Home Protection Ballot" (Bordin 1981, 117–39). By encouraging local and state unions to act upon and set their own reform priorities, Willard allowed for local control within a cohesive national structure. Thus, WCTU members could variously focus on gaining local dry laws, promoting censorship of impure literature, fighting for women's right to vote, establishing boarding houses for wage-earning women, working with the Knights of Labor in favor of an eight-hour day, or on recruiting black and immigrant women as WCTU members. In addition, the national WCTU's endorsement in 1881 of what Frances Willard brilliantly termed the "Home Protection Ballot" allowed women to link their role as mothers or potential mothers—whose first priority was protecting children—to their demand for the vote. By moving the argument for woman suffrage away from potentially threatening natural rights and equality positions, and toward an argument for suffrage based on women's unique differences, Willard greatly increased the number of women lobbying for the right to vote. Whereas the National American Woman Suffrage Association (NAWSA) had only 13,000 members in the mid-1890s, the WCTU had over 150,000 members by that time.

Of all the late 19th-century national women's organizations, only the WCTU actively recruited black women as members. In 1883, Frances Willard appointed a prominent black woman, Frances Watkins Harper, to be national superintendent of the Department of Work Among Colored People. A former abolitionist and a celebrated author, Harper had turned her focus to temperance and woman suffrage after the Civil War. As a WCTU national superintendent, she built up the organization's black membership. Although the WCTU was the most inclusive women's group of its time, black women still encountered racism and resistance. The national WCTU refused, for instance, to lobby Congress for national anti-lynching legislation.

Finding that their attempts at building genuine interracial alliances were unsuccessful, black clubwomen formed their own organization in 1896. In the 1890s, moreover, lynchings of African Americans were at their peak, and the Supreme Court ruled, in *Plessy v. Ferguson* (1896), that segregation laws did not violate the Constitution. Black clubwomen met at a conference in Washington, D.C. in 1896 to form the National Association of Colored Women (NACW). The NACW's first president, Mary Church Terrell, was an Oberlin College graduate, the first black member of the District of Columbia's School Board, a clubwoman, and a suffragist. Terrell explained: "We denominate ourselves colored, not because we are narrow, and wish to lay special emphasis on the color of the skin . . . but . . . because our peculiar status in this country at the present time seems to *demand* that we stand by ourselves in the special work for which we have organized" (Jones 1990, 134). Like Frances Willard, Terrell emphasized black women's public and political responsibilities as mothers. When advocated by black women—whose claims to true womanhood were continually denied by the dominant white culture—maternalism became a subversive rhetorical tool. As a whole, black women were negatively stereotyped by white Americans as impure, uneducated, unrefined, and poor. The NACW's motto, "lifting as we climb," emphasized the necessity of a cross-class alliance among black women. If middle-class black women wanted to break down hateful and ignorant stereotypes, they recognized that they had to work with all black women to improve their conditions and to assert their rightful place as true women. Black clubwomen were necessarily Progressive reformers who hoped to help their children by advocating federal funding for public schools and anti-lynching laws at the national level, as well as kindergartens, nurs-

Mary Church Terrell, an African American suffragist, was president of the National Association of Colored Women and a charter member of the National Association for the Advancement of Colored People. (Library of Congress)

ery schools, day care facilities, and settlement houses for black women and men at the local level.

The settlement house movement epitomized many of the main characteristics of Progressive reform. Hull House, the first settlement in the United States, was founded in 1889 by two well-off white women, Jane Addams and Ellen Gates Starr, in a poor immigrant community on Chicago's west side. During a tour of Europe, Addams had visited Toynbee Hall, in which educated reformers lived in London's East End, helping the immigrants and poor people who lived there. She was inspired by this visit, saying, "our consciences are becoming tender in regard to the lack of democracy in social affairs" (Elshtain 2002, 95). Settlement house residents were generally single, college educated, reform-oriented women who lived together in poor neighborhoods to learn directly about the problems there and begin to develop solutions. Settlement house residents established English classes, encouraged workers to organize for better health and safety regulations, set up kindergartens and after-school programs for children, established

Mary Church Terrell

Born in Memphis, Tennessee in 1863, as the daughter of light-skinned former slaves, Mary Eliza Church (1863–1954) had more advantages than did most freed slaves and their descendants. Her family's wealth came first from her mother's beauty parlor and then from her father's saloon and investments in Memphis real estate. One of only a handful of black women in America to do so, Mary Church graduated in 1884 from Oberlin College, the first institution of higher education in the U.S. to admit blacks and women. In 1891, she married Robert Heberton Terrell, a graduate of Harvard University who became a lawyer and the first black municipal court judge in Washington, D.C. Mary Terrell taught high school, and, in 1895, was the first black woman to be appointed to a school board in the United States; she served on the Washington, D.C. school board for 11 years. Throughout her long life, Mary Church Terrell helped found several important reform organizations, including the National Association of Colored Women (NACW), the National Association for the Advancement of Colored People (NAACP), and the Coordinating Committee for the Enforcement of the D.C. Anti-Discrimination Laws decades later, in the early 1950s.

After concerted attempts at interracial work and a series of rebuffs from white women, Mary Church Terrell, Frances Harper, Josephine St. Pierre Ruffin, and many of their fellow black clubwomen decided to organize separately. During her presidency of the new National Association of Colored Women, from 1896–1901, Terrell focused on uplifting poor and working-class black families with a self-help reform agenda. Appealing to the broadest possible audience of African American club women, by organizing them as mothers and potential mothers who were concerned about children, Terrell hoped that black women could mobilize in large numbers, while fending off criticisms that their reform work was unwomanly or overly political. One of the most prominent woman suffrage proponents in the black community in the late 1890s, Terrell built support for women's voting rights among rank-and-file National Association of Colored Women members.

By the early 1900s, Terrell moved to the forefront of working against institutionalized racism, arguing that white laws and attitudes played a more central a role in stunting opportunities for black youths than did their impoverished home environments. In 1906, Terrell, W. E. B. DuBois and the white reformer John Milholland formed the Constitution League, a group that monitored violations of citizens' constitutional rights and called for the full enforcement of the Constitution by federal, state, and local authorities. By 1909, she was a member of the Committee of Forty on Permanent Organization, which founded the interracial civil rights group, the National Association for the Advancement of Colored People. Terrell continued to follow her conscience, becoming a member of the Board of Directors of the NAACP and traveling extensively under its auspices as a public lecturer, promoting its antiracism campaigns, especially anti-lynching. Through her public speaking, Terrell served as a liaison bringing "the goals of the NAACP before white organizations" (Salem 1990, 156).

boarding houses for single wage-earning women, and offered cooking classes, as well as courses in the traditional arts and crafts of the immigrant groups in the neighborhood. Settlement residents favored an increased regulatory role for local, state, and federal governments, such as mandating maximum work hours, inspecting factories for safety violations, and setting a minimum wage.

Women of the Gilded Age and the Progressive Era explained their involvement in a wide array of social reforms, including the campaign to abolish child labor, on the basis of their maternal qualities and their special role in protecting children and families. This poster was produced by the National Child Labor Committee to protest child labor in the cotton mills, c. 1906. (Library of Congress)

Settlement house workers advocated good government campaigns for civic improvement, including direct primary elections, civil service examinations, and the referendum. Recognizing that the infant mortality rate was higher in her neighborhood than in most others, for instance, in 1894 Jane Addams organized the neighborhood's better-established Irish-American clubwomen (not the Italian or Russian new arrivals who were focusing on sheer survival) to survey conditions, including the frequency of waste removal by the city and the rate of infant mortality on a block-by-block basis. Addams' progressive critique of corruption in local government was based, in part, on her arduous attempt to get better garbage removal in the neighborhood. Urban machine politics, she charged, allowed incompetent cronies to gain vital government jobs as rewards for political loyalty rather than on the basis of their qualifications. Addams presented the women's findings in sophisticated, statistical charts to Chicago's City Hall. Rather than relying on the more sentimental language of maternal concern for child welfare, these seemingly neutral statistics helped settlement house workers argue for better services based on science. Her campaign against the negligent political appointee who was in charge of waste disposal in her west side neighborhood inspired Addams to put in an ultimately successful bid to be the first woman and the first reformer to hold the position of chief garbage inspector for her district.

The Hull House became a model for over 400 settlements across the United States by 1910. Although native-born white settlement house workers willingly tried to improve the lives of European immigrants, they often refused to offer services to African Americans, Jews, and Hispanics, who subsequently formed their own settlements. Ida B. Wells-Barnett, for instance, established the Negro Fellowship League in 1910 to serve Chicago's south side black population, especially men and boys, many of whom were migrants from the South like her. As settlement houses spread, the voluntary work of the residents became professionalized. By 1920, there were 30,000 social workers in the United States, and most of them were female.

Settlement house residents led a variety of state-level reform campaigns, including those for safety regulations in factories. Florence Kelley, for instance, who earned a law degree from Northwestern University while living at the Hull House, successfully won a maximum-hours law for women, and a ban on child labor in Illinois in 1893. Arguing for "a rigid inspection service" to enforce "all laws relating to the employment of women and children," Kelley won appointment as chief factory inspector for the state (Sklar 1995, 233). In 1899, Kelley took on the leadership of the National Consumers' League (NCL), a group that harnessed the purchasing power of middle-class and elite women, as consumers, to demand better conditions for female workers. The NCL guided consumer spending by issuing "white labels" for products that were made under good working conditions and "white lists" of stores that treated their female employees fairly. Kelley shifted the direction of the NCL to the fight for protective labor laws for women and children, including shorter-hours legislation and a minimum wage. NCL members provided essential research support for lawyer Louis Brandeis' brief in favor of the state of Oregon's maximum-hours law for women. On the grounds that women needed more protection as mothers and potential mothers, the U.S. Supreme Court sanctioned protective labor laws for women in *Muller v. Oregon* in 1908.

Workers in the Gilded Age and Progressive Era

At the start of the Gilded Age, both wage-earning women and farmwomen suffered from the lack of a political voice and access to organizations that could articulate their rights as workers, as farmers, and as women. The Farmers' Alliances of the late 1870s and 1880s attempted to create farmers' cooperatives to compete against the railroad monopolies. The Alliances united isolated farmwomen, bringing them together for social and political purposes. In the 1880s, the Knights of Labor went one step further by bringing all producers—farmers, workers, and small business owners—into one union. This union, run by Terence V. Powderly, accepted unskilled and skilled workers, resisting attempts to divide members of the working classes based on race or gender. It began accepting women in 1881, with 50,000 female members by 1886. An Irish immigrant widow, Leonora M. Barry, began working in the hosiery industry to support her young children. Determined to improve women's horrible pay and working conditions, Barry worked out of the Knight's national headquarters in Philadelphia, in a paid job as the "general instructor and director of women's work" (Wertheimer 1977, 186–89). Traveling widely, she organized working women into unions, started cooperative shirt factories, gave temperance and woman suffrage lectures, and fought for state-level factory inspection laws.

The Knights of Labor gained its greatest support by organizing workers to fight for an eight-hour day; many workers affiliated with the Knights went on strike throughout the 1880s. In 1886, the Knights supported a strike for an eight-hour day at the McCormick Reaper Works in Chicago. A rally the next day for the striking workers in Chicago's Haymarket Square ended with a bombing that resulted in the deaths of seven police officers. Eight anarchist labor leaders, who were not involved in the bombing, were arrested, charged, and convicted of murder. Labor opponents wrongly smeared the Knights as a radical, violent organization simply because workers affiliated with the union had participated in the strike and rally. Later that year, in a show of solidarity, Frances Willard and the Woman's Christian Temperance Union reached out to Powderly and the Knights of Labor. Reflecting her involvement in the Social Gospel movement, Willard wanted the "political machinery to dethrone those who reap the fruits but have not sown the seeds of industry" (Bordin 1986, 138). Appreciating the Knights' support of woman suffrage and equal pay for equal work, her organization offered to support their struggle for the eight-hour day in return for the Knights' support of prohibition and social purity. Already sympathetic to these reforms and to expanding women's rights, Powderly and the Knights agreed to this collaboration.

By the 1890s, farmers and workers decided to create a third national political party, called the People's or Populist Party. Unlike the two mainstream political parties, the Democrats and Republicans, the Populists welcomed black and white women as full members and endorsed woman suffrage. Kansan Mary Lease, whose husband had failed as a farmer, was a member of both the WCTU and the Knights of Labor before her involvement with the Populists. Lease gave approximately 160 speeches for Populist Party candidates in the months before they swept the 1890 election in Kansas. In her speeches, she declared, "I hold to the theory that if one man had not enough to eat three times a day and another man has $25 million, that last man has something that belongs to the first" (Edwards 2000, 60). Lease helped launch the Populist Party nationally in 1892, giving well-attended speeches across the country for the party and its presidential candidates. Several women toured the country on behalf of the Populist Party, yet its support remained concentrated in the West.

Even as they involved themselves in party politics, wage-earning women also searched for a new home within the labor movement. Women workers had participated in work stoppages and strikes, and had joined unions since their early days in the textile mills in the 1830s and 1840s, but they now found themselves unable to join the rising American Federation of Labor (AFL), which limited its membership to skilled white men in order to have more bargaining power with employers. During a convention of the AFL in 1903, where only four working women were in attendance, the National Women's Trade Union League (WTUL) was founded to encourage working women to organize. Settlement house residents and other women reformers brought the unionizing of wage-earning women and protective labor issues to the attention of the men's trade union movement. In New York and other states across the country, the WTUL formed local leagues to train wage-earning women to become union organizers "and persuade the labor movement to integrate women into its ranks" (Dye 1980, 2).

The Women's Trade Union League was a cross-class alliance that brought middle- and upper-class women reformers together with mostly Jewish and Italian immigrant young women wage earners, on the idea that women of all classes could unite for protective labor laws and voting rights. The WTUL's greatest accomplishment was its encouragement of the 1909 "uprising of the twenty thousand." Between 20 and 40 thousand mostly teenaged workers walked off their jobs in New York City's shirtwaist industry for over two months, demanding better conditions, pay increases, and recognition for their unions. The WTUL did not initiate the strike, but funded striking women workers and helped them gain publicity. "Mink brigades" of elite women visited the picket lines and helped contain police violence against the strikers. This cross-class alliance was strained when elite leaders tried to tamp down the socialist ideas of working-class labor organizers.

Workers at the Triangle Shirtwaist factory had joined the 1909 uprising of the twenty thousand, but had been forced to return to work without gaining union representation, new fire safety regulations, or new fire escapes. The subsequent Triangle factory fire of 1911, which resulted in the tragic deaths of 146 workers, mostly women and girls, intensified calls for unions and for safety regulations in factories. The deaths were preventable: the company routinely locked the doors from the outside (so that the workers could not take breaks, talk with union organizers, leave the premises, or take any materials from the factory), thereby trapping the workers when the fire broke out.

In the 1912 "Bread and Roses" strike in Lawrence, Massachusetts, approximately 25,000 textile workers from at least 30 different countries—over half of them girls and women—struck against their employers, in spite of significant ethnic, religious, and language barriers. Young girls and women carried picket signs, poignantly articulating their desire for a higher quality of life: "We want bread and roses too" (Kornbluh 1988, 164). The strike had strong female leadership, including Elizabeth Gurley Flynn, a dynamic organizer for the International Workers of the World (IWW), or the Wobblies, a radical union that was dedicated to organizing the unskilled, immigrants, and women. Radical labor organizer Mother Jones (Mary Harris Jones) developed the Children's Campaign to highlight the needs of the children by bringing them directly into the public eye. Impoverished children of the striking workers traveled to different cities asking for support; some even got a hearing before members of Congress. The IWW's dynamic radicalism threatened the staid American Federation of Labor; its skilled male workers offered to compromise with the employers, a move intended to damage the rising strength and popularity of the IWW. After witnessing police brutality against women and children, middle-class allies in the WTUL came out to the picket lines to help protect the workers. After less than two months, the strikers defied the odds and won concessions from their employers.

Feminists in the 1910s

During the 1910s, a small subset of women began to self-identify as feminists, a term that had its origins in the French language and meant a shared commitment to women's rights, individualism, free speech, economic and psychological independence, and sexual freedom. Feminists rejected female subservience in the family and in society, and believed in wage earning as a way to achieve independence. Unlike clubwomen and reformers who tried to make change without overtly challenging women's traditional roles, feminists purposefully did so; as a result, they were viewed as radicals by the wider culture. Several prominent feminists lived and worked in New York City's Greenwich Village, creating a space for themselves to experiment with ideas about free love, equality, and pro-labor radicalism.

Emma Goldman, a Russian Jewish immigrant, became radicalized by the Haymarket Tragedy of 1886, when authorities rushed to prosecute leading anarchist immigrants, whom they smeared as un-American. Goldman's first arrest and imprisonment, for allegedly trying to incite a riot, came during the economic crisis of 1893, when she urged unemployed workers to protest their conditions. In prison, she became interested in nursing, and subsequently used her skills in the tenements, where she witnessed married immigrant women suffering and dying from frequent pregnancies. Goldman advocated women's control over their own bodies. In 1906, her feminist, anarchist publication, *Mother Earth*, fought for better wages and conditions for workers, as well as for women's right to enjoy sex outside of marriage and reproduction. Her participation in the 1915–1916 movement for legalized birth control resulted in her arrest for distributing birth control literature, and confirmed her reputation as a champion of free speech. During World War I, Goldman helped organize No-Conscription Leagues against the draft, was arrested, and was charged with obstructing the draft. Acting as her own attorney, Goldman noted that "To charge people with having conspired to do something which they have been engaged in doing most of their lives, namely their campaign against war, militarism and conscription as contrary to the best interests of humanity, is an insult to human intelligence" (Goldman 2004, 292–94). After her imprisonment and release, Goldman was among those immigrants targeted by Attorney General A. Mitchell Palmer for deportation during the Red Scare of 1919. Suspected of being a sympathizer with the Bolshevik revolution of 1917, she was forced to return to Soviet Russia, where she found the communist regime to be disappointingly repressive. Her criticisms of the Soviet Union led to her deportation from that country as well.

Margaret Sanger, a young nurse and socialist with a working-class background, met the famous Emma Goldman in 1911 and was deeply influenced by her radical advocacy of women's sexuality and erotic desires. Sanger viewed "birth control" (a term she coined) as a mode of liberation for the many married immigrant women who were suffering under the strains of repeated pregnancies: "Three hundred thousand mothers . . . lose their babies every year from poverty and neglect . . . Are the cries of these women to be stifled?" (Gordon 1974, 223). Wanting to empower working-class women, Sanger identified birth control as fundamentally an issue of equal rights—of women's control over their own bodies. In 1912 and 1913, Sanger contributed a weekly column titled "What Every Girl Should Know" to the *Call*, a socialist newspaper. The pro-censorship crusader, Anthony Comstock, inadvertently turning birth control into a popular free speech cause, threatened to block the *Call* from the federal mails, unless it stopped publishing her column. Frustrated by her own lack of knowledge about contraceptive options, Sanger researched contraceptive devices in Europe. In 1914, she launched the journal the *Woman Rebel* and was charged with violating the 1873 Comstock Act, which labeled the dissemination of birth control information as obscene. Sanger fled to Europe to escape federal charges but returned in 1916 to introduce the vaginal diaphragm to the United States. Opening a free medical clinic in Brooklyn, New York, Sanger was arrested after having seen 464 married women in nine days. Her imprisonment gained public sympathy for her cause.

Unlike Emma Goldman, over time, Sanger chose to moderate her political stance and narrow her focus. Instead of advocating socialism or anarchism, she concentrated on challenging legal restrictions to birth control. Moving away from her radical roots and from advocacy of women's free expression of sexuality, Sanger's American Birth Control League (1921–1938) cultivated alliances with male medical doctors by convincing them to support laws that allowed married couples to receive birth control only when provided by a licensed physician. This strategy allowed doctors to see the legalization of birth control at the state level as an increase in their professional responsibilities and authority. Margaret Sanger's phrase, "planned parenthood," emphasized the respectable effort to control reproduction within marriage, rather than single women's sexual expression. Through Sanger's persistent efforts, more married women gained access to safe and legal birth control than ever before.

Women's Voluntary Efforts in World War I

World War I marked an important turning point for women, as workers, reformers, clubwomen, and feminists. When the Great War first began in

Women add to a pile of peach stones in this World War I advertisement for the unusual drive for peach stones, which were used as filters in gas masks, Boston, 1918. (National Archives and Records Administration)

Europe, many American women favored peace and arbitration rather than what they viewed as the barbaric, uncivilized nature of war. In 1915, Jane Addams presided over the first meeting of the Women's International League for Peace and Freedom in The Hague, Netherlands, to try to bring about a fair and equitable peace. Pacifists who supported U.S. neutrality risked their reputations by continuing to support pacifism after the United States declared war on Germany in 1917. Representative Jeannette Rankin, for instance, lost her seat in Congress by voting with a small minority of congressional representatives against U.S. entry into WWI. Jane Addams found herself marginalized and even demonized for her continued pacifism. She won the Nobel peace prize in 1931 in recognition of her courageous work.

Once the U.S. Congress declared war on Germany, most Americans set aside their isolationist tendencies and fully embraced the war effort. Clubwomen and suffragists alike supported the war by volunteering to knit socks, roll bandages, sell war bonds, and limit their family's food consumption. As increasing numbers of American men fought in the war, wage-earning women proved their patriotism and earned better wages by shifting from, for instance, sex-segregated jobs in domestic work or the textile industry to new jobs in factories and munitions plants. Women's participation in vital war work bolstered their demands for the right to vote, a goal that they finally achieved after the war's end, when the Nineteenth Amendment was ratified in 1920.

Conclusion

During the Gilded Age and Progressive Era, clubwomen, reformers, laborers, and feminists asserted their right to participate in the public, political sphere. Whether they intended to further their education, improve society, gain better working conditions, or control their own bodies, women expanded traditional gender roles and played an important role in transforming their society. Most significantly, the guarantee of voting rights provided by the Nineteenth Amendment marked a major milestone in the history of the struggle for women's rights. While women made important advances in other areas as well, many of the goals of turn-of-the-century reformers and feminists—for economic justice, racial equality, and women's full emancipation—remained unrealized, and would be left for subsequent generations of women to continue to pursue as the 20th century unfolded.

References and Further Reading

Addams, Jane. *Twenty Years at Hull House: With Autobiographical Notes.* 1910. New York: Signet Classics, 1999.

Blair, Karen J. *The Clubwoman as Feminist: True Womanhood Redefined, 1868–1914.* New York: Holmes & Meier Publishers, 1980.

Bordin, Ruth. *Frances Willard: A Biography.* Chapel Hill: University of North Carolina Press, 1986.

Bordin, Ruth. *Woman and Temperance: The Quest for Power and Liberty, 1873–1900.* Philadelphia: Temple University Press, 1981.

Brown, Victoria Bissell. *The Education of Jane Addams.* Philadelphia: University of Pennsylvania Press, 2004.

Cash, Floris Barnett. *African American Women and Social Action: The Clubwomen and Volunteerism from Jim Crow to the New Deal, 1896–1936.* Westport, CT: Greenwood Press, 2001.

Christie, Victoria. "Jeanette Rankin: Peace at any Cost." In *Women Who Speak for Peace,* ed. Colleen Kelley and Anna L. Eblen, 53–70. Lanham, MD: Rowman & Littlefield Publishers, 2002.

Cott, Nancy F. *The Grounding of Modern Feminism.* New Haven, CT: Yale University Press, 1987.

Croly, Jane Cunningham, *Sorosis: Its Origin and History.* 1886. Reprinted in *The Leisure Class in America,* ed. Leon Stein. New York: Arno Press, 1975.

Dye, Nancy Schrom. *As Equals and As Sisters: Feminism, the Labor Movement, and the Women's Trade Union League of New York.* Columbia: University of Missouri Press, 1980.

Edwards, Rebecca. "Mary Lease and the Sources of Populist Protest." In *The Human Tradition in the Gilded Age and Progressive Era,* ed. Ballard C. Campbell, 53–68. Wilmington, DE: SR Books, 2000.

Elshtain, Jean Bethke. *Jane Addams and the Dream of American Democracy: A Life*. New York: Basic Books, 2002.

Flanagan, Maureen A. *America Reformed: Progressives and Progressivisms, 1890s–1920s*. New York: Oxford University Press, 2007.

Gilmore, Glenda Elizabeth. *Gender & Jim Crow: Women and the Politics of White Supremacy in North Carolina, 1896–1920*. Chapel Hill: University of North Carolina Press, 1996.

Goldberg, Michael L. *An Army of Women: Gender and Politics in Gilded Age Kansas*. Baltimore, MD: Johns Hopkins University Press, 1997.

Goldman, Emma. "Address to the Jury in *U.S. v. Emma Goldman and Alexander Berkman*, by Emma Goldman, July 9, 1917." Reprinted in *Voices of a People's History of the United States*, ed. Howard Zinn & Anthony Arnove, 292–94. New York: Seven Stories Press, 2004.

Gordon, Linda. *Woman's Body, Woman's Right: A Social History of Birth Control in America*. New York: Penguin Books, 1974.

Gusfield, Joseph. *Symbolic Crusade: Status, Politics, and the American Temperance Movement*. Urbana: University of Illinois Press, 1963.

Guy-Sheftall, Beverly. *Daughters of Sorrow: Attitudes toward Black Women, 1880–1920*. Brooklyn, NY: Carlson Publishing, 1990.

Hale, Grace Elizabeth. *Making Whiteness: The Culture of Segregation in the South, 1890–1940*. New York: Vintage Books, 1998.

Hammond, Wendy F. "The Woman's National Loyal League: Feminist Abolitionists and the Civil War." *Civil War History* 35, no. 1 (1989): 39–58.

Hine, Darlene Clark, and Kathleen Thompson. *A Shining Thread of Hope: The History of Black Women in America*. New York: Broadway Books, 1998.

Jones, Beverly Washington, ed. *Quest for Equality: The Life and Writings of Mary Eliza Church Terrell, 1863–1954*. Brooklyn: Carlson Publishing, 1990.

Joslin, Katherine. *Jane Addams: A Writer's Life*. Urbana: University of Illinois Press, 2004.

Knight, Louise W. *Citizen: Jane Addams and the Struggle for Democracy*. Chicago: University of Chicago Press, 2005.

Kornbluh, Joyce. *Rebel Voices: An IWW Anthology*. Chicago: Charles H. Kerr Publishing, 1988.

Mattingly, Carol. *Well-Tempered Women: Nineteenth-Century Temperance Rhetoric*. Carbondale: Southern Illinois University Press, 1998.

McGerr, Michael. *A Fierce Discontent: The Rise and Fall of the Progressive Movement in America*. New York: Oxford University Press, 2003.

Orleck, Annelise. *Common Sense and a Little Fire: Women and Working-Class Politics in the United States, 1900–1965*. Chapel Hill: University of North Carolina Press, 1995.

Parker, Alison M. *Purifying America: Women, Cultural Reform, and Pro-Censorship Activism, 1873–1933.* Urbana: University of Illinois Press, 1997.

Salem, Dorothy. *To Better Our World: Black Women in Organized Reform, 1890–1920.* Brooklyn, NY: Carlson Publishing, 1990.

Schechter, Patricia A. *Ida B. Wells-Barnett and American Reform, 1880–1930.* Chapel Hill: University of North Carolina Press, 2001.

Schneider, Dorothy, and Carl J. Schneider. *American Women in the Progressive Era, 1900–1920.* New York: Facts on File, 1993.

Shaw, Stephanie J. *What a Woman Ought to Be and to Do: Black Professional Women Workers during the Jim Crow Era.* Chicago: University of Chicago Press, 1996.

Sklar, Kathryn Kish. *Florence Kelley and the Nation's Work: The Rise of Women's Political Culture, 1830–1900.* New Haven, CT: Yale University Press, 1995.

Smith, Karen Manners. "New Paths to Power, 1890–1920." In *No Small Courage: A History of Women in the United States,* ed. Nancy F. Cott, 353–412. New York: Oxford University Press, 2000.

Stansell, Christine. *American Moderns: Bohemian New York and the Creation of a New Century.* New York: Owl Books/Henry Holt & Co., 2000.

Stivers, Camilla. *Bureau Men, Settlement Women: Constructing Public Administration in the Progressive Era.* Lawrence: University Press of Kansas, 2000.

Stone, Geoffrey R. *Perilous Times: Free Speech in Wartime, from the Sedition Act of 1798 to the War on Terrorism.* New York: W. W. Norton & Co., 2004.

Stromquist, Shelton. *Re-inventing "The People": The Progressive Movement, the Class Problem and the Origins of Modern Liberalism.* Urbana: University of Illinois Press, 2006.

Tax, Meredith. *The Rising of the Women: Feminist Solidarity and Class Conflict, 1880–1917.* 1980. Reprint, Urbana: University of Illinois Press, 2001.

Terrell, Mary Church. *A Colored Woman in a White World.* 1940. Reprint, Washington, DC: National Association of Colored Women's Clubs, 1968.

Traxel, David. *Crusader Nation: The United States in Peace and the Great War, 1898–1920.* New York: Alfred A. Knopf, 2006.

Varon, Elizabeth R. *Southern Lady, Yankee Spy: The True Story of Elizabeth Van Lew, a Union Agent in the Heart of the Confederacy.* New York: Oxford University Press, 2003.

Wertheimer, Barbara Mayer. *We Were There: The Story of Working Women in America.* New York: Pantheon Books, 1977.

Wood, Mary I. *The History of the General Federation of Women's Clubs, for the First Twenty-Two Years of its Organization.* 1912. Reprint, Farmingdale, NY: Dabor Social Science Publications, 1978.

Modern Women in the 1920s | 8

Susan Goodier

The end of World War I brought vast and exciting, yet conflicting and ambiguous, changes for women in the United States. During the first two decades of the 20th century, women increasingly received college educations, worked outside the home, joined reform organizations, and broke some social barriers. On August 26, 1920, the Nineteenth Amendment granted women the right to vote. The following decade firmly ushered the United States into the modern era. Among the developments that Americans witnessed in the 1920s were the maturation of the industrial corporate economy, the expansion of urban populations, the growth of a mass consumer culture and mass media techniques, and the increasing predominance of scientific authority in many areas of public and private life. Many Americans eagerly embraced the changes associated with modernity. Others anxiously sought to stem the tide of social change, thereby rousing religious fundamentalism, resurgent racism and nativism, and political conservatism.

The modern woman was shaped by and helped create these complex social changes; for many Americans, she epitomized the promises and dangers of modernity itself. Building on the gains of earlier generations of women's rights activists, suffragists, and feminists, women of the 1920s enjoyed more opportunities for independence and equality than ever before in U.S. history. They also faced a range of challenges—some familiar, some new—as they struggled to claim more rights and freedoms in a nation simultaneously enthusiastic and wary about the arrival of the modern age.

After the Vote, What?: Women in Politics and Reform in a Post-Suffrage Age

The decade began with enthusiasm for women's newly won political power. To celebrate the passage of the Nineteenth Amendment, Alice Paul and the executive committee of the National Woman's Party (NWP) commissioned feminist and well-known sculptor Adelaide Johnson to sculpt Lucretia Mott, Elizabeth Cady Stanton, and Susan B. Anthony for a commemoration monument. Paul and the NWP revived an earlier National American Woman Suffrage Association (NAWSA) project, paying Johnson $2,000 to complete the monument for placement in the Capitol crypt. Representatives from more than 100 women's organizations attended the ceremony, held on the anniversary of Susan B. Anthony's birthday, February 15, 1921. Sara Bard Field, the west coast suffragist and reformer who presented the monument to the Speaker of the House, claimed that the statues represented the "body and the blood of a great sacrificial host . . . the body and blood of Revolution, the body and blood of Freedom herself" (Cook 1978, 58).

Other speeches during the three-day convention following the ceremony made it clear that voting was only a single step on the path to true equality for women. As NAWSA president Carrie Chapman Catt had predicted, "Winning the vote did not end the woman's campaign for equality and justice. Many a hard fought battle lies ahead and its field will be found in unexpected places" (Wilson 2007, 9). Former suffragists expressed confidence that women would use the vote to further advance their rights and improve society. Initially, this optimism seemed well founded, as women registered to vote and cast their ballots, formed and joined organizations devoted to promoting women's political activity and securing women's rights, participated in party politics, ran for political office, and lobbied federal, state, and local governments for social reforms.

Having grown up thinking that voting was a male concern , and needing time to learn how to be politically active, many activist women expressed ambivalence regarding membership in the major political parties. After all, after opposing woman suffrage for decades, neither the Republican nor Democratic parties had endorsed it with enthusiasm. Instead, two organizations led the way in coordinating and influencing the direction of women's political energies. Alice Paul had already reorganized the Congressional Union as the suffrage-focused NWP, in 1916; from 1921, it sought to achieve women's equal rights in political, social, and economic life. Proudly identifying themselves as "feminists," NWP members initially advanced an agenda that included attention to nationality laws, employment opportunities, and jury service for women, but their priority quickly became the Equal Rights Amendment (ERA).

Meanwhile, Carrie Chapman Catt had begun the process of reorganizing the NAWSA as the League of Women Voters (LWV) in anticipation of the ratification of the Nineteenth Amendment. The objectives of the League included educating women in their new civic responsibilities, promoting social welfare bills and protective legislation for women, eliminating discriminatory laws, and promoting international cooperation to prevent war. Although the League encouraged its members to join the existing political parties, Catt made it clear that the new League "must be nonpartisan and all partisan" to accommodate party women, as well as those who resisted joining parties (Van Voris 1987, 157–58). Politicians welcomed and encouraged women's work for the parties, but fearing a women's voting bloc, they barred women from holding any real power within the parties. As Eleanor Roosevelt

Marble statue of suffragists Susan B. Anthony, Lucretia Mott, and Elizabeth Cady Stanton at the U.S. Capitol. (Library of Congress)

pointed out in 1928, "Beneath the veneer of courtesy and outward show of consideration universally accorded women, there is a widespread male hostility—age-old perhaps—against sharing with them any actual control" (Freeman 2000, 149). Nevertheless, women worked within the party structure at the local, state, and national levels throughout the decade.

Although women had held political offices before the passage of the Nineteenth Amendment, the number of those who campaigned for or accepted appointments to political office increased substantially after its passage. Sophonisba Breckinridge, a women's rights activist with a doctorate in political science, showed that county and local positions as mayors, comptrollers, city clerks, and city council members were far more available to women than positions higher up on the political ladder. Certain governmental offices, especially those relating to education, welfare, and record keeping at state, county, or local levels, came to be seen as particularly appropriate for women. The first woman elected to Congress was Jeannette Rankin of Montana, who served from 1917 to 1919 and again in the early 1940s. Alice Robertson, a former antisuffragist, was the first woman elected to the House of Representatives after national enfranchisement. Altogether, 11 women served in Congress during the decade. In 1925, Nellie Tayloe Ross of Wyoming was elected the first female governor in the United States, replacing her husband, who had died in office. Later that year, Texans elected Miriam A. (Ma) Ferguson as the first female governor of their state. By 1929, at least 149 women served in the legislatures of 38 states.

Women also continued their social reform efforts during the 1920s, working through existing organizations, as well as newly established organizations. Activists sought more opportunities for women in education, the professions, and the industrial workforce. The National Federation of Business and Professional Women's Clubs (BPW), for example, focused on equality in pay and employment opportunities for women in the white-collar job sector. The Women's Trade Union League (WTUL) and National Consumers' League (NCL) continued their efforts to improve labor conditions for working-class women, although these organizations became less important as unions took over. The WTUL and the NCL did pressure the government to establish the Women's Bureau in the Department of Labor in 1920 to promote governmental action to benefit working women. Mary Anderson, formerly of the WTUL, ran the agency, but because it was poorly funded, the agency primarily gathered women's employment data.

In addition to focusing some federal attention on the needs of working women, reformers met with limited success in lobbying efforts on behalf of mothers and children. The Children's Bureau began its work in 1912 to reduce deaths related to childbearing. Under the capable leadership of Julia Lathrop, a close friend of Jane Addams, agency workers gathered statistics on the high rates of maternal and infant deaths in the United States. Lathrop, her successor Grace Abbott, and their colleagues sponsored lectures on child health, and prepared informational pamphlets on maternity, childbearing, and childcare. The agency proposed a maternity and infancy act and eventually found support from Senator Morris Sheppard and Representative Horace Mann Towner. The 1921 act, commonly called the Sheppard-Towner Maternity and Infancy Act, provided matching federal grants to individual states for lectures on nutrition and health, prenatal and child health clinics, and visiting nurses for pregnant women and new mothers. Many women's organizations endorsed the broadly popular act.

In 1920, Maud Wood Park, President of the LWV, gathered representatives of 10 major women's groups to consolidate women's political activity. They created the Women's Joint Congressional Committee (WJCC) to oversee federal-level lobbying efforts for social reform. The WJCC did not support any particular legislative program, but if five or more member organizations supported a specific piece of legislation, the WJCC would establish a subcommittee to coordinate lobbying efforts on its behalf. Subcommittees in the early years included infancy and maternity protection, child labor, increased appropriations for education, industrial legislation, independent citizenship for married women, regulation of the meatpacking industry, social hygiene, prohibition, and opposition to the ERA. By 1924, 21 organizations representing 12 million women belonged to the WJCC.

Because black women were frequently excluded from white women's organizations, they founded local Phillis Wheatley Clubs, the National Colored Parent-Teachers Association, and other organizations. Members of black women's clubs continued to work through the National Association of Colored Women (NACW), as well as through the male-dominated National Association for the Advancement of Colored People (NAACP). Their efforts usually focused on racial equality—"racial uplift"—rather than on gender equality, however. At the forefront of the black women's agenda were efforts to secure a federal anti-lynching law. In 1922, Mary B. Talbert founded the Anti-Lynching Crusade to coordinate women's support for the NAACP's campaign against lynching. Its goals included fundraising, publicity, pressuring Congress and state legislatures to enact and enforce anti-lynching laws, and support for legal investigations. Efforts to stop lynching had begun 30 years before and would continue for decades.

Those efforts provoked cooperation between some black and white women to eliminate racism and intolerance. Some, including Charlotte Hawkins Brown, joined the Council for Interracial Cooperation (CIC), founded in Memphis, Tennessee in October 1920. Speaking on behalf of African American women, Brown argued that white women must control the violence of their men: "The negro women of the South lay everything that happens to the members of her race at the door of the Southern white woman . . . We feel that so far as lynching is concerned that, if the white women would take hold of the situation, that lynching would be stopped" (Lerner 1973, 470). Although ongoing racial tensions allowed for little progress during the decade, the Council did initiate a nascent cooperation between middle-class black and white women.

Despite the success of some of their lobbying and reform efforts, and their inroads into electoral and party politics, women activists experienced some significant disappointments during the 1920s. Differing concerns among groups of women voters, disagreements between women activists about the meaning of gender equality, and a conservative backlash hostile to a progressive reform agenda all contributed to the fracturing of a broad, coordinated movement on behalf of women's rights, although an organized women's movement did not disappear.

The concentration on acquiring woman suffrage as a right of citizenship had effectively erased the differences among activist women during the Progressive Era. Once they achieved voting rights, the differences among them surfaced, affecting their organizational efforts. Factors such as class, race, educational level, religious affiliation, geographical region, and political ideology influenced more women than their gender. Thus, it did not take long for women activists, or male political figures for that matter, to realize that women did not all vote the same way on what were deemed to be women's issues. Furthermore, disenfranchisement remained problematic in some regions of the country, especially in the South, where poll taxes, literacy tests, and long waiting periods prevented many black women from voting. In spite of some interracial cooperation, white women activists rarely took up the issue of restrictions on black women's voting rights.

In addition to the social and ideological differences dividing women voters, the organized women's movement was especially compromised by disagreements about the nature of gender equality and how best to achieve it. Members of the NWP gathered extensive information on state laws that discriminated against women in areas of education, work, marriage and divorce, birth control, and child custody. They introduced the Equal Rights Amendment—"Men and women shall have equal rights throughout the United States and every place subject to its jurisdiction. Congress shall have

Crystal Eastman

Crystal Eastman (1881–1928) received her bachelor's degree from Vassar College (1903), a Master of Arts degree in economics and sociology from Columbia University (1904), and a PhD from New York University Law School (1907). She was an activist who sought worker safety, birth control access, mothers' endowments, and equality for women and men. Under a commission created by Governor Charles Evans Hughes of New York, she helped develop the first workers' compensation program in the country. Eastman cofounded, with Alice Paul, the Congressional Union for Woman Suffrage, which became the National Woman's Party in 1916, and cofounded the Woman's Peace Party (WPP) in 1915, encouraging Jane Addams to accept the presidency. The WPP became the U.S. section of the Women's International League for Peace and Freedom in 1919. She also co-founded the National Civil Liberties Bureau during World War I. The Bureau represented conscientious objectors and worked to protect free-speech rights, and soon became the American Civil Liberties Union (ACLU).

After the ratification of the Nineteenth Amendment, Eastman helped author the Equal Rights Amendment, introduced to Congress in 1923. She published articles on a broad range of feminist topics, and with her brother, Max Eastman, founded and edited *The Liberator,* a socialist journal. In one of her articles addressing the difference between the women's movement and socialism, Eastman wrote that "the true feminist, no matter how far to the left she may be in the revolutionary movement, sees the woman's battle as distinct in its objects and different in its methods from the workers' battle for industrial freedom." Equality between men and women, as Eastman perceived it, necessitated raising "feminist sons" to share the "business of home-making" (Cook 1978, 55–56). The Federal Bureau of Investigation kept Eastman's activities under surveillance, recording her speeches, and adding her to the blacklist of other activist women. Eastman died of nephritis, an acute inflammation of the kidneys never properly diagnosed or treated, on July 8, 1928. Unabashedly feminist, radical, and militant, Crystal Eastman devoted her life to the cause of making women free.

the power to enforce this article by appropriate legislation"—in December 1923. ERA supporters perceived protective labor laws for women, especially those that limited the hours they could work or prohibited them from working at night, as unfairly discriminating against women as a class and denying them their rights as individuals to freedom of contract. Feminist Crystal Eastman pointed out that "a good deal of tyranny goes by the name of protection" (Cook 1978, 156). She and other supporters of the ERA contended that protective legislation should apply to both women and men.

Outside of the NWP, women who had long been active in social reform argued for political, legal, social, and economic equality but feared the loss of protective labor legislation for women. Opposing the ERA, they argued that because of women's historically disadvantaged status in the workforce, and because all women were mothers or potential mothers, women required special protections under the law. As Florence Kelley, who resigned her position with the NWP because she believed the ERA would endanger protective labor legislation, put it, "The cry Equality, Equality, where Nature has created inequality, is as stupid and as deadly as the cry Peace, Peace, where there is no Peace" (Lemons 1990, 185). The Women's Bureau and the WJCC also opposed the ERA for the same reasons. The disagreements between the two factions of activists over the ERA rendered both groups less effective in advancing women's rights during the decade.

Women's political activity during the 1920s was most fundamentally thwarted by a conservative political climate that was adverse to a progressive reform agenda. Promoting this climate were fears that surfaced as the population shifted from rural to urban areas and as the economy shifted from an agricultural to an industrial base. Many commentators argued that urbanites, many of them immigrants and the children of immigrants, rejected basic American values, thereby encouraging the rise of antiradical groups and the strengthening of fundamentalist associations. In addition, three Republican presidents each served one term during the 1920s: Warren G. Harding, Calvin Coolidge, and Herbert Hoover. Their primary policies supported big business and opposed government regulation of the economy; Congress only passed laws that supported big business. Until the stock market crash in October 1929, making money seemed more important than reform. The apparent prosperity of the decade undermined many of the reform goals that had once been so important to women.

Additional hostility to women's reform efforts and feminism stemmed from the Red Scare and fears of Bolshevism, or communism, following the end of World War I and coinciding with the Russian Revolution. Many Americans believed that their own country was vulnerable to communism, the antithesis of free-market capitalism. They convinced themselves that Bolshevism would result in "unnatural gender roles" and "immoral sexual values," and that women represented the weak link allowing foreign influences to penetrate the nation (Nielson 2001, 28). Any hint of radical behavior was cause for alarm. Feminism was especially vulnerable to criticism as a subversive ideology; protection against radicalism could only come from powerful men and the patriarchal family. Red Scare antifeminists exhibited hostility toward government bureaucracy, social welfare policies, and women in positions of authority in government. Their efforts helped to undermine the public policy efforts of feminists and women reformers during the 1920s.

Several women's groups fostered the conservative political climate. One prominent example was the Women of the Ku Klux Klan (WKKK), which brought together thousands of native-born Protestant white women committed to a crusade against Catholics, Jews, immigrants, and blacks. The WKKK recruited members through the Woman's Christian Temperance Union (WCTU), a church-based movement that did not challenge existing gender relations but that often targeted Catholic and immigrant populations, and through nativist and patriotic societies. Many women joined to support the efforts of their husbands, family members, and friends already involved in the KKK. The women spread rumor or slander and organized consumer boycotts, serving as a vocal and economic complement to the night riding and gang terrorism of male Klan members. By the end of the decade, membership in the Klan had decreased, not because racism and xenophobia had diminished, but because restrictive laws resulted in a curtailment of immigration, and because fewer people supported the Klan's methods. While the WKKK was one of the most extreme right-wing groups, it symbolized the growing conservatism of the decade.

Women reformers' clout was also compromised by their ongoing association with the unpopular cause of Prohibition. When the Eighteenth Amendment went into effect in January 1920, saloons all over the country closed, although enforcement of the ban on liquor was uneven. Speakeasies, where illegal liquor was readily available, opened to replace them. Men wore hip flasks filled with booze; women carried flasks in their handbags. Drinking became a problem on many college campuses. Many people thought it was incongruous that alcohol was illegal in a decade marked by so many social freedoms, and Prohibition was generally considered a joke and a failure. Although women and men widely opposed the amendment, some women reformers continued to support Prohibition, thereby arousing resistance to their efforts to achieve broader social reforms.

By the mid-1920s, the WJCC and other women-run organizations and governmental agencies were spending more time fending off the criticism of right-wing groups than promoting the legislative interests of their members. The 1924 publication of the "Spider Web Chart," which accused the WJCC, the NWP, and other women's groups of communist connections, undermined women's organizational work. Prompted by a New York legislative investigation into radical and subversive activities, Lucia R. Maxwell, the librarian of the Chemical Warfare Service of the War Department, had created the chart. She distorted the records collected by the Military Intelligence Division, which had compiled information on the political activities of women, especially those of suffragists who had opposed World War I, and the groups to which they belonged. The chart labeled 15 women's groups and leading women activists linked to the WJCC and the National Council for the Prevention of War as subversives and communists. Discrediting these women's organizations served well the economic goals of business and manufacturing interests that objected to protective legislation.

Another organization that suffered from being targeted by the Spider Web Chart was the Women's International League for Peace and Freedom (WILPF), organizationally connected to the National Woman's Peace Party. Pacifist women, reeling from the horror, destruction, and waste of the Great War, blamed the war on the greed of men in power. In their rhetoric urging peace, members of the WILPF promoted the League of Nations, a world court, greater involvement of women in international peacemaking, and outlawing war. Peace activism, however, provoked criticism, hostility, and merciless surveillance. Ultimately, the WILPF was condemned as antipatriotic. In response, the League cleansed itself of Crystal Eastman and other radical leaders, and shifted its emphasis from peace to the economic causes of war.

Other important women's reform efforts also faltered, some failing entirely. For example, in spite of its popularity and the support of most women's organizations, the Sheppard-Towner Act drew the censure of organizations such as the American Medical Association (AMA), which claimed it was a step in the direction of socialized medicine. Ultra-conservative women's groups agreed, but also opposed the act on the basis of their disapproval of women holding posts in governmental agencies. The Woman Patriots, an organization that emerged from the remnants of the National Association Opposed to Woman Suffrage, helped lead the opposition to the efforts of the Children's Bureau. Funding for Sheppard-Towner lapsed in June 1929, in spite of the fact that rural, working class, and middle-class women all over the United States had gratefully utilized the much-needed healthcare services it had provided.

The WJCC also encountered a great deal of resistance to its support of the Child Labor Amendment. Congress passed the amendment in 1924, limiting the labor of children under the age of 18. As the WJCC worked to assure the ratification of the amendment in the states, adversaries such as the National Association of Manufacturers (NAM), backed by plenty of money, opposed it on the grounds that any regulation of child labor would lead to greater federal regulation of industry and severely limit industrial autonomy. Fears of radicalism and communism were strong enough to ensure the defeat of the amendment two years later.

The 1920s was a decade of challenges, contrasts, and changes for women as political actors. The sometimes-rampant conservatism of the era existed alongside the excitement generated by the innovativeness of the period. Although there was initial support for women to expand their political expertise and involvement, fears of change in the wider culture hampered the efforts of many reform-minded women. Furthermore, there was a general turning away from politics and a decline in voting rates overall as Americans increasingly embraced leisure and consumption. Finally, the controversy over protective legislation and equal rights sharply divided feminist and activist women. An organized women's movement was thus seriously stymied during the 1920s by opposition from without and disagreements from within. Even so, many activist women managed to sustain their commitments both to women's rights and to other social reform goals, thereby continuing the struggle for women to claim an equal role in the political life of the nation.

Working Women

As was the case with women's experiences in politics and reform, women made some gains and faced ongoing challenges in their efforts to achieve greater economic opportunity and independence in the 1920s. The United States emerged from World War I relatively unscathed, with powerful capabilities for utilizing innovative technologies to produce all kinds of exciting consumer goods. Industrial production increased by 64 percent during the decade, up from a mere 12 percent increase in the previous decade. As a greater proportion of the population moved into urban areas, more people sought individual satisfaction through participation in a mass consumer culture. However, economic growth and prosperity remained unevenly distributed on the basis of geography, class, ethnicity, and race. The economic order of the 1920s enabled some women to claim a place for themselves in the predominantly male world of work, while simultaneously reinforcing expectations and experiences of female difference and dependence.

During World War I, women had competently filled all kinds of jobs, vacated by men away at war and in newly opened war factories. But when the war ended, many of those opportunities were closed to them. As a result, women made few advances toward eradicating the sex-segregation and gender-biased differentiations in the workplace. Nevertheless, in 1920, 23.7 percent of women over the age of 15 were employed; that number rose to 24.8 percent by the end of the decade. Married women constituted 9 percent of the women gainfully employed in 1920; that number rose to 11.7 percent by 1930. Daughters of European immigrants and middle-class white women alike eagerly sought jobs as stenographers, typists, clerks, and bookkeepers in corporate and government offices, seeing the jobs as more profitable and respectable than factory or domestic work. Because they naturally under-stood, supposedly, what female consumers wanted, women initially seemed ideal for the exciting new field of advertising, as it stimulated the mass-market economy. Relying on scientific ideas of behaviorists such as John B. Watson, advertising accounted for more than half of the output of printing presses during the decade. Racism kept black women from both clerical and advertising jobs. For all women, pay remained low and opportunities for ad-vancement were limited, as office work formed part of an increasingly femi-nized job sector. Indeed, the office environment became an extension of the home, where women and men still maintained separate spheres.

A greater percentage of women attended college in the 1920s, and the numbers of women obtaining professional degrees steadily increased during the decade. For example, in 1920, 122 women obtained medical degrees; by 1930, that number had risen to 204. Women graduating from law schools in-creased from 177 in 1920 to 411 in 1930. Just 1,396 women earned graduate degrees in 1920; that number increased to 6,139 by 1930. Only 90 women received PhDs in 1920, whereas 311 received their doctorates in 1930. Still, as domestic values reemerged in the greater society, even some of the most rigorous women's colleges relaxed their academic standards to include home economics in their curriculum.

With the greater availability of graduate training, a small but widely pub-licized number of women pursued professional careers. By 1920, no state except Delaware forbade women from practicing law, and women could practice as doctors in every state. Women worked as teachers, nurses, and in businesses such as banking and investment firms that sought female cus-tomers. Professionally trained social workers replaced settlement house reformers and moved out of immigrant communities. Yet men increasingly filled the administrative positions at the top of the social work bureaucracy. Even as more women entered a widening range of fields, their salaries re-mained lower than those of men in the same professions, and few of them rose through the ranks. Members of the National Federation of Business and Professional Women's Clubs, founded in 1919, sought to coordinate the needs of women working in the various professions. Lena Madesin Phillips, the first executive secretary, described the organization as formed of "women who individually had exercised so great an influence yet who were as a class non-gregarious" cooperating "to increase the value of the group to themselves, their respective communities, and society at large" (Cott 1987, 89).

Feminists pressed the argument that women needed to work to obtain economic independence from men. Doris Stevens, who wrote *Jailed for Freedom* (1920) about the NWP's role in the suffrage movement, contended that activist women must concentrate on obtaining economic equality next. Even so, relatively few women expected to have a professional career, for the prevailing notion was that marriage was the ultimate goal for women, an idea reinforced by magazine articles and movies throughout the decade. According to the Secretary of Labor James Davis, working women violated the natural order and threatened familial and social stability. Woman, he argued, is "by her very nature . . . the standard of morality . . . the stabilizer of the home" (Cott 1987, 137). Nevertheless, the idea that women would spend a part of their lives in the workforce slowly gained acceptance. Some men and women conceded that women's work was appropriate if it helped their current or future family and if they worked before marriage, or, at the most, before they bore children. Whatever any individual woman might have thought about the matter, though, it remained impossible for most working women to achieve economic independence. The average clerical worker earned $1,200 annually, when the average salary for all workers was $2,010.

African American women faced racism in office work and the professions, just as they did in other realms of life. Elizabeth Ross Haynes, the first black woman elected to the YWCA national board (serving 1924–1934), was the Domestic Service Secretary of the United States Employment Service from 1920 to 1922. Dominant in three types of occupations—domestic and personal service, agriculture, and manufacturing and mechanical industries— black women were "restricted in opportunities to get and hold jobs," Haynes concluded, but remained optimistic that they, too, would find "economic independence" and "places in the ranks with other working women" (Lerner 1973, 260). Whatever her social status, the average African American woman worked outside her home as she struggled to meet the needs of her family and her community in racist and sexist surroundings.

Like black women, Mexican American women also faced the double burdens of racism and sexism in the workforce. Propelled by the Mexican Revolution (1910–1920) and World War I, 1.5 million Mexicans, usually in family groups, had moved to the United States by 1930. Many Mexican Americans worked in agribusiness, notorious for its low wages and heavy use of child labor. Women could contribute to the economic benefit of their families by bearing many children to help with wage labor. Although women also worked in agriculture, their husbands received their wages. Racism and sexism kept other Mexican women in domestic labor or unskilled factory work. Poor Mexican American families faced living conditions as appalling as their working conditions, placing additional heavy physical burdens on women.

The American Federation of Labor (AFL) and other industrial unions were not interested in improving working conditions for Mexican women, black women, or white women, although women's locals, the WTUL and the

Women's Bureau all attempted to help women workers. While the Women's Bureau advocated for government action to benefit working women, the WTUL sought to organize working women into trade unions, lobbied for legislation improving working hours and conditions, and educated workers on the benefits of organization and legislation. From 1921 to the mid-1930s, the Summer Schools for Women Workers created by M. Carey Thomas and Hilda Smith of Bryn Mawr College constituted one of the most intriguing worker education programs. As articulated in the 1923 mission statement, the schools would provide "young women in industry opportunities to study liberal subjects and to train themselves in clear thinking; to stimulate an active and continued interest in the problems of our economic order; to develop a desire for study as a means of understanding and of enjoyment in life" (Hollis 1994, 34). Benefiting from an innovative pedagogy, the participants took courses in labor organizing and negotiating. Some eventually assumed leadership roles in later labor struggles.

Social and Private Lives

Despite persistent hurdles, women made some significant advances toward greater equality and autonomy in the public spheres of politics and work during the 1920s. The changes women experienced in their private lives were as transformative and complex. Mass production and mass consumption stimulated new habits and ways of thinking for both women and men. Materialism and a desire for the good life replaced old ideas of thrift and moderation. People could now use credit to acquire goods of all types. Young women coming of age, and wives and mothers alike, shed the submissiveness, self-sacrifice, and purity required of the true woman and embraced a modern standard for femininity emphasizing personal pleasure, individual fulfillment, and sexual expression. Media voices exuberantly proclaimed that the liberation of the modern woman was at hand, even as they sent messages establishing limits on her freedom. Women strove to navigate this contradictory terrain and faced some hard lessons as they continued to struggle to achieve gender equality.

The icon of emancipated modern womanhood in the 1920s was the young single woman, or "flapper." Cartoonist and illustrator John Held, Jr. specialized in drawing youthful, slender, long-legged girls with cropped hair and young men wearing galoshes and raccoon coats. His drawings of women sitting on men's laps, drinking from flasks, smoking cigarettes, and dancing with abandon illustrate the fads and the fashions of the Jazz Age. In addition to cutting her hair, the flapper wore cosmetics, bound her breasts, wore loosely fitting blouses, shortened her skirts, rolled her stockings below her knees, and shocked her elders as she "flaunted her sexuality" (Evans 1989, 175). The flapper debuted on the Broadway stage in playwright Rachel Crothers's comedy *Nice People* (1922). Later, actress Anita Loos characterized the flapper as rather empty-headed, but still charming in the popular play *Gentlemen Prefer Blondes* (1926).

The flapper exemplified young women's newfound opportunities for sexual freedom, even as she reckoned with the persistent double standard.

John Held Jr.'s cover for the February 18, 1926 issue of *Life* captured the image of the flappers: young women of the 1920s who flouted social norms, bobbing their hair, elevating their hemlines, and dancing the night away. (Library of Congress)

Since the turn of the century, working-class youths, feminists, intellectuals, and scientists had posed challenges to the Victorian code of sexual restraint. During the 1920s, new behaviors and ideas moved into the mainstream as white middle-class young women embraced the ethic of heterosexual freedom. Young people from all social classes now regularly frequented amusement parks, dance halls, and movie theaters in pursuit of heterosocial interactions away from the watchful eyes of their parents. The prevalence of Ford's Model T automobiles made it easy to find private places for what was called "petting." On college campuses, more young women experimented with new forms of physical intimacy. Nevertheless, sexual expression usually stopped short of claiming a woman's virginity; dating and petting meant marriage would soon follow. A 1925 article on the topic of petting on college campuses claimed that most girls drew a sharp line between petting and "actual illicit relations between the petters" (Wembridge 1925, 394). Young women remained responsible for keeping young men's sexual urges in check and were expected to maintain their own sexual respectability. In addition to delineating heterosexual expression, the new sexual freedom of the 1920s did not condone lesbian relationships. In fact, the growing emphasis on heterosexual coupling made friendships between women increasingly suspect.

Expectations for marriage changed considerably during the 1920s, although most women continued to believe that true fulfillment would come from marriage and domesticity. Influenced by a spate of social-scientific literature touting the benefits of what was called "companionate marriage," many women dreamed their marriages would be based on romance, sexual pleasure, and friendship, and less on patriarchy. As the old separate spheres ideas for women and men collapsed and more women had access to sexual and birth control information, expectations for personal satisfaction in marriage increased. At the same time, popular views rejected the same-sex relationships and the close extended-family ties typical of previous generations, resulting in the escalating importance of marital commitments.

Laborsaving devices for cleaning and cooking made housework less burdensome for many urban women and some rural women, as electricity and indoor plumbing reached a majority of homes in the 1920s. Electric devices replaced servants, as fewer women were available to hire for domestic work (except in the South, where black women had limited earning options). Vacuum cleaners, washing machines, refrigerators, electric stoves, irons, and coffeemakers became commonplace, and could be bought on credit. The modernized home and availability of all the new labor-saving devices raised expectations for cleanliness, with the result that women often spent more time engaged in household cleaning tasks. Modernization also set new standards for childbearing and childrearing. Women increasingly gave birth to their babies in hospitals, assisted by doctors, rather than at home, assisted by midwives. Advice columns encouraged women to give up club work and devote their lives to raising their children without too much emotional attachment, on a scientifically designed schedule. Proper motherhood necessitated trained professionals and relied less on simply doing what came naturally.

As mothers relied on doctors and psychologists to tell them how to raise their children, so they had to rely on physicians to distribute birth control. As a result, middle- and upper-class women had greater access to birth control than did poor women. While Margaret Sanger initially advocated birth control as a means for poor and working-class women to improve their lives, in the 1920s, birth control became more broadly accepted as a means to an ideal marriage. Birth control separated sex from reproduction and allowed for women's sexual expression in marriage, free from the fear of pregnancy. It contributed to smaller families, which resulted in a lessening of some aspects of domestic work for women. Nevertheless, the association of birth control with the medical profession and marriage kept many poor and single women from realizing its promises of sexual and reproductive freedom.

The popular culture of the 1920s offered single and married women alike an abundance of images of female freedom to emulate, although messages women received from the consumer culture and the mass media remained ambivalent. The first Miss America pageant, held in Atlantic City in 1921, epitomizes this ambivalence. Although the pageant organizers tried to convey a message of female "athleticism rather than exhibitionism," the display of the female body suggested immorality to some critics (Collins 2003, 346). Changing standards of fashion and female beauty allowed women expanded opportunities for self-expression and sexual expression, while narrowing definitions of beauty around a new set of norms and associating the acquisition of beauty with the purchase of consumer goods. Fashions changed during the decade from the tightly corseted Gibson Girl look to the boyish, straight-waist look, exposing women's arms and legs. Where once only prostitutes would apply makeup to enhance their beauty, now women of all classes enthusiastically wore cosmetics. Elizabeth Arden and Helena Rubenstein sold face powder, rouge, and lipstick, making their fortunes in the cosmetic industry. The tobacco industry marketed cigarettes to women, as well, and by the end of the decade, smoking in public had become acceptable. Advertisers insinuated that women would only be free of the restrictions of past generations if they bought the products advertisers promoted. Movies, like advertisers, demonstrated the use of the new products and fashions, and especially targeted young people.

The immensely popular films of the era also sent conflicting messages about the modern woman. Sound films replaced silent films, as the movie industry became the fifth-largest industry in the country. About 100 million people attended movie theaters every week, and girls between the ages of 8 and 19 saw an average of 46 films a year as they idolized the movie stars. Stars like Gloria Swanson in *Why Change Your Wife* (1920) illustrated just how women could become properly modern, helping to transform social behavior. Many of the films explicitly informed women that they would have to become flappers to win happiness and husbands. Other films, such as *Charge It* (1921), *Gimme* (1923), and *Ladies Must Dress* (1927), not only encouraged women to be flappers, but to increase their consumerism. Sexuality was a favorite theme of the movies, and virtually every female star of the decade played a scene in lingerie. Bebe Daniels wore lingerie in *Stranded in Paris* (1926) and Clara Bow played a salesgirl selling lingerie in *It* (1927). Joan Crawford exuded sexual energy and joie de vivre as she danced the Charleston in *Our Dancing Daughters* (1928). Quite a few films, such as *Bertha the Sewing Machine Girl* (1926), depicted the progress of working women and legitimized their new roles. Films like *Ankles Preferred* (1927) and *Soft Living* (1928), however, showed the boredom and brevity of women's typical jobs.

In movies such as *Gentlemen Prefer Blondes* (1928), *Five and Ten Cent Annie* (1928), and *The Girl in the Glass Cage* (1929), women worked only until they could marry rich men.

The movie theater was not the only place where women enthralled spectators. Able to draw audiences like a movie star, the beautiful Aimee Semple McPherson founded the Angeles Temple in Los Angeles in 1923, and quickly made a fortune with her Four-Square Gospel. The temple held an audience of 5,300 for the Sunday night performances that included a band, choir, and religious extravaganzas. Through her popular radio show, McPherson gained a reputation as a faith healer across the United States. She skillfully used the media to claim a public voice, reflecting the increasing freedoms and influence women experienced in the larger society. McPherson lost most of her influence, however, when it was rumored that she had run off with a lover. McPherson thus represents many of the limits and contradictions experienced by the emancipated woman of the 1920s.

In their lives and work, women novelists and artists also contributed new and sometimes conflicting ideas about women's liberation to the wider culture. In 1921, Edith Wharton became the first woman to win the Pulitzer Prize for a novel with the publication of *The Age of Innocence* (1920). She published more than 40 volumes of writing, including novels, short stories, nonfiction, and poetry, often criticizing the limitations of a strict social code for upper-class women. Zona Gale was the first woman to receive the Pulitzer Prize for drama, also in 1921, for her play, *Miss Lulu Betts* (1920). With a Master of Arts degree from the University of Wisconsin, the prolific Gale set many of her novels, plays, and short stories in Wisconsin and the Midwestern states. The prairie states and the southwest often formed the settings of Willa Cather's stories, and in 1923, she won the Pulitzer Prize for her novel, *One of Ours* (1922). In the novel, a mother is relieved that her son, a soldier during the Great War, died still believing in the glorious cause of war, which he would not have believed had he survived. Cather's novels *One of Ours*, *The Professor's House* (1925) and *Death Comes for the Archbishop* (1927) all exemplify the postwar melancholy that many people of the decade felt. Other writers celebrated the exhilaration and new sexual freedom of the decade. Edna St. Vincent Millay exemplified the thoroughly modern woman in her life and writing. A 1917 graduate of Vassar College, she had already published several collections of poems and an antiwar play when she received the Pulitzer Prize for poetry in 1923 for *The Ballad of the Harp-Weaver, A Few Figs from Thistles,* and eight sonnets published in *American Poetry, 1922, a Miscellany.*

Authors and artists alike reflected excitement, modern ideas, and American dynamism. Georgia O'Keeffe painted cityscapes of New York, abstract landscapes, and gigantic, richly detailed flowers, which some critics saw as sexual allusions, making her the most controversial female artist of the decade. Less famous artists connected with the O'Keeffe circle included Marion Beckett, Katharine Rhoades, and Florine Stettheimer. These artists all challenged the male-dominated field of art, becoming worthy role models for future artists.

African American women artists re-imagined meanings of black womanhood, including black women's sexuality, attempting to influence a broader public with their work. They were part of an effort "toward communal revitalization and self-determination," as well as resistance to white racist stereotypes (Stavney 1998, 533). Most black women writers enjoyed connections with the nation's dynamic center for black culture in the Harlem neighborhood of New York City, and participated in the energetic and creative vitalization of African American artistic and intellectual expression known as the Harlem Renaissance. Nella Larson wrote *Quicksand* (1928) and *Passing* (1929), both exploring the struggles of mixed-race women seeking their place in society. Jessie Redmon Fauset worked as an editor of W.E.B. DuBois's *Crisis,* from 1919 to 1926, continually encouraging the creativity of young black writers. Probably the first black woman to attend Cornell University (Fauset graduated Phi Beta Kappa in 1905), she wrote novels such as *Plum Bun* (1929), about a young woman who abandons her darker sister to pass for white. In 1925, Zora Neale Hurston began her studies in anthropology at Barnard College. She collected valuable black folklore, some of which influenced the novels she would write in the next decade. It would take until the 1960s for the novels of these black women to receive the acclaim they deserved.

The Harlem Renaissance heavily influenced the kind of music people enjoyed during the 1920s. Women performed as musicians, orchestra conductors, and singers at clubs, cabarets, the integrated Savoy Ballroom, or the tremendously popular Cotton Club. Gertrude Pridgett "Ma" Rainey, who introduced "the blues" to the public, and Bessie Smith, who filled her songs with social protest and a "woman's determination to protect herself and her self-respect," expressed the culture of black America through their lyrics (Hine and Thompson 1999, 210). Ethel Waters also sang in clubs in Harlem, and by the end of the decade became a Broadway star with her performance in *Africana* (1927). Appealing to both black and white audiences, blues music is closely related to jazz, another type of music profoundly informed by black culture.

Exciting new music ushered in a new recreational craze—dancing. The shimmy and the toddle were dances left over from the war years, and as the decade progressed new dances included "the collegiate," the Charleston, "the black bottom," and the tango. People would travel 100 miles or more to dance to the music played by bands, and people in remote areas danced to music played on radios and records. Most college social functions included dancing, as did many high-school functions. Older enthusiasts danced at clubs and speakeasies. The craze for dancing continued through the decade, becoming increasingly energetic and stimulating. Women and men loved the sexual and social freedom popular dancing represented.

Women challenged the former limits to their physicality off the dance floor as well. The 1920s marked a period of increasing interest in sports. For example, in 1926, Gertrude Ederle swam the English Channel, breaking the record by two hours. It was just one of 29 world and United States records she broke during the 1920s. Tad (Barbara Inez Barnes) Lucas became a professional cowgirl in 1922, winning major prizes for her trick riding, bronco riding, and relay racing in the U.S. and abroad. Many other young women performed on the rodeo circuit during the decade. Helen Wills Moody was at the top of women's tennis, winning the national singles title six times, the

Josephine Baker

Josephine Baker (1906–1975) was born Freda Josephine McDonald in St. Louis, Missouri. She took the name of her second husband, whom she married in 1921. The 1917 race riot in East St. Louis influenced her lifelong efforts to achieve racial equality. Her career as a performer began in tent shows touring the American southern states, but her big break came when she was hired as a dresser by Noble Sissle and Eubie Blake for their tremendously popular touring show, the musical production of *Shuffle Along*. Although not hired to dance, Baker learned all the songs and dances for the show, and finally appeared onstage when a member of the chorus line got pregnant. Entertaining audiences during 504 performances, including several on Broadway, the show introduced jazz to musical theater. In 1924, Baker appeared in the Broadway musical comedy, *The Chocolate Dandies*. Soon after the show closed, she moved to France to escape the racism she faced in the United States. In Paris, Baker appeared in the all-black show, *La Revue Nègre*, which opened at the Théâtre des Champs Elysées and eventually transferred to Berlin. Everywhere she appeared, her fluid and magnificent dancing captivated audiences. Her notorious banana skirt costume for *La Folie du Jour*, worn while appearing at the Folies Bergère, also created a sensation.

Having established her stage prestige, in 1926 Baker established her social prestige at *Chez Joséphine,* her nightclub in Paris where she sometimes prepared food for her customers. She enjoyed entertaining her international guests with dancing, singing, and jokes. Novelists and poets wrote about her, and intellectuals, sculptors, and painters were all intrigued by her. Innovations she made to her dancing inspired chorographers throughout Europe. Her combination of comedy and eroticism appealed to the broader European public.

Josephine Baker was more than a performer, however, as she was involved in politics and antiracist causes, sometimes at great danger to herself. She joined the French Resistance from the very beginning of the German occupation during the Second World War, and she enthusiastically served as a correspondent for the French military intelligence, writing notes in invisible ink on her sheet music. Although she also raised money for the Resistance and earned the Medal of the Resistance with Rosette for her contributions, she perceived entertaining soldiers as her primary wartime work.

Racism in the United States kept Baker living most of her life in Europe as an American expatriate. Between 1954 and 1965, she and her fourth husband adopted 12 children of various ethnic and religious backgrounds, considering their "Rainbow tribe" to be an experiment in racial harmony (Rose 1989, 231). In 1963, Robert Kennedy helped Baker obtain a visa so she could participate in the March on Washington, the largest civil rights demonstration in U.S. history. Wearing her Women's Auxiliary of the French Air Force uniform and her Medal of the Resistance, she spoke at the rally, sharing the podium with Martin Luther King, Jr.

Josephine Baker symbolizes the powerful limitations of racism in the 20th-century United States, yet she is remarkable for her persistence in rising to international fame and for her visionary view of a world where people of different cultures, religions, and races could live in harmony.

Wimbledon singles three times, the French singles twice, and gold medals for both singles and doubles at the 1924 Paris Olympics.

Zora Neale Hurston, anthropologist, author, and prominent figure of the Harlem Renaissance. (Library of Congress)

Aviation was another popular sport in the 1920s, and many women trained as pilots in the years before men came to dominate aviation. Bessie Coleman had to get her pilot's license at the French *Fédération Aéronautique Internationale* after American schools rejected her. At the time, she was the only licensed African American female pilot in the world, becoming famous for her aerial acrobatics. She refused to perform anywhere that discriminated against blacks. Coleman fell to her death during a practice flight in 1926. Her grieving friends fulfilled her life's dream by founding an aviation school for blacks in Los Angeles. Amelia Earhart may have been the most famous woman aviator of the time, and she began setting world records in 1922. But she was only one of 99 licensed female pilots who met at Curtiss Field, Long Island, New York in November 1929 to found the Ninety-Nines, an organization of female pilots still in existence.

Conclusion

The 1920s represent a period of significant contrasts for women. While they gained the right to vote by federal amendment, their reform efforts were circumscribed by conflicts over the ERA, as well as by a conservative backlash. Although more women sought economic gains through employment, they were often relegated to low-paying jobs and faced criticism for working outside the home. Black women and Mexican American women additionally faced racism, which severely constrained their efforts for gainful employment. A newly ascendant mass and consumer culture promoted women's social and sexual freedom, while reinforcing older double standards for behavior, and rendering women vulnerable to new forms of objectification and exploitation. Thus, many aspects of modern life promised women greater opportunities for equality, autonomy, and freedom than ever before. And yet, the ongoing revolution in women's rights—to which Sara Bard Field referred at the dedication of the monument commemorating the suffrage pioneers—remained far from complete at decade's end, even as the advent of modernity confronted women with a new set of challenges with which to wrestle as the 20th century continued to unfold.

References and Further Reading

Alonso, Harriet Hyman. *Peace as a Women's Issue: A History of the U.S. Movement for World Peace and Women's Rights.* Syracuse, NY: Syracuse University Press, 1993.

Andersen, Kristi. *After Suffrage: Women in Partisan and Electoral Politics before the New Deal.* Chicago: University of Chicago Press, 1996.

Banner, Lois W. *Women in Modern America: A Brief History.* 4th ed. Belmont, CA: Thomson Wadsworth, 2005.

Baritz, Loren, ed. *The Culture of the Twenties.* Indianapolis: Bobbs-Merrill, 1970.

Bernikow, Louise. *The American Women's Almanac: An Inspiring and Irreverent Women's History.* New York: Berkley Books, 1997.

Blee, Kathleen M. *Women of the Klan: Racism and Gender in the 1920s.* Berkeley: University of California Press, 1991.

Breckinridge, Sophonisba P. *Women in the Twentieth Century: A Study of Their Political, Social and Economic Activities.* 1933. Reprint, New York: Arno Press, 1972.

Collins, Gail. *America's Women: 400 Years of Dolls, Drudges, Helpmates, and Heroines.* New York: Harper Collins, 2003.

Comstock, Sarah. "Aimee Semple McPherson: Prima Donna of Revivalism." *Harper's Magazine* (December 1927): 11–19.

Cook, Blanche Wisen, ed. *Crystal Eastman on Women and Revolution.* New York: Oxford University Press, 1978.

Coontz, Stephanie. *Marriage, A History: From Obedience to Intimacy or How Love Conquered Marriage.* New York: Viking, 2005.

Corn, Joseph J. "Making Flying 'Thinkable': Women' Pilots and the Selling of Aviation, 1927–1940." *American Quarterly* 31, no. 4 (Autumn 1979): 556–71.

Cott, Nancy F. *The Grounding of Modern Feminism*. New Haven, CT: Yale University Press, 1987.

Davis, Thadious M. "Larsen, Nella." In *The Oxford Companion to African American Literature,* ed. William L. Andrews, Frances Smith Foster, and Trudier Harris, 427–28. New York: Oxford University Press, 1997.

Drowne, Kathleen Morgan, and Patrick Huber. *The 1920s*. Westport, CT: Greenwood Publishing, 2004.

Dumenil, Lynn. *The Modern Temper: American Culture and Society in the 1920s*. New York: Hill and Wang, 1995.

Evans, Sara M. *Born for Liberty: A History of Women in America*. New York: Simon & Schuster, 1989.

Fass, Paula S. *The Damned and the Beautiful: American Youth in the 1920s*. New York: Oxford University Press, 1977.

Freeman, Jo. *A Room at a Time: How Women Entered Party Politics*. Lanham, MD: Rowman & Littlefield Publishers, 2000.

Goldberg, Ronald Allen. *America in the Twenties*. Syracuse, NY: Syracuse University Press, 2003.

González, Rosalinda M. "Chicanas and Mexican Immigrant Families 1920–1940: Women's Subordination and Family Exploitation." In *Decades of Discontent: The Women's Movement, 1920–1940,* ed. Lois Scharf and Joan M. Jenson, 59–84. Boston: Northeastern University Press, 1987.

Hamm, Richard F. *Shaping the Eighteenth Amendment: Temperance Reform, Legal Culture, and the Polity, 1880–1920*. Chapel Hill: University of North Carolina Press, 1995.

Haney, Lynn. *Naked at the Feast: A Biography of Josephine Baker*. New York: Dodd, Mead & Co., 1981.

Hine, Darlene Clark, and Kathleen Thompson. *A Shining Thread of Hope: The History of Black Women in America*. New York: Broadway Books, 1999.

Hollis, Karyn. "Liberating Voices: Autobiographical Writing at the Bryn Mawr Summer School for Women Workers, 1921–1938." *College Composition and Communication* 45, no. 1 (Feb. 1994): 31–60.

Hummer, Patricia. *The Decade of Elusive Promise: Professional Women in the United States, 1920–1930*. Ann Arbor: UMI Research Press, 1979.

Jacoby, Robin Miller. "The Women's Trade Union League and American Feminism." *Feminist Studies* 3, no. 1/2 (Autumn 1975): 126–40.

Jessup, Josephine Lurie. *The Faith of Our Feminists: A Study in the Novels of Edith Wharton, Ellen Glasgow, Willa Cather*. New York: R. R. Smith, 1950.

Ladd-Taylor, Molly. *Mother-Work: Women, Child Welfare, and the State, 1890–1930*. Urbana: University of Illinois Press, 1994.

Ladd-Taylor, Molly. *Raising a Baby the Government Way: Mothers' Letters to the Children's Bureau, 1915–1932*. New Brunswick: Rutgers University Press, 1986.

Lecompte, Mary Lou. *Cowgirls of the Rodeo: Pioneer Professional Athletes*. Champaign: University of Illinois Press, 1999.

Lemons, J. Stanley. *The Woman Citizen: Social Feminism in the 1920s*. Charlottesville: University Press of Virginia, 1990.

Lerner, Gerda, ed. *Black Women in White America: A Documentary History*. New York: Vintage House, 1973.

Lunardini, Christine A. *From Equal Suffrage to Equal Rights: Alice Paul and the National Woman's Party, 1910–1928*. New York: New York University Press, 1986.

McCallum, Jack, and Richard O'Brien. "An American Original." *Sports Illustrated* 88, no. 1 (Jan. 12, 1998): 32.

McLendon, Jacquelyn Y. "Fauset, Jessie Redmon." In *The Oxford Companion to African American Literature*, ed. William L. Andrews, Frances Smith Foster, and Trudier Harris, 269–70. New York: Oxford University Press, 1997.

Milford, Nancy. *Savage Beauty: The Life of Edna St. Vincent Millay*. New York: Random House, 2001.

Nielson, Kim E. *Un-American Womanhood: Antiradicalism, Antifeminism, and the First Red Scare*. Columbus: Ohio State University Press, 2001.

Peiss, Kathy. *Cheap Amusements: Working Women and Leisure in Turn-of-the-Century New York*. Philadelphia: Temple University Press, 1986.

Perrett, Geoffrey. *America in the Twenties: A History*. New York: Simon and Schuster, 1982.

Rhodes, Chip. *Structures of the Jazz Age: Mass Culture, Progressive Education, and Racial Discourse in American Modernism*. London: Verso, 1998.

Rose, Phyllis. *Jazz Cleopatra: Josephine Baker in Her Time*. New York: Doubleday, 1989.

Ryan, Mary P. "The Projection of a New Womanhood: The Movie Moderns in the 1920s." In *Decades of Discontent: The Women's Movement, 1920–1940*, ed. Lois Scharf and Joan M. Jenson, 113–30. Boston: Northeastern University Press, 1987.

Schneider, Dorothy, and Carl J. *American Women in the Progressive Era, 1900–1920: Change, Challenge and the Struggle for Women's Rights*. New York: Anchor Books, 1993.

Shaw, Arnold. *The Jazz Age: Popular Music in the 1920s*. New York: Oxford University Press, 1987.

Stavney, Anne. "'Mothers of Tomorrow': The New Negro Renaissance and the Politics of Maternal Representation." *African American Review* 32, no. 4 (Winter 1998): 533–61.

Stevens, Doris. *Jailed for Freedom*. New York: Boni & Liveright, 1920.

Terborg-Penn, Rosalyn. *African American Women in the Struggle for the Vote, 1850–1920*. Bloomington: Indiana University Press, 1998.

Van Voris, Jacqueline. *Carrie Chapman Catt: A Public Life*. New York: Feminist Press, 1987.

Wandersee, Winifred D. "The Economics of Middle-Income Family Life: Working Women During the Great Depression." In *Decades of Discontent: The Women's Movement, 1920–1940*, ed. Lois Scharf and Joan M. Jenson, 45–58. Boston: Northeastern University Press, 1987.

Wembridge, Eleanor. "Petting and the College Campus." *Survey* 54 (July 1, 1925): 393–94.

White, Deborah Gray. *Too Heavy a Load: Black Women in Defense of Themselves, 1894–1994*. New York: W. W. Norton & Co., 1999.

Wilson, Jan Dolittle. *The Women's Joint Congressional Committee and the Politics of Maternalism, 1920–1930*. Urbana: University of Illinois Press, 2007.

Women Facing the Emergencies of the Great Depression and World War II: Women's Rights in the 1930s and 1940s

Gillian Nichols-Smith

9

The 1930s and 1940s are often understood as decades in which the women's rights movement was stalled in the wake of the suffrage victory in 1920 and the conservatism of the decade that followed it. However, during these years, women continued to struggle for their rights, and they made significant advances by the use of their leadership and participation in a multitude of social and labor movements. The 1930s and 1940s in the United States were decades of both crisis and national purpose. The Great Depression and World War II formed the historical circumstances under which women would play unprecedented roles in the federal government, steward their families through the challenges of material want, enter the workforce in record numbers, and help the nation win World War II. Even as the exigencies of economic depression and war opened up new opportunities for women in political, economic, and social life, however, the realities of gender and racial discrimination in the workforce, as well as the persistence of assumptions about the primacy of women's domestic roles and responsibilities, constituted formidable barriers to the achievement of gender equality throughout these periods of national emergency and beyond.

1930s—The Great Depression

Women at Work

In 1929, the U.S. stock market crashed and the money of approximately nine million families disappeared as one-fifth of U.S. banks failed. The result was the national economic catastrophe that came to be known as the Great Depression. Businesses and industries shut down, leading to massive unemployment and plummeting wages. Without income, people were unable to pay their mortgages, resulting in widespread foreclosures. Lacking a federal unemployment program, people were struggling for their very survival.

In the early 1930s, at the onset of the Great Depression, it seemed women's gains in the 1920s—especially those having to do with the acceptance of women continuing to work for wages after marriage—would be eroded. Whether in terms of a living wage, the self-respect from an honest day's work, or the sense of social dislocation caused by unemployment, the impact of the economic disaster was largely understood in terms of male loss. Male unemployment at the height of the Depression stood at 30 percent (significantly, female unemployment figures were not tabulated), and as the Depression wore on, with men out pounding the pavement for jobs, the employment of married women struck many as unjust. Men were still viewed as the family breadwinners, and women were accused of stealing jobs from men, despite that fact that numerous women were employed before the Depression. In particular, black women faced a 50 percent unemployment rate in Chicago and a 75 percent unemployment rate in Detroit.

Opinion polls revealed that Americans overwhelmingly opposed married women's employment. George Gallup claimed that he had never seen respondents "so solidly united in opposition as on any subject imaginable including sin and hay fever" (Scharf 1980, 50). It was within this social context that the American Federation of Labor (AFL) passed a resolution stating, "Married women whose husbands have permanent positions should be discriminated against in the hiring of employees" (Schatz 1983, 126). In addition, Congress passed section 213 of the 1932 Economy Act, the married persons clause, which stipulated that whenever personnel reductions were necessary among government employees, married persons were to be the first discharged if their spouses were also federal government employees. The bill was ostensibly gender-neutral, but was intentionally aimed at eliminating married women from government positions. Professional women also suffered. Women's numbers among the ranks of schoolteachers, social workers, lawyers and PhD recipients all declined between 1930 and 1940. Women as a percentage of undergraduates also declined, from 43 percent to 40 percent of enrolled students.

The assault on working wives galvanized women's organizations, which, over the course of the 1920s and early 1930s, had become embroiled in battles among themselves over how best to achieve women's equality. On one side was The National Woman's Party (NWP), which pursued an equalitarian feminism. The NWP agitated for passage of an Equal Rights Amendment (ERA), and sought the same legal and political rights for women that were explicitly guaranteed to men in the Constitution. Other organizations, such as the League of Women Voters (LWV), believed that women workers needed labor legislation to protect them from the extremes of industrial capitalism, particularly laws that would govern women's work hours and safety conditions in mines, laundries, and other dangerous occupations. This kind of social feminism called for special treatment for women, even as it sought equal pay for equal work. However, when national and state governments began to call for discrimination against married working women, virtually all women's groups, including The American Association of University Women (AAUW), the National Federation of Business and Professional Women's Clubs (BPW), and even the American Home Economics Association (AHEA) united on the question of women's right to work. The attack on working wives was seen as an assault on the economic freedom of all women. In May of 1933, representatives of nine women's organizations met with President Roosevelt's budget director, Lewis Douglas, to demand an end to the government dismissals. The NWP warned that the economic crisis was being used to "place a brake on the steady advance in the gainful employment of women" (Scharf 1980, 51). Unfortunately, the meeting did little to alleviate the gender discrimination against married women.

Women also sought to advance their rights as workers by joining labor unions. Between 1930 and 1940, women's union membership increased 300 percent, to approximately eight hundred thousand women. The International Ladies Garment Workers' Union (ILGWU) and the Amalgamated Clothing Workers (ACW) used these new numbers to win better labor protections in the garment industry's codes of fair competition. In 1935, several of the smaller unions within the American Federation of Labor, including the ILGWU, left to form the Congress of Industrial Organizations (CIO), and began unionizing unskilled industrial workers. This, in part, accounted for the significant increase of women workers in unions. Nevertheless, in general, unions' official lines were that women should not be employed outside the home, and most unions prioritized male workers' needs over those of female workers. For example, in addition to the AFL's resolution against married women workers, the United Automobile Workers (UAW) created separate job classifications with lower wages for women. In other unions, such as the Minneapolis Teamsters, women were relegated to subordinate (but essential) support roles during strikes, like nursing the wounded and cooking.

Between 1930 and 1934, the Communist Party of the USA(CPUSA) received approximately sixty thousand membership applications. A great deal of this interest was spurred by massive unemployment demonstrations by the CPUSA in 1929, and by the nothing-left-to-lose mentality of CPUSA strike leaders during the Depression. Under communist leadership, the UAW organized a massive sit-down strike at General Motors in 1937 in Flint, Michigan, in which women participated in nontraditional ways. Genora (Johnson) Dollinger was a union organizer who worked at Briggs Manufacturing Company. Besides simply having women deliver food to male strikers, Dollinger founded the Women's Auxiliary and headed its militant division: the Women's Emergency Brigade. One historian describes how these women bravely supported the strikers: they wore "red armbands and red tams, they marched and sang, broke windows when their men were gassed, and put their bodies in front of threatening police" (Cook 1992, 428). In the 1930s, this emerging militancy rapidly spread among the different union movements. In the CPUSA, some women became influential leaders, including "Mother" Bloor and Elizabeth Gurley Flynn. Nonetheless, problems specific to women were often neglected by the CPUSA, such as childcare, sexual harassment, and wage equality.

Despite the social and political barriers facing them, working women increased their numbers over the course of the 1930s. Women went from 22 percent to 25 percent of the workforce. Meanwhile, the proportion of working, married women grew from 12 to 15 percent, and they increased their share of the female work force from 29 to 35.5 percent. Both married and single women worked out of economic necessity. With wages declining and male unemployment rising, families' survival increasingly depended upon women's paid labor. Nevertheless, sex-segregation of the job market was ongoing, and women were "concentrated in service, clerical, and retail jobs where layoffs were less severe" (Babson 1999, 55).

Women's unpaid economic contributions to the family increased as well. Among the poor and working classes, women's abilities in the home became critical to family survival in ways that were reminiscent of the pre-industrial era: they patched and remade clothes, sewed old sheets together to make new ones, made over children's clothes from adult garments, re-lined coats, planted home gardens, canned vegetables, and made meals out of the slimmest of ingredients. This kind of recycling and home production could mean the difference between barely surviving and total destitution. They also took in boarders and washing, or prepared food and clothing to sell. Extended families moved in together following evictions, pushing housing capacities to their limits. Wives and mothers were expected to be perfect homemakers, and in the face of the extreme economic hardship, they were required to take on ever-more demanding tasks and circumstances to ensure their families' survival.

The financial insecurities of the Great Depression resulted in significantly changing family demographics. Many young couples postponed marriage. Divorce rates declined because it was too expensive to divorce lawfully; instead, men deserted their wives and children at an alarming rate. The birthrate dropped, with only 75.7 of every 1,000 women of childbearing age actually having children, and approximately 25 percent of women in their twenties did not have any children. Meridel LeSueur, an activist and single mother, described women's general attitude during the Great Depression: "I don't want to marry. I don't want any children. So they all say. No children. No marriage. They arm themselves alone, keep up alone" (Evans 1989, 200). In 1936, a federal appeals court overturned the Comstock Act, which classified contraception as obscene, thus prohibiting sending it through the mail, in a case called *United States v. One Package.* Although several state anticontraceptive laws remained valid, birth control was exceedingly common, simply because people did not want to have children they could not afford.

Black women—whether mothers, wives, or singles—suffered some of the worst deprivation and economic distress of any group during the Depression. Historically, black women had been employed outside the home more than white women. As wages and job opportunities withered across the social and economic spectrum, substantial numbers of black women were forced out of higher-paying jobs and into domestic labor. In some cities, black women were reduced to waiting on corners for a day to get a few hours' work, often for 10–15 cents an hour. Many worked only for room and board. In 1935, two black women from the NAACP investigated this phenomenon in New York, dubbing it the "Bronx Slave Market." They learned that lower-middle-class women were hiring cheap domestic help for the first time. From 1930 to 1940, private domestic workers increased by

25 percent. While in 1930 about half of domestic workers were not white, by 1940, almost two-thirds of domestic workers were not white.

From 1930 to 1940, the number of Mexican citizens in the United States was cut in half. In the 1930s, 500,000 Mexican citizens and their U.S. citizen children were deported to Mexico. Many Mexican and Mexican American families were denied emergency aid and had to leave the United States in order to survive. Mexican, Mexican American, and white migrant farm workers were forced into a desperate struggle to earn enough to live on during the Depression. In rural areas, families commonly did not even receive $100 per year in wages. Previously, Mexican American women had not been employed outside the home as often as other women had, but during the 1930s, their employment paradoxically increased. As unemployed fathers and husbands could no longer exert their traditional authority, daughters and wives went to work in New Deal programs and industry jobs.

Women in Politics

Women played a crucial role in designing and enacting the New Deal programs of the 1930s, gaining unprecedented positions in the federal government. In March 1933, President Franklin D. Roosevelt took office, and Eleanor Roosevelt assumed the role of First Lady. While only 12 women served in Congress during the 1930s, women were central to President Roosevelt's New Deal policies, forming a powerful network in the executive branch. This network was composed of 28 social feminists, including Molly Dewson, Frances Perkins, Ellen Sullivan Woodward, and Mary Anderson. Congresswomen Mary T. Norton and Caroline O'Day were also part of the women's network. Black women, with the guidance of Mary McLeod Bethune, also gained unprecedented power during President Roosevelt's presidency.

Eleanor Roosevelt's background prepared her to coordinate revolutionary reforms. She was born into privilege, and when she was young, she volunteered in a settlement house and with the National Consumers' League. In 1905, she married Franklin Roosevelt, and in the ceremony, her uncle, then President Theodore Roosevelt, gave her away. Over the next 10 years, she gave birth to six children (one died as a baby). After her husband's affair with her social secretary, Lucy Mercer, Eleanor stayed married to Franklin, but their relationship was transformed into that of formidable political partners. Eleanor Roosevelt established her own political identity through her work with the League of Women Voters, the Women's Trade Union League, and the peace crusade. In addition, she volunteered in the women's division of the New York Democratic Committee and was otherwise active in the Democratic Party. As First Lady, she held press conferences for only women journalists, and wrote about women's unique challenges in her daily column "My Day," which was syndicated in newspapers nationwide. She was an influential advocate for unemployed women and minorities, motivating thousands of people to write letters to her and the president. In one letter, Mrs. Blanche Crumbly sent in her pay stubs from a textile mill and wrote, "I want to let you see that they didn't pay me enough. I worked eight

Frances Perkins (1880–1965)—U.S. Secretary of Labor

Frances Perkins served as the first women member of the U.S. Cabinet and was the longest-sitting Secretary of Labor in U.S. history, from 1933 to 1945. She was a social worker and a professional political figure in New York before serving in President Franklin D. Roosevelt's administration.

As a young woman, Perkins volunteered in two Chicago settlement houses: Hull House and Chicago Commons. In 1910, she accepted a fellowship to work in Hell's Kitchen in New York while earning a Master of Arts degree from Columbia University. She then joined the Consumers' League, lobbying for workers' rights legislation and investigating the Triangle Shirtwaist Fire in 1911, which killed 146 people. In 1918, Governor Al Smith appointed Perkins to the State Industrial Commission, and she became the chairman in 1926. In 1928, Governor Franklin Roosevelt made her the Industrial Commissioner of New York.

Perkins's social and political past with President Franklin Roosevelt and First Lady Eleanor Roosevelt led her to be named Secretary of Labor in 1933. Perkins advocated for women to be appointed to leadership positions in the new administration. She was also essential to developing New Deal legislation, including the Fair Labor Standards Act and the Social Security Act. The labor movement viewed Perkins as an ally of social reformers, and businesses were hostile to her efforts to improve working conditions. In 1939, she weathered an impeachment attempt. Perkins resigned from the cabinet when President Roosevelt died in 1945, but she served on the Civil Service Commission under President Harry Truman from 1946 to 1953, and lectured at universities after she retired.

hours a day and you will see they have me marked up forty hours a week and didn't pay twelve dollars and by law they were supposed to" (Kessler-Harris 2000, 420). Eleanor Roosevelt was able to use her distinctive position in the White House to represent poor people's needs and to advocate for innovative New Deal legislation. A social-welfare state was established that included the Public Works Administration (PWA), with a $3.3 billion budget for construction projects, and the Civil Works Administration (CWA), which eventually employed over four million people.

Eleanor Roosevelt also built strong ties with labor and civil rights movements. For example, she developed connections with the UAW's founders, the Reuther brothers, following their organization of the massive General Motors sit-down strike. In February 1937, Roy, Walter, and Victor Reuther emerged victorious when General Motors formally recognized the UAW-CIO. Eleanor Roosevelt met with union organizers that month and wrote in her "My Day" column that their demands for a living wage, a 40-hour work week, and adequate termination notice appeared very reasonable. She defended women's right to work, contending that people cannot insist "that married women should stay out of the gainful occupations. The contention that they create unemployment will not hold. It happens that in good times there is work enough for everybody, however large the labor supply, and in times of depression there is idleness, no matter how small the supply" (Cook 1992, 421). In 1938, the First Lady brought the civil rights and labor movements together when she helped form the Southern Conference for Human Welfare with the National Committee for the Defense of Political Prisoners' southern representative, Joseph Gelders, and the CIO's southern field representative, Lucy Randolph Mason. She also invited black leaders to meetings at the White House and championed projects aimed at eradicating black poverty. In addition, she worked with the NAACP to expand the interracial movement against lynching. She lobbied one of the movement's most prominent leaders, Jessie Daniel Ames, to support federal anti-lynching legislation. In these and other acts on behalf of civil and workers' rights, Eleanor Roosevelt transformed the role of First Lady from that of being the country's hostess into an influential platform for social change.

Moreover, Eleanor Roosevelt's connections with the social feminists assisted her in moving numerous other women into leadership roles in the federal government. For instance, Molly W. Dewson served as the Director of the Women's Division of the Democratic National Committee from 1932 to 1934; the Chairman of the Women's Division Advisory Committee from 1934 to 1937; and a Member of the Social Security Board from 1937 to 1938. Her background was grounded in the New York branch of the National Consumers' League, and she met Eleanor Roosevelt when the First Lady was a member of the Women's Division of the New York Democratic Party. Dewson was a successful advocate for the appointment of many women to President Roosevelt's administration, including Frances Perkins. Perkins became the first woman cabinet member when President Roosevelt appointed her Secretary of Labor in 1933. Previously, Perkins had served as the Industrial Commissioner of New York, and she had worked with the Consumers' League. In turn, Perkins was able to bring numerous women into the Labor Department. A former social worker, she played a central role in formulating the majority of the New Deal's social welfare legislation. For example, she chaired the committee that drafted the 1935 Social Security Act, which provided aid to dependent children, as well as federal unemployment and old-age insurance, for the first time. In 1938, the Fair Labor Standards Act was passed, legislating minimum wages and maximum hours for male and female workers, and banning most child labor. Nevertheless, Perkins could not prevent gender discrimination from infiltrating the New Deal. Perkins declared in a paper titled *Resolution on Unemployment and Working Women* that "[t]hey have been thrown out of jobs as married women, refused relief as single women, discriminated against by the N.R.A. [National Recovery Act] and ignored by the C.W.A. [Civil Works Administration]" (Cott 2000, 464).

Another vital member of the network was Ellen Sullivan Woodward, who was active in social and political movements in Mississippi. She became Director of the Women's Division of the Federal Emergency Relief Administration (FERA), from 1933 to 1936; Director of Women's and Professional Projects of the Works Progress Administration (WPA), from 1936 to 1938; and Member of the Social Security Board, from 1938 to 1946. Intended to create jobs, the FERA had a budget of $500 million, and the WPA had an unprecedented budget of $4.88 billion. Woodward used her leadership positions within these powerful agencies to provide jobs for millions of unemployed women. Despite Woodward's efforts, gender discrimination was inherent in most New Deal jobs programs, with men given job preference over women, because men were still seen as the family breadwinners. Women were also limited to jobs with domestic underpinnings like sewing, food preparation, heath care, clerical work, and domestic service. Another major figure was Mary Anderson. A former shoe factory worker and a member of the Chicago branch of the Women's Trade Union League, she served as the Chief of the Women's Bureau in the U.S. Department of Labor from 1920 to 1944.

Mary McLeod Bethune was the Director of the Negro Division of the National Youth Administration (NYA), from 1936 to 1944. President Roosevelt did not have black appointees until 1936, which was two years after Eleanor Roosevelt began speaking out on black rights. Bethune became the leader of these appointees, known as the "Black Cabinet," and a vocal advocate for civil rights. Both as an educator and as an activist, Bethune was a pioneer. She had established and become president of Bethune-Cookman College. She was the president of the National Association of Colored Women and, in 1935, founded the National Council of Negro Women. Bethune felt responsible for promoting the expansion of black women's leadership in government, writing to President Roosevelt that "[i]n the ranks of Negro womanhood in America are to be found ability and capacity for leadership, for administration as well as routine tasks, for the types of service so necessary in a program of national defense" (McCluskey 1999, 174). Bethune succeeded in guaranteeing that the NYA supported black universities and established a scholarship fund for black college students. However, racial discrimination in New Deal policies and programs remained rampant, with white administrators routinely refusing job placement and relief services to poor African Americans. In the 1930s, 90 percent of black women worked in domestic service or agriculture, occupations that were not covered by either Social Security or the minimum wage and maximum-hour protections of the New Deal.

Popular Culture

The movies of the 1930s starred tough, confident characters played by actresses like Greta Garbo, Marlene Dietrich, Joan Crawford, and Bette Davis. These independent women were strong enough to handle the struggles of the Great Depression, but in doing so, they stepped out of women's traditional roles, and were perceived as threatening men's power. As a result, these movies commonly ended in a Taming of the Shrew fashion, with the feisty woman being either verbally or physically abused, or overpowered, by a man. One of the most famous examples is from *Gone with the Wind* (1939), in which the strong-willed Scarlett O'Hara is raped into obedience by Rhett Butler.

During the 1930s, the portrayal of black women in movies was mainly limited to the stereotype of the black mammy. The mammy character was shown as forever "[s]tanding proud, she offers her many services on a tray and is the daily dispenser of nourishment to all who enter her; her body invites invasion and knows no privacy" (Taylor 1989, 168). In *Gone with the Wind*, the fittingly named Mammy, played by Hattie McDaniel, conformed to

Norma Jeane Dougherty was discovered while working in a war production factory. Under the name Marilyn Monroe, she rose to fame as a film star. Her bombshell looks, breathy voice, and personal mystique caused her fame to soar far beyond her talents as an actress, leading her to become the icon of femininity in the postwar period. (The Illustrated London News Picture Library)

the southern romanticized image of a happy slave, and she served the white family with the fussy, energetic pleasure of a busy mother. McDaniel won an Oscar for this role, becoming the first African American to accept an Academy Award. Despite this civil rights victory being diminished by the Mammy stereotype, it still served as an inspiration to all people that racial equality could be reached. In her acceptance speech, McDaniel said, "I sincerely hope I shall always be a credit to my race and to the motion picture industry. My heart is too full to tell you just how I feel. And may I say thank you and God bless you" (Watts 2005, 179).

During the 1930s, women were able to take the desperate times of the Great Depression and forge new ways to ensure their fiscal survival through social and labor movements. Women entered politics, took the reigns of the federal government, and passed some of the most revolutionary social legislation in American history. Yet even as women began to secure government support of their rights, gender and racial stereotypes limited their ability to take advantage of new opportunities. Discrimination stifled women political

Norma Jeane Dougherty/Marilyn Monroe (1926–1962)—War Worker/Movie Star

In 1944, Norma Jeane Dougherty was an 18-year-old war bride living with her in-laws, while her husband Jim Dougherty was a Merchant Marine serving in the Pacific. Norma Jeane was doing her part for the war effort on the home front, working 10 hours a day packing parachutes at the Radioplane Company in Burbank, California. In a letter, Norma Jeane wrote the following to her friend, Grace McKee: "I am saving almost everything I earn (to help pay for our future home after the war). The work isn't easy at all for I am on my feet all day and walking quite a bit" (Yellin 2004, 55). In the fall of 1944, her potential for a more glamorous life was revealed when the Army's First Motion Picture Unit arrived at her war production plant with orders to photograph beautiful women on the assembly line, partly in order to alleviate social gender anxiety by publicizing the femininity of women war workers.

Photographer and army corporal David Conover quickly focused on Norma Jeane (still a brunette at the time), and after the motion picture shooting was completed, he arranged to take some still color photographs of Norma Jeane at the plant. She posed for him several times over the following weeks, and again in the summer of 1945. On June 26, 1945, Norma Jeane appeared on the cover of the Army magazine *Yank*. She signed with a modeling agency (which recommended she dye her hair blonde) and, over the next year, she was on the cover of 33 magazines, including *Laff, Stars and Stripes,* and *Family Circle*. In August 1946, she signed with Twentieth Century Fox, under the name Marilyn Monroe, and began an acting career that would propel her from being an anonymous war worker to being a beloved celebrity renowned for her particularly feminine roles.

leaders' attempts to provide all women and people of color with equal access to government relief and economic opportunity. In sum, women's rights took major steps forward due to the need for drastic changes in response to the Great Depression, but gender discrimination continued to present a formidable challenge throughout the 1930s and into the 1940s.

1940s—World War II

Women at Work

On December 8, 1941, the United States entered World War II. One of the most remarkable aspects of the war effort was the sudden change in governmental and, subsequently, social attitudes towards women's participation in the workforce. As one commentator put it, "the war caused a greater change in women's status and outlook than a prior century of reform and rhetoric had been able to achieve" (Chafe 1991, 121). By 1943, with men away at war, the combination of an almost-full labor force participation on the part of single women and the demands of war production meant that housewives and mothers were now acceptable industrial workers. When World War II ended, the percentage of employed married women had risen from 15 to 25 percent of all married women. For about one-third of employed married women, their wartime job was the first time they had worked outside of the home.

Just as remarkable was the radical shift in beliefs about what jobs women were capable of performing. Prior to the war, women in industrial jobs, by a universal but unspoken rule, were limited to using tools that weighed less than two pounds, and were consigned to the most tedious and repetitive of tasks. Seemingly overnight, women became precision toolmakers in shipyards, maneuvered giant overhead cranes, ran lathes, read blueprints, and became blacksmiths, drill press operators, and welders. These jobs not only provided women with newfound status, they also provided for instant access to upward mobility. In 1942, Kay Wells from Pittsburgh talked about making nuts and bolts for airplanes, saying, "[t]hey started you out at $1.72 per hour. That was a lot of money. So many women were working. We learned how to do a lot of things. People were shocked. The women were not going to sit at home. Our boys were doing a job, and we were going to work" (Yellin 2004, 46). More women were making more money, and they were controlling their money, resulting in groundbreaking economic independence for women war workers.

Black women, for the first time, had widespread opportunities in industry, overcoming employers' discrimination, because all other laborers were already employed or unavailable. From 1940 to 1944, black women's percentage of the factory workforce increased from 6.5 percent to 18 percent. The number of black female farm workers decreased by 50 percent as they migrated to cities to work in war industry. Nevertheless, black women were limited to the lowest-paying and most dangerous industrial jobs. Furthermore, many black women were able to move out of domestic work or farm labor, and into federal agency white-collar jobs, clerical work, and nursing careers. In the apparel industry, black women's employment increased by 350 percent. However, black women faced a double bind of both gender and racial discrimination, which the civil rights and feminist activist Pauli Murray termed "Jane Crow." During the 1940s, black women actively resisted this double discrimination. For instance, in 1942 and 1943, black women joined with the United Automobile Workers in Detroit to demonstrate against Ford Motor Company's racially discriminatory practices.

Women's entry into the war industry was encouraged by a ceaseless propaganda campaign by the government and the media. Radio stations sponsored a "working women win wars week." There were national broadcasts by Commando Mary. "Why do we need women workers?" the broadcast would ask. "Because you can't build ships and planes and guns without them" (Streitmatter 2008, 148). In November 1941, advertising agencies were frustrated by losing accounts due to the drop in consumer goods manufacturing and the absence of any federal assistance to make up for the drop in business. In response, they established the War Advertising Council (WAC). In 1942, President Roosevelt created the Office of War Information (OWI). Both the WAC and the OWI defined their purposes as merely presenting war information to the public, but these organizations were unequivocally influential propaganda machines. In 1943, the OWI's director, Elmer Davis, declared, "The easiest way to inject a propaganda idea into most people's minds is to let it go in through the medium of an entertainment picture when they do not realize that they are being propagandized" (Koppes 1977, 88).

The recruitment of women into industry jobs and military service was a major WAC campaign, and it was carefully managed by the OWI. Perhaps the most famous image from these campaigns was Rosie the Riveter with her "We Can Do It!" caption, originally drawn by Norman Rockwell. Like other propaganda images of working women from World War II, Rosie's picture in magazines (as well as other advertisements featuring women in overalls and lipstick) were meant to not only encourage women to work in industry jobs, but to show that those jobs did not threaten a woman's femininity. The propaganda also stressed that women were only replacing men for the duration of the war, increasingly showing women happy to give up their jobs to returning soldiers. In 1944, the national Women in the War project was launched, an extensive joint endeavor between the WAC, the OWI, and a number of military agencies. This enormous campaign included a saturation of posters, booklets, films, and fiction literature, with the pictures and stories of beautiful, feminine women adeptly handling heavy labor in industrial and military occupations. In addition, the advertisements also emphasized the temporary nature of women working in industrial jobs, and pushed the agenda that once men returned from war, women should happily relinquish their jobs. Magazines constituted a large part of this propaganda, publishing tales of war, work, and inevitable romance in the *Saturday Evening Post* and pulp magazines like *True Story.*

Even as women entered the workforce as full-time laborers, they were expected to maintain their domestic responsibilities with little assistance. This meant that women were expected to spend a full day at work and then come home to cook and clean. Moreover, childcare during the day was a major concern for working mothers. The Lanham Act was passed by Congress in 1942, and over three years, $51.9 million was spent on 3,102 childcare centers serving 600,000 children. However, the need drastically outweighed federal funding, and only 10 percent of working mothers ever used the centers. Many women relied on family, friends, and limited corporate childcare centers. In 1943, *Fortune* magazine pointed out how women were overwhelmed with responsibilities, writing, "The problems do not stop with child care. A working mother still has marketing, cooking, laundering, and cleaning to attend to. These stretch her working day another four to six hours. Unless she receives concessions, not normally given, it is questionable how long she can stand up under a twelve- or fourteen-hour day" (Yellin 2004, 59–61). These women were overburdened, as society demanded that they fulfill both the role of full-time breadwinner and that of homemaker with limited outside aid.

During the war, however, industry itself changed in response to women's arrival on the shop floor. Management took the opportunity to practice what is called job dilution or de-skilling, the introduction of mechanization that requires workers to do lighter tasks more often, rather than several tasks that require more movement. A manager at Vultee Aircraft described the gendered justifications used by the company: "[i]t definitely was in Vultee's favor that the hiring of women was started when production jobs were being simplified to meet the needs of fast, quantity production . . . Special jigs were

"We Can Do It," a poster by J. Howard Miller, is the quintessential image of the female defense worker during World War II. The image of the factory woman, depicted in many ways and popularized as "Rosie the Riveter," became a national symbol of American unity and patriotism. At once feminine and strong, "Rosie" was expected to make a contribution to the war effort without fundamentally challenging conventional gender roles. (National Archives)

added to hold small tools, such as drills, so that women could concentrate on employing more effectively their proven capacity for repetitive operations requiring high digital dexterity" (Milkman 1987, 60). Management had wanted to introduce many of these changes for a long time, but had hesitated because of fears of union resistance. In part because of the de-skilling of jobs and in part because women worked for less money than men did, unions responded to the introduction of women into the workforce with hostility.

Despite union hostility towards women, women's participation in unions increased as female employment increased and women demanded the same protections from labor organizations as men. From 1940 to 1944, women's percentage of union participation increased from 9.4 percent to 21.8 percent, about 3 to 3.5 million women members out of 15 million total union memberships. The CIO had always admitted women workers and, as women's employment increased, so did their union membership. The AFL once again united with the woman-dominated ILGWU, adjusted its policies in the 1940s, and admitted more women. Unions like the UAW and the United Electrical, Radio, and Machine Workers of America (UE) began to stand up for female workers in order to protect wages for male workers, who were viewed as eventually returning to those jobs. As a consequence, these unions were able to successfully defend against wage reductions and achieve equal pay for women workers who were working in formerly male-only occupations. Unions became even more disposed to admit and support women members when the War Labor Board ruled that women workers must be paid the same as men workers.

Women on the Home Front

In addition to going out to work in war industries, women served in other ways on the home front. Many women volunteered towards the war effort, working for organizations like the Red Cross. The marriage rate jumped as young couples rushed to take their vows before war separated them. Close to two million weddings took place in 1942 alone. These brides joined other war wives and mothers forced to take care of their families without their spouses, in increasingly difficult times. Women faced government rationing of sugar, coffee, and red meat, as well as shortages of butter, milk, and eggs. Many women grew Victory Gardens, and learned canning to make up for the lack of fruits and vegetables. In 1944, a pregnant newlywed named Rose Truckey described how women learned to rely on each other and themselves, to get through the shortages. She explained, "You could always make sure that somebody would be there if you needed them because you couldn't depend on a man, there weren't any around. So it was really what we could do for ourselves" (Yellin 2004, 20). Women were gaining new independence and confidence by taking on these staggering responsibilities, even as they endured insecurity and loneliness.

Women also provided emotional support by writing letters to their sons, brothers, boyfriends, fiancés, and husbands serving abroad. Through their writings, women sought to encourage their loved ones, send stories to remind them of home, and share their heartache. The government encouraged women to keep their letters to military personnel positive, but amid such adversity, it was nearly impossible for life's realities not to enter women's correspondence. In October 1944, Natalie Mirenda wrote to her husband Frank Maddalena, who was killed in action a month later, saying, "I see you everywhere—in the chair, behind me, in the shadows of the rooms. Everyplace I go you are always with me in the back of my mind. I seem to have a continuous headache because I'm so worried about you" (Yellin 2004, 33). The letters women received from their men were assurances that they were still alive. Following the Japanese bombing of Pearl Harbor in 1942, Alice Woods received (almost a month later) her first piece of mail from her brother-in-law, Ray Woods, who was wounded in the attack. She wrote back, "I couldn't put down on paper how we felt when we received your letter (Dec. 29th). To say we were elated is putting it mild. It just seemed like a black cloud was suddenly lifted. Like hearing from someone we thought (and prayed not) didn't exist anymore" (Litoff 1991, 7). Overall, the mail served as the principal means for men and women to stay connected and share their hardship during World War II.

Women in the Military

Approximately 350,000 women served in the U.S. military during World War II. Many women served and experienced combat overseas as members of the Army Nurse Corps (ANC) and the Navy Nurse Corps (NNC). In addition, there were women's branches, in which 140,000 women served in the Army (WACs), 100,000 in the Navy (WAVES), 13,000 in the Coast Guard (SPARS), and 23,000 in the Marines (MCWR). The 1,000 women who served as Women's Airforce Service Pilots (WASP) had civilian status during the war and were granted veteran status in 1977. A book published in 1943, titled *The WAVES: The Story of the Girls in Blue,* stated the following:

> A few months ago the very word WAVES was a kind of joke, and the thought of women in uniform was barely acceptable to the so-called protective male animal. But the organization is functioning now, developing surely and fast, and wiping out laughter about itself as it goes. (Treadwell 1954, 22)

Many women joined the military for the same the reasons that men did: to overcome the limitations of their civilian lives, serve their country, and see the world. However, they were denied full military status, including not having authorization to carry weapons. Navy personnel were limited to shore duty, and members of the WASP were restricted to American airspace. In addition, women in the military faced vicious rumors of widespread promiscuity and venereal disease, rumors that essentially accused them of having no other purpose than to sexually service male personnel. Despite these obstacles, women served bravely in North Africa, Europe, and the Pacific.

As in the industrial workforce, black women also faced harsh discrimination in the military during World War II, but in 1941, 56 black female nurses were permitted to join the ANC. These nurses were only allowed to treat black patients and prisoners of war, but by 1945, the ANC included around 500 black women, due to the advocacy of civil rights groups. Despite these advances in the Army, only four black women served in the Navy Nurse Corps during World War II.

Women of Japanese Descent

In February 1942, President Franklin D. Roosevelt issued Executive Order 9066, commanding the internment of 120,000 Japanese American people living in the western United States at 10 relocation camps. Fifty thousand were Japanese American women. Forty percent were Issei, or people born in Japan and denied U.S. citizenship, and the remaining 60 percent were Nisei, or citizens born in the United States. Upon relocation, Japanese Americans were allowed to take only what they could carry and, consequently, they had to sell real and physical properties at a drastic loss. Akiko Mabuchi Toba was 19 when she and her family were relocated. She described the trip to the relocation camp as follows:

> [t]he train was one of those rickety old trains, a real antique. It was awful. It hardly moved and it was hot. And then they made us keep the shades down.

A World War II poster invites women to join the WAVES, the first female division of the U.S. Navy. Women Accepted for Volunteer Emergency Service was established through Eleanor Roosevelt's lobbying of Congress in August 1942. (Library of Congress)

I don't know why. Maybe they didn't want us to see anything. We were told we were going to Topaz, Utah. We heard it was in the middle of the desert. But you don't really realize how bad it is until you get there. (Yellin 2004, 269)

When they got to the relocation camps, many Japanese Americans encountered 20-by-25-foot rooms in which eight people would sleep, and communal bathrooms shared by 250 people, all surrounded by barbed-wire fences and armed guards. Even though Japanese American women had higher employment rates than white women, both men and women experienced the disconcerting deterioration of traditional gender roles, as men no longer worked to support their families, and women struggled to care for their families with minimal resources. For almost three years, until the end of World War II, Japanese Americans remained imprisoned in these miserable conditions.

After the War—Reconversion

On August 14, 1945, Japan surrendered, World War II ended, and the reconversion began. The reconversion consisted of U.S. government propaganda and measures aimed at persuading and coercing women to leave their wage-paying jobs and return to the domestic sphere. On April 18 and 19 of 1945, the Women's Bureau of the UAW convened a conference, during which women delegates reported their overwhelming desire to continue working in their wartime jobs. One union survey of shipyard employees revealed that 98 percent of women wanted to keep their jobs, and another survey of New York factory employees found that 82 percent of women wanted to keep their jobs. In 1945, Ottilie Juliet Gattuso wrote to President Harry Truman after she was fired, stating, "I happen to be a widow with a mother and son to support . . . I would like to know why after serving a company in good faith for almost three and a half years, it is now impossible to obtain employment with them. I am a lathe hand and was classified as skilled labor, but simply because I happen to be a woman I am not wanted" (Yellin 2004, 68). Despite their resistance, women were fired from these well paying jobs as factories closed and industries moved from manufacturing war materials to consumer goods. The amount of women working in the Detroit automobile industry decreased from 25 percent to 7.5 percent. Millions of women left their jobs, many turning to unpaid labor in the home. Yet, in 1946, 75 percent of women who worked during the war were employed in some fashion, and 45 percent of those women still had their wartime jobs. However, nearly 9 out of 10 had experienced a wage decrease. The remaining 55 percent of those women had to seek employment in lower-paying, female-dominated industries like hat making and clerical work.

Women took to the picket lines to protest, but usually did so without the backing of unions. However, Mildred Jeffrey and Lillian Hatcher were in charge of the Women's Bureau of the United Automobile Workers and, under their interracial leadership, the UAW became an influential postwar advocate for women. As members of the Council of Women Delegates at a UAW convention in 1946, Jeffrey and Hatcher raised the pressing issue of the classification of jobs as either male or female, which consistently resulted in lower pay and separate seniority lists for women. Consequently, the Women's Bureau was allied with the UAW's Fair Practices and Anti-Discrimination Department, and women in the UAW suddenly possessed a powerful platform from which they could coordinate a labor movement focused on women's rights.

Conclusion

During the 1930s and 1940s, women's roles radically changed, even as old expectations about women's place in society persisted. For example, concerning employment, women both had lost jobs and had worked for wages for the first time during the Great Depression of the 1930s. Many women gained higher paying wartime jobs in the early 1940s, but then a lot of these women lost the status of those higher-paying industrial jobs during the postwar reconversion. By the end of these two decades, women had experienced a certain degree of equality in politics, the workforce, and the military. Moreover, social and labor movements underwent vital transformations in the 1930s and 1940s that would have a notable impact as those movements continued to evolve in the 1950s. Women were not going to give up their new rights and freedoms without a fight.

References and Further Reading

Anderson, Karen Tucker. "Last Hired, First Fired: The Black Woman Workers during World War II." *Journal of American History* 69 (June 1982): 82–97.

Babson, Steve. *The Unfinished Struggle: Turning Points in American Labor, 1877–Present.* Lanham, MD: Rowman & Littlefield Publishers, 1999.

Chafe, William H. *The Paradox of Change: American Women in the 20th Century.* New York: Oxford University Press, 1991.

Churchwell, Sarah Bartlett. *The Many Lives of Marilyn Monroe.* New York: Metropolitan Books, 2004.

Cook, Blanche Wiesen. *Eleanor Roosevelt, Volume 1: 1884–1933.* New York: Penguin Books, 1992.

Cott, Nancy F. *The Grounding of Modern Feminism.* New Haven, CT: Yale University Press, 1987.

Cott, Nancy F., ed. *No Small Courage: A History of Women in the United States.* New York: Oxford University Press, 2000.

Evans, Sara M. *Born for Liberty: A History of Women in America.* New York: The Free Press, 1989.

Hartmann, Susan M. *The Home Front and Beyond: American Women in the 1940s.* Boston: Twayne Publishers, 1982.

Honey, Maureen. *Creating Rosie the Riveter: Class, Gender, and Propaganda during World War II.* Amherst: The University of Massachusetts Press, 1984.

Hooks, Janet M. *Women's Occupations through Seven Decades.* Women's Bureau Bulletin, No. 218. Washington, DC: U.S. Government Printing Office, 1947.

Jones, Jacqueline. *Labor of Love, Labor of Sorrow: Black Women, Work, and the Family from Slavery to the Present.* New York: Basic Books, 1985.

Kessler-Harris, Alice. *Out to Work.* New York: Oxford University Press, 1982.

Kessler-Harris, Alice. "Providers: Gender Ideology in the 1930s." In *Women's America: Refocusing the Past,* ed. Linda K. Kerber and Jane Sherron De Hart, 418–26. New York: Oxford University Press, 2000.

Koppes, Clayton R., and Gregory D. Black. "What to Show the World: The Office of War Information and Hollywood, 1942–1945." *The Journal of American History* 64 (June 1977): 87–105.

Litoff, Judy Barrett, and David C. Smith, eds. *Since You Went Away: World War II Letters from American Women on the Home Front.* Lawrence: University Press of Kansas, 1991.

McCluskey, Audrey Thomas, and Elaine M. Smith, eds. *Marcy McLeod Bethune: Building a Better World, Essays and Documents.* Bloomington: Indiana University Press, 1999.

Milkman, Ruth. *Gender at Work: The Dynamics of Job Segregation by Sex during World War II.* Urbana: University of Illinois Press, 1987.

Milkman, Ruth. "Organizing the Sexual Division of Labor: Historical Perspectives on 'Women's Work' and the American Labor Movement." *Socialist Review* 49 (January–February 1980): 128–33.

Orleck, Annelise. *Common Sense and a Little Fire: Women and Working-Class Politics in the United States, 1900–1965.* Chapel Hill: University of North Carolina Press, 1995.

Pasachoff, Naomi E. *Frances Perkins: Champion of the New Deal.* New York: Oxford University Press, 2000.

Scharf, Lois. *To Work and to Wed: Female Employment, Feminism, and the Great Depression.* Westport, CT: Greenwood, 1980.

Schatz, Ronald W. *The Electrical Workers: A History of Labor at General Electric and Westinghouse 1923–60.* Urbana: University of Illinois Press, 1983.

Straub, Eleanor Ferguson. "United States Government Policy towards Civilian Women during World War II." *Prologue* 4 (Winter 1973): 240–54.

Streitmatter, Rodger. *Mightier than the Sword: How the News Media Have Shaped American History.* Boulder, CO: Westview Press, 2008.

Taylor, Helen. *Scarlett's Women: Gone with the Wind and its Female Fans.* New Brunswick, NJ: Rutgers University Press, 1989.

Treadwell, Mattie E. *United States Army in World War II, Special Studies: The Women's Army Corps.* Washington, DC: U.S. Government Printing Office, 1954.

Ware, Susan. *Beyond Suffrage: Women in the New Deal.* Cambridge, MA: Harvard University Press, 1981.

Watts, Jill. *Hattie McDaniel: Black Ambition, White Hollywood.* New York: HarperCollins Publishers, 2005.

Women Union Leaders Speak. U.S. Women's Bureau Union Conference, April 18–19, 1945. Washington, DC: U.S. Department of Labor, 1945.

Yellin, Emily. *Our Mothers' War: American Women at Home and at the Front during World War II.* New York: Free Press, 2004.

Homemakers and Activists in the 1950s

10

Kathleen A. Laughlin

An estimated twelve million women were members of gender-segregated social, religious, or civic associations after World War II. Modest and uncontroversial projects, the promise of self-improvement, and the availability of friendship networks drew women into voluntary associations in unprecedented numbers, transforming the elite study clubs of the turn of the century into a movement for civic engagement. The large number of disparate, active women's clubs in the 1950s reflected an affiliation mania among women who embraced domesticity but also believed in responsible citizenship. Unions, civil rights organizations, and political parties provided other pathways to women who had multiple allegiances and identities. Through various organizational affiliations, women were able to develop important leadership skills and achieve some measure of political agency during a decade characterized as repressive and reactionary.

But this engagement was paradoxical: while these women did not live in quiet desperation in the suburbs, they were unable to transform mainstream politics or challenge gender norms in the 1950s. Organized women failed to shape public policy on the federal level, and remained on the margins of mainstream politics in the 1950s—a stasis that reflected not only the political conservatism and the power of social custom in postwar America, but also the fractures among national women's organizations divided by class, race, religion, and ideology. But women did not retreat from public life either, for World War II altered the missions and programs of organizations. In postwar America, a critical mass of housewives and working women maintained the high levels of civic engagement and voluntary services demanded during wartime, engaging in multifaceted forms of political activism without courting opprobrium for upending traditional gender roles. They did not completely foreswear individual achievement, nor did they question female difference or repudiate domesticity. They were housewives *and* activists.

Return to Domesticity

Several social, economic, and political changes in the postwar world contrived and reinforced women's domestic roles during the 1950s. The 1950s encompassed both anxiety of the atomic age and the exuberance of a booming consumer economy; these two seemingly contradictory impulses endowed a powerful ideology that celebrated the American way of life. Fear of communism and the potential for atomic warfare increased feelings of vulnerability in postwar America. World War II taught Americans that the days of isolation from the rest of the world were at an end. The burden of maintaining American values in an unstable world fell on women, who were practically compelled to make full-time and unwavering commitments to domestic life. In this age of anxiety, women's role as "moral force" within the family was elevated and politicized by experts, politicians, and in the popular media (Kaledin 1984, preface). Public opinion was generally unsympathetic toward any expansion of women's role; pundits and experts not only discouraged women from entering public life, but also often condemned expressions of personal ambition. Many social scientists lent scientific credence to the domestic ideal. Prescriptive literature at its most extreme warned of the dangers to the future of the nation if women assumed traditional male roles. The implications of the domestic ideology were explored by Betty Friedan in her best-selling book, *The Feminine Mystique,* published in 1963. Friedan's content analysis of popular media and her survey of the attitudes and life choices of her graduating class at Smith College supported an assessment of middle-class white women as being no more than victims of prescriptive literature and diminishing economic and educational opportunities.

The Baby Boom and the emergent suburban lifestyle transformed the domestic ideal into reality for a significant percentage of white women. These women chose family life during this period, either by freely abandoning employment, or in response to limited opportunities for job and career advancement, after government policies and employer and labor union practices effectively restored the rigidly sex-segregated labor market. Whatever the reason for a retreat to domestic life, women married at younger ages and had more children. The median age for marriage for women was 20. The fertility rate increased significantly to 122.9 per 1,000 women, up from 79.9 in 1940. The rapid expansion of the suburbs to accommodate commitments to the nuclear family placed insular domesticity at the forefront of American life. Federal policies contributed to this change by placing the suburban lifestyle within reach for millions of Americans. The Servicemen's Readjustment Act of 1944, popularly known as the GI Bill of Rights, mandated low-interest mortgages, and financed the educational pursuits of returning veterans. Federally subsidized road building projects, including an interstate highway system completed during the Eisenhower administration, stimulated building outside of urban centers. In the 1950s, suburbs grew by 45 percent, while the population of cities remained static. Suburban homes were locations for nuclear family units, breaking the bonds of extended families and community networks of urban life. This transformation further segmented the U.S. population by race and class; white men benefited from the GI Bill of Rights while men of color encountered barriers to economic and educational advancement.

Paid Employment and Voluntarism

Revised histories of the 1950s have suggested that women had social, political, and economic agency, despite the potency of the domestic ideal. Women's lives were far more complicated and not nearly as bleakly isolating as Betty Friedan suggested in her feminist polemic. Public opinion influenced the worldview of middle-class Americans during the 1950s, but women asserted themselves in marriage, and relationships between husbands and wives were characterized by a "contested egalitarianism" rather than a passive acquiescence to traditional gender roles (Weiss 2000, 16). Relationships within the family were fluid rather than static. Nor was the media monolithic; popular magazines legitimized the domestic ideal but also publicized and celebrated women's individuality. Women readers were not necessarily discouraged from pursuing wage work or entering politics.

Labor shortages in a rapidly expanding consumer economy eased barriers to married women's employment. Married women with children pursued paid work in the 1950s to supplement family incomes because additional wages were needed to maintain middle-class status, albeit in acceptable sex-typed jobs in the service and clerical sectors. African American women were able to take advantage of changes in the labor market. In the North, black women in greater numbers left low-paid agricultural and domestic-service jobs for higher paid clerical and factory jobs. Women who remained in college pursued traditional female fields as social workers, librarians, and teachers. Ironically, government policies also facilitated the movement of women into the labor market, but without challenging sex roles. The National Manpower Commission at Columbia University legitimized women's wage work as essential to continued economic growth in *Womanpower,* published in 1957. The Women's Bureau of the U.S. Department of Labor relied on *Womanpower* and internal studies documenting women's need and desire to work to promote policies to encourage women to enter the labor force. In collaboration with the National Federation of Business and Professional Women's Clubs (BPW), Women's Bureau director Alice Leopold created Earning Opportunity Forums to train women how to seek employment and introduce them to employers. By the early 1960s, 41 percent of women between the ages of 25 and 44 were in the labor force.

Upper- and middle-class women who did not seek paid employment also wanted to combine family life with meaningful contributions to society. Nationalistic collective identity, so powerful during World War II, continued in the 1950s, as containment of communism required a recommitment to civic duty. Women's clubs, inclined to work on inconsequential study programs focusing on art and literature or charitable projects prior to World War II, intensified efforts to encourage members to become active, alert citizens during the 1950s. These efforts were punctuated with pleas from national officers to the rank and file to combine study with action. Discouraged from entering mainstream party politics by the antifeminist machinery of the 1950s, women embraced voluntary associations as locations for exercises in citizenship, especially in communities where the emphasis was on providing services. *The Ladies' Home Journal* and other publications publicized club activities and encouraged women to engage in nonpartisan community betterment projects.

Federal civil defense agencies charged to prepare citizens for home defense in the atomic age also legitimized women's civic engagement. The newly established Federal Civil Defense Administration (FCDA) relied on public action to implement procedures and policies. Home defense initiatives presented women with another rationale for active civic engagement. Katherine Howard, President Dwight D. Eisenhower's director of women's affairs and advisor to the FCDA, was a leading advocate for a partnership between government and women's organizations. Meetings, conferences, and training sessions organized by civil defense advisors and government agencies in Washington, D.C. legitimized the programs of hundreds of women's organizations.

Although most national women's organizations maintained longstanding commitments to nonpartisanship throughout the 1950s, the politicalization and militarization of domestic life in the Cold War era placed politics at the forefront of programs and activities. After World War II, many national organizations became complex, bureaucratic political groups, subsidized through the membership dues of the millions of women seeking some form of involvement outside of the home. Organizational innovations to accommodate growing memberships stimulated political activism on all levels of government. The League of Women Voters reorganized from a loose collection of state associations into a powerful national body that instigated community activism. The National Council of Jewish Women (NCJW) and the BPW hired professional lobbyists to work in Washington, D.C. Professional staff, through publications, workshops, and institutes, provided training in active citizenship. Although critics of women's organizations found this emphasis on study and training frivolous, clubwomen took their responsibilities seriously. A renewed commitment to mainstream politics after the dislocation of the Great Depression and World War II revitalized the dormant Women's Joint Congressional Committee (WJCC), a coalition group formed in 1920 to organize newly enfranchised women into a potent voting bloc. During the late 1940s and throughout the 1950s, the WJCC advocated legislation that furthered women's interests as a group.

The importance of the United Nations in contributing to increasing political awareness among women during this period cannot be underestimated. Eleanor Roosevelt's emergence as a spokesperson and leader for the UN inspired women to become thoroughly informed about international relations. New international bodies and alliances offered women a foothold in public discourses about world affairs. After losing her appointment as U.S. ambassador to the United Nations with the election of Republican Dwight D. Eisenhower as President, Roosevelt created a grassroots campaign of support for the UN. Groups as disparate as the Women's International League for Peace and Freedom and the Republican-dominated BPW joined together to actively promote the policies of the United Nations and lobby for federal legislation to facilitate world understanding and free trade. International branches of national women's organizations also facilitated collaboration abroad. At the same time, isolationist mothers' groups formed in the 1930s opposed the United Nations. However, the extremist mothers' movement, with its combination of anti-Semitism and anticommunism, found few adherents. Former isolationist activists sought an institutional home within more mainstream Republican women's clubs.

Women engaged in autonomous political activism that combined an awareness of international events with action at home. The desire of suburban whites to construct homogenous enclaves elevated the importance of local governments and local issues. Local governments erected zoning laws and provided desperately needed educational, recreational, and municipal services. Community betterment efforts drew women into politics in significant numbers. Civic engagement to improve services, for families and children in particular, enabled women to enter public life without explicitly challenging the domestic ideal. At the same time, both women and men residing in the suburbs expected national, state, and local governments to be responsive to their concerns as citizens, homeowners, and parents. This well-developed sense of rights and responsibilities in postwar America led to an unprecedented commitment to civic and national life.

Female leaders in the Democratic and Republican parties sought to redirect womanpower into party work in the suburbs. Even though women made few inroads in mainstream politics in the 1950s and were denied leadership positions within both parties, activists continued to engage in partisan politics, marshalling an effective grassroots volunteer effort. A loose coalition of Republican women's clubs organized under the auspices of the Republican National Committee orchestrated structural changes in the postwar years that paralleled the organizational adjustments of the League of Women Voters. In 1950, the National Federation of Republican Women became an autonomous national organization endeavoring to organize housewives into a political force to be reckoned with by the Republican leadership. Unconvinced that the League of Women Voters, the Women's Joint Congressional Committee, and other national women's organizations were truly nonpartisan, Betty Farrington, president of the National Federation of Republican Women, attempted to introduce the Republican Party agenda to millions of organized women she believed were covertly aligned with the Democratic Party.

Even though the Democratic National Committee (DNC) disbanded its Women's Division in 1953, female leaders remained party loyalists committed to addressing the ascendancy of the Republican Party with the election of Dwight D. Eisenhower in 1952. Democratic women hoped to disprove the perception that women were responsible for Eisenhower's election, but, like women in the Republican Party, they organized outside of the party apparatus by working with Democratic women's auxiliaries and clubs. Under the leadership of Katie Lochheim, head of the Office of Women's Activities, a poor substitute for the Women's Division, women became central to local organizing. Women's role in partisan politics during the 1950s was largely

Kathryn (Kay) Frederick Clarenbach (1920–1994)

With a graduate degree in political science from the University of Wisconsin, Kathryn Frederick took advantage of the employment opportunities for women during World War II, and moved to Washington, D.C. to work as an analyst with the War Production Board. After the war, she returned to the University of Wisconsin to pursue a PhD, which she completed in 1946. She married Henry G. Clarenbach, and like many white, middle-class women in the 1950s, she left the labor market to raise children but remained involved in public life as a volunteer. While caring for her three children, Clarenbach joined the League of Women Voters and ascended to the state board of the Missouri League of Women Voters in the mid-1950s. Clarenbach reentered the labor market in 1962, becoming a pioneer in continuing education for women at the University of Wisconsin. Her efforts on behalf of women in Wisconsin led to her appointment as chair of the Wisconsin Commission on the Status of Women, a post she held from 1964 to 1969 and from 1971 to 1979.

At a national conference for state commissions on the status of women convened by the Women's Bureau, U.S. Department of Labor, in 1966, Clarenbach met women's rights activists who were impatient with the federal government's reluctance to enforce the prohibition against sex discrimination stipulated by the 1964 Civil Rights Act. A small group of conference attendees discussed plans to establish a national organization to pursue civil rights for women, which became the National Organization for Women (NOW). Clarenbach's involvement with NOW propelled her into feminist activism. She served as the first president of the National Association of Commissions of Women in 1970, and in 1971 chaired the organizing conference for the Women's Political Caucus. In 1977, she became the Executive Director of the National Commission on the Observance of International Women's Year. She remained a passionate and committed feminist until her death in 1994 at the age of 73. Her career represents a political life cycle that began with volunteer work in the 1950s.

confined to traditional voluntarism—registering voters, raising funds, distributing information and staffing offices.

Women in the Labor Movement and the Civil Rights Movement

The labor movement became influential and politically powerful even during the conservative period of the 1950s, especially within the Democratic Party. In 1955, the newly merged American Federation of Labor and the Congress of Industrial Organizations (AFL-CIO) represented 18 million workers, composing 35 percent of the nonagricultural workforce. Collective bargaining agreements expanded health and welfare benefits and raised wages, propelling blue collar, unskilled workers into the ranks of the middle class. Labor leaders abandoned militant postures characteristic of the 1930s

Rosa Parks is fingerprinted in Montgomery, Alabama. Parks's arrest for refusing to give up her seat on a bus to a white man on December 1, 1955, inspired the Montgomery Bus Boycott, a prolonged action against the segregated Montgomery, Alabama, bus system by African American riders and their white supporters. (Library of Congress)

and embraced mainstream politics as another means to represent workers. The importance of legislation in determining the future of the labor movement became dramatically apparent with the passage of anti-union legislation, the Taft-Harley Act (1947), and the Landrum-Griffin Act (1959). In the 1950s, labor unions became a location for the development of activist political agendas.

In much the same way as voluntary associations, unions offered women a means to enter public life where few opportunities existed. After World War II, the United Auto Workers' (UAW) acquiesced to the demands of its female members and created a women's bureau, which became a department within the union in 1955. The UAW Women's Department supported a cadre of feminist activists who used similar strategies as women's clubs to encourage the rank and file to become involved in union affairs. National conferences, training institutes, and publications solidified women's presence within the labor movement. Other unions followed suit. The United Packing House Workers Union created an Anti-Discrimination Department in 1949. Women comprised 35 percent of the membership in the International Union of Electrical Workers (IUE), a presence that gave them political clout within the union. Union organizing also occurred in the female-dominated labor market.

Dorothy I. Height (1912–)

Dorothy Height joined the Young Women's Christian Association (YWCA) while a teenager in Pennsylvania, an involvement that began a lifetime of organizational and political work on behalf of the oppressed and disenfranchised. During the Great Depression, she accepted a position with the YWCA and continued to work for the organization in various positions with increasing responsibility until the 1970s. In the post–World War II years, Height became one of the architects of the YWCA's commitment to racial equality. She directed the YWCA's Department of Racial Justice during the civil rights era. While working for the YWCA, Height became involved in the National Council of Negro Women (NCNW), founded by Mary Mc-Leod Bethune in 1935. In 1957, she became president of the NCNW and brought her substantial organizational skills to bear on a moribund organization. Under Height's leadership, the NCNW engaged in civil rights and women's rights activism, and joined other women's organizations in a coalition for progressive social change.

Telephone operators, waitresses, teachers, and flight attendants considered the advantages of collective bargaining agreements. In addition, union auxiliaries, established in the 1930s to support striking workers, became powerful federations, an expansion of power and influence that mirrored changes in the women's club movement. Women's federations, like women's clubs, elected officers and held conferences.

This activist cohort within the AFL-CIO promoted a legislative program to combat sex discrimination and extend benefits that would make it possible for women to remain in the labor market. These "labor feminists" sought to achieve "full industrial citizenship," through provisions such as amendments to the federal tax code, to allow tax deductions for childcare and household help, and equal pay for equal work legislation (Cobble 2004, 4). A loose coalition of women's organizations, trade unions, and the Women's Bureau of the U.S. Department of Labor promoted the gender justice issue of the 1950s—equal pay for equal work. African American union leaders worked for both racial and gender equity. Addie Wyatt (United Packing House Workers of America), Gloria Johnson (IUE), and Lillian Hatcher (UAW) actively participated in coalition politics with women's organizations.

In the 1950s, African American women provided organizational support and leadership within the emerging civil rights movement. Rising expectations of real social change after World War II shaped the agendas of women's groups and civil rights organizations. The potential for meaningful change in the area of civil rights after World War II led to the creation of interracial coalition groups to lobby Congress for a permanent commitment to the fair-employment practices embodied in temporary wartime measures. The landmark Supreme Court ruling in 1954 invalidating the separate but equal doctrine in education, *Brown v. Board of Education of Topeka, Kansas*, spurred direct action to end *de jure* segregation in the South. In 1955, women in Montgomery, Alabama organized a grassroots effort that sustained a bus boycott for 381 days. Boycott leaders Jo Ann Robinson and Rosa Parks were longstanding civil rights activists; Robinson was an educator and leader of a black women's club in Montgomery, and Parks was a former secretary of the National Association for the Advancement of Colored People (NAACP). NAACP lawyer Constance Baker Motley fought to end segregation through the courts. During the 1950s, Shirley Chisholm and other black women sought social change through mainstream politics. Dorothy Height, president of the National Council of Negro Women, led behind-the-scenes efforts to fund fledgling civil rights organizations and worked with white women's organizations to promote civil rights and protect civil liberties.

Progressive Impulses and Alternative Communities

The burgeoning civil rights movement occurred within the unlikely context of conservative Cold War politics. The decade began with world events that deepened the resolve of social critics and politicians to protect national security at all costs. National security issues dominated political discourses with the rise of communist China, war in Korea, the changing political landscape in Eastern Europe, and the Soviet Union's success in testing nuclear weapons. In the period of extreme anxiety, civil liberties were sacrificed in order to end perceived communist influence in the United States. The Internal Security Act of 1950 required the registration of Communists, and established the Subversive Control Board to investigate un-American activities. The House Committee on Un-American Activities focused more intently on revealing communist infiltration of organizations, unions, governments, and universities during the 1950s. In 1952, with the Republican electoral victory in the Senate, Senator Joseph McCarthy, Republican from Wisconsin, used his chairmanship of an investigative committee on government operations to intensify Communist purges within government. Red baiting put liberal and progressive political interest groups, including many women's organizations, on the defensive, but that did not mean that progressive ideologies and politics failed to develop.

Even though the decade is known for demands for conformity and virulent anticommunism, which had a chilling effect on many progressive political interest groups, active, progressive subcultures and networks nurtured ideas and ideals that would flourish during the 1960s. Several women's groups remained stalwart advocates of peace and defenders of civil rights and civil liberties during the 1950s Red Scare. By cloaking their politics in the domestic ideal, women's organizations promoted peace and justice issues without inviting scrutiny. The Women's International League for Peace and Freedom's membership dropped precipitously during the decade, and, as a result, the organization adopted a defensive posture. Despite sensitivity to the label Communist, the WILPF continued to decry the nuclear arms race, but did so by appealing to housewives and mothers. Able to avoid the communist label without completely shedding its progressive ideals, the WILPF survived the decade to witness the rise of antiwar sentiment during the 1960s.

Other organizations composed of middle-class housewives, such as the National Council of Jewish Women, the National Council of Negro Women, and the YWCA, promoted racial justice and defended free speech, often by building a "postwar progressive coalition" around specific issues (Lynn 1994, 105).

Women in the Communist Party of the USA (CPUSA) faced more daunting challenges during this period, but were able to change the ideological direction of the party to include a thoroughgoing gender analysis that anticipated the radical feminism of the 1970s. Women from all political persuasions and walks of life were galvanized by expanded opportunities to enter public life during World War II. World War II was also a watershed for women in the Communist Party. Although organized women failed to achieve a permanent transformation of women's traditional roles after World War II, the postwar period, contrary to previous assumptions about the 1950s, inspired gender-conscious political activity by increasing the number of national women's organizations, such as the BPW, the NCJW, and the American Association of University Women. Left-wing women were emboldened to craft a gender analysis as well. The short-lived Congress of American Women (CAW), active in the late 1940s, comprised of female activists within the Communist Party, promoted a political agenda quite similar to mainstream women's organizations: equal pay for equal work and amendments to existing New Deal legislation, the Fair Labor Standards Act and the Social Security Act, to cover occupations dominated by African American women, domestic service and agricultural labor. Yet CAW members recognized that women's economic success was tied to their social roles as wives and mothers. Unlike mainstream women's organizations, the CAW advocated a critical analysis of gender relations. By the early 1950s, the discourses within CPUSA included male chauvinism and the oppression of women.

Lesbians, forced to confront the shame of engaging in a lifestyle that was reviled as abnormal and deviant, felt the repression of the 1950s more acutely than did the victims of political red baiting. They sought succor from repression in alternative communities in urban areas after World War II, as the suburbs were burnishing the normative nuclear family. Much like the legions of organized women denied opportunities to explore their full potential, lesbians succeeded in creating a self-consciousness community of interest, but bars and private homes provided a sense of solidarity in the absence of political and social organizations. Locations that allowed the freedom of personal expression sustained a community identity that eventually found a political voice on the heels of the civil rights and women's movements.

Preconditions for Mass-Based Activism

Women's organizations were not uniform in their adjustments to the imperatives of Cold War America, and differences in missions, goals, and political ideologies prevented potential coalitions from forming around the promotion of national policies. Racial, ethnic, class, and ideological differences contributed to rifts within the post–World War II women's movement. Deep divisions of personal identity made ongoing coalitions untenable. The BPW and the General Federation of Women's Clubs (GFWC) committed resources to national security, especially civil defense, and were fiercely anticommunist. These Republican-dominated women's clubs composed of white, middle-class women, alienated other, more progressive women's organizations, such as the National Councils of Jewish, Catholic, and Negro Women. White, ethnic women from immigrant backgrounds, and African American women were steadfast in their progressivism and far more likely to view anticommunist hysteria as a threat to civil liberties. These differences were exacerbated over debates of the efficacy of the Equal Rights Amendment (ERA). Trade union women joined progressively-inclined groups to oppose the ERA as a threat to protective legislation regulating working conditions and establishing minimum wages and maximum hours for working women. Conversely, BPW and GFWC members believed that the ERA was the only way to address persistent inequalities between the sexes. Consequently, women as a group were unable to change the course of mainstream politics or to shape policy debates in the 1950s.

Yet coalitions did emerge, usually around less controversial goals that all groups could support, as national bodies attempted to fuse civic engagement with mainstream political activism. Even though the fractured women's movement could not surmount barriers to passing national antidiscrimination laws in the conservative climate of the 1950s, state and local groups succeeded in achieving modest legislative victories and appointments of women to policy-making bodies, and, more importantly, they remained organized around gender-conscious activities.

Bureaus, divisions, commissions, and offices to study the status of women were established in local, state, and federal governments; in unions, universities, and women's organizations; and within political parties, thereby providing a formidable institutional base for grassroots feminism in the 1960s. The CPUSA had a commission on the status of women. In 1947, the Women's Status Bill was introduced in Congress, which became the blueprint for the eventual creation, in 1961, of President John F. Kennedy's Commission on the Status of Women, a body credited with launching the liberal branch of the women's movement. Labor unions nurtured female activists by creating separate departments and bureaus. Think tanks produced studies on women's labor force participation, and universities introduced pilot programs to encourage women to return to higher education.

Before the women's movement in the late 1960s and early 1970s, women from all walks of life were already making personal choices that challenged conventional gender norms. The Baby Boom peaked in 1957. The number of women in college had begun to rise prior to resurgent feminism. Black women willingly and without apology sought elective office and engaged in public protest. Lesbians defied the repressive constraints of 1950s America. Women in left-wing organizations were ideologically ahead of their time. Women living more conventional lives engaged in political behavior that was quietly transformative. By the 1960s, isolated communities and fractured coalitions came together around unabashedly feminist goals.

References and Further Reading

Alonso, Harriet Hyman. "Mayhem and Moderation: Women Peace Activists during the McCarthy Era." In *Not June Cleaver: Women and Gender in Postwar America, 1945–1960*, ed. Joanne Meyerowitz, 128–150. Philadelphia: Temple University Press, 1994.

Brodkin, Kim. "'We are neither male nor female Democrats': Gender Difference and Women's Integration within the Democratic Party." *Journal of Women's History* 19, no. 2 (Summer 2007): 111–37.

Cobble, Dorothy Sue. *The Other Women's Movement: Workplace Justice and Social Rights in Modern America*. Princeton, NJ: Princeton University Press, 2004.

Cohen, Lizabeth. *A Consumers' Republic: The Politics of Mass Consumption in Postwar America*. New York: Alfred A. Knopf, 2003.

Deslippe, Dennis A. *"Rights Not Roses": Unions and the Rise of Working-Class Feminism, 1945–1980*. Urbana: University of Illinois Press, 2000.

Friedan, Betty. *The Feminine Mystique*. New York: Norton, 1963.

Harrison, Cynthia. *On Account of Sex: Public Policies on Women's Issues, 1945–1970*. Berkeley: University of California Press, 1989.

Kaledin, Eugenia. *Mothers and More: American Women in the 1950s*. Boston: Twayne Publishers, 1984.

Kennedy, Elizabeth Lapovsky, and Madeline D. Davis. *Boots of Leather, Slippers of Gold: A History of a Lesbian Community*. New York: Routledge, 1993.

Laughlin, Kathleen A. "Kathryn Clarenbach." In *Notable American Women: A Biographical Dictionary: Completing the Twentieth Century*, ed. Susan Ware and Stacy Braukman, 122–24. Cambridge, MA: Harvard University Press, 2005.

Laughlin, Kathleen A. *Women's Work and Public Policy: A History of the Women's Bureau, U.S. Department of Labor, 1945–1970*. Boston: Northeastern University Press, 2000.

Lyman, Darryl. *Great African-American Women*. New York: Jonathan David Company, 2005.

Lynn, Susan. "Gender and Progressive Politics: A Bridge to Social Activism of the 1960s." In *Not June Cleaver: Women and Gender in Postwar America, 1945–1960*, ed. Joanne Meyerowitz, 103–137. Philadelphia: Temple University Press, 1994.

McEnaney, Laura. *Civil Defense Begins at Home: Militarization Meets Everyday Life in the 1950s*. Princeton, NJ: Princeton University Press, 2000.

Meyerowitz, Joanne. "Beyond the Feminine Mystique: A Reassessment of Postwar Mass Culture, 1946–1958." In *Not June Cleaver: Women and Gender in Postwar, 1945–1960*, ed. Joanne Meyerowitz, 229–262. Philadelphia: Temple University Press, 1994.

Murray, Sylvie. *The Progressive Housewife: Community Activism in Suburban Queens, 1945–1965.* Philadelphia: University of Pennsylvania Press, 2003.

National Manpower Council. *Womanpower.* New York: Columbia University Press, 1957.

Rymph, Catherine E. *Republican Women: Feminism and Conservatism from Suffrage through the Rise of the New Right.* Chapel Hill: University of North Carolina Press, 2006.

Ware, Susan. "American Women in the 1950s: Nonpartisan Politics and Women's Politicalization." In *Women Politics and Change,* ed. Louisa A. Tilly and Patricia Gurin, 281–99. New York: Russell Sage Foundation, 1992.

Weigand, Kate. *Red Feminism: American Communism and the Making of Women's Liberation.* Baltimore, MD: Johns Hopkins University Press, 2001.

Weiss, Jessica. *To Have and To Hold: Marriage, the Baby Boom and Social Change.* Chicago: University of Chicago Press, 2000.

White, Deborah Gray. *Too Heavy a Load: Black Women in Defense of Themselves, 1894–1994.* New York: W. W. Norton and Company, 1999.

Feminists of the 1960s and 1970s | 11

Natasha Zaretsky

In the 1960s and 1970s, feminists created one of the most influential social movements in the history of the United States. Over a 20-year period, feminists generated a revolution in public policy, restructured older institutions, established new ones, and changed American culture. Feminists compelled people to reflect more deeply on gender relations, and, in the process, they expanded the meaning of freedom for both men and women. The women who comprised the movement differed along lines of race, class, and sexuality, and they did not always share the same strategies. For example, some sought to insure that women gained equality within preexisting institutions (such as the workplace and schools), while others sought to politicize issues (such as reproduction and rape) that had been excluded from the realm of public debate. But these diverse goals were what made feminism such a powerful force in the 1960s and 1970s. By the early 1980s, the movement had radically altered the politics, culture, and society of the United States.

Origins of Feminism

The feminist movement that emerged in the 1960s originated in changes that took place in the United States after World War II. The first change concerned the growing presence of women in the paid labor force. During the war, women had entered wage labor in unprecedented numbers, and the trend continued after 1945. A dominant postwar ideology emphasized women's domestic duties as wives and mothers. But this ideology was belied by the fact that it was increasingly married women and mothers who sought paid employment. In 1950, married women accounted for 36 percent of the female labor force; by 1960, the number had jumped to 52 percent. Between 1940 and 1960, the number of dual income families—families comprised of both a husband and wife employed in the paid labor force —increased by over 200 percent. The reasons for women's increased participation in the labor force varied along lines of class and race. Working-class women labored in order to sustain their families economically, while other women worked in order to secure their families' position among the ranks of the middle class. For African American women, wage labor was a necessity, since by the mid-1960s, they were heading 25 percent of all African American families.

Despite these different motives, all women confronted pervasive discrimination and inequality in the postwar American workplace. The labor force was segregated along gender lines, with women often seeking employment as secretaries, waitresses, housecleaners, and retailers. Job listings that appeared in newspapers were divided by sex. Employers had separate pay scales for women and men; by 1966, women's wages averaged only 60 percent of those of men. Meanwhile, women were excluded from academia, law, and medicine. Women also encountered uninvited sexual attention from male coworkers and bosses, and they had no way to fight back against male advances. Working women who became pregnant had no rights and could be fired on a whim. While these various forms of job discrimination hurt all women, they exacted the heaviest toll on racial minorities, who were consigned to the lowest-paying jobs. As late as 1970, one-third of all nonwhite working women were employed as private household workers. Postwar women thus confronted a contradiction: they were entering the workforce in increasing numbers, yet gender discrimination remained rampant.

The rise of working women was related to changes within the family. Divorce became more frequent in the decades after World War II; by 1973, the national divorce rate had approached the 50 percent mark. This rise meant that increasingly children were growing up in homes without their fathers. These changes in the family reflected a broader shift away from an earlier family wage economy (defined by a male breadwinner's ability to support a stay-at-home wife and children) to a dual-earner economy in which both men and women would need to enter the labor market in order to survive. Within this new economy, women (whether married, single, or divorced) would have to secure employment outside the home. Yet labor legislation and economic policy continued to marginalize women economically. This was a contradiction that would spark feminist activism in the 1960s.

The feminist movement also had its origins in cultural changes that occurred in American life during the postwar years. The 1950s inaugurated a new era of openness surrounding female sexuality. In 1948, biologist Alfred Kinsey published the first of two volumes on sexual behavior, in which he reported that as sexual beings, men and women actually had much in common. In 1960, the federal government approved the use of the birth control pill, which gave women greater freedom to have nonprocreative sex. Two years later, Helen Gurley Brown wrote her bestselling *Sex and the Single Girl*, which encouraged young women to defer marriage and motherhood in favor of economic independence and sexual experimentation. In the 1950s and early 1960s, scientific research, birth control legislation, and popular culture undermined earlier ideologies of female sexuality, which tied women to restraint and their maternal role, in ways that would help pave the way for feminism.

The social movements of the postwar era also set the stage for feminist resurgence. After World War II, and especially after the 1954 *Brown versus Board of Education* Supreme Court decision (calling for school desegregation), African Americans became increasingly mobilized in their longstanding fight for racial equality. Throughout the 1950s and 1960s, civil rights activists articulated a powerful rhetoric of freedom, equality, and justice. Meanwhile, activists in the New Left and the antiwar movement pursued a politics that combined a critique of U.S. policies with a quest for personal authenticity. In the years ahead, feminists would put forth a politics that combined these dual conceptions of freedom—on the one hand, a civil rights conception that linked freedom to the eradication of discrimination, and on the other, a New Left conception that linked it to the pursuit of personal authenticity.

The Fight for Women's Rights

The feminist revolution of the 1960s and 1970s was made up of two distinct but overlapping political movements: the Women's Rights Movement and the Women's Liberation Movement. The Women's Rights Movement emerged in the mid-1960s. Rooted in the large-scale social transformations that had taken place since World War II, the movement was also linked to certain short-term causes. Between 1960 and 1965, policymakers and commentators began paying greater attention to the injustices that limited American women's lives. In 1961, President John F. Kennedy created a Commission on the Status of Women. Under the leadership of former First Lady Eleanor Roosevelt, the commission (made up of representatives from unions, governmental agencies, and women's organizations) evaluated women's place in the economic and legal system. It uncovered employment discrimination against women, as well as a dearth of adequate childcare options for working mothers. Published in 1963, the commission report had three immediate effects. First, President Kennedy issued a 1963 executive order requiring the federal civil service to hire for career positions without regard to sex. Second, Congress passed the Equal Pay Act, which made it illegal to set different pay rates for women and men for the same work. Finally, commissioners decided to establish state commissions that conducted their own investigations into discriminatory laws.

In 1963, Betty Friedan published her bestselling book *The Feminine Mystique*. Born in 1921, Friedan was a wife, mother, and journalist who had spent her early literary career writing for leftist and labor movement publications. In 1957, Friedan attended her 15th reunion at Smith College, where she surveyed her fellow women graduates. The President's Commission focused on the contradiction between women's workplace participation and the persistence of sexism, but Friedan turned to a second contradiction: white, middle-class women received the early benefits of higher education, but their later lives were circumscribed by motherhood and marriage. The consequence, Friedan argued, was that these women were leading lives characterized by depression and personal frustration. Friedan's study addressed the experiences of a narrow demographic group: white, middle class women

Pauli Murray

A descendant of slaves, slaveholders, and Native Americans, Pauli Murray devoted her life to analyzing the connections between race and gender discrimination. Born in 1910 and orphaned at a young age, Murray grew up in Durham, North Carolina in the era of Jim Crow segregation. A brilliant young student, she was denied admission to the University of North Carolina in 1938 because of her race. Six years later, she was denied admission to Harvard Law School because of her sex. Eventually receiving her law degree at Howard University, Murray devoted her legal career to combating racial and gender discrimination, which she insisted were deeply interconnected. Coining the term "Jane Crow" to describe the ways in which African American women were doubly victimized by racism and sexism, Murray contended, "The rationalizations upon which this sex prejudice rests are often different from those supporting racial discrimination in label only" (Maclean 2006, 120). The battle against race and sex was particularly crucial for African American women, she maintained, who often had to work outside the home to support their families. She fought for the inclusion of sex in the Civil Rights Act of 1964, contending that if sex were not part of the bill, it would include "only one half of the Negroes" (121). Two years later, she helped to found the National Organization for Women. By refusing to choose between the civil rights and feminist struggles, and insisting on a synthesis between them, Murray expanded the meanings of freedom and justice for all women.

who resided in the nation's suburbs. But Friedan had set an important precedent for feminist politics by using women's accounts of their own experience as a basis for a wider social critique.

A third watershed during these years was the passage of the Civil Rights Act of 1964. Title VII of that act defined discrimination on the grounds of "race, color, religion, sex, or national origin" as an "unlawful employment practice." Activists in the Civil Rights Movement had fought to secure a federal promise of fair employment for African Americans, and women's rights activists soon discovered that Title VII could be used as a significant tool for combating sexism as well. Attorney Pauli Murray recognized the power of Title VII for challenging both racism and sexism simultaneously. When Southern Congressman Howard Smith proposed that sex discrimination be added to Title VII (possibly hoping to derail the bill), Murray drafted a memorandum that she distributed to every member of Congress. In it, she wrote, "If sex is not included, the civil rights bill would be including only half of the Negroes." The inclusion of sex was particularly important for African American women, Murray contended, because they were the "heads of families in more than one fifth of all nonwhite families" (MacLean 2006, 121). The inclusion of sex in Title VII was significant for several reasons. First, Title VII represented an advance over the Equal Pay Act of 1963, which had only addressed the problem of wage discrimination for men and women employed in the same work. The larger economic obstacles confronting women revolved around sex segregation within the labor force (that is, that women were ghettoized into low-wage sectors of the economy). Second, Title VII

National Organization for Women president Betty Friedan and feminists march in New York City on August 26, 1970. The march commemorated the 50th anniversary of the passage of the Nineteenth Amendment, which granted American women full suffrage. (JP Laffont/Sygma/Corbis)

acknowledged the reality of women's employment and thus challenged a family wage ideal that identified men as the exclusive breadwinners within the family. Finally, Title VII's inclusion of sex meant that women workers could appeal to the Equal Employment Opportunity Commission (EEOC), a newly formed federal agency that provided workers with a vehicle for suing employers who violated their right to fair treatment.

Soon after the EEOC opened in 1965, women workers began reporting to the agency the numerous obstacles that typified sex discrimination in the American workplace. Indeed, complaints from women workers made up 25 percent of the total number received by the EEOC. But most agency employees were initially unwilling to take women's complaints seriously. The executive director of the EEOC described the inclusion of sex in Title VII as "a fluke" (MacLean 2006, 125). Yet only three years later, the agency's employees had come to recognize the legitimacy of sex discrimination complaints. What had changed between 1965 and 1968?

Tish Sommers

At the age of 57, Tish Sommers found herself in a vulnerable position. Newly divorced after 23 years as a wife, mother, and homemaker, she did not know how she would support herself financially. Spurred on by the women's movement of the late 1960s and early 1970s, Sommers transformed her personal challenge into a basis for political activism. In 1973, she founded NOW's Task Force on Older Women and coined a new term, "displaced homemakers," to describe women who faced life alone after years of marriage and motherhood. Joining with older women, church women, and feminists, Sommers went to the California State Legislature and fought for a bill to protect displaced homemakers. The bill was soon passed, creating a pilot project in California for a center where widowed and divorced women could come for job training and counseling. By the late 1970s, the program was being emulated in 16 other states, and 12 states had passed displaced homemakers laws. Using her own life struggle as the basis for analyzing and fighting against social injustice, Sommers emerged in her later life as a champion of the rights of older women. She famously proclaimed, "Don't agonize, organize!" (Hartmann 1989, 127).

The answer was that women activists demanded the enforcement of Title VII provisions. In June 1966, at the Third National Conference of Commissions on the Status of Women, approximately two dozen women, including Betty Friedan, formulated a resolution urging the EEOC to take seriously the problem of sex discrimination. When conference leaders responded that they could not issue a directive to a federal agency, the women formed the National Organization for Women, an organization committed to the fight for legal equality for women. The following October, NOW held its first conference, at which 300 men and women put forth the group's statement of purpose, which demanded an end to occupational segregation and pay disparities, an end to discrimination in education and the professions, and the creation of a national system of childcare. The stated aim of NOW was "To take action to bring women into full participation in the mainstream of American society now, assuming all the privileges and responsibilities thereof in truly equal partnership." By the end of 1967, the organization had over 1,000 members.

The 1966 founding of NOW inaugurated a period of feverish women's rights organizing. While NOW's membership climbed, other feminist groups were formed. Women who opposed NOW's support of abortion rights broke away from the organization in 1968 to form the Women's Equity Action League (WEAL), which focused on ending sex discrimination in employment and education. Also emerging out of NOW was the Center for Women's Policy Research, a think tank devoted to women and public policy. The National Women's Political Caucus was founded in 1971 with the aim of supporting women political candidates, and a Professional Women's Caucus was formed in 1970.

Between 1966 and 1976, these groups, along with others, facilitated a revolution in law and public policy. In 1967, President Lyndon Johnson added gender discrimination to a 1965 executive order that prohibited discrimination by the federal government and by private employers. From that point on, affirmative action programs would address gender as well as race. By the early 1970s, Congress and the federal courts were also responding to feminist demands. Between 1971 and 1974, Congress prohibited sex discrimination in medical training programs, extended employment benefits to married women employed by the government, challenged gender discrimination in Social Security and other pension programs, prohibited creditors from discriminating against women, and passed a Women's Equity Act designed to support women's training programs. Activists also successfully fought for an amendment that extended to domestic workers the rights included in the Fair Labor Standards Act, a victory that was particularly meaningful for working-class and minority women. In 1972, Title IX of the Educational Amendments Act banned sex discrimination in education.

Meanwhile, both the upper and lower courts challenged sex-labeling of jobs, affirmed the principle of equal pay for equal work, and banned the press from referring to sex in job advertisements. Recognizing the significance of litigation to women's rights organizing, feminists formed legal defense funds. The cumulative effect of this litigation was profound, in part because activists pursued industry wide (rather than individual) cases. In one landmark case, the EEOC brought a sex discrimination suit against AT&T. By the early 1970s, the Bell System (of which AT&T was a part) was the largest employer of women in the nation; it also barred women from jobs as linemen, classified all of its jobs according to sex, and denied women the benefits and promotions it accorded to men. Indeed, by 1970, the EEOC had received 1,500 complaints from women workers at AT&T (seven percent of the agency's total). A government report on the case contended, "The Bell monolith is, without doubt, the largest oppressor of women workers in the United States" (MacLean 2006, 132). In 1972, the suit was settled out of court, when AT&T agreed to a multimillion-dollar payment to women workers and promised to implement a plan to end sex segregation at the company. The case reflected the power of litigation to change working women's lives in dramatic and permanent ways; these transformations in the law, in turn, altered the way women workers saw themselves. As one female guard at a U.S. Steel plant recalled, "When I first took this job, I had to prove to them [the men] that women could handle it . . . Before this, I had been brought up to think women were inferior and I believed it. It wasn't actually until I started doing what they considered a man's job and found out that I could do it just as well that I actually began to believe" (145–46).

These victories were also accompanied by feminist defeats. Among them was the failure to ratify the Equal Rights Amendment. Support for a constitutional amendment guaranteeing women's equality had been part of NOW's early agenda, President Richard Nixon came out in support of the amendment in June 1970, and it won Congressional approval in 1972. But as the amendment moved through the states for ratification, grassroots activists launched a movement to defeat it. Responding to public ambivalence about recent changes in gender roles, ERA opponents like Phyllis Schlafly argued that the amendment would jeopardize the security of housewives who lacked

Pauli Murray, priest, lawyer, educator, and writer, 1946. A nearly lifelong activist for racial and gender equality, Murray became the first African American woman to be ordained as an Episcopal priest in 1977. (Library of Congress)

job skills, that it represented a frightening encroachment of government power over family life, and that it would overturn federal laws that excluded women from the military draft. These arguments proved effective enough to derail the state ratification process, and by 1982, the ERA was dead.

A second feminist defeat revolved around childcare. A coalition of labor feminists, women's rights advocates, and civil rights veterans had rallied successfully for the Congressional passage of the 1971 Comprehensive Child Development Act, which would have provided childcare on a sliding scale basis to working parents. Yet Nixon vetoed the act, arguing that it represented an endorsement of "communal approaches to childrearing" (Rosen 2000, 90). Like the defeat of the ERA, the failure to secure a national childcare program reflected both a deep ambivalence about shifting gender roles and a growing antigovernment sentiment in the 1970s.

Both academic and popular accounts of the women's rights movement have critiqued mainstream feminist organizations like NOW for being dominated by white, middle-class women, and for failing to address the needs of working-class women and women of color. Yet the critique overlooks two significant facts. First, African American women were in the vanguard of the women's rights movement when it came to issues like employment and public policy. Because African American women had been excluded from the family wage system, they had an acute sense of the need to combat sex, along with race segregation, in the workplace. Recognizing that racial and gender discrimination were interconnected, African American women like Pauli Murray helped to found NOW, and Fannie Lou Hammer and Shirley Chisholm (the first African American woman elected to the House of Representatives in 1968) were recruited to the organization. Aileen Hernandez, who had been among the first to fight against sex discrimination as an employee within the EEOC, succeeded Betty Friedan as NOW's president in 1970. When it came to issues of workplace discrimination, in other words, African American women were trailblazers in implementing a feminist agenda.

NOW and other mainstream feminist organizations also formed coalitions with working-class women in the 1960s and 1970s. Women staffers of the United Auto Workers, like Olga Mader and Dorothy Haener, were involved in NOW from the start, and in 1974, they helped form the Coalition of Labor Union Women (CLUW), an organization designed to make unions more responsive to women's needs. Organizations like Women Employed in Chicago, and the Boston-based group Nine to Five, mobilized women who were employed in the clerical and service industries. These groups helped define feminism's legislative agenda. It was the UAW's Dorothy Haener who urged NOW to fight for paid maternity leave for all working mothers, and in 1972, the organization successfully pressured the EEOC into issuing appropriate maternity leave guidelines. Six years later, women from the labor movement joined with feminists to persuade Congress to pass the Pregnancy Discrimination Act, which protected pregnant women from unfair treatment. Like African Americans, working-class women were in the vanguard of legislative reform.

This is not to suggest that there were no divisions within organizations like NOW. For example, women of different classes were divided over the issue of the Equal Rights Amendment, since union women feared that the amendment would eliminate gender-based protective labor legislation that had been secured by the labor movement. And although African American women had been on the vanguard of feminist reform, they, along with other women of color, also encountered racism within feminist groups, and felt compelled to create their own autonomous organizations. The North American Indian Women's Association was founded in 1970, the first National Chicana Conference was held in 1971, the first Conference of Puerto Rican Women took place the following year, and the National Black Feminist Organization was founded in 1973. The question of sexuality also threatened to split feminists. In 1969, Betty Friedan infamously described lesbianism as a "lavender menace" that undermined the larger aims of the women's movement. The organization repudiated Friedan's position by passing a resolution recognizing the civil rights of lesbians, and Friedan later reversed herself, publicly declaring her support for lesbian rights at the 1977 National Women's Conference in Houston, Texas.

The Women's Liberation Movement

The divisions within the women's rights movement, over whether issues like abortion and lesbianism should be included in feminist organizing, reflected an attempt by organizations like NOW to focus on legal and institutional reform. But for some women, organizations like NOW did not go far enough when it came to analyzing, interpreting, and eventually uprooting women's oppression. A desire to expand the definition of "the political" gave rise to a second movement in the late 1960s: the women's liberation movement. While the women's rights movement focused on eradicating gender discrimination in an array of institutions, the women's liberation movement sought to redefine the relationship between the public and the private by insisting on the political nature of issues once seen as solely personal: issues like abortion, female psychology, and lesbianism.

The women's liberation movement emerged in the late 1960s, and the women who were drawn to it tended to be somewhat younger in age, college educated, white, and middle class. Many had first become political through their activism in the Civil Rights, New Left, and antiwar movements of the era. Within these movements, they learned valuable organizing skills; at the same time, they encountered certain contradictions. In the Civil Rights movement, they were inspired by the struggle for racial justice and equality, and were exposed to models of female leadership in figures like Rosa Parks, Diane Nash, and Ella Baker. In the antiwar movement, women joined with men in indicting the Vietnam War. And within the New Left, young women worked with men to articulate a vision of participatory democracy that could combat the alienation they perceived within society. Yet within all of these movements, women were marginalized in certain ways. They were often expected to do traditional women's work like cooking, laundry, and typing, and their crucial organizational roles were often obscured as male leaders assumed center stage. Sexual dynamics between men and women sometimes meant that women were treated as sexual objects. In a range of ways, the rhetoric of justice and equality within these movements was belied by women's objectification and marginalization.

By the late 1960s, many women broke away from these movements and began organizing on their own behalf. They had come to believe that the problem of women's oppression needed to be addressed on its own terms. They began to form their own political groups, including New York Radical Women, the Redstockings, the Chicago Women's Liberation Union, the Westside Group of Chicago, and D.C. Women's Liberation. There were substantive differences between these various groups. Some activists believed that women's oppression had its origins in capitalism, and thus argued that women's groups should be tied to a larger leftist movement. Others argued that male supremacy was so pervasive that it required a complete break with leftist organizations. But they all shared a commitment to developing a more radical critique of women's oppression than that put forth by organizations like NOW.

There were two crucial tools that women's liberation activists used to analyze women's oppression. The first was writing. Feminists circulated manifestos, essays, and position papers in which they reflected on the ways that women had been denied their full humanity: by media portrayals that treated women as sex objects, by the disproportionate responsibility for housework assigned to women, and by the male promulgation of myths that denied women their experience of sexual pleasure. In 1968, New York Radical Women published their papers under the title *Notes from the First Year*. Two years later, in 1970, feminist Robin Morgan published a feminist anthology called *Sisterhood is Powerful*, and Shulamith Firestone published *The Dialectic of Sex*, which argued that women's oppression was rooted in biological reproduction. In all of these writings, activists explored themes that challenged the traditional division between public and private: female body image, the politics of housework, women's sexuality, and reproduction.

The second political tool developed by women's liberation activists was consciousness-raising (CR). Consciousness-raising was spearheaded by younger feminists who believed that overthrowing male supremacy required a psychological revolution no less than it required changes in law and policy. By bringing women together in small groups to discuss their personal experiences, feminists could link psychological problems to larger structures of oppression. As one feminist described it, consciousness-raising allowed for "the political reinterpretation of one's personal life" (Echols 1989, 83). As CR groups spread throughout the country, women began to recognize collective patterns of sexism. At the same time, CR groups obscured differences of race and class among women.

As feminists used writing and consciousness-raising to explore sexism, they developed strategies such as public protests for calling attention to their cause. For example, New York Radical Women organized a protest of the 1968 Miss America Pageant. On the day of the pageant, women protestors gathered on the Atlantic City boardwalk and carried signs that read "No More Beauty Standards" and "Welcome to the Cattle Auction." They even crowned a sheep as queen to underscore the absurdity of the pageant. At the center of the protest was a "Freedom Trash Can," in which women threw away items that symbolized their oppression: dish detergent, false eyelashes, magazines, high heels, and bras (Rosen 2000, 160). The protest succeeded at bringing unprecedented public attention to the movement. On August 26, 1970, 50,000 women marched in New York City to commemorate the 50th anniversary of the woman suffrage amendment. Protestors draped a banner over the Statue of Liberty that read "Women of the World Unite," and other women held marches and rallies in cities and towns throughout the country. The Women's Strike for Equality was the largest women's demonstration in the United States since the suffrage movement.

Protests brought the feminist cause to the attention of the mass media and the wider public. But the most enduring legacy of women's liberation was the creation of new institutions that changed women's relationships to themselves, their families, and their communities. Feminists founded women's bookstores, coffee shops, music festivals, and summer camps with the aim of honoring and celebrating what they saw as a distinct women's culture. In response to the male domination of the medical field, activists opened health clinics designed to address the specific needs of women patients. As more

Over 200 women, organized by the group New York Radical Women, picket the 1968 Miss America Pageant in one of the most well-known demonstrations of the feminist movement. (UPI-Bettmann/Corbis)

and more women began to speak out about their experiences with rape and domestic violence, activists opened battered women's shelters and launched rape hotlines that provided assistance and refuge to women in crisis.

This institution-building reflected the dialectical relationship between the women's rights movement and the movement for women's liberation, and the extent to which activists from both groups often worked in tandem. The fight for women's reproductive freedom provides an illustrative example. Even before the 1973 *Roe versus Wade* decision (which constitutionally guaranteed a woman's right to an abortion), several states had begun liberalizing abortion laws. But beginning in the late 1960s, activists recast abortion as a feminist issue. Both activists in organizations like NOW and radical feminists disrupted legislative hearings, picketed, and organized sit-ins in which women could testify about their experiences with illegal abortion. While some activists focused on repealing abortion laws, other activists empowered women to learn more about their bodies. In 1969, a group of women in Boston began studying women's anatomy, physiology, and sexuality. By 1971, they compiled all of their notes and lectures, a compilation eventually published in 1973 as *Our Bodies, Ourselves*. By the late 1970s, the Boston collective had been emulated in other cities and towns, and a national women's health network existed that provided healthcare to women.

The women's health movement highlighted the different histories that white women and women of color brought to the struggle for reproductive freedom. While white women conceived of reproductive freedom in terms of access to legal abortion and the right to prevent childbearing, women of color, who historically had been the victims of forced sterilization, insisted that the campaign for abortion rights be coupled with an attack on sterilization abuse. Thus, a multiracial coalition of feminists formed the Committee for Abortion Rights and Against Sterilization Abuse, which demanded that states enact strict consent laws for sterilization procedures.

The emphasis on institution-building reveals the invaluable contribution of lesbians to the feminist movement. It was often lesbians who launched feminist bookstores and ran women's health clinics; they sustained these institutions into the 1980s and beyond. The place of lesbianism in the women's liberation movement was complex. Women's liberation activists were divided around the question of lesbianism, with some radical lesbians contending that lesbianism was a necessary political choice for feminists, while other activists insisted that continued heterosexual relations with men did not compromise their feminist politics. Through speak-outs and consciousness-raising sessions, lesbian activists fought back against the homophobia they perceived within the feminist movement. Like women of color who had to balance their loyalties to feminism with their loyalties to their own racial communities, lesbians moved between feminism and gay liberation. Yet it was lesbians who often sustained the multiple feminist institutions that left such a lasting mark on American society and culture.

Conclusion

The feminist movement of the 1960s and 1970s was among the most influential social movements in American history. As the country made the transition from an industrial to a postindustrial society, women entered the labor force in unprecedented numbers. By the late 1960s, the contradiction between women's presence in the workforce and the persistence of sex discrimination unleashed a movement for women's rights. Feminists took their inspiration from two primary sources: a Civil Rights Movement emphasis on equality, freedom, and justice, and a leftist emphasis on the quest for personal authenticity. Feminists transformed law and public policy, while creating new institutions that brought private issues into the public realm. Feminists were not always successful at bridging divisions of race, class, and sexuality. Yet it was African American women, working class women, and lesbians who propelled the movement forward and sustained it. Because of their exclusion from the family wage economy, African American women and working-class women were in the vanguard of the fight against workplace sexism. Meanwhile, it was often lesbians who supported feminist institutions over decades. The cumulative effect was that by the early 1980s, American society was dramatically different from what it had been only two decades earlier. Working together, millions of women created a feminist revolution, the outcome of which is still unfolding.

References and Further Reading

Boston Women's Health Collective. *Our Bodies, Ourselves: A Book by and for Women*. New York: Simon and Schuster, 1973.

Breines, Wini. *The Trouble between Us: An Uneasy History of White and Black Women in the Feminist Movement*. New York: Oxford University Press, 2006.

Brown, Helen Gurley. *Sex and the Single Girl*. New York: Pocket Books, 1962.

Echols, Alice. *Daring to Be Bad: Radical Feminism in America, 1967–1975*. Minneapolis: University of Minnesota, 1989.

Evans, Sara. "Beyond Declension: Feminist Radicalism in the 1970s and 1980s." In *The World the 60s Made: Politics and Culture in Recent America*, ed. Van Gosse and Richard Moser, 52–66. Philadelphia: Temple University Press, 2003.

Evans, Sara. *Personal Politics: The Roots of Women's Liberation in the Civil Rights Movement and the New Left*. New York: Vintage Books, 1979.

Firestone, Shulamith. *The Dialectic of Sex: The Case for Feminist Revolution*. New York: Morrow, 1970.

Friedan, Betty. *The Feminine Mystique*. New York: Norton, 1963.

Gerhard, Jane. *Desiring Revolution: Second Wave Feminism and the Rewriting of American Sexual Thought, 1920 to 1982*. New York: Columbia University Press, 2001.

Hartmann, Susan. *From Margin to Mainstream: American Women and Politics since 1960*. New York: Knopf, 1989.

Horowitz, Daniel. *Betty Friedan and the Making of* The Feminine Mystique: *The American Left, the Cold War, and Modern Feminism*. Amherst: University of Massachusetts Press, 1998.

Keniston, Kenneth. *All Our Children: The American Family under Pressure*. New York: Harcourt Brace Jovanovich, 1977.

Kinsey, Alfred C., Wardell B. Pomeroy, Clyde E. Martin, and Paul H. Gebhard. *Sexual Behavior in the Human Female*. Philadelphia: Saunders, 1953.

Kinsey, Alfred C., Wardell B. Pomeroy, and Clyde E. Martin. *Sexual Behavior in the Human Male*. Philadelphia: W.B. Saunders, 1948.

Maclean, Nancy. *Freedom Is Not Enough: The Opening of the American Workplace*. Cambridge, MA: Harvard University Press, 2006.

Mansbridge, Jane. *Why We Lost the ERA*. Chicago: University of Chicago Press, 1986.

Morgan, Robin. *Sisterhood Is Powerful: An Anthology of Writings from the Women's Liberation Movement*. New York: Random House, 1970.

Murray, Pauli. "The Liberation of Black Women." In *Voices of the New Feminism*, ed. Mary Lou Thompson, 87–102. Boston: Beacon Press, 1970.

Nicholson, Linda. *The Second Wave: A Reader in Feminist Theory.* New York: Routledge, 1997.

Rosen, Ruth. *The World Split Open: How the Women's Movement Changed America.* New York: Penguin Books, 2000.

Rosenberg, Rosalind. *Divided Lives: American Women in the Twentieth Century.* New York: Hill and Wang, 1992.

Springer, Kimberly. *Living for the Revolution: Black Feminist Organizations, 1968–1980.* Durham, NC: Duke University Press, 2005.

Woloch, Nancy. *Women and the American Experience.* New York: McGraw Hill, 2000.

Third Wave Feminists: The Ongoing Movement for Women's Rights

12

Janice Okoomian

> The problem is that, while on a personal level feminism is everywhere, like fluoride, on a political level the movement is more like nitrogen: ubiquitous and inert.
>
> —Baumgardner and Richards 2000, 18

Introduction: The "Wave" Metaphor

"Third Wave feminism" is a term "generally used to describe three interconnected concepts: generational age, ideological position, and historical moment" (Henry 2004, 34). Third Wavers are usually younger feminists, born in the early 1960s or later, who have a distinct set of political or ideological beliefs arising from the social and historical conditions of their era. This chapter traces the rise of the Third Wave as an historical movement. The metaphor of feminist waves helps us to identify commonalities and differences between large groups of feminists who differ by age, historical period, and ideology. Nevertheless, it is important as we proceed to keep in mind the drawbacks of the waves framework. For one thing, this framework may imply that feminist disagreements are trivial mother/daughter squabbles rather than genuine political debates. The waves model also tends to exaggerate ideological and historical differences, when in fact there is considerable continuity in Second and Third Wave feminisms. It is more accurate to think of Third Wave feminism as *both* a departure from *and* a continuation of Second Wave feminism. This view yields a more complex and historically rich picture of U.S. feminism over the past 40 years.

Background: Postfeminism and Backlash

By the late 1980s, feminism was dead—or so the media had repeatedly claimed. Writer Erica Jong discovered, for instance, that between 1969 and 1998, *Time* magazine announced the demise of feminism 119 times. The 1980s were declared to be a postfeminist era. Feminists expected to meet resistance from conservatives, but by the end of the 1980s, even moderates and liberals seemed to have lost enthusiasm for feminism. A crushing defeat of the ERA (Equal Rights Amendment) in 1982 was followed in 1984 by the defeat of Geraldine Ferraro, the first woman to run for Vice President on a major party ticket. Second Wave feminists were bitterly disappointed by these losses. A deep cultural anxiety about feminism and its attacks on male privilege had taken hold.

Two main strands of thinking fueled the belief that feminism was obsolete. According to some, feminism was no longer necessary because it had accomplished its main goals. More women had entered the workforce, especially in nontraditional fields. Sexual harassment had been declared a form of job discrimination. Some states had passed victim protection laws for rape victims. Women had legal access to reproductive choices, including birth control and abortion. The federal Title IX statute prohibited sex discrimination in education. The problem of domestic violence had been brought to the attention of the public.

Others believed that feminism had failed because it was too radical. In the media, feminism was blamed for the high divorce rate. Many accused feminists of creating hordes of depressed, lonely, single women who had opted for careers instead of families. Feminists were said to have duped married women into delaying childbirth, thereby creating an infertility epidemic. One *Newsweek* writer complained, "The truth is, a woman can't live the true feminist life unless she denies her child-bearing biology. She has to live on the pill, or have her tubes tied at an early age . . . [to] keep up with guys with an uninterrupted career" (Ebeling 1990, 9). Others complained that the new rape, sexual harassment, and sexual abuse laws feminists had fought for unfairly imposed a rigid standard of sexual correctness, a specific form of political correctness.

Both strands of reasoning can be traced to what journalist Susan Faludi termed "backlash" in her 1991 book of the same name. Faludi provided a wealth of evidence that the radical right and the Reagan/Bush administrations, along with the cooperation of the media, had undone much of what Second Wave feminism had accomplished. For instance, Faludi writes, "Just when women were starting to mobilize against battering and sexual assaults, the federal government stalled funding for battered-women's programs, defeated bills to fund shelters, and shut down its Office of Domestic Violence—only two years after opening it in 1979" (Faludi 1991, xix).

The harshest forms of backlash in the 1980s were already well known to feminists. Among the most notorious antifeminists were televangelists like Jerry Falwell, Pat Robertson, and Jim Bakker. Robertson claimed, in a 1992 fund raising letter, that "[t]he feminist agenda is not about equal rights for women. It is about a socialist, anti-family political movement that encour-

Norma McCorvey (right), known as Jane Roe in the landmark U.S. Supreme Court case, stands with a young friend at an Operation Rescue rally on January 22, 1997. Though she instigated the enormously controversial decision that legalized abortion nationwide, McCorvey is now an opponent of the pro-choice movement and works with the anti-abortion group Operation Rescue. (AP/ Wide World Photos)

ages women to leave their husbands, kill their children, practice witchcraft, destroy capitalism and become lesbians" (Boston 1996, 164). Antiabortion protesters also became increasingly vocal during the 1980s, some resorting to violence. Groups like Operation Rescue staged blockades to prevent women from entering abortion clinics. Between 1977 and 1989, 77 family planning clinics were bombed or burned by antiabortion activists, and numerous attacks and death threats were made on providers.

The most radically antifeminist groups never gained the support of the majority of Americans. Indeed, despite media reports of the feminist movement's failure, Faludi reported that in national surveys taken in the 1980s, "75 to 95 percent of women credit the feminist campaign with *improving* their lives, and a similar proportion say that the women's movement should keep pushing for change" (Faludi 1991, xv). What was more shocking to readers of *Backlash* was the revelation that despite the popular belief that things were getting better for women, this was far from the reality. Although there were indeed more women in the workforce, 80 percent still worked in low-paying, traditionally female sectors, including secretarial, sales clerking, and the lowest levels of the service industry. The glass ceiling—an invisible barrier of sex discrimination—prevented women from reaching the highest positions in business, government, and the professions. In 1989, 75 percent of high schools were still in violation of Title IX regulations.

Then, in the presumedly post-feminist climate of the early 1990s, a new source of criticism arose against feminism, in the form of several well-publicized, sweeping criticisms by self-described feminists. Criticism from within its ranks was not new to feminism—Second Wave feminists had been grappling with claims of racism, classism, homophobia, and other ideological differences for years. However, three new writers in the 1990s received national attention for their criticism of feminism: Camille Paglia, Katie Roiphe, and Naomi Wolf. These writers critiqued feminists for focusing too much on victimization, and Wolf coined the term "power feminism" as an antidote to "victim feminism." Power feminists refused to dwell on victimization and, claimed these writers, were likely to be more successful, empowered, and effective as a result. Some feminists appreciated this distinction, but others believed power feminism to be nothing more than "the voice of the father in his latest disguise" (Heywood and Drake 1997, "We Learn America," 50).

"I'm Not a Feminist, But . . ."

This period, full of contradictory claims and interpretations of feminism's value, was the era when Generation X (usually referring to those born between 1961 and 1981) came of age. Young women had never known a time in which they did not have legal access to contraception and abortion; protection from forced sterilization (especially for women of color and poor women); greater access to education and jobs than there had been for their mothers; shelters and legal support for victims of rape and domestic violence; and Women's Studies courses in many colleges.

But as events in politics and law during the late 1980s and 1990s showed, the work of feminism was not yet finished. In 1991, law professor Anita Hill testified before the Senate Judiciary Committee that she had been sexually harassed by her former boss, Supreme Court justice nominee Clarence Thomas. The Thomas confirmation hearings were televised and widely reported by the media, but the Senate Judiciary Committee refused to believe Hill's testimony. The Thomas hearings served as a wake-up call for feminists both white and black. Reproductive rights were also being compromised during this period. The Supreme Court upheld restrictions on abortion in the *Webster v. Reproductive Health Services* (1989), *Rust v. Sullivan* (1991), and *Planned Parenthood v. Casey* (1992) cases. These rulings paved the way for restrictions such as mandatory waiting periods for women seeking abortions, parental notification and consent laws for minors seeking abortions, and gag rules preventing doctors from discussing abortion as a valid option for patients.

In light of these new assaults on women's rights and status, Second Wave feminists began to criticize what they perceived to be a lack of feminist consciousness in the young women of Generation X. Some older feminists were dismayed at the numbers of young women who not only did not self-identify as feminists, but took the hard-won gains of Second Wave feminism for granted. There was a "girl power" movement in the early 1990s, but many Second Wavers saw this movement as backlash-driven and politically apathetic.

In fact, however, many younger women *did* identify as feminists and were very much aware of the gains made by Second Wavers. In their Third Wave tract *Manifesta,* Jennifer Baumgardner and Amy Richards describe the cultural mood in which they were children as an exhilarating one. Theirs was the generation that "took its first breath of air in a new atmosphere, one where women's expectations and freedoms were soaringly, thrillingly different" (Baumgardner and Richards 2000, 12). Some were raised in feminist families, while others learned about principles of gender equality at school. Girls could play on Little League teams. Boys as well as girls were taught about girls' rights. Many Gen Xers did not encounter sexism until they were older, so they did not have occasion to understand the dynamics of patriarchy as soon in life as many Second Wavers had.

Baumgardner and Richards argued that the comparative invisibility of young feminists should not be taken as a sign that they did not exist. In fact, they claimed, "Third Wave women have been seen as nonfeminist when they are actually living feminist lives" (48). If feminist principles were embedded in younger women's lives and guided their choices, it was because this generation grew up in a culture more infused with feminist principles than any other. However, a 1998 *Time*/CNN poll found that over 50 percent of women in the 18–34-year-old range did not call themselves feminists, despite believing in central goals of feminism, such as reproductive rights and wage equity. The reason for this contradiction, as Baumgardner and Richards noted, is that, while younger women had feminist values, they often lacked a feminist consciousness.

Third Wave Consciousness

Feminist consciousness, as Baumgardner and Richards imply, includes an awareness of the history of women's rights and feminist movements, an understanding of how one's own life experience could be viewed using feminist interpretive lenses, and a willingness to call oneself a feminist. In young women, all three components were not always present. They were often, for instance, unaware of the history of feminism. Audre Lorde famously said in 1984 that, without a significant understanding of what has gone before, women expend their energies *re-creating* feminism again and again, instead of being able to devote themselves to advancing its goals. Second Wavers did not want to expend energy re-inventing feminism; but the younger generation, lacking historical knowledge, was not ready to proceed with the Second Wavers' agenda.

Young women were also less likely than their elders to have thought about feminism in relation to their own lives. Second Wavers had participated in consciousness-raising sessions, where they could explore what feminism was and what it meant to them. In conversations with others, women discussed the ways in which sexism permeated U.S. culture in the mass media, the political realm, and the work world; they made connections between the conditions of their personal lives and a larger social system of patriarchy. Younger women arrived on the scene after this important work had been done by older women, but not in time to participate in it. As Baumgardner and Richards pointed out, this meant that younger women did not have an awareness of how sexism and patriarchy affected their own their lives.

Because they lacked the first two components of feminist consciousness, many young women did not adopt the third component—a willingness to self-identify as feminist. However, even those young women who *did* identify as feminists sometimes felt at odds with the Second Wave movement. Feminist organizations' agendas grew out of Second Wavers' articulation of feminist values. Raised under different historical conditions, younger feminists sometimes had different priorities. Yet they found themselves comparatively voiceless in feminist organizations in which Second Wavers were the established leaders. Third Wavers criticized NOW, *Ms.*, and other prominent feminist organizations for ignoring, even excluding, younger feminists.

One significant difference in the perspective of Third Wave feminism was its multiracial focus. Third Wavers were more likely to identify as biracial, to have biracial friends, and to date across racial lines than were Second Wavers. Multiracial consciousness thus was more prevalent in Generation X than in any previous generation. This heightened multiracial consciousness among Third Wavers did not, however, mean that Third Wave feminism had become fully racially inclusive. Indeed, some young women of color remained alienated by the ongoing whiteness of feminism. For instance, Veronica Chambers critiqued fellow Third Waver Naomi Wolf for failing to discuss "how the tyranny of the beauty myth had scarred so many women of color—not only black women, but Asian, Latina and American Indian women as well" (Chambers 2001, 26). Likewise, Rebecca Hurdis argued that Baumgardner and Richards' *Manifesta* failed to include a sustained discussion of women of color feminism. Thus, while multiracial consciousness was more intrinsic to the Third Wave, there continued to be a privileged focus on the needs and concerns of white women.

The popularity of poststructuralist theories of identity had also caused a shift in the way Third Wavers approached feminism. Poststructuralists like Jacques Derrida, Michel Foucault, and Jacques Lacan had argued that identities are not fixed, not biological, not essential, but rather are fluid, socially constructed, and performative. These theories had been appropriated by 1970s feminist theorists such as Julia Kristeva and Luce Irigaray to deconstruct notions not only of women's inferiority, but also of gender identity itself. Queer theorists like Judith Butler used poststructuralism to argue that sexualities are numerous and fluctuating, that identities like "homosexual," "heterosexual" and "bisexual" are social constructions created and maintained by the "performance" of individual subjects and regulated by the institutions of social power (Butler 1990). Third Wave college students were exposed to these concepts in their Women's Studies classes and tended to integrate them into their own feminist beliefs. Thus, Third Wavers were more likely to take a stance of playful disruption toward gender and sexual categories, performing

Queen Latifah

Grammy-winning Rap artist and television and film actress Queen Latifah has used her celebrity status to advocate for feminism in terms that are accessible to many Third Wavers. Latifah (born Dana Evans) grew up poor and black in Newark, New Jersey, a child of divorced parents. She skyrocketed to fame as a young rapper, eventually branching out to film and television. As an artist, she has used her voice to speak out against race, class, and gender inequalities. For instance, in the following lyrics to her hit song "U.N.I.T.Y.," Latifah takes male rappers to task for their misogynistic representations of women:

> Instincts lead me to another flow
> Every time I hear a brother call a girl a
> bitch or a ho.
>
> —(Latifah 1999, 3)

The theme of women's strength and value is explored in other songs, such as "Ladies First." Queen Latifah also appeared in movies as a plus-size sexy woman. In her public persona, she appears comfortable with her body and speaks out against beauty standards that ruin women's self-esteem and body images. Her autobiography, *Ladies First,* is full of pro-women stories and advice. She refers to God as "the Original Queen and Creator of All" (Latifah 1999, p. ix). However, despite the fact that she shares an interest in feminist issues, Latifah does not self-identify as feminist. Most recently, she has become a spokesperson for weight-loss company Jenny Craig.

Queen Latifah presents an interesting object of reflection for feminists. On the one hand, she is clearly an outspoken advocate of women, one who combines a successful public career with an independent voice. On the other hand, her disinclination to identify as a feminist means that she is not connected with networks of women working on similar issues. Latifah may feel that feminism is still a white women's movement, but neither has she affiliated herself with Womanist or Black Feminist organizations or groups. Some feminists might hold her up as a role model, while others might point out the limits of the effect an unaffiliated celebrity can have on social policy.

gender or not as they wished, often with a sense of irony, as in the appropriation of such performative props as lipstick and high heels. This seemed frivolous and trivializing to some Second Wavers, who thought that Third Wavers viewed personal identity and experience "as a focus in its own right and not as a route to theoretical insights and structural change" (Fixmer and Wood 2005, 248). Yet Third Wavers also thought seriously about the implications of poststructuralist theory for feminism. "We must recognize that there can be no single representative subject of feminism, while, at the same time, we must continue to speak in a collective voice that articulates political demands on behalf of a group called 'women,'" writes Deborah L. Siegel. "This" she continues, "is the paradox that faces women of my generation: It is not easy for 'third wave' feminists to say 'we,' yet we must" (Siegel 1997, 61–62).

Men's consciousness and relation to feminism likewise underwent a shift in the Third Wave. Men had been involved in both the First and Second Waves of U.S. feminism. But Gen X men, like Gen X women, had grown up with feminism in the form of slogans of gender equality that had permeated the popular culture. Some Generation X college-educated men came out of college having taken at least one Women's Studies course, so their knowledge of feminist principles was generally more in-depth than that of other men in their cohort. Gender Studies classes offered the ability to explore theories of gender and identity, the ways in which patriarchy privileged men, and the history of women's lives and activism. The influence of Women's Studies in the lives of men extended into their later lives and professional activities, with some highly visible results. For instance, Gen Xer Joss Whedon, the creator of the 1990s cult television show *Buffy the Vampire Slayer,* is a self-described feminist himself, who was raised by a feminist mother. The inspiration for *Buffy* came from Whedon's observation that horror movies typically include a scene in which a lone girl is attacked in a dark alleyway; Whedon wondered what it would be like if that girl could fight back. *Buffy* became a huge success, popular with the Gen-X audience (female and male alike), in part because of its depiction of a heroine who could kick ass.

An increase in feminist consciousness among young women also arose out of popular culture phenomena like the Riot Grrls. Riot Grrls came into being during the summer of 1991, when two all-girl bands, Bratmobile and Bikini Kill, transplanted themselves from Olympia, Washington to Washington, D.C. There, they gained quick prominence in the Indie (independently produced) pop scene, started a fanzine (an amateur-produced magazine for fans of a particular group or genre), and circulated slogans such as "Revolution Girl Style Now." A movement was ignited. Riot Grrl chapters sprang up around the country, holding consciousness-raising meetings and workshops. Central to the Riot Grrl agenda was claiming the stage for women in the male-dominated world of Indie pop. Through their music, which reclaimed punk as a protest form, and their song lyrics and zines, which addressed a range of feminist topics, the Riot Grrl movement generated an upsurge of feminist consciousness among fans.

All of these social developments created a significant shift in the way younger women experienced and thought about gender identity and feminism. To some Second Wavers, it looked as though Third Wavers had blunted the edge of feminist criticism and action. However, Third Wavers writing about their perspectives described experiencing identity as increasingly complex. As Rebecca Walker put it, "For us the lines between Us and Them are often blurred, and as a result we find ourselves seeking to create identities that accommodate ambiguity and our multiple positionalities: including more than excluding, exploring more than defining, searching more than arriving" (Walker 1995, xxxiii).

Third Wave Activism

Activism in the Third Wave manifests itself differently than did Second Wave activism. The most notable difference is that Third Wavers tend to engage in the popular culture rather than rejecting it, as Second Wavers did, taking "cultural production and sexual politics as key sites of struggle, seeking to use desire and pleasure as well as anger to fuel struggles for justice" (Heywood and Drake 1997, *Third Wave Agenda,* 4). Another difference in Third Wave activism is that it appears leaderless. Yet this apparent leaderlessness is really a sign of the heterogeneity of the Third Wave and its tendency to be expressed in a diversity of local contexts or quietly integrated within the framework of numerous other activities. In a culture that recognizes social and political movements only if they have a hierarchical leadership structure, with a few individuals at the top serving as spokespersons, Third Wavers have resisted the urge to narrow the scope of the movement, instead valuing the very diffuseness that makes it hard for the media to identify a superleader.

Some highly visible organizations do exist to advance the goals of the Third Wave, nevertheless. For instance, The Feminist Majority Foundation has a widespread college-campus program. Affiliated groups on college campuses receive support and resources from the Foundation as they organize to work on campus feminist issues such as Title IX compliance, access to contraceptives, student voter registration, and establishing sweatshop-free policies. Perhaps the most celebrated birth of a Third Wave organization took place in 1992, when Rebecca Walker declared in the pages of *Ms.* that "I am not a post-feminist feminist; I am the Third Wave" (Walker 1992, 41). *Ms.* was flooded with letters from young women who wanted to be part of the Third Wave. Shortly thereafter, Walker and Shannon Liss founded The Third Wave Direct Action Corporation to promote young women's feminist activism. By 1997, the Corporation had morphed into the Third Wave Foundation, whose purpose is to make grants to organizations that benefit women, girls, and transgendered people. One such grantee organization is the California-based "Khmer Girls in Action," which worked in 2008 to defeat a bill that would have required parental notification for California minors seeking abortions. These organizations are but two example of activism in the Third Wave; through these and other vehicles, Third Wavers address the issues most important to them.

Reproductive Rights

The 1990s and 2000s saw the chipping away of reproductive rights, fueled by the *Webster* and *Casey* Supreme Court decisions. Thus, reproductive rights remain high on the Third Wave feminist agenda. College campuses are active sites of organized activism, sometimes sponsored by student activities boards of the colleges. Some campus feminist groups receive organizational help from national groups such as NARAL (National Abortion & Reproductive Rights Action League) Pro-Choice America. Students Organizing Students (SOS) was founded in the wake of the *Webster* decision, and within one year had established 150 chapters at high schools and colleges. Groups like New York's Women's Action Coalition (WAC), launched in response to the Clarence Thomas/Anita Hill hearings, joined forces to resist the tactics of Operation Rescue. Medical Students for Choice, founded in 1993, coordinates efforts by medical students to make sure that abortion procedure training remains a part of medical school education, fighting the attempts of anti-choice groups to have that training eliminated from medical school curricula.

Abortion is still a legal right, and *Roe v. Wade* has not yet been overturned, but assaults on women's reproductive freedom continue, so Third Wavers maintain ongoing vigilance and activism in this area.

Body Image and Eating Disorders

Second Wavers identified disordered eating and body image as feminist issues, and interpreted the power relations underlying them. Third Wavers continue the struggle over how big the female body is permitted to be, how much space it can take up, and what it should look like. Some feminists question whether struggling with an eating disorder is a form of political activism, since it does not involve attempts to change laws, institutional politics, or social policy, and it is largely a personal struggle rather than a collective one. On the other hand, Third Waver Abra Fortune Chernik, a one-time anorexic and bulimic, asserts, "Gaining weight and getting my head out of the toilet bowl was the most political act I have ever committed" (Chernik 2001, 81). Third Wave activism about body image occurs through media like autobiography, visual art, theater, song lyrics, and blogs. Feminist artists and social critics use these forms to create alternative representations of the female body and to promote dialogue and consciousness-raising about body image.

Sexuality

The Third Wave is insistently sex-positive. Whereas Second Wavers focused on preventing sexual victimization of women, Third Wavers want to explore the domain of sexual activity free of all judgments. They critique Second Wavers for losing sight of women's pleasure as a goal in their battles against date rape and pornography. Third Wavers, by contrast, are likely to celebrate or produce female-centered pornography, rather than supporting the prohibition of male-centered pornography. As Debbie Stoller writes, "from fucking around to cursing like sailors to watching porn to shaking our booties at the local strip joint, we are sexual adventuresses who, unlike our foremothers, don't dare to assume that we know what 'female sexuality' is all about" (Stoller 1999, 84). Third Wavers have critiqued government-funded abstinence-only sex education programs in the public schools. Feminists charge that these programs rely upon the sexist virgin/whore dichotomy, give out misinformation about contraception, and prohibit the teaching of safe-sex practices. Jessica Valenti puts it like this: "The government is spending $178 million a year to tell young women they're big whores if they give it up, and various other untruths" (Valenti 2007, 21). Third Wavers also work for gay marriage and adoption rights, as well as rights for transgendered people.

Work

Third Wavers came of age in an economic climate rather different from that of Second Wavers, particularly white middle-class Second Wavers. Middle-class Third Wavers grew up assuming that they would have careers, and there are, indeed, more opportunities for women in many professions and trades. However, there is still a gender wage gap: women earned 76 percent of what men earned in 1998. While college-educated women's earnings rose between 1980 and 2000, by about 22 percent, there was little or no increase in earnings for women without a college education during the same period. Third Waver Michelle Sidler writes that, whereas Second Wave activism "took the shape of hard work in positions that pushed on a glass ceiling, a third wave activism might take the form of denying or resisting corporate America by starting worker-friendly businesses or by helping employees unite to buy out their companies, thus returning the wealth and capital of the company to those who fostered it" (Sidler 1997, 36). Third Wavers also mobilize to support working-class women's needs for workplace protections. In 2003, for instance, thanks to grassroots feminist activists, the New York City Council passed a bill (the first in the country) protecting domestic workers against exploitation.

The Mommy Wars—women's struggles to balance work and family—continue to be an area of feminist activism as well. In recent years, a flurry of books about motherhood has been published, including Judith Warner's *Perfect Madness* (2005), Susan J. Douglas and Meredith W. Michaels' *The Mommy Myth* (2004), Susan Maushart's *The Mask of Motherhood* (1999), and the anthologies *The Mommy Wars* (Steiner 2006) and *The Bitch in the House* (Hanauer 2002). These books cover ground familiar to Second Wavers—busting the Supermom stereotype and describing their struggles to maintain a healthy balance between working and mothering. But if the issues are not new, it is nevertheless significant that younger women are beginning to speak up in greater numbers and louder voices. It is likely that, as more Third Wavers confront motherhood/work issues in their own lives, these issues will become a more significant focus of Third Wave activism.

Transnational Feminism

Raised in an era of globalization, Third Wavers are more likely to be conversant with global feminist issues than Second Wavers may have been. Many gender studies courses now incorporate a global perspective into the curriculum. Feminists from the United States and other western industrialized nations confront the thorny matter of how to engage with women in cultures whose practices are perceived to be misogynist. Respect for cultural self-determination and the desire not to impose western cultural values conflict with feminist desires to raise the consciousnesses of Third World women about such practices as honor killings and female genital mutilation. Transnational feminist activists direct their efforts in areas such as sweatshop labor, education and literacy for women and girls, women's health, human trafficking, genocide, and the environment. The Feminist Majority Foundation, for instance, has a "Global Women's and Reproductive Rights" campaign, focused on engaging young women in global activism. Participating student activists educate fellow students on their home campuses about women's health and reproductive rights, violence against women, and the connections between environmentalism and feminism, all in a transnational context.

Media

Much of Third Wave action is to be found in journalism, the Internet, and the arts. In print media, young women started zines—small, self-published, grassroots magazines—over which they maintained total editorial control. Both *Bitch* and *BUST,* for instance, began as zines, each of them eventually going national. *BUST,* launched in 1993, describes itself as "fierce, funny, and proud to be female," offering "an uncensored view on the female experience" (*BUST* Web site, http://www.bust.com/index.php, http://www.bust.com/info/about.html). *Bitch: Feminist Response to Pop Culture,* launched in 1996, is "about critically examining the images of things like femininity, feminism, class, race, and sexuality that are thrown at us by the media" (*Bitch: Feminist Response to Pop Culture* Web site, http://www.bitchmagazine.org, http://www.bitchmagazine.org/about/). Other, larger magazines with national circulation were pitched for Third Wavers who found *Ms.* unexciting and for girls, as an alternative to fashion magazines. *Sassy,* (published 1988–1994) was an alternative teen magazine. Its young editors steered clear of content about dieting, boys, and celebrities, instead writing hip and candid articles about sexuality and the real lives of girls. *Hues,* an acronym for "Hear Us Emerging Sister" (published 1992–1997), situated multicultural and multiracial feminism at its center, and used the subtitle "A Woman's Guide to Power and Attitude," not explicitly declaring itself feminist, in order to reach those who had been turned off to feminism by the forces of backlash. Despite not using the F word, however, the *Hues* editorial staff thought of its agenda as resolutely feminist.

The impact of the Internet on the Third Wave has been profound. Third Wavers, often more computer literate than their Second Wave sisters, have launched a number of online resources for feminists. These online sites use cyberspace to create feminist communities, in which feminists can discuss political beliefs, share personal experiences, create agendas for political action, and share information about reproductive technologies or other matters of mutual concern. The Internet is as much a site of consciousness-raising for the Third Wave as meeting with speculums in someone's living room was in the Second Wave. *BUST* magazine, for instance, hosts a Web site with a variety of chat rooms on topics like media, fads, love and dating, body image, work, relationship, global politics, and teens. Women enter these chat rooms with a range of perspectives and feminist consciousness. For newcomers to feminism, online chatting may be a way to learn about and explore feminist ideas. The range of topics itself indicates an expansion of feminist belief—that one might reconcile a taste in S/M or B/D sex with one's feminist principles, for instance. Moreover, the Internet has engendered new forms of technology-assisted activism. For instance, HollaBack organizations in cities around the world host Web sites on which they post cell-phone photographs of street harassers sent in by victims.

The Internet can be a democratizing force for those with Internet access. Anyone can launch a Web site, create a blog, or post a video on YouTube. Yet, feminists disagree about whether what is touted as "cyberfeminism" is truly

Eve Ensler and the *Vagina Monologues* Phenomenon

In 1996, playwright, actress, and feminist Eve Ensler first performed her Obie-Award-winning one-woman play, *The Vagina Monologues*. Based on over two hundred interviews with women of different ages, races, and sexualities, the monologues cover a wide range of topics: some women speak of being raped or sexually abused, some about feeling disconnected from their bodies, some about the joy they take in experiencing sexual pleasure. In speaking so explicitly about women's bodies, Ensler's goal was to overcome the shame and silences that are connected with women's sexual experience.

The play sparked a movement. Ensler and a group of activists organized an event called "V-Day" to raise funds for groups that work to fight violence against women. At the first V-Day, held in New York on February 14th, 1998, *The Vagina Monologues* was performed by a host of famous women, including Whoopi Goldberg, Susan Sarandon, and Glenn Close. From there, the movement spread. Every year, students produce *The Vagina Monologues* on college campuses around the U.S., to raise awareness and often to raise funds for local organizations that fight violence against women. The national V-Day fund supports similar grassroots efforts in numerous countries around the world.

The V-Day movement continues to thrive through annual benefit performances, and to work towards the eradication of violence against women in communities all over the globe. V-Day and *The Vagina Monologues* have also bridged the gap between Second and Third Wave feminists. Drawing upon Third Wave sensibilities, *The Vagina Monologues* takes a resolute and joyful pro-sex stance, while also upholding a vigorous standard of activism characteristic of the Second Wave.

feminist, or whether it merely repackages western consumerism in the guise of girl power. Some critics have argued that cyberfeminism offers a fantasy of global sisterhood rather than a reality. As Stacy Gillis writes, "That fewer than 20 percent of global households have electricity—let alone Internet access—raises the question of whose politics this fantasy obscures" (Gillis 2004, 191).

Third Wavers have expressed their politics and activism not only through journalism and the Internet, but also through conventional artistic media as well. One notable example is Eve Ensler's play, *The Vagina Monologues*, which debuted in 1996. *The Vagina Monologues* was a national hit, won an Obie award, and spawned an international activist movement to end violence against women. Every year, the play is produced on college campuses around the country on Valentine's Day. Proceeds from ticket sales benefit domestic abuse advocacy organizations. Lilith Fair, an all-woman rock festival organized by musician Sarah McLachlan, traveled and performed from 1997–1999. The tour earned over $16.4 million in its first year, and gave $20,000 (on average) to battered women's shelters or social service agencies in each locale in which it performed. Examples like Lilith Fair and *The Vagina Monologues* demonstrate that feminist art projects can garner significant national attention and acclaim, and that they can draw enough audience support to create a sizeable purse for feminist-based activism.

Eve Ensler, author of *The Vagina Monologues,* poses in her dressing room at the Booth Theatre before performing her new one-person Broadway show, *The Good Body,* 2004. (AP/Wide World Photos)

Conclusion

It is clear that much of what Second Wave feminism tried to accomplish has yet to be realized, due to resistance from antifeminist forces in the United States. But the vitality and scope of Third Wave feminism is proof of the ongoing commitment of the younger generation of women to fight for the rights of women. If the movement is quieter, that may not mean that it is less effective. The authors of *Manifesta* write, "Whether casting spells or *Bitch*ing, it's a sign of the times that feminists today are more likely to be individuals quietly (or not so quietly) living self-determined lives than radicals on the ramparts. They are experts in their fields—media, politics, advertising, business—rather than expert feminists (though they are often that, too)" (Baumgardner and Richards 2000, 36). It may be that the integration of feminist values into the domestic, social, and professional fabric of U.S. society will be the most important contribution of the Third Wave towards advancing the cause of equality for women. Collective activism—in the form of a visible social movement—may not be in evidence until a fourth wave comes into being.

References and Further Reading

Baumgardner, Jennifer, and Amy Richards. *Manifesta: Young Women, Feminism, and the Future.* New York: Farrar, Strauss and Giroux, 2000.

Baumgardner, Jennifer, and Amy Richards. "Who's the Next Gloria? The Quest for the Third Wave Superleader." In *Catching a Wave: Reclaiming Feminism for the 21st Century,* ed. Rory Dicker and Alison Piepmeir, 159–70. Boston: Northeastern University Press, 2003.

Boston, Robert. *The Most Dangerous Man in America: Pat Robertson and the Rise of the Christian Coalition.* Amherst, NY: Prometheus Books, 1996.

The Boston Women's Health Collective. *Our Bodies, Ourselves: For the New Century.* New York: Simon & Schuster, 1998.

Bowler, Mary. "Women's Earnings: An Overview." *Monthly Labor Review* 122 (1999): 13–21.

Butler, Judith. *Gender Trouble: Feminism and the Subversion of Identity.* New York: Routledge, 1990.

Chambers, Veronica. "Betrayal Feminism." In *Listen Up: Voices from the Next Feminist Generation,* 2nd ed., ed. Barbara Findlen, 258–64. Seattle, WA: Seal Press, 2001.

Chernik, Abra Fortune. "The Body Politic." In *Listen Up: Voices from the Next Feminist Generation,* 2nd ed., ed. Barbara Findlen, 103–11. Seattle, WA: Seal Press, 2001.

Douglas, Susan J., and Meredith W. Michaels. *The Mommy Myth: The Idealization of Motherhood and How It Has Undermined All Women.* New York: Free Press, 2004.

Ebeling, Kay. "The Failure of Feminism." *Newsweek,* 116 no. 21 (1990): 9.

Ensler, Eve. *The Vagina Monologues.* The V-Day ed. New York: Villard, 2001.

Faludi, Susan. *Backlash: The Undeclared War against American Women.* New York: Crown, 1991.

Findlen, Barbara, ed. *Listen Up: Voices from the Next Feminist Generation.* 2nd ed. Seattle: Seal Press, 2001.

Fixmer, Natalie, and Julia T. Wood. "The Personal is *Still* Political: Embodied Politics in Third Wave Feminism." *Women's Studies in Communication* 28, no. 2 (2005): 235–57.

Friedan, Betty. "Twenty Years after the Feminine Mystique." *New York Times,* February 27, 1983, late edition (East Coast), A35.

Gillis, Stacy. "Neither Cyborg Nor Goddess: The (Im)Possibilities of Cyberfeminism." In *Third Wave Feminism: A Critical Exploration,* ed. Stacy Gillis, Gillian Howie, and Rebecca Munford, 185–96. New York: Palmgrave Macmillan, 2004.

Hall, Elaine J., and Marnie Salupo Rodriguez. "The Myth of Postfeminism." *Gender and Society* 17 (2003): 878–902.

Hanauer, Cathi, ed. *The Bitch in the House: 26 Women Tell the Truth About Sex, Solitude, Work, Motherhood, and Marriage.* New York: William Morrow, 2002.

Havens, Candace. *Joss Whedon: The Genius Behind Buffy.* Dallas, TX: Benbella Books, 2003.

Henry, Astrid. *Not My Mother's Sister: Generational Conflict and Third Wave Feminism.* Bloomington: Indiana University Press, 2004.

Heywood, Leslie, and Jennifer Drake. "We Learn America Like a Script: Activism in the Third Wave; or Enough Phantoms of Nothing." In *Third Wave Agenda: Being Feminist, Doing Feminism,* ed. Leslie Heywood and Jennifer Drake, 40–54. Minneapolis: University of Minnesota Press, 1997.

Heywood, Leslie, and Jennifer Drake, eds. *Third Wave Agenda: Being Feminist, Doing Feminism.* Minneapolis: University of Minnesota Press, 1997.

Hurdis, Rebecca. "Heartbroken: Women of Color Feminism and the Third Wave." In *Colonize This!: Young Women of Color on Today's Feminism,* ed. Daisy Hernández and Bushra Rehman, 279–92. New York: Seal Press, 2002.

Jervis, Lisa. "Goodbye to Feminism's Generational Divide." In *We Don't Need Another Wave: Dispatches from the Next Generation of Feminists,* ed. Melody Berger, 12–18. New York: Seal Press, 2006.

Jong, Erica. "Ally McBeal and *Time* Magazine Can't Keep the Good Women Down." *New York Observer,* July 13, 1998, Front Page, 19.

Klein, Melissa. "Duality and Redefinition: Young Feminism and the Alternative Music Community." In *Third Wave Agenda: Being Feminist, Doing Feminism,* ed. Leslie Heywood and Jennifer Drake, 207–25. Minneapolis: University of Minnesota Press, 1997.

Latifah, Queen. *Ladies First: Revelations of a Strong Woman.* New York: William Morrow, 1999.

Lorde, Audre. *Sister Outsider: Essays and Speeches.* Freedom, CA: The Crossing Press, 1984.

Maushart, Susan. *The Mask of Motherhood: How Becoming a Mother Changes Our Lives and Why We Never Talk About It.* New York: Penguin Books, 1999.

Naples, Nancy A., and Manisha Desai, eds. *Women's Activism and Globalization: Linking Local Struggles and Transnational Politics.* New York: Routledge, 2002.

Paglia, Camille. *Sex, Art, and American Culture.* New York: Vintage, 1992.

Poo, Ai-jen, and Eric Tang. "Domestic Workers Organize in the Global City." In *The Fire This Time: Young Activists and the New Feminism,* ed. Vivien Labaton and Dawn Lundy Martin, 150–65. New York: Anchor Books, 2004.

Pough, Gwendolyn. *Check It While I Wreck It: Black Womanhood, Hip-Hop Culture, and the Public Sphere.* Boston: Northeastern University Press, 2004.

Roiphe, Katie. *The Morning After: Sex, Fear, and Feminism on Campus.* Boston: Little, Brown and Company, 1993.

Sidler, Michelle. "Living in McJobdom." In *Third Wave Agenda: Being Feminist, Doing Feminism,* ed. Leslie Heywood and Jennifer Drake, 25–39. Minneapolis: University of Minnesota Press, 1997.

Siegel, Deborah L. "Reading Between the Waves: Feminist Historiography in a 'Postfeminist' Moment." In *Third Wave Agenda: Being Feminist, Doing Feminism,* ed. Leslie Heywood and Jennifer Drake, 55–82. Minneapolis: University of Minnesota Press, 1997.

Steiner, Leslie, ed. *Mommy Wars: Stay-at-Home and Career Moms Face Off on Their Choices, Their Lives, Their Families.* New York: Random House, 2006.

Stoller, Debbie. "Sex and the Thinking Girl." In *The Bust Guide to the New Girl Order,* ed. Marcelle Karp and Debbie Stoller, 75–84. New York: Penguin, 1999.

Valenti, Jessica. *Full Frontal Feminism: A Young Woman's Guide to Why Feminism Matters.* Emeryville, CA: Seal Press, 2007.

Walker, Rebecca. "Becoming the Third Wave." *Ms.* (January 1992): 39–41.

Walker, Rebecca. "Being Real: An Introduction." In *To Be Real: Telling the Truth and Changing the Face of Feminism,* ed. Rebecca Walker, xxix–xl. New York: Anchor Books, 1995.

Warner, Judith. *Perfect Madness: Motherhood in the Age of Anxiety.* New York: Riverhead Books, 2005.

Wolf, Naomi. *The Beauty Myth: How Images of Beauty Are Used against Women.* New York: William Morrow, 1991.

Wolf, Naomi. *Fire with Fire: The New Female Power and How It Will Change the 21st Century.* New York: Random House, 1993.

Web Sites for Further Reference

Bitch: Feminist Responses to Pop Culture. http://www.bitchmagazine.org.

BUST. http://www.bust.com/index.php.

Feminist Majority Foundation. http://www.feministcampus.org.

HollaBack NYC. http://www.hollabacknyc.blogspot.com/.

Third Wave Foundation. http://www.thirdwavefoundation.org.

Primary Source Documents

The Witchcraft Examination of Bridget Bishop

Bridget Bishop was a widow in her early fifties who had faced witchcraft accusations in 1680, but was acquitted at the conclusion of her trial. These prior witchcraft accusations likely made Bishop more susceptible to renewed accusations in 1692. Also, Bishop's age and widowhood might have made her a target. During the Salem witchcraft outbreak, Mercy Lewis, Ann Putnam Jr., and other young women charged Bishop's likeness or "specter" with physically torturing and possessing them. Salem authorities arrested Bishop and placed her on trial. In the following trial testimony, Bishop faces her accusers and continues to protest her innocence. Upon the conclusion of her trial, Bishop was found guilty and hanged on June 10, 1692.

THE EXAMINATION OF BRIDGET BISHOP, APRIL 19, 1692

(The examination of Bridget Bishop before the Worshipfull John Harthon and Jonathan Curren esq'rs)

Bridget Bishop being now coming in to be examined relating to her accusation of Suspicon of sundry acts of witchcrafts the afflicted persons are now dreadfully afflicted by her as they doe say.

(Mr. Harthon): Bishop what doe you say you here stand charged with sundry acts of witchcraft by you done or committed upon the bodyes of mercy Lews and An Putnam and others.

(Bishop): I am innocent I know nothing of it I have done no witchcraft

(Mr. Har): Looke upon this woman and see if this be the woman that you have seen hurting you. Mercy Lewes and An Putnam and others doe [doe] now charge her to her face with hurting of them.

(Mr. Harthon): What doe you say now you see they charge you to your face

(Bish): I never did hurt them in my life I did never see these persons before I am as innocent as the child unborn

(Mr. Harth): is not your coate cut

(Bish): [RECORDER'S NOTE: answers no but her garment being Looked upon they find it cut or toren two wayes Jonathan walcoate saith that the sword that he strucke at goode Bishup with was not naked but was within the scabbord so that the rent may very probablie be the very same that mary walcoate did tell that she had in her coate by Jonathans stricking at her apperance The afflicted persons charge her, with having hurt them many wayes and by tempting them to sine to the devils Booke at which charge she seemed to be very angrie and shaking her head at them saying it was false they are all greatly tormented (as I conceive) by the shaking of her head]

(Mr Har): good Bishop what contract have you made with the devill

(Bish): I have made no contract with the devill I never saw him in my life. An Putnam sayeth that shee calls the devill her God

(Mr. Har): what say you to all this that you are charged with can you not find in your heart to tell the truth

(Bish): I doe tell the truth I never hurt these persons in my life I never saw them before.

(Mercy Lewes): oh goode Bishop did you not come to our house the Last night and did you not tell me that your master made you tell mor than you were willing to tell

(Mr Har): tell us the truth in this matter how comes these persons to be thus tormented and to charge you with doing

(Bish): I am not come here to say I am a witch to take away my life

(Mr H): who is that that doth it if you doe not they say it is your likenes that comes and torments them and tempts them to write in the booke what Booke is that you tempt them with.

(Bish): I know nothing of it I am innocent.

(Mr Harth): doe you not see how they are tormented you are acting witchcraft before us what doe you say to ths why have you not an heart to confese the truth

(Bish): I am innocent I know nothing of it I am no witch I know not what a witch is.

(Mr H): have you not given consent that some evill spirit should doe this in your likeness.

(B): no I am innocent of being a witch I know no man woman or child here

(Marshall Herrik): how came you into my bed chamber one morning then and asked me whether I had any curtains to sell shee is by some of the aflicted persons charged with murder

(Mr Harth): what doe you say to these murders you are charged with

(B): I am innocent I know nothing of it now she lifts up her eyes and they are greatly tormented again

(Mr Har): what doe you say to these things here horrible acts of witch craft (Bish) I know nothing of it I doe not know whither be any witches or no

(Mr Har): no have you not heard that some have confessed.

(Bish): no I did not.

[RECORDER'S NOTE: two men told her to her face that they had told her here shee is taken in a plain lie now shee is going away they are dreadfully afflicted 5 afflicted persons doe charge this woman to be the very woman that hurts them This is a true account of what I have taken down at her examination according to best understanding and observation I have also in her examination taken notice that all her actions have great influence upon the aflicted persons and that they have been tortored by her]

Ezekiel Cheever

Source: Famous American Trials Website, by Douglas Linder, "Salem Witchcraft Trials 1692." http://www.law.umkc.edu/faculty/projects/ftrials/salem/ASA_BISX.HTM.

Letter from Narragansett Indian Sarah Simon to Eleazar Wheelock

The following letter, penned by Narragansett Indian Sarah Simon and sent to Eleazar Wheelock, founder of Lebanon, Connecticut's Moor's Indian Charity School, appears rather unremarkable upon first glance. Yet there is a great deal of history bound up in Simon's simple request to return home in order to care for her ailing mother. Rhode Island's Narragansett Indians had been major players in Southern New England's diplomatic arena during the early colonial period. King Philip's War (1675–1676) proved devastating for the tribe, however, and inaugurated a long period of painful adjustment. The English destroyed the Narragansetts' main village during the war, then disease and subsequent conflicts reduced their numbers dramatically. The Great Awakening, then, held a great deal of appeal to a people who were not only struggling to survive, but also struggling to make sense of their dramatically changed world. The majority of surviving Narragansetts converted to Christianity during the 1740s and established a church on their small reservation.

The tribe also sent several of its children to Moor's County Charity School, which was later moved to Hanover, New Hampshire, and renamed Dartmouth College. However, these efforts to educate area Indians, which was a major component of early Indian policy, ultimately bore little fruit. Because of a general lack of economic resources, reformers like Wheelock often spent far more time on fundraising efforts than in the classroom. Still, as evidenced by Sarah Simon's letter, many of these Indians managed to learn to read and write. Although Simon's letter seems rather crudely written, a closer look reveals a shrewd mind at work, capable of couching her request to return home in language that a reformer and educator would have found irresistible. First of all, Wheelock is referred to in the third person, as an indication of deference. Then Simon assures Wheelock that she has no desire to return home on a permanent basis, and concludes by attesting not only to her commitment to God but also to her commitment to Wheelock's mission to save her "poor Parishing Brethren."

Lebanon Apral 4th 1769

Revend and Honrd Sir

as I have Receved many kind favours I desire to bag one homble request ond that is whether the Doctor would be willing to let me go to my home if I would not be gone no longer then if I only want to Mohegin. for I wont very much to See my Mother I understand She has mate with trouble latly and She wants see me and she is not able to come See me. and tharfore I think it my gret Duty to go and See hir.

for I donot think that she is long for this world I have no Reson to thing so. for She is very weekly and always Sick. my Parant is very near and Dear to me: and being I do not desine to Ever to go home and live with hir again, I Desire to beg that favour to go and see hir as ofen as the Doctor is willing I should for I dont want to ofand the Doctr in the least. but I feel willing to do any thing Sir that you think is bast for me.

Oh how I orto Blease and adore that grat and kind God that put it in the hands of some of his Pepple to take so much Care of the poor indions nee above all the rast. it Seems to me I could go any where or do any thing if it would do any good to my poor Parishing Brethren.

So I desire to Subscrib mysilfe your
Ever Dutyfull Sarvent

Sarah Simon

Source: Colin G. Calloway, ed., The World Turned Upside Down: Indian Voices from Early America *(Boston: Bedford/St. Martin's, 1994), 64.*

Esther DeBerdt Reed, "The Sentiments of an American Woman"

In May of 1780, George Washington reported that his troops were facing serious shortages of supplies, and immediate relief was needed. A group of women in Philadelphia, led by Esther DeBerdt Reed and Sarah Bache Franklin, formed the Ladies Association of Philadelphia, and went from house to house soliciting support. This was one of the first times American women organized to raise money on behalf of a public cause. They were immensely successful; according to a letter from Reed to Washington, they raised more than $300,000 in paper currency.

This broadside, attributed to Reed, explains, defends, and encourages women's fundraising efforts for the Patriot cause. It sets out examples of women's patriotic deeds in the near and distant past to justify women's involvement in political action and encourage women to make sacrifices to serve the public good.

ON the commencement of actual war, the Women of America manifested a firm resolution to contribute as much as could depend on them, to the deliverance of their country. Animated by the purest patriotism, they are sensible of sorrow at this day, in not offering more than barren wishes for the success of so glorious a Revolution. They aspire to render themselves more really useful; and this sentiment is universal from the north to the south of the Thirteen United States. Our ambition is kindled by the same of those heroines of antiquity, who have rendered their sex illustrious, and have proved to the universe, that, if the weakness of our Constitution, if opinion and manners did not forbid us to march to glory by the same paths as the Men, we should at least equal, and sometimes surpass them in our love for the public good. I glory in all that which my sex has done great and commendable. I call to mind with enthusiasm and with admiration, all those acts of courage, of constancy and patriotism, which history has transmitted to us: The people favoured by Heaven, preserved from destruction by the virtues, the zeal and the resolution of Deborah, of Judith, of Esther! The fortitude of the mother of the Macchabees, in giving up her sons to die before her eyes: Rome saved from the fury of a victorious enemy by the efforts of Volumnia, and other Roman Ladies: So many famous sieges where the Women have been seen forgeting the weakness of their sex, building new walls, digging trenches with their feeble hands, furnishing arms to their defenders, they themselves darting the missile weapons on the enemy, resigning the ornaments of their apparel, and their fortune, to fill the public treasury, and to hasten the deliverance of their country; burying themselves under its ruins, throwing themselves into the flames rather than submit to the disgrace of humiliation before a proud enemy.

Born for liberty, disdaining to bear the irons of a tyrannic Government, we associate ourselves to the grandeur of those Sovereigns, cherished and revered, who have held with so much splendour the scepter of the greatest States, The Batildas, the Elizabeths, the Maries, the Catharines, who have extended the empire of liberty, and contented to reign by sweetness and justice, have broken the chains of slavery, forged by tryants in the times of ignorance and barbarity. The Spanish Women, do they not make, at this moment, the most patriotic sacrifices, to encrease the means of victory in the hands of their Sovereign. He is a friend to the French Nation. They are our allies. We call to mind, doubly interested, that it was a French Maid who kindled up amongst her fellow-citizens, the flame of patriotism buried under long misfortunes: It was the Maid of Orleans who drove from the kingdom of France the ancestors of those same British, whose odious yoke we have just shaken off; and whom it is necessary that we drive from this Continent.

But I must limit myself to the recollection of this small number of atchievements. Who knows if persons disposed to censure, and sometimes too severely with regard to us, may not disapprove our appearing acquainted even with the actions of which our sex boasts? We are at least certain, that he cannot be a good citizen who will not applaud our efforts for the relief of the armies which defend our lives, our possessions, our liberty? The situation of our soldiery has been represented to me; the evils inseparable from war, and the firm and generous spirit which has enabled them to support these. But it has been said, that they may apprehend, that, in the course of a long war, the view of their distresses may be lost, and their services be forgottten. Forgotten! never; I can answer in the name of all my sex. Brave Americans, your disinterestedness, your courage, and your constancy will always be dear to America, as long as she shall preserve her virtue.

We know that at a distance from the theatre of war, if we enjoy any tranquility, it is the fruit of your watchings, your labours, your dangers. If I live happy in the midst of my family; if my husband cultivates his field, and reaps his harvest in peace; if, surrounded with my children, I myself nourish the youngest, and press it to my bosom, without being affraid of feeing myself separated from it, by a ferocious enemy; if the house in which we dwell; if our barns, our orchards are safe at the present time from the hands of those incendiaries, it is to you that we owe it. And shall we hesitate to evidence to you our gratitude? Shall we hesitate to wear a cloathing more simple; hair dressed less elegant, while at the price of this small privation, we shall deserve your benedictions. Who, amongst us, will not renounce with the highest pleasure, those vain ornaments, when-she shall consider that the valiant defenders of America will be able to draw some advantage from the money which she may have laid out in these; that they will be better defended from the rigours of the seasons, that after their painful toils, they will receive some extraordinary and unexpected relief; that these presents will perhaps be valued by them at a greater price, when they will have it in their power to say: *This is the offering of the Ladies.* The time is arrived to display the same sentiments which animated us at the beginning of the Revolution, when we renounced the use of teas, however agreeable to our taste, rather than receive them from our persecutors; when we made it appear to them that we placed former necessaries in the rank of superfluities, when our liberty was interested; when our republican and laborious hands spun the flax, prepared the linen intended for the use of our soldiers; when exiles and fugitives we supported with courage all the evils which are the concomitants of war. Let us not lose a moment; let us be engaged to offer the homage of our gratitude at the altar of military valour, and you, our brave deliverers, while mercenary slaves combat to cause you to share with them, the irons with which they are loaded, receive with a free hand our offering, the purest which can be presented to your virtue,

By An *AMERICAN WOMAN.*

Source: The Sentiments of an American Woman *(Philadelphia, 1780). The Library of Congress, American Memory Website, "An American Time Capsule: Three Centuries of Broadsides and Other Printed Ephemera." http://hdl.loc.gov/loc.rbc/rbpe.14600300.*

The Declaration of Sentiments

Principally drafted by Elizabeth Cady Stanton and approved by the delegates at the first women's rights convention, held in Seneca Falls, New York, in July of 1848, the Declaration of Sentiments became the foundational document in the organized movement for women's rights in the United States. Stanton and the delegates purposely modeled their manifesto on the Declaration of Independence. The first part of the Declaration, excerpted below, outlined women's civil, social, legal, religious, and political grievances. This was followed by a series of Resolutions, which proclaimed for women the same rights and responsibilities men enjoyed as citizens of a democracy.

Reaction to the Declaration of Sentiments was decidedly mixed, even among supporters of women's rights. Many feared that the document's emphasis on woman suffrage might impede the fight for other rights for women, including married women's property rights. Other, far more critical, observers chastised the female convention participants for dangerously overstepping the bounds of woman's sphere. Women's rights advocates fully expected that their bold statement would be summarily mocked and dismissed. They nonetheless continued to rely on the Declaration of Sentiments as a source of inspiration and direction as they bravely forged ahead in the struggle for gender equality in the decades to come.

When, in the course of human events, it becomes necessary for one portion of the family of man to assume among the people of the earth a position different from that which they have hitherto occupied, but one to which the laws of nature and of nature's God entitle them, a decent respect to the opinions of mankind requires that they should declare the causes that impel them to such a course.

We hold these truths to be self-evident: that all men and women are created equal; that they are endowed by their Creator with certain inalienable rights; that among these are life, liberty, and the pursuit of happiness; that to secure these rights governments are instituted, deriving their just powers from the consent of the governed. Whenever any form of government becomes destructive of these ends, it is the right of those who suffer from it to refuse allegiance to it, and to insist upon the institution of a new government, laying its foundation on such principles, and organizing its powers in such form, as to them shall seem most likely to effect their safety and happiness. Prudence, indeed, will dictate that governments long established should not be changed for light and transient causes; and accordingly all experience hath shown that mankind are more disposed to suffer, while evils are sufferable, than to right themselves by abolishing the forms to which they were accustomed. But when a long train of abuses and usurpations, pursuing invariably the same object, evinces a design to reduce them under absolute despotism, it is their duty to throw off such government, and to provide new guards for their future security. Such has been the patient sufferance of the women under this government, and such is now the necessity which constrains them to demand the equal station to which they are entitled.

The history of mankind is a history of repeated injuries and usurpations on the part of man toward woman, having in direct object the establishment of an absolute tyranny over her. To prove this, let facts be submitted to a candid world.

He has never permitted her to exercise her inalienable right to the elective franchise.

He has compelled her to submit to laws, in the formation of which she had no voice.

He has withheld from her rights which are given to the most ignorant and degraded men—both natives and foreigners.

Having deprived her of this first right of a citizen, the elective franchise, thereby leaving her without representation in the halls of legislation, he has oppressed her on all sides.

He has made her, if married, in the eye of the law, civilly dead.

He has taken from her all right in property, even to the wages she earns.

He has made her morally, an irresponsible being, as she can commit many crimes with impunity, provided they be done in the presence of her husband. In the covenant of marriage, she is compelled to promise obedience to her husband, he becoming, to all intents and purposes, her master—the law giving him power to deprive her of her liberty, and to administer chastisement.

He has so framed the laws of divorce, as to what shall be the proper causes, and in case of separation, to whom the guardianship of the children shall be given, as to be wholly regardless of the happiness of the women—the law, in all cases, going upon a false supposition of the supremacy of man, and giving all power into his hands.

After depriving her of all rights as a married woman, if single, and the owner of property, he has taxed her to support a government which recognizes her only when her property can be made profitable to it.

He has monopolized nearly all the profitable employments, and from those she is permitted to follow, she receives but a scanty remuneration. He closes against her all the avenues to wealth and distinction, which he considers most honorable to himself. As a teacher of theology, medicine, or law, she is not known.

He has denied her the facilities for obtaining a thorough education, all colleges being closed against her.

He allows her in Church, as well as State, but a subordinate position, claiming Apostolic authority for her exclusion from the ministry, and, with some exceptions, from any public participation in the affairs of the Church.

He has created a false public sentiment by giving to the world a different code of morals for men and women, by which moral delinquencies which exclude women from society, are not only tolerated but deemed of little account in man.

He has usurped the prerogative of Jehovah himself, claiming it as his right to assign for her a sphere of action, when that belongs to her conscience and to her God.

He has endeavored, in every way that he could, to destroy her confidence in her own powers, to lessen her self-respect, and to make her willing to lead a dependent and abject life.

Now, in view of this entire disfranchisement of one-half the people of this country, their social and religious degradation—in view of the unjust laws above mentioned, and because women do feel themselves aggrieved, oppressed, and fraudulently deprived of their most sacred rights, we insist that they have immediate admission to all the rights and privileges which belong to them as citizens of the United States.

In entering upon the great work before us, we anticipate no small amount of misconception, misrepresentation, and ridicule; but we shall use every instrumentality within our power to effect our object. We shall employ agents, circulate tracts, petition the State and National legislatures, and endeavor to enlist the pulpit and the press in our behalf. We hope this Convention will be followed by a series of Conventions embracing every part of the country.

Source: Elizabeth Cady Stanton, Susan B. Anthony, and Matilda Joslyn Gage, eds., History of Woman Suffrage, *vol. 1, 1881. Rochester, NY: Charles Mann, 1887, 70–71.*

Buffalo Bird Woman Laments the Losses Experienced by the Hidatsa People

The following oral history offers a window into how Native women likely felt about the gradual loss of their tribes' subsistence base during the 19th century, as well as the cultural fallout that accompanied this development. Buffalo Bird Woman, a Hidatsa Indian, describes the profound sense of loss and alienation felt by those Indians who recognized all too well the fact that their lives had been changed forever by colonization, and that they were likely the worse for it.

I am an old woman now. The buffaloes and black-tail deer are gone, and our Indian ways are almost gone. Sometimes I find it hard to believe that I ever lived them.

My little son grew up in the white man's school. He can read books, and he owns cattle and has a farm. He is a leader among our Hidatsa people, helping teach them to follow the white man's road.

He is kind to me. We no longer live in an earth lodge, but in a house with chimneys; and my son's wife cooks by a stove.

But for me, I cannot forget our old ways.

Often in summer I rise at daybreak and steal out to the cornfields; and as I hoe the corn I sing to it, as we did when I was young. No one cares for our corn songs now.

Sometimes at evening I sit, looking out on the big Missouri. The sun sets, and dusk steals over the water. In the shadows I seem again to see our Indian village, with smoke curling upward from the earth lodges; and in the river's roar I hear the yells of the warriors, the laughter of little children as of old. It is but an old woman's dream. Again I see but shadows and hear only the roar of the river; and tears come into my eyes. Our Indian life, I know, is gone forever.

Source: Colin G. Calloway, ed., Our Hearts Fell to the Ground: Plains Indian Views of How the West Was Lost *(Boston: Bedford/St. Martin's, 1996), 156.*

Zitkala-Sa, School Days of an Indian Girl

Zitkala-Sa [Gertrude Simmons Bonnin] (1876–1938) was born on a South Dakota Indian reservation and was educated at a Quaker missionary school in Indiana. As an adult, she became a writer and devoted herself to reform work for Native American rights and culture. In addition to political activism, she wrote about the tensions she and other Native Americans felt between maintaining their traditions and becoming acculturated to the larger society in the United States.

The following excerpt from *The School Days of an Indian Girl* recollects Native American experiences at Indian boarding schools. In this selection, a young girl describes her first days at the boarding school where her teachers sought to civilize her by changing her appearance. Female reformers often thought education could be used to help other women better their positions in society. But the actions of the European-American reformers whom Zitkala-Sa describes show how education could be used to impose one set of beliefs and values on a subordinate group. At the same time, education enabled Zitkala-Sa to become a leader for her people.

Late in the morning, my friend Judewin gave me a terrible warning. Judewin knew a few words of English, and she had overheard the paleface woman talk about cutting our long, heavy hair. Our mothers had taught us that only unskilled warriors who were captured had their hair shingled by the enemy. Among our people, short hair was worn by mourners, and shingled hair by cowards!

We discussed our fate some moments, and when Judewin said, "We have to submit, because they are strong," I rebelled.

"No, I will not submit! I will struggle first!" I answered.

I watched my chance, and when no one noticed I disappeared. I crept up the stairs as quietly as I could in my squeaking shoes,—my moccasins had been exchanged for shoes. Along the hall I passed, without knowing whither I was going. Turning aside to an open door, I found a large room with three white beds in it. The windows were covered with dark green curtains, which made the room very dim. Thankful that no one was there, I directed my steps toward the corner farthest from the door. On my hands and knees I crawled under the bed, and cuddled myself in the dark corner.

From my hiding place I peered out, shuddering with fear whenever I heard footsteps near by. Though in the hall loud voices were calling my name, and I knew that even Judewin was searching for me, I did not open my mouth to answer. Then the steps were quickened and the voices became excited. The sounds came nearer and nearer. Women and girls entered the room. I held my breath, and watched them open closet doors and peep behind large trunks. Some one threw up the curtains, and the room was filled with sudden light. What caused them to stoop and look under the bed I do not know. I remember being dragged out, though I resisted by kicking and scratching wildly. In spite of myself, I was carried downstairs and tied fast in a chair.

I cried aloud, shaking my head all the while until I felt the cold blades of the scissors against my neck, and heard them gnaw off one of my thick braids. Then I lost my spirit. Since the day I was taken from my mother I had suffered extreme indignities. People had stared at me. I had been tossed about in the air like a wooden puppet. And now my long hair was shingled like a coward's! In my anguish I moaned for my mother, but no one came to comfort me. Not a soul reasoned quietly with me, as my own mother used to do; for now I was only one of many little animals driven by a herder.

Source: Zitkala-Sa, "School Days of an Indian Girl," Atlantic Monthly 85, no. 508 (February 1900), 185–94.

Emma Goldman, "The Tragedy of Women's Emancipation"

In March 1906, Emma Goldman became publisher, and also coedited, the monthly magazine, *Mother Earth*. Goldman's partner and sometimes lover, Alexander Berkman, became its editor in March 1907. The journal was intended to promote literary radicalism and anarchist ideas but included more extensive discussions of free speech once the police began confiscating the magazine. Goldman published *Mother Earth* from 1906 to 1917, making it one of the longest-running anarchist publications in the United States. She raised most of the funds for its survival, including funds to pay lawyers to defend herself and her coeditors from charges ranging from obscenity to inciting a riot.

The general social antagonism which has taken hold of our entire public life to-day, brought about through the force of opposing and contradictory interests, will crumble to pieces when the reorganization of our social life, based upon the principles of economic justice, shall have become a reality.

Peace and harmony between the sexes and individuals does not necessarily depend on a superficial equalization of human beings; nor does it call for the elimination of individual traits or peculiarities. The problem that confronts us to-day, and which the nearest future is to solve, is how to be oneself, and yet in oneness with others, to feel deeply with all human beings and still retain one's own innate qualities. This seems to me the basis upon which the mass and the individual, the true democrat and the true individuality, man and woman can meet without antagonism and opposition. The motto should not be forgive one another; it should be, understand one another . . .

Emancipation should make it possible for her to be human in the truest sense. Everything within her that craves assertion and activity should reach its fullest expression; and all artificial barriers should be broken and the road towards greater freedom cleared of every trace of centuries of submission and slavery.

This was the original aim of the movement for woman's emancipation. But the results so far achieved have isolated woman and have robbed her of the fountain springs of that happiness which is so essential to her . . .

Liberty and equality for woman! What hopes and aspirations these words awakened when they were first uttered by some of the noblest and bravest souls of those days. The sun in all its light and glory was to rise upon a new world; in this world woman was to be free to direct her own destiny, an aim certainly worthy of the great enthusiasm, courage, perseverance and ceaseless effort of the tremendous host of pioneer men and women, who staked everything against a world of prejudice and ignorance.

My hopes also move towards that goal, but I insist that the emancipation of woman, as interpreted and practically applied to-day, has failed to reach that great end. Now, woman is confronted with the necessity of emancipating herself from emancipation, if she really desires to be free. This may sound paradoxical, but is, nevertheless, only too true.

What has she achieved through her emancipation? Equal suffrage in a few states. Has that purified our political life, as many well-meaning advocates have predicted? Certainly not. Incidentally it is really time that persons with plain, sound judgment should cease to talk about corruption in politics in a boarding-school tone. Corruption of politics has nothing to do with the morals or the laxity of morals of various political personalities. Its cause is altogether a material one. Politics is the reflex of the business and industrial world, the mottoes of which are: 'to take is more blessed than to give'; 'buy cheap and sell dear'; 'one soiled hand washes the other.' There is no hope that even woman, with her right to vote, will ever purify politics . . .

The right to vote, equal civil rights, are all very good demands, but true emancipation begins neither at the polls nor in courts. It begins in woman's soul. History tells us that every oppressed class gained its true liberation from its masters through its own efforts. It is necessary that woman learn that lesson, that she realize that her freedom will reach as far as her power to achieve her freedom reaches. It is therefore far more important for her to begin with her inner regeneration, to cut loose from the weight of prejudices, traditions, and customs. The demand for various equal rights in every vocation in life is just and fair, but, after all, the most vital right is the right to love and be loved . . . Indeed if the partial emancipation is to become a complete and true emancipation of woman, it will have to do away with the ridiculous notion that to be loved, to be sweetheart and mother, is synonymous with being slave or subordinate . . .

A true conception of the relation of the sexes will not admit of conqueror and conquered; it knows of but one great thing: to give of one's self boundlessly in order to find oneself richer, deeper, better. That alone can fill the emptiness and replace the tragedy of woman's emancipation with joy, limitless joy.

Source: Emma Goldman, "The Tragedy of Women's Emancipation," Mother Earth *1, no. 1 (March 1906), 9–18.*

"Why Women Should Vote"

This list of 12 reasons why women should vote was included in one of the Blue Books published by the National American Woman Suffrage Association in 1917. These books were distributed to state and local chapters to help them in their campaigning. The books contained essays and information that women could use to convince an audience, whether a lecture hall full of people or simply their husbands, to support woman suffrage. Notice that both equality and difference rationales are used to justify women's claims for suffrage.

Twelve Reasons Why Women Should Vote

1. BECAUSE those who obey the laws should help to choose those who make the laws.
2. BECAUSE laws affect women as much as men.
3. BECAUSE laws which affect women are now passed without consulting them.
4. BECAUSE laws affecting children should include the woman's point of view as well as the man's.

5. BECAUSE laws affecting the home are voted on in every session of the legislature.

6. BECAUSE women have experience which would be helpful to legislation.

7. BECAUSE to deprive women of the vote is to lower their position in common estimation.

8. BECAUSE having the vote would increase the sense of responsibility among women toward questions of public importance.

9. BECAUSE public-spirited mothers make public-spirited sons.

10. BECAUSE about 8,000,000 women in the United States are wage workers, and the conditions under which they work are controlled by law.

11. BECAUSE the objections against their having the vote are based on prejudice, not on reason.

12. BECAUSE to sum up all reasons in one—*it is for the common good of all.*

Source: Björkman, Frances M., and Annie G. Porritt, eds., "The Blue Book": Woman Suffrage, History, Arguments and Results, rev. ed. (New York: National Woman Suffrage Publishing Co., 1917), 231–32. The Library of Congress, American Memory Website, "Votes for Women: Selections from the National American Woman Suffrage Association Collection, 1848–1921." http://hdl.loc.gov/loc.rbc/rbnawsa.n4862.

Carrie Chapman Catt, "Woman Suffrage Only an Episode"

This article by Carrie Chapman Catt, president of the National American Woman Suffrage Association from 1900 to 1904 and 1915 to 1920, was published as part of a symposium on The New Woman. Throughout the first decade of women being able to vote, there was much discussion about whether or not women were bringing about the changes to politics that they had long advocated would come with women's enfranchisement. Catt, long a moderate voice in women's rights activism, offers her assessment of the campaign for equal rights for women.

There was no "rise" of the woman suffrage movement in the usual sense of that expression. Instead, it "emerged" from the broader woman movement, but it did so through the deliberate design of certain bold spirits, already leaders in the women's agitation, who called a convention in America in 1848 . . . The campaign, grown stronger each year, at length became so insistent in its appeals that the general public took notice of it and imagined it has sprung "full armed," officered and organized upon the public stage . . .

The vote won, some women ask, "Has it been worth the trouble it cost?" Some men ask, "What good has it done?" "What change has it wrought?" "Is the new way better than the old?"

The first and chief effect of woman suffrage is one the general public has probably not noticed, or if so, has not comprehended. A vast army has been demobilized . . . Every woman discharged from the suffrage campaign merely stepped back into the ranks of the broader woman movement from which she and her predecessors emerged some seventy-five years ago with the definite object of eliminating one discrimination against women. Having achieved the aim women now have a new demand. It is a demand for equality of opportunity between the sexes. It means that when and if a woman is as well qualified as a man to fill a position, she shall have an equal and unprejudiced chance to secure it . . .

What will bring the revolt to a close? Women have freedom of education, but restricted opportunities to use it. Women have the vote, but the old prejudices still rise to forbid freedom of action within the political parties. Nothing but time and many small skirmishes will change these conditions. Absolute equality of opportunity only will satisfy and therefore close the woman movement . . .

The direct results of the enfranchisement of women in its brief trial may be enumerated as follows:

1. The vote has been used in all the States to secure the removal of discriminations against women under the law, to prevent the passing of other proposed discriminations and to improve the legislation which concerns women and children.

2. Women vote in numbers surprisingly approaching that of man voters. Examination indicates it is not true that women, more than men, are neglecting their political opportunities of expressing their opinions at the polls.

3. The testimony is general that the presence of women at the polls in the capacity of voters and election officials has quite altered the character of election day, making it a peaceful and dignified function.

4. The service of women in high positions to which they have been appointed by the Federal, State and local governments, or elected as members of Legislatures, national, State, county and local officials, has been satisfactorily intelligent and in accord with the public good.

5. Civilization has always been lopsided, being strong where men's ambitions are keenest and lamentably weak where women's interests are strong. A careful investigation of the results of woman suffrage reveals the fact that women voters are most active and most effective in efforts to adjust this abnormal development of civilization. An enormous number of women have been called into service within the field of health, care of maternity, children, old people and dependents of every kind. Women are building strong, well thought out, constructive programs concerning public welfare and are thus using their vote to do what has always been the acknowledged specific work of women.

To sum up: The woman suffrage campaign has been only an incident in the age-old woman movement, always aiming at opportunity. The campaign destroyed legal barriers to the political freedom of women, but it did not convince the minority, who also carry on. Now and then some one from this minority writes an article, makes a speech, or publishes an editorial filled with fiery resentment at something women voters have or have not done . . . They are only symptoms of the pains of surrender.

The irritations within the political parties which most voters experience are also normal. Political managers are shocked to discover that women are not content to vote any ticket and support any platform which a few leaders have decided upon in a convention boardroom, and women partisans are disturbed because their welcome into the party is only into the outside vestibule . . . Woman suffrage, man suffrage, politics are all normally, wholesomely moving forward. The anxiety comes only from the critics who are reluctant to become reconciled to the march of events.

Source: Carrie Chapman Catt, "Woman Suffrage Only an Episode in Age-Old Movement," Current History *27, no. 1 (October 1927), 1–6.*

Letter to Eleanor Roosevelt

During the economic crisis of the 1930s, black women worked outside the home more than did white women, but were confronted with massive unemployment. Many lost higher paying jobs and were forced to do domestic work, for which wages were plummeting to as little as 15 cents an hour. Furthermore, New Deal programs, designed to offer unemployment relief during the Great Depression, openly discriminated against black women. President Franklin D. Roosevelt and First Lady Eleanor Roosevelt received hundreds of letters from black women that described how the New Deal agencies had failed them, asking for relief. In the following letter, a young woman writes to First Lady Eleanor Roosevelt, pleading for a job after being fired from the National Youth Administration, a New Deal agency.

New Orleans, Louisiana

April 18, 1941

Mrs. F. D. Roosevelt

Dear Mrs.

I'm a Negro girl of 25 yrs. I'm sick. I been sick 4 months. I'm in need of food and closes. I don't have any relative at all so help me. I hop I'm not asking so much of you, but I hop you would help me, Mrs. Roosevelt. I'm righting you this morning I don't have food for the day. I gose to the hospital. The dr say all my sickes is from not haveing food.

I was working on the NYA [National Youth Administration] . . . I work there 10 month. They lad me off because I was sick and diden give me nothing to live off after tune me off . . . They was so hard every time I get a job I get sick but I try to keep them anyway but after all I lose them. Mrs. Roosevelt I'm rooming with an old lade she dont have a husban. She give me food when she have it but she dont have it all the time. I own her 5 month rent right now. She have to pay rent her silf. She was asking me when I was going to pay her. If I dont be able to pay her in 2 week she going to put me out. I dont have nobody to go to for help and no where to go what I going to do if she put me out.

Could you do something for me help me to fine something. Tell me what to do if you could give me some to do in the hospital or in a hotel or any where I will do it. I I will take a day job are a night job anything. Please help me. You can see I'm in need of help Mrs. Roosevelt. Will you please help me

I can live much longer without food.—have lot of micine to take I do take it but it wont do me any good without food and if the lady put me out I just no I will die because I don't have no where to go . . . Mrs. Roosevelt if you can get me a job in the post office anywhere it will do. Please wright at once as soon as you can. I be looking for a letter from you.

Please do what every you can for me. I'm in need of help bad . . . Thank you. Your kindes will never be foregoting.

Yours sincerely.

Mabel Gilvert

1225 Poydres St. New Orleans, La.

Please do some thing for me at once any thing. Pleasanywhere. pleas.

Source: Gerda Lerner, ed., Black Women in White America *(New York: Vintage Books, 1973), 403–4.*

Yoshiko Uchida, Desert Exile

During World War II, all people of Japanese heritage on the West Coast were forced to register with the U.S. Government and were given family numbers for identification purposes. In 1942, they were confined in relocation camps. At the time, the popular sentiment among white Americans was that this massive violation of human rights was not comparable to Nazi activities. The real experience, however, was quite different. The following excerpt is from *Desert Exile*, an autobiography by Yoshiko Uchida, an American citizen from Berkeley, California. She was in her twenties in 1942 when she and her family were ordered from their homes and into confinement because of their Japanese ancestry. In this passage, Uchida discusses her first impression of the relocation camp she has been sent to along with her mother, father, and sister. They were family number 13453.

We were entering the edge of the Sevier Desert . . . and the surroundings were now as bleak as a bleached bone. In the distance there were mountains rising above the valley with some majesty, but they were many miles away. The bus made the turn into the heart of the sun-drenched desert and there in the midst of nowhere were rows and rows of squat, tar-papered barracks sitting sullenly in the white, chalky sand. This was Topaz, the Central Utah Relocation Center, one of ten such camps located throughout the United States in equally barren and inaccessible areas . . .

The entire camp was divided into forty-two blocks, each containing twelve barracks constructed around a mess hall, a latrine-washroom, and a laundry. The camp was one mile square and eventually housed 8,000 residents . . . Everyone looked like pieces of flour dusted pastry. In its frantic haste to construct this barrack city, the Army had removed every growing thing, and what had once been a peaceful lake bed, now churned up into one great mass of loose flour-like sand. With each step we sank two to three inches deep, sending up swirls of dust that crept into our eyes and mouths, noses and lungs . . .

Each barrack was one hundred feet in length, and divided into six rooms for families of varying sizes. We were assigned to a room in the center, about twenty by eighteen feet, designed for occupancy by four people. When we stepped into our room it contained nothing but four army cots and mattresses . . . Cracks were visible everywhere in the siding around the windows, and although our friends had swept out our room before we arrived, the dust was already seeping into it again from all sides.

Source: Yoshiko Uchida, Desert Exile: The Uprooting of a Japanese-American Family *(Seattle: University of Washington Press, 1982), 106–9. Courtesy of the Bancroft Library, University of California, Berkeley.*

Report of the National Council of Jewish Women

The "Report of the National Committee on Education and Social Action, October 28-November 2, 1951" of the National Council of Jewish Women indicates a commitment to political action, especially on the local and state levels. Concerns ranged from federal legislation to ensure permanent social change after World War II, such as advocacy for a permanent Fair Employment Practices Committee, to local programs to improve the lives of children. A professional lobbyist in Washington, D.C., Olya Margolin, and staff assigned to the Committee on Education and Social Action organized and sustained political activism within Sections (local and state branches) of the National Council of Jewish Women.

The effect of the Korean War on state legislation has not been as apparent or as abrupt as it has been on national legislation. The demand, however, for economy has been a recurrent theme in the state legislatures, and in many states important social services that might have been instituted this past year were lost in the need to appropriate funds for civil defense programs, roads and increased salaries to meet increased living costs. On the other hand, there appeared to be some feeling that if hospitals, schools and other institutional programs were to be started or completed, it must be done while construction materials and labor were still available. These programs had lagged badly as a result of the Second World War, and the states were just beginning to make up for the lost time during that period.

Perhaps because the states are not as intimately tied up with defense expenditures, and also because the elected representatives are frequently more responsive to public pressure at home, there is a greater opportunity for citizens to influence the course of good legislation on the state and local level then there appears to be in Congress at this time.

We are happy to report that Sections have expressed an increasing interest in our State Legislation program. Reports from all of the Regional Conferences this past year indicated a growing eagerness to participate in the program. The growth of the program has been due to stimulate by the National office as well as to a growing awareness of the importance of state issues. We have been in communication with 40 Chairmen of State Legislation, the largest number we have ever had.

Some of the issues in which Council Sections expressed their views were Fair Employment Practices Commission, housing, teacher's salaries, oleomargarine, mental hygiene, juvenile delinquency, cerebral palsy, minimum wage legislation, rent control, and constitutional reform. In an effort to secure the passage of desirable legislation on these and other programs, Chairmen have been cooperating increasingly with other community organizations, a highly desirable objective in itself.

The picture in state legislation now is greatly changed from that existing three years ago, when we first engaged a professional to concentrate on the program. There were then not more than two or three successful programs, and never more than about ten Chairmen functioning at any one time.

Source: "Report of the National Committee on Education and Social Action to the National Board of Directors, October 12–17, 1947," Part I Administration Files, Box 14, Folder: National Board 1947, National Council of Jewish Women, National Office Records, Library of Congress, Washington, D.C.

"No More Miss America"

In August 1968, women's liberation activists staged a protest against the Miss America Pageant in Atlantic City, New Jersey. In their invitation to the protest, a section of which is reprinted below, organizers list the reasons why they believe pageants degrade women. The protest demonstrated the growing effectiveness of feminist organizing, and the ways that activists effectively used the media to spread their message.

The Ten Points

We Protest:

1. *The Degrading Mindless-Boob-Girlie Symbol.* The Pageant contestants epitomize the roles we are all forced to play as women. The parade down the runway blares the metaphor of the 4-H Club county fair, where the nervous animals are judged for teeth, fleece, etc., and where the best "specimen" gets the blue ribbon. So are women in our society forced daily to compete for male approval, enslaved by ludicrous "beauty" standards we ourselves are conditioned to take seriously.

2. *Racism with Roses.* Since its inception in 1921, the Pageant has not had one Black finalist, and this has not been for a lack of test-case contestants. There has never been a Puerto Rican, Alaskan, Hawaiian, or Mexican-American winner. Nor has there ever been a *true* Miss America—an American Indian.

3. *Miss America as Military Death Mascot.* The highlight of her reign each year is a cheerleader-tour of American troops abroad—last year she went to Vietnam to pep-talk our husbands, fathers, sons and boyfriends into dying and killing with a better spirit. She personifies the "unstained patriotic American womanhood our boys are fighting for." The Living Bra and the Dead Soldier. We refuse to be used as Mascots for Murder.

4. *The Consumer Con-Game.* Miss America is a walking commercial for the Pageant's sponsors. Wind her up and she plugs your product on promotion tours and TV—all in an "honest, objective" endorsement. What a shill.

5. *Competition Rigged and Unrigged.* We deplore the encouragement of an American myth that oppresses men as well as women: the win-or-you're-worthless competitive disease. The "beauty contest" creates only one winner to be "used" and forty-nine losers who are "useless."

6. *The Woman as Pop Culture Obsolescent Theme.* Spindle, mutilate, and then discard tomorrow. What is so ignored as last year's Miss America? This only reflects the gospel of our society, according to Saint Male: women must be young, juicy, malleable—hence age discrimination and the cult of youth. And we women are brainwashed into believing this ourselves!

7. *The Unbeatable Madonna-Whore Combination.* Miss America and Playboy's centerfold are sisters over the skin. To win approval, we must be both sexy and wholesome, delicate but able to cope, demure yet titillatingly bitchy. Deviation of any sort brings, we are told, disaster: "You won't get a man!!"

8. *The Irrelevant Crown on the Throne of Mediocrity.* Miss America represents what women are supposed to be: inoffensive, bland, apolitical. If you are tall, short, over or under what weight The Man prescribes you should be, forget it. Personality, articulateness, intelligence, and commitment—unwise. Conformity is the key to the crown—and, by extension, to success in our Society.

9. *Miss America as Dream Equivalent To-?* In this reputedly democratic society, where every little boy supposedly can grow up to be President, what can every little girl hope to grow to be? Miss America. That's where it's at. Real power to control our own lives is restricted to men, while women get patronizing pseudo-power, an ermine clock and a bunch of flowers; men are judged by their actions, women by appearance.

10. *Miss America as Big Sister Watching You.* The Pageant exercises Thought Control, attempts to sear the Image onto our minds, to further make women oppressed and men oppressors; to enslave us all the more in high-heeled, low-status roles; to inculcate false values in young girls; women as beasts of buying; to seduce us to prostitute our selves before our own oppression.

NO MORE MISS AMERICA

Source: Robin Morgan, ed., Sisterhood is Powerful: An Anthology of Writings from the Women's Liberation Movement *(New York: Random House, 1970), 521–24.*

Letter from the Editors of BUST

The following is the preface to The BUST Guide to the New Girl Order, a collection of articles originally published in BUST magazine. BUST began in 1993 as a zine (a self-published and self-distributed grassroots publication). One of the most long-lasting of Third Wave endeavors, BUST is still in publication, now as a nationally-circulated magazine with an active Web community. Here, founders and editors

Marcelle Karp and Debbie Stoller convey a sense of the social, political and aesthetic context in which Generation X feminists were situated, and give voice to the perspectives shared by many Third Wavers.

There's been a lot of talk lately of defining our generation, this generation of late twenties, early thirties, non baby-boomer slackers. They call us Generation X. They talk about our difficulty committing to jobs, difficulty taking on responsibilities, difficulty becoming adults. But there has been very little talk about Generation XX, we women slackers, the girls having a difficult time becoming women, and the adult fears that are particular to being female: having children, fear of becoming "spinsters," dealing with men who can't "commit," being way more than two boys away from being virgins, aging and our body image, to name a few. There are a ton of women's magazines out there, but they all seem to tell us that being an adult woman is a major bummer. They tell us to exercise, just say no, decorate your apartment, get a facial, diet diet diet, how to deal with the married man, how to deal with the single man, cooking, how to keep your man, how to avoid sexual harassment at the office, how to avoid date rape, etc. Only *Sassy* magazine, devoted to the newly found freedom and sexuality of the teenage girl, seems to understand that being a girl can be really fun. That being independent is a cool thing, that girls make great friends, that boys are only part of the story, that the way you look doesn't matter all that much and that beauty comes in many shapes and colors, that you buy clothes because it's fun to buy things you like, fun to listen to music that floats your boat, excellent super fun to say yes to cute boys, yes to wild car rides, and yes to life.

Those of us older girls who get off on reading *Sassy* do it as a sort of guilty pleasure: sure, it makes us feel good, but it also makes us feel like losers because the only magazine we can relate to is meant for teenagers! One by one we think to ourselves: why didn't I grow up to be the type of woman who relates to *Mademoiselle* or *Essence?* What kind of weirdo am I? And mostly, we get to feeling really lonely, and really afraid. We are the women who were raised on feminism, who pitied our mothers for being choicelessly house bound, and looked down on those girls we went to high school with who got married to the first guy they fucked, had kids, and worked in shoe stores. We wanted to have choices, to have careers, to not be tied down, to hold onto our freedom, and to become sexually "experienced." And we were sure that neither our gender nor our race would stop us. But somewhere, somewhere in our girl-brains the idea had been planted—when we were young, when we watched "The Brady Bunch," when we were forced to take "homemaking" while the boys took "shop"—that we would, of course, be married to successful men and be ready to have families by the time we were, well, at least definitely by the time we were thirty!!

Instead we find ourselves nearing or past thirty, still in dating hell, still trying to figure out our sexual identities, still sleeping too late, forgetting to do the fucking laundry and wearing dirty underwear, not knowing how to cook, worrying about the electricity being turned off again, being in debt to our creditors, not having any savings, and hearing the TICK TICK TICK of our goddamned biological clocks. When we were in our early twenties we thought that

that biological clock and "juggling career and family" stuff was yuppie bullshit for women who wore beige stockings or relaxed their hair. We knew better. We would figure it all out, in our own radical bohemian thrift-store ways. Surely it would happen to us in its own time. Surely we'd figure out what we wanted to be when we grew up. Surely. And yet it hasn't. We haven't figured it out. And now here we are. But look around you—there are a lot of us here. Lots and lots of us. It's not just me, it's not just you, there are a whole heap of us late twenties early thirties groovy girl-women. And we need to hear each other. We need to help each other. We need to laugh at each other. We need to speak to each other. So speak. We wanna read you. We wanna recognize ourselves and laugh. We wanna have fun. We wanna get mad. We wanna BUST!

Source: "Pre-Introductory Material," from The BUST Guide to the New Girl Order *by Marcelle Karp and Debbie Stoller, copyright © 1999 by Bust Magazine Enterprises, Inc. Used by permission of Viking Penguin, a division of Penguin Group (USA), Inc.*

Journal Entry of Bushra Rehman

Bushra Rehman included this journal entry in *Colonize This!: Young Women of Color on Today's Feminism*, which she coedited with Daisy Hernández in 2002. Like many Third Wavers, Rehman writes about her own experience to convey the complicated relationship between the personal and the political. Her journal entry explores the contradictions that arise from being a young feminist in a post-9/11 United States complicated not only by misogyny, but also by racism, homophobia, terrorism, and nationalism. She uses the term "women of color feminism" to indicate the centrality of race in her feminism.

December 7, 2001

This morning I woke up to the news radio. Women were throwing off their veils in Afghanistan and I thought about how for years the women I have known have wanted this to happen. But now what a hollow victory it all is. I am disgusted by the us-and-them mentality. "We" the liberated Americans must save "them" the oppressed women. What kind of feminist victory is it when we liberate women by killing their men and any woman or child who happens to be where a bomb hits? I feel myself as a Muslim-American woman, as a woman of color fearing walking down the street, feeling the pain that my friends felt as they were beaten down in the weeks after September 11th. Solemnly, we counted as the numbers rose: two, five, seven . . . My friend telling me: They told me I smelled—they touched me everywhere— and when I talked back, they made fun of me, grabbed me, held my arms back, told me to go back to my country, took my money and ran. My other friend telling me: they punched me, kicked me, called me queer—they had found the pamphlets in my bag, and I'm here on asylum, for being a queer activist—my papers were just going through—I'm not safe in this country as a gay man. My other friends telling me: We didn't want to report it to the police, why just start another case of racial profiling? They're not going to find the guys who did it. They're just going to use our pain as an excuse for more violence. Use our pain as an excuse for more violence. It's what I hear again and again in a city that is grieving, that is beginning to see what other countries live every day.

But where does women of color feminism fit into all of this? Everywhere. As women of color feminists, this is what we have to think about.

Source: Bushra Rehman and Daisy Hernández, "Introduction." Colonize This! Young Women of Color on Today's Feminism, *ed. Daisy Hernández and Bushra Rehman (New York: Seal Press, 2002), xvii–xviii.*

Academies (also known as seminaries or institutes) varied in style and offerings. While some focused on training in female accomplishments, others offered the most advanced education available to young women of the upper and middle classes in all regions of antebellum America.

Adams, Abigail (1744–1818) was the wife of America's second president, John Adams, and one of his closest advisers. She corresponded with a network of patriotic men and women and advocated for broader opportunities for women.

Addams, Jane (1860–1935) was a founder of the Hull House, the first settlement house in the United States. She was the first president of the Women's International League for Peace and Freedom, and also became the first American woman to be awarded a Nobel Peace Prize, in 1931.

AIM (American Indian Movement) was founded in 1968 with the goals of combating police brutality against Indian peoples, encouraging Indian self-sufficiency, and promoting Indian self-determination. AIM was largely responsible for two widely publicized demonstrations in the early 1970s: the occupation of the Bureau of Indian Affairs offices in Washington, D.C., and the occupation of the site of the 1890 Wounded Knee Massacre on South Dakota's Pine Ridge reservation.

Allen, Paula Gunn (1939–2008) was a Laguna, Sioux, and Lebanese writer, editor, educator, and activist, and is widely considered to be among the most important Native American intellectuals and artists of the 20th century.

The **American and Foreign Anti-Slavery Society** (AFASS) was founded in 1840 by Lewis Tappan and other conservative abolitionists. The AFASS formed out of opposition to William Lloyd Garrison and the association of women's rights with the abolitionist cause.

The **American Anti-Slavery Society** (AASS) was organized in 1833 by William Lloyd Garrison and other abolitionists. Garrisonian abolitionists advocated for the immediate and unconditional abolition of slavery and equal rights for African Americans, as well for women's rights. Women served as members, speakers, and leaders in the AASS. Conflict over women's participation in abolitionism led to a split in the movement at the end of the 1830s.

The **American Colonization Society** (ACS) was founded in 1817 by abolitionists who believed emigration of blacks to Africa would solve the problems inherent in abolition. Supporters of the ACS believed the races were incompatible.

The **American Equal Rights Association** (AERA) was founded in 1866 by Susan B. Anthony, Elizabeth Cady Stanton, and other women's rights activists to advocate for universal suffrage.

The **American Federation of Labor** (AFL) was founded in 1886 and was one of the first labor unions in the United States. During the first half of the 20th century, it was one of the largest unions, and organized only skilled workers.

American Revolutionary War (1775–1783)—After years of escalating tension, armed conflict broke out between Britain and the 13 American colonies in 1775. Independence was declared in July of 1776, and the war ended with the Treaty of Paris in 1783.

The **American Woman Suffrage Association** (AWSA) was formed in 1869 by Lucy Stone and Henry Blackwell after the split in the American Equal Rights Association. It was less radical than the National Woman Suffrage Association, which was also established in 1869.

Anarchists, such as Emma Goldman, rejected government and its compulsory laws as harmful to the people, who should have been able to associate freely and collectively. Anarchists generally accepted violence as a means to overthrow the state.

Anderson, Mary (1972–1964) was Chief of the Women's Bureau from 1920 to 1944.

The **Anita Hill/Clarence Thomas hearings** were nationally televised hearings of the United States Senate Judiciary Committee to determine whether the nomination of Clarence Thomas to the Supreme Court should be confirmed. Anita Hill, a law professor and former colleague of Thomas's, testified that Thomas had sexually harassed her on the job.

Anthony, Susan B. (1820–1906) was one of the most famous of the suffrage activists. Anthony served as the president of the National American Woman's Suffrage Association, from its creation until 1900. The Nineteenth Amendment is often called the Susan B. Anthony Amendment, in honor of Anthony's work in the suffrage struggle.

Anti-lynching legislation was repeatedly introduced in Congress by black and white civil rights advocates from 1882 to 1968, yet no law was ever passed to make lynching a federal crime.

Anti-seduction laws criminalized seduction. In the antebellum period, moral reformers formed associations, such as the New York Female Moral Reform Society, to grant women legal protection from sexual abuse.

Arbitration was a goal of American pacifists, including Jane Addams and Jeanette Rankin, who joined European women in the Women's International League for Peace and Freedom to advocate negotiation and dialogue between nations as a viable alternative to war.

Baby Boom is the term most often used to describe the significant increase in birth rates from 1946 until 1957.

Backlash refers to reactions (in word or action) against feminism and feminists. Backlash tends to arise when feminism has made, or is thought to have made, gains toward the equality of women.

Bacon's Rebellion was a revolt, mainly of former indentured servants, led by Nathaniel Bacon. It took place in Virginia in 1676. The group first attacked Indians, and then attacked Jamestown. Women took part on both sides of the rebellion, but their participation was limited to informal means.

Barnett-Wells, Ida B. (1862–1931) was an African American anti-lynching crusader and suffrage activist.

Beecher, Catharine (1800–1878) founded female seminaries in Hartford and Cincinnati and authored numerous influential manuals for American housewives. Beecher argued the importance of an expanded domesticity for women and promoted women as the ideal teachers to staff America's schools.

Bethlehem Female Seminary (now Moravian College) opened in 1742 in Bethlehem, Pennsylvania as the first boarding school for young women in the country. It was founded by the Protestant Moravian church, and was inspired by the educational ideas of Moravian Bishop John Comenius.

Bethune, Mary McLeod (1875–1955) founded the Daytona Educational and Industrial School for Negro Girls in 1904. As the Negro Affairs Director for the National Youth Administration from 1936 to 1944, and as the founder of the National Council of Negro Women, Bethune became an active national figure, fighting for the rights of African Americans.

Birth control and **planned parenthood** were terms coined by Margaret Sanger to simplify and clarify the goals of the American birth control movement by shifting the discussion from obscenity and sin to responsible family planning.

Blackwell, Henry (1825–1909) was the husband of suffragist Lucy Stone and the brother of Elizabeth Blackwell (the first female doctor in the United States). He was an abolitionist and suffrage advocate, helping Stone to organize the American Woman Suffrage Association.

Boissevain, Inez Milholland (1886–1916) led the Washington, D.C. suffrage parade in 1913. She later died while on a lecture tour and was mourned by many as a martyr to the suffrage cause.

Bradstreet, Anne (1612–1672) was a prolific poet who came to Massachusetts in 1630. Her poetry provides insight into the lives of everyday Puritan women, although as a poet, she was participating in an activity usually reserved for men.

Burns, Lucy (1879–1966) was a militant suffrage leader in the National Woman's Party. Burns spent more time in jail than any other suffragist.

Campbell, Maria (b. 1940) is a Métis writer, educator, and activist from Saskatchewan. She is perhaps best known as the author of *Halfbreed*, published in 1973, which details her upbringing during a period of transition for the Métis, a period marked by social and cultural turmoil.

Castas were racial classifications for people in the Spanish colonies. The term *mestizo* is an example of a *casta*.

Catt, Carrie Chapman (1859–1947) was the president of the National American Woman Suffrage Association when the Nineteenth Amendment became law.

The **Charleston** was a type of dance in 4/4 time with syncopated rhythms, introduced in the 1923 Broadway musical, *Runnin' Wild*, along with a song, "The Charleston," by James P. Johnson. It was apparently based on a style of dance of African Americans living off the coast of South Carolina.

Civic housekeeping allowed women reformers at the turn of the century to rhetorically apply their domestic talents to clean up corrupt city governments and improve impoverished immigrant neighborhoods. Reformers used a maternalist vocabulary to legitimize and provide a rationale for their political activism.

Civil Defense refers to military preparedness among civilians during the Cold War.

The **Civil Rights Act of 1964** outlawed discrimination in the United States based on race, color, religion, sex, or national origin in voting, employment, and public services.

The **Civil Works Administration** (CWA) was a New Deal project under the Federal Emergency Relief Administration (FERA) that provided approximately 4 million construction jobs building bridges, schools, and roads during the winter of 1933.

Clarke, Dr. Edward H. (1820–1877) was a Harvard Medical School physician and professor whose 1873 book, *Sex in Education; Or, A Fair Chance for the Girls,* argued that the pursuit of higher education endangered the health of young women.

The **Coalition of Labor Union Women** was formed in 1974 to address the needs of unorganized working women and to demand that labor unions be more responsive to the specific needs of working women.

The **Cold War** was the ongoing conflict between the United States and the Soviet Union, from the end of World War II until the collapse of the Soviet Union in the 1990s.

The **Commission on Interracial Cooperation** (CIC) was founded in Atlanta, Georgia to develop programs, inform the public of black achievements, and oppose the Ku Klux Klan and lynching. In 1920, the CIC and the National Association of Colored Women met to discuss black women's issues, but subsequent meetings and publications focused primarily on lynching.

The **Commission on the Status of Women** was formed by the Kennedy Administration in 1961 to look at women's status within the American economy and law. The commission was comprised of labor unions, women's organizations, and governmental agencies.

The **Common Schools** of the 1830s and 1840s were envisioned as free schools open to girls and boys of all classes that would teach a common curriculum to prepare all students for citizenship and give them an equal chance in life.

Common Sense, a book by Thomas Paine, was published in January of 1776. It was wildly popular, and shifted the mood in the American colonies toward open revolt and a declaration of independence.

The **Communist Party of the USA** (CPUSA) was an influential political party in the 1930s that advocated for the rights of workers. While there were several prominent women leaders, feminism was considered less important than the socialist revolution. By the early 1950s, CPUSA social critiques began to include discussions about the oppression of women.

The **Comprehensive Child Development Act** was passed by both houses of Congress in 1971, which would have provided childcare on a sliding scale to working parents. President Richard Nixon vetoed the act on the grounds that it endorsed "communal approaches to childrearing."

The **Comstock Act,** passed in 1873, was named after its chief promoter, the morals crusader Anthony Comstock. The act declared contraceptives to be obscene and prohibited their dissemination through the U.S. mail.

The **Congressional Committee** was the committee of the National American Woman Suffrage Association that dealt with lobbying for a national amendment in Washington, D.C.

The **Congressional Union** (CU) was a group formed by Alice Paul and Lucy Burns in 1913 with the aim of pressuring Congress to pass a woman suffrage amendment. The CU became the National Woman's Party in 1916.

The **Congress of Industrial Organizations** (CIO) was formed in 1935 when smaller organizations within the AFL, including the International Ladies Garment Workers' Union, left to form a labor organization composed mainly of unskilled industrial workers.

Consciousness-raising was a political tool developed by radical feminists. The aim was to bring women together in small groups to discuss their experiences as women in order to make connections between their personal stories and wider structures of patriarchal oppression.

Coverture was a doctrine of English common law that stipulated that women lost their separate legal status when they married. The result was that married women could not own their own property, enter into contractual relationships, or write wills to pass on property. Because they were not independent persons, they also could not vote or hold political office.

Crandall, Prudence (1803–1890) opened a school for African American girls in Canterbury, Connecticut in 1831. In the face of an 1834 Connecticut law making it illegal to provide free education for black students, as well as hostility from the local community, the school soon closed.

Creole was a term used in the Spanish and French colonies to refer to a person born in the Americas whose parents were born in Europe.

Criados were Indians who were ransomed from other Indians and were raised in Spanish households in the Spanish colonies of the present-day southwestern United States. *Criados* were usually women and children, and they performed the duties of servants.

Croly, Jane Cunningham (1829–1901) was an author and journalist. In the 1850s, she became the first woman with a syndicated column. Croly founded the women's club Sorosis, the New York Woman's Press Club, and the General Federation of Women's Clubs.

The **Daughters of Liberty** was a Boston organization that organized boycotts and spinning bees to support the wearing of homespun clothing in the years leading up to the American Revolution.

The **Dawes Severalty Act** (1887) was a policy mandating the allotment of communally held Indian lands to individual Indians and their immediate families. The policy was one component of the federal government's strategy to force the assimilation of Indian peoples into the Euro American mainstream. The act had the dual benefit, from the perspective of policymakers, of opening up Indian lands for white settlement. The policy remained on the books until 1934, when policymakers officially deemed it a failure and reversed it via the Wheeler-Howard Act.

The **Declaration of Sentiments (American Anti-Slavery Society)** is the founding document of the American Anti-Slavery Society.

The **Declaration of Sentiments and Resolutions** (of the 1848 Women's Rights Convention) is the founding document of the women's rights movement in the United States. It was purposely modeled on the Declaration of Independence and named for the American Anti-Slavery Society's Declaration of Sentiments.

Deer, Ada (b. 1935) is a social worker, educator, and activist, perhaps best known for her crusade to have Wisconsin's Menominee Indians' trust status restored after a disastrous experience with the federal government's termination policies. Deer co-founded DRUMS, or Determinations of Rights and Unity for Menominee Shareholders, and for much of her life, she has devoted herself to myriad causes on behalf of Native peoples, particularly in the arenas of education, health, and legal services.

Dewson, Mary "Molly" W. (1874–1962) is best known for being the head of the Women's Division of the Democratic Party in President Franklin D. Roosevelt's administration.

Dix, Dorothea (1802–1887) worked to reform treatment of prisoners and the mentally ill. Her efforts led to the establishment of state hospitals and institutions for the mentally insane.

Douglass, Fredrick (1818–1895) was an abolitionist and early supporter of women rights. He was a signer of the Declaration of Sentiments and helped to found the American Equal Rights Association.

Dower was the one-third of a husband's estate that was given to a widow under English law.

Dowry was a woman's property that was transferred to her husband or shared by both spouses at marriage. This often included land, animals, and houses.

Dress reform refers to the effort during the antebellum period to introduce a more natural form of female dress. In the early 1850s, several women's rights activists briefly adopted some version of the "Bloomer costume," so named after the reformer Amelia Bloomer, who promoted a new style of female dress, consisting of pantaloons and a loose-fitting shortened skirt.

Dry laws were local and state laws regulating (and sometimes banning) the licensing, distribution, and sale of alcohol. These were promoted by many women reformers, including those in the Woman's Christian Temperance Union.

EEOC v. AT&T was a landmark sex discrimination case settled out of court. The largest single employer of women in the United States in the early 1970s, AT&T agreed in 1972 to a multimillion dollar payment to women workers and the implementation of a program to end longstanding company policies that discriminated against women.

Eight-hour day—At the turn of the 20th century, most unions focused on reducing the 10–16 hour work day, with the slogan "Eight Hours for Work, Eight Hours for Rest, and Eight Hours for What We Will."

Embodiment is the manifestation of social constructs in one's physical body. For instance, anorexia is the embodiment in a woman's body of the social pressure for women to be small, invisible, and powerless.

The **Enlightenment** was a cultural and philosophical movement in Europe that focused on rational thought, empirical inquiry, and a belief that the physical world is knowable. It is often associated with a rejection of tradition and religious skepticism.

Ensley, Elizabeth (1848–1919) organized within the African American community, helping to guarantee a vote in favor of woman suffrage in Colorado.

The **Equal Employment Opportunity Commission** (EEOC) was a federal agency formed by the Civil Rights Act of 1964. The agency was given the power to bring suit on behalf of workers who claimed that employers had violated their right to fair treatment.

The **Equal Pay Act** was passed by Congress in 1963, making it illegal to set different rates of pay for women and men who did the same work.

The **Equal Rights Amendment** (ERA) was first introduced in Congress in 1923. Written by Alice Paul, it would have guaranteed equal protection under the law for all Americans, regardless of sex. Although the amendment was approved by Congress in 1972, it was never ratified by the states.

Erdrich, Louise (b. 1954) is an author of Chippewa and German descent, and a member of North Dakota's Turtle Mountain band of Chippewa Indians. Erdrich first earned wide recognition with the publication of her novel *Love Medicine* in 1984, including a National Book Critics Circle Award.

Essentialism refers to any belief in a fixed identity arising from nature (of either the physical body or the soul), as in the belief that women are natural nurturers.

Euro-American describes a U.S. resident or citizen who is of European descent, and is often used as a synonym for "white American."

The **Factory Girls Association** was formed in 1836 by textile workers in Lowell, Massachusetts. It served as model for similar organizations in factory towns throughout New England.

The **Fair Labor Standards Act** (FLSA), enacted in 1938, provided for minimum wages, maximum hours, and rules for overtime pay for men and women engaged in production for interstate commerce. It also outlawed most forms of child labor.

The **Federal-Aid Highway Act of 1956,** also known as the National Interstate and Defense Highway Act, provided federal appropriations for an interstate highway system.

The **Federal Emergency Relief Administration** (FERA) was a New Deal program that provided $3.1 billion to relief and work projects, providing employment for over 20 million people.

Feminazis is a backlash term, coined by conservative talk radio personality Rush Limbaugh, suggesting a comparison between feminists and Nazis.

The Feminine Mystique (1963) was a bestselling book written by Betty Friedan that described the malaise and boredom afflicting the white, middle-class wives and mothers of her generation.

The **Fifteenth Amendment** (1870) prohibits the restriction of the right to vote on the basis of "race, color, or previous condition of servitude."

The **First National Women's Conference** was held in Houston, Texas in 1977. Twenty thousand women from all 50 states gathered to pass a National Plan of Action designed to advance feminist goals.

The First Wave of Feminism refers to the era of women's rights activism that was inaugurated with the Seneca Falls Convention of 1848 and ended with the passage of the Nineteenth Amendment in 1920.

Flapper was the name given to the young women of the 1920s who wore shortened skirts, bound their breasts, bobbed their hair, smoked, drank, wore cosmetics, and engaged in behavior reflecting the new sexual freedom of the era.

The **Fourteenth Amendment** (1868) formally defines citizenship and guarantees the civil rights of American citizens regardless of race.

Free love was advocated by feminists such as Victoria Woodhull and Emma Goldman, who embraced the idea that both men and women could (and should be able to) experience sexual pleasure, including outside the system of marriage.

Free produce refers to the movement to abstain from the products of slave labor. The first American female antislavery societies were free produce associations.

Friedan, Betty (1921–2006) was the author of the influential feminist polemic, *The Feminine Mystique,* published in 1963, and a leader of the liberal branch of the modern women's movement.

Gannett, Deborah Sampson disguised herself as a man to fight in the American Revolution.

Generation X is the generation born immediately after the Baby Boom. It is usually said to include those born between 1961 and either 1974 or 1981.

The **GI Bill of Rights** was the popular name for the Servicemen's Readjustment Act of 1944, legislation that guaranteed low-interest home loans and education subsidies to returning veterans.

Girlie Feminism embraces a playful love of traditionally feminine behaviors, such as wearing lipstick and high heels.

Girl Power refers to the transmutation of Riot Grrls feminism into a more popular and palatable celebration of girlhood.

The **Glass Ceiling** is an invisible barrier of sexism that prevents most women from reaching the highest levels of business, the professions, or government.

Goldman, Emma (1869–1940) was a Lithuanian-born Jewish anarchist who left Russia in 1885 for the United States. By 1889, Goldman was living on the Lower East Side of New York, speaking to workers about anarchism and the need to overthrow the capitalist state. She also championed free love and women's right to birth control. Goldman was deported in 1919, a victim of the Red Scare.

Gone with the Wind (1939) is a popular film set during the U.S. Civil War about a strong-willed woman named Scarlett O'Hara.

Goodwife was a term and title to describe an honorable woman in Puritan society. A Puritan goodwife was pious, pure, obedient, and industrious.

The Great Awakening was a series of religious revivals that occurred in England and the English colonies in the 1730s through the 1770s. Women were important church members prior to The Great Awakening, they participated in large numbers in The Great Awakening, and they continued to play major roles in the religious education of their families after the revivals.

Grimké, Angelina (1805–1879) was the daughter of a South Carolina judge and slaveholder. She joined the Society of Friends (Quakers) and became an outspoken abolitionist and women's rights advocate. In 1838, she married fellow activist Theodore Weld. Though she had hoped to continue her reform work, Grimké eventually gave up public activism to care for her family.

Grimké, Sarah (1792–1873) was the sister of Angelina Grimké. Like her sister, she joined the Society of Friends and became an abolitionist and advocate for women's rights. Throughout the 1830s, Grimké fought for the immediate abolition of slavery and for the rights of women to speak in public.

Haley, Margaret (1861–1939), the daughter of Irish immigrants, worked as a teacher and organizer for the Chicago Teachers Federation. She fought for better pay and working conditions for teachers, and allied them with causes such as woman suffrage and child labor legislation.

Harjo, Joy (b. 1951) is a musician, performer, educator, and poet whose work has focused heavily on her Creek heritage. She has received the most acclaim, however, for her seven volumes of poetry.

Harper, Frances Watkins (1825–1911) was a free black from Baltimore, Maryland, who wrote abolitionist poetry and fiction, and lectured for the American Anti-Slavery Society. Harper became national superintendent of the department of Work Among Colored People in the Woman's Christian Temperance Union (1883–1890).

Ho is a rapper's slang term, derived from "whore."

Hogan, Linda (b. 1947) is a poet, novelist, essayist, and educator of Chickasaw heritage, whose work has typically reflected her interest in feminism, environmentalism, spirituality, and Native American history. Hogan was nominated for a Pulitzer Prize in 1991 for her novel *Mean Spirit.*

Huguenots were French Protestants who often faced persecution in France. There were several Huguenot attempts to settle in the present-day United States, most notably in the Jacksonville, Florida area.

Hull House was a settlement house founded in 1889 by Jane Addams and Ellen Gates Starr on Chicago's poor, immigrant-dominated west side. It offered services ranging from classes on nutrition and English, to a kindergarten and assistance in promoting child-labor laws and work-safety laws, among others.

Hungry Wolf, Beverly (b. 1950) was born on the Blood Indian Reserve in Canada, and is a member of the Blackfoot Nation. Hungry Wolf's writings demonstrate a particular interest in chronicling the life stories of older Native American women, including her mother, aunt, and various elders within the Blackfoot Nation.

Hutchinson, Anne (1591–1643) was a Puritan woman who held meetings in her Massachusetts home to discuss the Bible and religion. She challenged the ministers and colonial leaders, and was exiled to Rhode Island.

Identity Politics involves a belief that one's social politics arise out of one's life experience in the social categories (woman, lesbian, person of color, etc.) that one inhabits.

Immediatism was the radical abolitionist movement that formed in England in the 1820s and in the United States in the 1830s. Immediatists sought an immediate end to slavery. The movement is typically dated to the first issue of William Lloyd Garrison's paper, *The Liberator;* however, immediatism developed earlier in England with the publication of Elizabeth Heyrick's antislavery tract, *Immediate, Not Gradual Abolition,* and with the early efforts of black abolitionists against the American Colonization Society.

Indentured servants signed a contract promising their labor to another person, and in return, the servant's passage to the American colonies was paid. More men than women came to the colonies as indentured servants, as colonists viewed male labor as more valuable. Women indentured servants faced difficult living conditions, hard labor, and high mortality rates. Also, laws punished women for becoming pregnant while they were servants.

The **Internal Security Act of 1950** was also known as the McCarran Act after its chief sponsor, U.S. Senator Patrick McCarran (R-Nevada). The act required communist organizations to register with the Department of Justice, and created the Subversive Control Board, authorized to investigate un-American activities.

The **International Ladies Garment Workers' Union** (ILGWU) was one of the first unions to have a majority female membership, even though its leadership was male. Its membership increased as a result of the Uprising of the Twenty Thousand in 1909–1910, and it revived unionizing by organizing by industry, instead of only skilled workers.

Jingoism was embodied by the unswerving patriotism of "100 percent Americanism" during World War I. Women's peace groups were condemned by jingoistic fanatics as disloyal.

Kelley, Florence (1859–1932) was a resident of the Hull House and a lawyer who championed protective labor laws for women and children, became a factory inspector for the state of Illinois, and a leader of the National Consumers' League.

The **Ladies Association of Philadelphia** was a group organized in Philadelphia by Esther DeBerdt Reed and Sarah Franklin Bache in 1780, which collected money and supplies for the Patriot troops under George Washington.

Laissez faire **capitalism**—To promote rapid economic growth and industrialization, businesses at the turn of the 20th century were almost entirely unregulated. Progressive reformers fought for more government regulation, such as safety laws, maximum hours and minimum labor laws, and a ban on child labor.

The **Lanham Act** of 1942 provided federal monies for childcare during World War II. Federal government funding for childcare ceased when the war ended.

The **League of Women Voters** was the organization formed by the National American Woman Suffrage Association after the Nineteenth Amendment enfranchised women. It was devoted to preparing women for their new role as enfranchised citizens. In addition, the league continued working for the social legislation that women reformers had long advocated.

Litchfield Female Academy was a school for girls, founded by Sara Pierce in Litchfield, Connecticut in 1792.

Locke, John (1632–1704) was a British philosopher whose ideas were immensely influential on the American colonies and early republic, both for his empiricism and his notions of the social contract.

A **Loyalist/Tory** was a person in the American colonies who remained loyal to the British. The name Tory came from one of the political parties in Britain.

Lyon, Mary (1797–1849) tirelessly raised funds to establish the Holyoke Seminary in Massachusetts in 1837. Holyoke provided women from modest backgrounds with academic and teacher training. Holyoke, which evolved into the present-day Mount Holyoke College, served as a model for other female academies and women's colleges.

Mankiller, Wilma (b. 1945) was born to a Cherokee father and Dutch-Irish mother, and went on to become the first female principle chief of the Cherokee Nation of Oklahoma. A noted activist and advocate for Indian rights, Mankiller has primarily focused on issues related to health care, economic development, and tribal self-determination.

Mann, Horace (1796–1859), often referred to as the "father of American education," served as Secretary of Education for Massachusetts (the first such position in the United States). He believed citizens must be literate and educated if the republic was to survive.

Married Women's Property Acts referred to the laws enacted by state legislatures to protect the property and income of married women.

Mary T. Norton (1875–1959) was the Democratic Congresswoman from New Jersey from 1925 to 1950. As Chairman of the Labor Committee, she helped pass the 1938 Fair Labor Standards Act.

McCarthy, Joseph R. (1908–1957), the Republican U.S. Senator from Wisconsin from 1947 to 1957, is most associated with the virulent anticommunism of the 1950s.

Mestizo was a Spanish term used in the colonies to describe a person with a Spanish and an Indian parent.

Metí was a French term used in the colonies to describe a person with a French and an Indian parent.

A **midwife** was a woman who delivered babies. She played a vital role in the female rituals and companionship that accompanied childbirth during the colonial era. Midwives' knowledge of herbs gave them high status, but this sometimes made them suspect in the eyes of community members, and vulnerable to accusations of witchcraft. During the course of the 18th century, doctors began to challenge the place of midwives in delivering babies, as doctors claimed superior training and the aid of technology, namely forceps.

A **milliner** was a creator or seller of hats. This was one of the few types of work outside of the home in which women could participate during the colonial period.

Minor v. Happersett—Suffragist Virginia Minor sued the registrar who refused to place her name on the voting lists in her hometown of St. Louis. Minor argued that the Fourteenth Amendment guaranteed her rights as a citizen of the United States, including the right to vote. The Supreme Court ruled in 1875 that although women were citizens of the United States, suffrage was not a right of citizenship.

The **Miss America Pageant of 1968** was the site of a feminist action organized by New York Radical Women, who protested the ways that the pageant demeaned and objectified women.

Moral Reform was a social reform movement of the antebellum period emphasizing evangelical ideas about women's innate sexual purity. It focused primarily on the crime of female prostitution and men's role in perpetuating the crime.

"Mother" (Mary Harris) Jones (c. 1837–1930) helped found the International Workers of the World in 1905. As a labor union organizer for the United Mine Workers, she generated favorable publicity for the workers by organizing demonstrations by the wives and children of the striking workers.

Mott, Lucretia Coffin (1793–1880) was a Quaker abolitionist. Mott was one of the organizers of the first woman's rights convention, held in Seneca Falls, New York, in 1848. Mott continued to speak for women's rights and the vote through out her life.

Muller v. Oregon was a Supreme Court case decided in 1908 that endorsed protective labor laws for women on the grounds that they were ostensibly weaker than men, and that their roles as mothers were essential to social and evolutionary progress.

Murray, Judith Sargent (1751–1820) was an essayist, playwright, poet, letter writer, and advocate for women's rights. Many of her works were published anonymously in a 1798 collection entitled *The Gleaner.*

The **National American Woman Suffrage Association** (NAWSA) was created in 1890 by the merger of the National Woman Suffrage Association and the American Woman Suffrage Association. The NAWSA was the largest suffrage organization in the United States, with a national office, as well as state and local branches.

The **National Association of Colored Women** (NACW) was formed in 1896 as a coalition of secular and religious groups headed by black women who had encountered resistance from white women in their attempts to work interracially for their mutual reform goals.

The **National Black Feminist Organization** (NBFO) was formed by African American women in New York in 1973 to explore their relationship to feminism as well as feminism's relationship to the black liberation struggle.

The **National Council of Jewish Women** (NCJW) is a social-welfare organization founded in 1893. After World War II, the NCJW became increasingly politically engaged in the cause of women's rights, civil rights, and civil liberties.

The **National Council of Negro Women** (NCNW) is an organization founded in 1935 by Mary McLeod Bethune to serve as a national clearinghouse for black women's organizations. The NCNW became involved in civil rights activism and progressive politics during the 1950s and 1960s under the leadership of its president, Dorothy I. Height.

The **National Federation of Business and Professional Women's Clubs** (BPW) is an organization founded in 1919 to support working women, including unwavering support for the Equal Rights Amendment. The group was instrumental in securing the passage of the Equal Pay Act of 1963 and the formation of state commissions on the status of women in the 1960s.

The **National Organization for Women** (NOW) is a civil rights organization founded in 1966 that advocates for women's full access to education, work, and political participation in American society.

The **National Woman's Party** (NWP) was first known as the Congressional Union, which was founded by Alice Paul and Lucy Burns in 1913 and renamed the NWP in 1916. The NWP relied on more militant tactics in advocating for the vote than did the National American Woman Suffrage Association, including picketing the White House. After women obtained the right to vote in 1920, the NWP focused on the Equal Rights Amendment. The single-issue focus of the NWP alienated working-class women and women of color, for the amendment would have eliminated protective legislation.

The **National Woman Suffrage Association** (NWSA) was the radical organization formed by Susan B. Anthony and Elizabeth Cady Stanton in 1869 after the demise of the American Equal Rights Association.

The **National Women's Political Caucus** (NWPC) is an organization founded in 1971 that aims to get more women elected to political office through both grassroots organizing and fundraising efforts.

The **National Women's Trade Union League** (NWTUL) was founded in 1903 by Mary Kenney O'Sullivan, a labor union organizer and settlement-house worker. The NWTUL allied elite, educated, and professional women reformers with poor, wage-earning women to fight for better wages and working conditions by organizing women into trade unions and by promoting protective labor legislation.

The **National Youth Administration** (NYA) was a New Deal program aimed at unemployed young people. It provided grants in exchange for work, so people could remain in high school and college. It also provided on-the-job-training for those not pursuing an education.

The **New Departure** was an argument advanced by some suffragists in the 1870s that contended that women were already enfranchised by the Fourteenth and Fifteenth Amendments, and therefore simply needed to go to the polls to exercise their right to vote.

The **Nineteenth Amendment,** added to the U.S. Constitution in August 1920, granted women the right to vote.

Ninety-Nines is an international organization of licensed women pilots that came into being in November 1929 at Curtiss Field, Long Island, New York. Its first president was Amelia Earhart and its purpose was (and remains) to support and advance women in aviation.

No-Conscription Leagues were set up by Alexander Berkman and Emma Goldman in 1917 to protest the U.S. government's entry into World War I, by encouraging men to resist the draft.

Normal Schools, which were founded in the 1830s to establish teaching standards or norms, trained teachers to staff the nation's growing school system throughout the 19th and early 20th centuries.

Occoquan Workhouse was the women's prison where members of the National Woman's Party were imprisoned after picketing the White House.

O'Day, Caroline (1869–1943) was Congresswoman-at-large from New York from 1935 to 1942. She was a social activist and worked with the Democratic Women's Committee of New York.

Our Bodies, Ourselves was written by the Boston Women's Health Collective and published in 1973. A testament to the growing women's health movement, it taught women readers about their bodies, with the aim of empowering them within the fields of health and medicine.

Patriots were American colonists who supported independence.

Paul, Alice (1885–1977) was the founder and leader of the National Woman's Party. She planned and organized militant demonstrations in order to gain the vote, and she spent time in jail for her suffrage activities. Paul authored the original Equal Rights Amendment and remained a staunch advocate for women's rights in the United States and around the world until her death.

Perkins, Frances (1880–1965) was the U.S. Secretary of Labor from 1933 to 1945, and the first woman cabinet member. Her efforts were central to forming New Deal policies.

Pinckney, Eliza Lucas (1722–1793) moved to South Carolina in 1738. She often managed her father's plantations while he was traveling, and she experimented with growing plants such as indigo.

Planned parenthood—see **birth control.**

Pocahontas (c. 1595–1617) was the daughter of Powhatan, who governed a powerful Indian confederacy in eastern Virginia. After the founding of the Jamestown Settlement by the English in 1607, Pocahontas became ever more deeply involved with the newcomers, culminating in her marriage, in 1614, to John Rolfe. She died in 1617 in England from an unknown illness.

Politically correct is a term originally used by antiracist, feminist, and other activists on the Left to refer to making one's behavior and language match one's ideals. It was appropriated by the Right and turned into a pejorative term implying that Left activists were rigid policers of behavior.

Postfeminism refers to a media-induced popular belief that the feminist movement was over, either because it had achieved its goals or because it was a bad thing that people had abandoned. Statistics show that women continued to believe in the need for feminism, and to identify as feminists, even during the height of the so-called postfeminist era of the 1980s and 1990s.

Poststructuralism is an academic cultural theory that holds identity and meaning to be fluid categories rather than essential ones. In feminism, it is used to combat the notion that there is an essential femininity.

The **Pregnancy Discrimination Act** was passed by Congress in 1978, protecting pregnant women from unfair treatment in the workplace.

Prohibition—The Woman's Christian Temperance Union fought for a constitutional amendment to prohibit the distribution and sale of alcohol in the United States. The Eighteenth Amendment was ratified in 1919 (and repealed by the Twenty-first Amendment in 1933).

Protective labor laws offered protections to women and children in the workplace. Women Progressive reformers lobbied successfully for a range of state-level protections for women and children from work-place dangers and exploitation. Protective laws for women were upheld by the Supreme Court's decision in *Muller v. Oregon* in 1908, and remained in place until the late 1960s.

The **Public Works Administration** (PWA) was a New Deal agency that provided jobs for people unemployed as a result of the Great Depression. It had a budget of $3.3 billion, to be spent on public works construction projects.

Puritans were Protestants from England who came to New England in the 17th century. Their religious views followed those of John Calvin, and they were dissatisfied with the Church of England, perceiving it to be incapable of reform. Puritans believed in a gendered hierarchy, and required that wives obey their husbands. As a result, women did not have formal authority in the church or government. Despite the hierarchy, Puritan society valued women's roles in the family as mothers and wives.

The **Quakers,** also known as the Religious Society of Friends, stressed a personal relationship with God, and tended to avoid hierarchy in their church, which gave women some authority in the church and society. Women could speak out at meetings, and played important roles in endorsing a couple's decision to marry. The Quakers who came to the present-day United States settled primarily in Pennsylvania and New Jersey.

Queer, queer theory—Once a pejorative term for homosexuals, "queer" was appropriated by gay and lesbian activists in the 1980s and turned into a positive self-descriptor. The term is based on poststructuralist understanding of sexual identity.

Querelle des femmes was the French term, widely adopted, for the continuous literary debate, which had been going on in Europe since the Renaissance, about the merits and flaws of women, and whether men or women were superior.

Radical Republicans were a group of Republicans in Congress who were opposed to slavery before the Civil War. After the war, they supported harsh penalties for ex-confederates, as well as equal rights for freed slaves.

Rankin, Jeannette (1880–1973) was a woman suffragist and a pacifist who became the first woman elected to the U.S. House of Representatives. She was the only member of Congress to vote against U.S. entry into World War I and World War II.

Reconstruction was the period directly after the Civil War when attempts were made to reconstruct the South and redefine national citizenship. The era was characterized by federal military occupation of the South and the political involvement of freed slaves, as well as by violent opposition to federal power and racial equality by white southerners. The period ended in 1877 with Southern Democrats resuming control over the governments of the former confederate states and the abandonment of the commitment by the Republican Party and the federal government to protect the civil and political rights of African Americans.

Red Scare of 1919—Fearful that the Bolshevik Revolution of 1917 was inspiring a radical workers' movement in the United States, Attorney General A. Mitchell Palmer arrested thousands of immigrants; hundreds of these, including Emma Goldman, were deported to Russia.

Referendum—Progressives campaigning for good government advocated the referendum as a tool to allow voters to adopt reform laws via petition campaigns and direct elections, without having to wait for their legislators to take action.

Republican Motherhood is the term for a concept that arose in the decades after the American Revolution. By emphasizing the desirability of educating mothers so that they might train their children to become quality citizens, this notion provided a powerful rationale for improving women's education. The concept emphasized the importance of women in the development of the early American republic, but it also limited their sphere of engagement.

Riot Grrls was a movement in the early 1990s to refer to all-girl Indie rock bands and their feminist politics. For a few years, the Riot Grrls galvanized activism among young women.

Roe v. Wade was the 1973 Supreme Court case in which the court ruled that a woman's right to an abortion was constitutionally guaranteed on the basis of her right to privacy.

Roosevelt, Eleanor (1884–1962) married Franklin D. Roosevelt in 1905, and was First Lady of the United States from 1933 to 1945. Her experience with social work in New York influenced her efforts to gain government leadership positions for women and support for New Deal legislation that benefited women and children. After World War II, she served as a spokesperson for the United Nations. In 1961, she served as the chair of the President's Commission on the Status of Women, which helped initiate the liberal branch of the women's movement.

Rush, Benjamin (1745–1813) was a physician, polemicist, and educator. One of the signers of the Declaration of Independence, he was an early proponent of education for women.

Sanger, Margaret (1879–1966) was a nurse who became a birth control advocate for poor immigrant women in the 1910s. She founded the American Birth Control League, which became the Planned Parenthood Federation of America in 1942.

The Second Great Awakening was a series of religious revivals that began in the 1790s and were particularly prominent in the Northeast. Revivalist ministers repudiated traditional Calvinist ideas, and exhorted their followers to seek a more personal relationship with a loving and merciful God. Moreover, they emphasized the importance of individual choice and action in determining eternal fate. The collective effect of moral individual choices would mitigate social evils such as poverty, intemperance, prostitution, and slavery, and lead to the perfection of American society.

The Second Wave of Feminism refers to the period of activism on behalf of women's rights and women's liberation that began in the early 1960s and continued through the 1970s.

Segregation was a social system that separated white and black Americans in the activities of daily life. The U.S. Supreme Court, in *Plessy v. Ferguson* (1896), allowed for Jim Crow segregation, based on the premise that forced separation of the races would work because separate facilities could still be equal. Public schools in both the North and South frequently segregated students until the historic *Brown v. Board of Education* decision in 1954.

Seneca Falls, New York was the site of the first women's rights convention held in 1848 and organized primarily by Lucretia Mott, Elizabeth Cady Stanton, Jane Hunt, and Mary Ann McClintock.

Separate Spheres is a descriptive term for a set of ideals originating with the middle class in the early 19th century. Women and men were believed to have distinct and contrasting natures and duties in the world. Women belonged in the private world of the home, whereas men were suited to activities in the public realm.

Settlement houses were pioneered in England in the 1880s and spread to the United States by 1890. Staffed primarily by middle- and upper-class women, settlement houses provided a range of social services for the urban poor, most of them immigrants, including kindergartens, English classes, and assistance with union organizing. The most prominent settlement house in the United

States was the Hull House, founded in Chicago in 1889 by Jane Addams and Ellen Gates Starr.

The **Seven Sisters** are colleges in the Northeast that include Barnard, Bryn Mawr, Mount Holyoke, Radcliffe, Smith, Wellesley, and Vassar Colleges. Founded in the late 19th century, these institutions were devoted exclusively to women's higher education and exerted national influence on women's education.

Sex-positive refers to the belief that a wide array of sex practices can be positive. A sex-positive stance encourages avoiding negative judgments about sex practices that women may find pleasure in, even if they seem to involve replicating sexist power relations.

Shaw, Anna Howard (1847–1919), the first female Methodist Minister, served as the president of the National American Woman Suffrage Association from 1904 to 1915.

Shaw, Anna Moore (1898–1975) was born on the Gila River Pima Reservation and is perhaps best known for her 1968 collection of stories, titled *Pima Indian Legends,* as well as her 1974 autobiography, entitled *A Pima Past.* Because of her efforts to encourage cross-cultural understanding and foster interracial harmony between whites and Native Americans, Shaw was posthumously inducted into the Arizona Hall of Fame.

The **Sheppard-Towner Maternity and Infancy Protection Act** was in effect from 1921 to 1929. Overseen by the Children's Bureau, the first agency of the Federal government managed by women, the act made block grants available to states to educate women about maternal and child health.

Silko, Leslie Marmon (b. 1948) is a novelist and essayist of Laguna Pueblo heritage who is perhaps best known for her novels *Ceremony* (1977) and *Almanac of the Dead* (1991). Her published works also include non-fiction, including articles on Native American issues and literary criticism.

Sisterhood is Powerful was a collection of feminist essays and manifestos edited by activist Robin Morgan and published in 1970.

Social Gospel Movement—During the last decades of the 19th century, Protestant reformers, including Frances Willard, supported reform legislation, such as child labor laws, as part of their mission to bring their Christian values into politics.

Socialism advocates that the means of production should be collectively owned, either by the workers or by the state on behalf of the workers.

Social purity—Women reformers in groups like the Woman's Christian Temperance Union fought for raising the state-level age of consent laws from 9 or 10 years old for girls in some states to 16 to 18 years old. They also fought against white slavery—the market for forced prostitution.

A **speakeasy** was a bar or restaurant that distributed illegal liquor. People were admitted on the basis of a personal introduction or by presenting a card.

Although speakeasies had been around since the 1890s, they became very popular in the 1920s, and were patronized by women as well as men.

Stanton, Elizabeth Cady (1815–1902) fought for a host of reforms to give women equal rights. She helped to organize the first women's rights convention in Seneca Falls, New York, and was the primary author of the Declaration of Sentiments. Stanton was also the president of the American Equal Rights Association, the National Woman Suffrage Association, and the National American Woman Suffrage Association, before her radical views, especially about women and religion, caused friction with the members of that organization. In contrast to reformers who emphasized women's differences from men, Stanton argued that women deserved equal rights because of their essential similarities to men.

Stone, Lucy (1818–1893) was a founder of the American Woman Suffrage Association. She created a sensation by retaining her maiden name after marriage; other women who followed her lead were referred to as "Stoners."

Temperance reform developed in the 1820s in response to a dramatic increase in the production and consumption of alcohol. Women were particularly drawn to temperance reform because of the impact of men's alcohol consumption on the family. Elizabeth Cady Stanton and Susan B. Anthony, who worked together to found the New York State Woman's Temperance Society in 1852, linked temperance reform to a broad program for women's rights, including divorce reform and woman suffrage. After the Civil War, temperance again became a major focus of women's political and reform efforts, spearheaded by the Woman's Christian Temperance Union, founded in 1874. Temperance advocates favored legal prohibition, which became the law of the land with the passage of the Eighteenth Amendment in 1919.

Termination referred to post-WWII federal Indian policies that were designed to hasten the assimilation of Indian peoples into mainstream American society by attacking their land base. Policymakers intended the termination policies to relieve the federal government of further responsibilities for Indian peoples by converting select Indian reservations into state-level municipalities that were subject to state laws. The termination policies proved devastating for targeted Indian groups, and remained on the books until the Nixon administration.

Terrell, Mary Church (1863–1954) was born to former slaves in Memphis, Tennessee. A graduate of Oberlin College, she was the first black woman appointed to the District of Columbia Board of Education (1885–1906). Terrell was an active suffragist and served as the first president of the National Association of Colored Women (1896–1901).

The **Third Wave of Feminism** refers to the period of women's right activism that began in the early 1990s.

The **Thirteenth Amendment** abolished slavery in the United States. It was passed by Congress in January 1865 and ratified by the states in December of that same year.

Thomas, M. Carey (1857–1935), who traveled to Europe to study for a PhD when universities in the United States denied her the privilege, served as Dean and then President of Bryn Mawr College. Thomas, an outspoken advocate for the rights of women, was determined to make her college as academically rigorous as any institutions open to men.

Title VII of the Civil Rights Act of 1964 described discrimination on the grounds of race, color, religion, sex, or national origin to be an "unlawful employment practice." Feminists used Title VII to pressure the government to enforce anti-discrimination laws.

Title IX of the Educational Amendment Act, passed by Congress in 1972, banned sex discrimination in education and prohibited the dispersal of federal funds to educational institutions that discriminated against women in admissions, athletics, or financial aid.

Trail of Tears is the label given to the forced march of Cherokee Indians during the winter of 1838–1839 from their home in the present-day American Southeast to lands west of the Mississippi in present-day Oklahoma. At least one-fourth of these Cherokee migrants perished while en route.

True Womanhood—the 19th-century cult of domesticity—idealized white middle-class women, in particular, as pure, pious, domestic and submissive. Because women were deemed more moral than men, they were responsible for protecting their children and husbands from the corrupting influences of the outside world.

Truth, Sojourner (c. 1797–1883) was a former slave who was active in the abolition movement and the suffrage movement.

Turn-out refers to a strike. In 1834, female textile workers in Lowell, Massachusetts turned out,—went on strike—when employers proposed a wage reduction.

The **United Nations** was founded in 1945 by 58 nations signing of the Charter of United Nations, to mediate conflicts between member nations.

United States v. One Package of Japanese Pessaries was a 1936 federal appeals case that undercut the power of the Comstock Act. The court decided that birth control is not inherently obscene and that doctors have the right to obtain birth control information and devices through the mail and to prescribe contraceptives to protect the health of their patients.

Victim Feminism/Power Feminism—"Victim feminism" is the term used by some to describe what they saw as an excessive focus in feminism on women as victims of male power. Naomi Wolf coined the term "power feminism" to suggest a feminist stance that would not be focused on the victimization of women.

Voluntary Motherhood was the term used by 19th-century women's rights activists to refer to women's right to control their reproduction by refusing sexual relations with their husbands.

WARN (Women of All Red Nations) was founded in the mid-1970s to tackle issues that many Native American activists felt were being ignored by AIM, including, especially, domestic violence and the involuntary sterilization of Indian women. Like AIM, however, WARN also concerned itself with protecting the rights and cultures of Indian peoples more generally.

Warren, Mercy Otis (1728–1814) was an American historian and political thinker, and the author of numerous political poems, pamphlets, and plays.

Willard, Emma Hart (1787–1870) founded the Troy Seminary, which offered a curriculum similar to that of leading male colleges, in New York, in 1821. Willard lobbied the New York state legislature to provide funds for female education, and argued that the health of the state demanded higher quality education for women.

Willard, Frances E. (1839–1898) was a strong suffragist who became a prominent leader of American women through her presidency of the largest women's organization of the 19th century, the Woman's Christian Temperance Union (1879–1898).

The **Winning Plan** was Carrie Chapman Catt's plan, devised in 1916, to campaign for suffrage at both the state and federal levels.

Witch Trials, Salem began in 1692 when several girls and women accused others of witchcraft. One hundred eighty-five people were accused of witchcraft, 59 were tried, 31 were convicted, and 19 were executed. Two-thirds of the accused were women.

Wollstonecraft, Mary (1759–1797) was a British writer and early feminist. She is best known for *A Vindication of the Rights of Woman*, published in 1792. Wollstonecraft argued that women only appeared inferior to men because they lacked education. *Vindication* served as a touchstone for many American women's rights advocates.

Womanism/Woman of Color Feminism—Both terms are meant to make racial inclusion central to feminism. "Womanism" was coined by writer Alice Walker in the 1980s. "Woman of Color Feminism," more recent, is used by some Third Wavers.

Womanpower was the term used to describe the increasing importance of women workers to economic prosperity in the booming consumer economy of the 1950s and 1960s.

The **Woman's Christian Temperance Union** (WCTU) was founded in 1874 and had over 150,000 members by the mid-1890s. President Frances Willard expanded the scope of the group from promoting Christian temperance to supporting woman suffrage and the 8-hour day, among other reforms.

The **Women's Bureau** was established by Congress in 1920 to represent the public policy needs of wage-earning women in the United States.

The **Women's Equity Action League** (WEAL) was formed in 1968 by women who opposed NOW's support of abortion rights and wanted to focus exclusively on legal and economic issues.

The **Women's International League for Peace and Freedom** (WILPF) was organized by Jane Addams and German and Dutch feminists. An outgrowth of the Woman's Peace Party, established in 1915, the group continues to work for permanent world peace, disarmament, and arbitration.

The **Women's Joint Congressional Committee** (WJCC) was founded in November 1920 by representatives of 10 national women's clubs, as an umbrella organization. Its task was to coordinate the legislative agendas of women's groups. By 1930, it had lost much of its public support. Revitalized in the late 1940s, at mid century it played an important role in advocating for legislation that advanced women's interests.

The **Women's Strike for Equality** was a march held on August 6, 1970 in New York City to celebrate the 50th anniversary of the woman suffrage amendment. Fifty thousand women marched in New York, and other marches were held throughout the country.

Woodward, Ellen Sullivan (1887–1971) was Works Progress Administration administrator from 1933 to 1938 and a member of the Social Security Board from 1938 to 1946.

The Young Ladies' Academy of Philadelphia was founded by John Poor in 1780 as one of the earliest and most popular female academies in the United States. One of its most famous trustees was Benjamin Rush.

The **Young Women's Christian Association** (YWCA) was formed in the mid-19th century to serve the interests of working women. By the mid-20th century, the YWCA increasingly focused its mission on promoting racial understanding.

zine/fanzine—a self-published, self-distributed magazine. A fanzine is a zine created by and for fans of a particular artist, text, or genre.

Zitkala-Sa [Gertrude Simmons Bonnin] (1876–1938) was a writer and political activist for the rights of Native Americans. She wrote about Indian Boarding Schools, which, in the name of civilizing Native American children, forced them to abandon their traditions in favor of Euro-American customs and values.

Bibliography

Adams, David Wallace. *Education for Extinction: American Indians and the Boarding School Experience, 1875–1928.* Lawrence: University Press of Kansas, 1995.

Allen, Paula Gunn. *The Sacred Hoop: Recovering the Feminine in American Indian Traditions.* Boston: Beacon Press, 1992.

Andersen, Kristi. *After Suffrage: Women in Partisan and Electoral Politics before the New Deal.* Chicago: University of Chicago Press, 1996.

Anderson, James D. *The Education of Blacks in the South, 1865–1935.* Chapel Hill: University of North Carolina Press, 1988.

Anderson, Karen Tucker. "Last Hired, First Fired: The Black Woman Workers during World War II." *Journal of American History* 69 (June 1982): 82–97.

Babson, Steve. *The Unfinished Struggle: Turning Points in American Labor, 1877–Present.* Lanham, MD: Rowman & Littlefield Publishers, 1999.

Bacon, Margaret Hope. *Mothers of Feminism: The Story of Quaker Women in America.* San Francisco: Harper and Row Publishers, 1986.

Bacon, Margaret Hope. *Valiant Friend: The Life of Lucretia Mott.* New York: Walker and Company, 1980.

Baker, Jean H., ed. *Votes for Women: The Struggle for Suffrage Revisited.* New York: Oxford University Press, 2002.

Bataille, Gretchen M., ed. *Native American Women: A Biographical Dictionary.* New York: Garland, 1993.

Bataille, Gretchen M., and Kathleen Mullen Sands, eds. *American Indian Women: Telling Their Lives.* Lincoln: University of Nebraska Press, 1984.

Baumgardner, Jennifer, and Amy Richards. *Manifesta: Young Women, Feminism, and the Future.* New York: Farrar, Strauss and Giroux, 2000.

Berger, Melody, ed. *We Don't Need Another Wave: Dispatches from the Next Generation of Feminists.* Emeryville, CA: Seal Press, 2006.

Berkin, Carol. *First Generations: Women in Colonial America.* New York: Hill and Wang, 1996.

Berkin, Carol. *Revolutionary Mothers: Women in the Struggle for America's Independence*. New York: Knopf, 2005.

Blair, Karen J. *The Clubwoman as Feminist: True Womanhood Redefined, 1868–1914*. New York: Holmes & Meier Publishers, 1980.

Blee, Kathleen M. *Women of the Klan: Racism and Gender in the 1920s*. Berkeley: University of California Press, 1991.

Bloom, Alexander, and Wini Breines, eds. *"Takin' it to the Streets": A Sixties Reader*. New York: Oxford University Press, 1995.

Bordin, Ruth. *Woman and Temperance: The Quest for Power and Liberty, 1873–1900*. Philadelphia: Temple University Press, 1981.

Boylan, Anne. *The Origins of Women's Activism: New York and Boston, 1797–1840*. Chapel Hill: University of North Carolina Press, 2002.

Branson, Susan. *Those Fiery Frenchified Dames: Women and Political Culture in Early National Philadelphia*. Philadelphia: University of Pennsylvania Press, 2001.

Breines, Wini. *The Trouble Between Us: An Uneasy History of White and Black Women in the Feminist Movement*. New York: Oxford University Press, 2006.

Brodkin, Kim. "'We are neither male nor female Democrats': Gender Difference and Women's Integration within the Democratic Party." *Journal of Women's History*. 19, no. 2 (Summer 2007): 111–37.

Brooks, James. *Captives and Cousins: Slavery, Kinship, and Community in the Southwest Borderlands*. Chapel Hill: University of North Carolina Press, 2002.

Brown, Kathleen M. *Good Wives, Nasty Wenches, and Anxious Patriarchs: Gender, Race, and Power in Colonial Virginia*. Chapel Hill: University of North Carolina, 1996.

Brown, Victoria Bissell. *The Education of Jane Addams*. Philadelphia: University of Pennsylvania Press, 2004.

Buhle, Mary Jo, and Paul Buhle, eds. *The Concise History of Woman Suffrage: Selections from History of Woman Suffrage*. Urbana: University of Illinois Press, 2005.

Calloway, Colin G. *First Peoples: A Documentary Survey of American Indian History*. Boston: Bedford/St. Martin's, 2004.

Campbell, Maria. *Halfbreed*. Toronto, Canada: McClelland and Stewart, 1973.

Canfield, Gae Whitney. *Sarah Winnemucca of the Northern Paiutes*. Norman: University of Oklahoma Press, 1983.

Cash, Floris Barnett. *African American Women and Social Action: The Clubwomen and Volunteerism from Jim Crow to the New Deal, 1896–1936*. Westport, CT: Greenwood Press, 2001.

Clark, Emily. *Masterless Mistresses: The New Orleans Ursulines and the Development of a New World Society, 1727–1834*. Williamsburg, VA: The Omohundro Institute for Early American History and Culture, 2007.

Clarke, Edward H. *Sex in Education; Or, A Fair Chance for the Girls*. 1873. Reprint, New York: Arno Press, 1972.

Cleary, Patricia. *Elizabeth Murray: A Woman's Pursuit of Independence in Eighteenth-Century America*. Amherst: University of Massachusetts Press, 2000.

Cobble, Dorothy Sue. *The Other Women's Movement: Workplace Justice and Social Rights in Modern America*. Princeton, NJ: Princeton University Press, 2004.

Cohen, Lizabeth. *A Consumers' Republic: The Politics of Mass Consumption in Postwar America*. New York: Alfred A. Knopf, 2003.

Cott, Nancy F. *The Bonds of Womanhood: "Woman's Sphere" in New England. 1780–1835*. New Haven, CT: Yale University Press, 1977.

Cott, Nancy F. *The Grounding of Modern Feminism*. New Haven, CT: Yale University Press, 1987.

Cott, Nancy F, ed. *No Small Courage: A History of Women in the United States*. New York: Oxford University Press, 2000.

Davies, Kate. *Catharine Macaulay and Mercy Otis Warren: The Revolutionary Atlantic and the Politics of Gender*. Oxford: Oxford University Press, 2005.

Dayton, Cornelia Hughes. *Women before the Bar: Gender, Law, and Society in Connecticut, 1639–1789*. Chapel Hill: University of North Carolina Press, 1995.

Deslippe, Dennis A. *"Rights Not Roses": Unions and the Rise of Working-Class Feminism, 1945–1980*. Urbana: University of Illinois Press, 2000.

Devens, Carol. *Countering Colonization: Native Women and Great Lakes Missions, 1630–1900*. Berkeley: University of California Press, 1992.

Diamante, Lincoln D., *Revolutionary Women in the War for American Independence: A One-volume Revised Edition of Elizabeth Ellet's 1848 Landmark Series*. Westport, CT: Praeger, 1998.

Dixon, Chris. *Perfecting the Family: Antislavery Marriages in Nineteenth-Century America*. Amherst: University of Massachusetts Press, 1997.

Douglas, Ann. *Terrible Honesty: Mongrel Manhattan in the 1920s*. New York: Noonday Press, Farrar, Straus and Giroux, 1995.

DuBois, Ellen Carol, ed. *Elizabeth Cady Stanton, Susan B. Anthony: Correspondence, Writings, Speeches*. Rev. ed. Boston: Northeastern University Press, 1992.

DuBois, Ellen Carol. *Woman Suffrage and Women's Rights*. New York: New York University Press, 1998.

Dumenil, Lynn. *Modern Temper: American Culture and Society in the 1920s*. New York: Hill and Wang, 1995.

Echols, Alice. *Daring to Be Bad: Radical Feminism in America, 1967–1975*. Minneapolis: University of Minnesota, 1989.

Edwards, G. Thomas. *Sowing Good Seeds: The Northwest Suffrage Campaigns of Susan B. Anthony*. Portland: Oregon Historical Society Press, 1990.

Erdrich, Louise. *Love Medicine: A Novel.* New York: Holt, Rinehart and Winston, 1984.

Evans, Sara. "Beyond Declension: Feminist Radicalism in the 1970s and 1980s." In *The World the 60s Made: Politics and Culture in Recent America,* ed. Van Gosse and Richard Moser, 52–66. Philadelphia: Temple University Press, 2003.

Evans, Sara M. *Born for Liberty: A History of Women in America.* New York: Free Press Paperbacks, 1997.

Evans, Sara. *Personal Politics: The Roots of Women's Liberation in the Civil Rights Movement and the New Left.* New York: Vintage Books, 1979.

Faludi, Susan. *Backlash: The Undeclared War against American Women.* New York: Doubleday, 1991.

Farnham, Christie Ann. *Education of the Southern Bell: Higher Education and Student Socialization in the Antebellum South.* New York: New York University Press, 1995.

Fass, Paula S. *The Damned and the Beautiful: American Youth in the 1920s.* New York: Oxford University Press, 1977.

Findlen, Barbara, ed. *Listen Up: Voices from the Next Feminist Generation.* 2nd ed. Seattle: Seal Press, 2001.

Fixmer, Natalie, and Julia T. Wood. "The Personal is *Still* Political: Embodied Politics in Third Wave Feminism." *Women's Studies in Communication* 28, no. 2 (2005): 235–57.

Ford, Linda G. *Iron Jawed Angles: The Suffrage Militancy of the National Woman's Party 1912–1920.* Lanham, MD: University Press of America, 1991.

Friedan, Betty. *The Feminine Mystique.* New York: Norton, 1963.

Garceau-Hagen, Dee, ed. *Portraits of Women in the American West.* New York: Routledge, 2005.

Gerhard, Jane. *Desiring Revolution: Second Wave Feminism and the Rewriting of American Sexual Thought, 1920 to 1982.* New York: Columbia University Press, 2001.

Gilley, Jennifer. "Writings of the Third Wave: Young Feminists in Conversation." *Reference & User Services Quarterly* 44, no. 3 (2005): 187–98.

Gillis, Stacy, Gillian Howie, and Rebecca Munford, eds. *Third Wave Feminism: A Critical Exploration.* New York: Palgrave Macmillan, 2004.

Ginzberg, Lori D. *Untidy Origins: A Story of Woman's Rights in Antebellum New York.* Chapel Hill: University of North Carolina Press, 2005.

Ginzberg, Lori D. *Women and the Work of Benevolence: Morality, Politics, and Class in the Nineteenth-Century United States.* New Haven, CT: Yale University Press, 1990.

Goldberg, Michael L. *An Army of Women: Gender and Politics in Gilded Age Kansas.* Baltimore, MD: Johns Hopkins University Press, 1997.

Goodsell, Willystine. *Pioneers of Women's Education in the United States.* New York: Macmillan, 1931.

Gordon, Ann D., Bettye Collier-Thomas, John H. Bracey, Ariene Voski Avakian, and Joyce Avrech Berkman, eds. *African American Women and the Vote, 1837–1965.* Amherst: University of Massachusetts Press, 1997.

Gordon, Linda. *Woman's Body, Woman's Right: A Social History of Birth Control in America.* New York: Penguin Books, 1974.

Gutiérrez, Ramón A. *When Jesus Came, The Corn Mothers Went Away: Marriage, Sexuality, and Power in New Mexico, 1500–1846.* Palo Alto, CA: Stanford University Press, 1991.

Haley, Margaret A. *Battleground: The Autobiography of Margaret A. Haley.* Ed. Robert L. Reid. Champaign: University of Illinois Press, 1982.

Hansen, Debra Gold. *Strained Sisterhood: Gender and Class in the Boston Female Anti-Slavery Society.* Amherst: University of Massachusetts Press, 1993.

Harrison, Cynthia. *On Account of Sex: Public Policies on Women's Issues, 1945–1970.* Berkeley: University of California Press, 1989.

Hartmann, Susan M. *The Home Front and Beyond: American Women in the 1940s.* Boston: Twayne Publishers, 1982.

Hartmann, Susan M. *From Margin to Mainstream: American Women and Politics Since 1960.* New York: Knopf, 1989.

Harvey, Sheridan. "Marching for the Vote: Remembering the Woman Suffrage Parade of 1913." *Library of Congress Information Bulletin* 57, no. 3 (March 1998), http://www.loc.gov/loc/lcib/9803/suffrage.html.

Henry, Astrid. *Not My Mother's Sister: Generational Conflict and Third-Wave Feminism.* Bloomington: Indiana University Press, 2004.

Hernández, Daisy, and Bushra Rehman, eds. *Colonize This!: Young Women of Color on Today's Feminism.* New York: Seal Press, 2002.

Hewitt, Nancy A. *Women's Activism and Social Change: Rochester, New York, 1822–1872.* Ithaca, NY: Cornell University Press, 1984.

Heyrick, Elizabeth. *Immediate, Not Gradual Abolition; Or, An Inquiry into the Shortest, Safest, and Most Effectual Means of Getting Rid of West Indian Slavery.* London: Hatchard & Son, 1824.

Heywood, Leslie, and Jennifer Drake, eds. *Third Wave Agenda: Being Feminist, Doing Feminism.* Minneapolis: University of Minnesota Press, 1997.

Hoffman, Nancy. *Woman's True Profession: Voices from the History of Teaching.* 2nd ed. Cambridge, MA: Harvard Education Press, 2003.

Hoffman, Ronald, ed. *Women in the Age of the American Revolution.* Charlottesville: University Press of Virginia (published for the United States Capitol Historical Society), 1989.

Hogan, Linda. *Mean Spirit: A Novel.* New York: Atheneum, 1990.

Honey, Maureen. *Creating Rosie the Riveter: Class, Gender, and Propaganda during World War II.* Amherst: University of Massachusetts Press, 1984.

Hooks, Janet M. *Women's Occupations through Seven Decades.* Women's Bureau Bulletin, no. 218. Washington, DC: U.S. Government Printing Office, 1947.

Hopkins, Sarah Winnemucca. *Life among the Paiutes: Their Wrongs and Claims.* Reno: University of Nevada Press, 1994.

Horowitz, Daniel. *Betty Friedan and the Making of the Feminine Mystique: The American Left, the Cold War, and Modern Feminism.* Amherst: University of Massachusetts Press, 1998.

Horowitz, Helen Lefkowitz. *Alma Mater: Design and Experience in the Women's Colleges from their Nineteenth-Century Beginnings to the 1930s.* New York: Alfred A. Knopf, 1984.

Horowitz, Helen Lefkowitz. *The Power and Passion of M. Carey Thomas.* New York: Alfred A. Knopf, 1994.

Hummer, Patricia M. *The Decade of Elusive Promise: Professional Women in the United States, 1920–1930.* Ann Arbor: University of Michigan Research Press, 1979.

Isenberg, Nancy. *Sex and Citizenship in Antebellum America.* Chapel Hill: University of North Carolina Press, 1998.

Jeffrey, Julie Roy. *The Great Silent Army of Abolitionism: Ordinary Women in the Antislavery Movement.* Chapel Hill: University of North Carolina Press, 1998.

Jones, Jacqueline. *Labor of Love, Labor of Sorrow: Black Women, Work, and the Family from Slavery to the Present.* New York: Basic Books, 1985.

Kaestle, Carl F. *Pillars of the Republic: Common Schools and American Society, 1780–1860.* New York: Hill and Wang, 1983.

Kaledin, Eugenia. *Mothers and More: American Women in the 1950s.* Boston: Twayne Publishers, 1984.

Kamen, Paula. *Feminist Fatale: Voices from the Twentysomething Generation Explore the Future of the Women's Movement.* New York: Donald L. Fine, 1991.

Karlsen, Carol F. *The Devil in the Shape of a Woman: Witchcraft in Colonial New England.* New York: W.W. Norton & Company, 1987.

Karp, Marcelle, and Debbie Stoller, eds. *The BUST Guide to the New Girl Order.* New York: Penguin, 1999.

Katz, Jane, ed. *Messengers of the Wind: Native American Women Tell Their Life Stories.* New York: Ballantine Books, 1995.

Kennedy, Elizabeth Lapovsky, and Madeline D. Davis. *Boots of Leather, Slippers of Gold: A History of a Lesbian Community.* New York: Routledge, 1993.

Kerber, Linda K. *Toward an Intellectual History of Women.* Chapel Hill: University of North Carolina Press, 1997.

Kerber, Linda K. *Women of the Republic: Intellect and Ideology in Revolutionary America.* Chapel Hill: University of North Carolina Press, 1980.

Kessler-Harris, Alice. *Out to Work: A History of Wage-Earning Women in the United States*. New York: Oxford University Press, 1982.

Kierner, Cynthia A. *Beyond the Household: Women's Place in the Early South, 1700–1835*. Ithaca, NY: Cornell University Press, 1998.

Klein, Laura F., and Lillian A. Ackerman, eds. *Women and Power in Native North America*. Norman: University of Oklahoma Press, 1995.

Koppes, Clayton R., and Gregory D. Black. "What to Show the World: The Office of War Information and Hollywood, 1942–1945." *The Journal of American History* 64 (June 1977): 87–105.

Labaton, Vivien, and Dawn Lundy Martin, eds. *The Fire this Time: Young Activists and the New Feminism*. New York: Random House, 2004.

Laughlin, Kathleen A. *Women's Work and Public Policy: The Policy Initiatives of the Women's Bureau, U.S. Department of Labor, 1945 to the 1960s*. Boston: Northeastern University Press, 2000.

Lemons, J. Stanley. *The Woman Citizen: Social Feminism in the 1920s*. Charlottesville: University Press of Virginia, 1990.

Lerner, Gerda. *The Grimké Sisters from South Carolina: Pioneers for Women's Rights and Abolition*. New York: Schocken Books, 1967.

Lunardini, Christine A. *From Equal Suffrage to Equal Rights: Alice Paul and the National Woman's Party, 1910–1928*. New York: New York University Press, 1986.

Lutz, Alma. *Crusade for Freedom: Women of the Antislavery Movement*. Boston: Beacon Press, 1968.

Maclean, Nancy. *Freedom is not Enough: The Opening of the American Workplace*. Cambridge, MA: Harvard University Press, 2006.

Mankiller, Wilma, ed. *Every Day is a Good Day: Reflections by Contemporary Indigenous Women*. Golden, CO: Fulcrum Publishing, 2004.

McCluskey, Audrey Thomas, and Elaine M. Smith, eds., *Mary McLeod Bethune: Building a Better World, Essays and Documents*. Bloomington: Indiana University Press, 1999.

McEnaney, Laura. *Civil Defense Begins at Home: Militarization Meets Everyday Life in the 1950s*. Princeton, NJ: Princeton University Press, 2000.

McGerr, Michael. *A Fierce Discontent: The Rise and Fall of the Progressive Movement in America*. New York: Oxford University Press, 2003.

Melder, Keith E. *Beginnings of Sisterhood: The American Woman's Rights Movement, 1800–1850*. New York: Schocken Books, 1977.

Meyerowitz, Joanne, ed. *Not June Cleaver: Women and Gender in Postwar, 1945–1960*. Philadelphia: Temple University Press, 1994.

Mihesuah, Devon Abbott. *Indigenous American Women: Decolonization, Empowerment, Activism*. Lincoln: University of Nebraska Press, 2003.

Milkman, Ruth. *Gender at Work: The Dynamics of Job Segregation by Sex during World War II.* Urbana: University of Illinois Press, 1987.

Milkman, Ruth. "Organizing the Sexual Division of Labor: Historical Perspectives on 'Women's Work' and the American Labor Movement." *Socialist Review* 49 (January–February 1980): 128–33.

Mitchell, Allyson, Lisa Bryn Rundle, and Lara Karaian, eds. *Turbo Chicks: Talking Young Feminisms.* Toronto: Sumach Press, 2001.

Morgan, Robin. *Sisterhood Is Powerful: An Anthology of Writings from the Women's Liberation Movement.* New York: Random House, 1970.

Murray, Judith Sargent. *The Gleaner: A Miscellaneous Production in Three Volumes.* 3 vols. Boston: L. Thomas and E. T. Andrews, 1798.

Murray, Sylvie. *The Progressive Housewife: Community Activism in Suburban Queens, 1945–1965.* Philadelphia: University of Pennsylvania Press, 2003.

Nam, Vickie. *Yell-Oh Girls: Emerging Voices Explore Culture, Identity, and Growing Up Asian American.* New York: Harper Collins, 2001.

Narrett, David. *Inheritance and Family Life in Colonial New York City.* Ithaca: Cornell University Press, 1992.

Nash, Margaret A. *Women's Education in the United States, 1780–1840.* New York: Palgrave Macmillan, 2005.

Neilsen, Kim E. *Un-American Womanhood: Antiradicalism, Antifeminism, and the First Red Scare.* Columbus: Ohio State University Press, 2001.

Nicholson, Linda. *The Second Wave: A Reader in Feminist Theory.* New York: Routledge, 1997.

Norton, Mary Beth. *Founding Mothers and Fathers: Gendered Power and the Forming of American Society.* New York: Vintage Books, 1996.

Norton, Mary Beth. *Liberty's Daughters: The Revolutionary Experience of American Women, 1750–1800.* Boston: Little, Brown, 1980.

Orleck, Annelise. *Common Sense and a Little Fire: Women and Working-Class Politics in the United States, 1900–1965.* Chapel Hill: University of North Carolina Press, 1995.

Painter, Nell Irvin. *Sojourner Truth: A Life, a Symbol.* New York: W. W. Norton & Company, 1996.

Parker, Alison M. *Purifying America: Women, Cultural Reform, and Pro-Censorship Activism, 1873–1933.* Urbana: University of Illinois Press, 1997.

Penney, Sherry H., and James D. Livingston. *A Very Dangerous Woman: Martha Wright and Women's Rights.* Amherst: University of Massachusetts Press, 2004.

Perdue, Theda. *Cherokee Women: Gender and Culture Change, 1700–1835.* Lincoln: University of Nebraska Press, 1998.

Perdue, Theda, ed. *Sifters: Native American Women's Lives.* New York: Oxford University Press, 2001.

Perrett, Geoffrey. *America in the Twenties: A History.* New York: Simon and Schuster, 1982.

Pipher, Mary. *Reviving Ophelia: Saving the Selves of Adolescent Girls.* New York: Grosset/Putnam, 1994.

Reger, Jo, ed. *Different Wavelengths: Studies of the Contemporary Women's Movement.* New York: Routledge, 2005.

Resch, John, and Walter Sargent. *War & Society in the American Revolution: Mobilization and Home Fronts.* DeKalb: Northern Illinois University Press, 2007.

Richter, Daniel K. *Facing East from Indian Country: A Native History of Early America.* Cambridge, MA: Harvard University Press, 2001.

Robinson, Harriet. *Massachusetts in the Woman Suffrage Movement.* Boston: Roberts Brothers, 1881.

Rosen, Ruth. *The World Split Open: How the Women's Movement Changed America.* Rev. ed. New York: Penguin Books, 2006.

Rosenberg, Rosalind. *Beyond Separate Spheres: Intellectual Roots of Modern Feminism.* New Haven, CT: Yale University Press, 1982.

Rosenberg, Rosalind. *Divided Lives: American Women in the Twentieth Century.* New York: Hill and Wang, 1992.

Ruiz, Vicki L. *From Out of the Shadows: Mexican Women in Twentieth-Century America.* New York: Oxford University Press, 1998.

Rymph, Catherine E. *Republican Women: Feminism and Conservatism from Suffrage through the Rise of the New Right.* Chapel Hill: University of North Carolina Press, 2006.

Salem, Dorothy. *To Better Our World: Black Women in Organized Reform, 1890–1920.* Brooklyn, NY: Carlson Publishing, 1990.

Salerno, Beth A. *Sister Societies: Women's Antislavery Organizations in Antebellum America.* DeKalb: Northern Illinois University Press, 2005.

Salmon, Marylynn. *Women and the Law of Property in Early America.* Chapel Hill: University of North Carolina Press, 1986.

Scharf, Lois. *To Work and to Wed: Female Employment, Feminism, and the Great Depression.* Westport, CT: Greenwood, 1980.

Scharf, Lois, and Joan M. Jenson, eds. *Decades of Discontent: The Women's Movement, 1920–1940.* Boston: Northeastern University Press, 1987.

Schechter, Patricia A. *Ida B. Wells-Barnett and American Reform, 1880–1930.* Chapel Hill: University of North Carolina Press, 2001.

Schneider, Dorothy, and Carl J. Schneider. *American Women in the Progressive Era, 1900–1920.* New York: Facts on File, 1993.

Shaw, Anna Moore. *Pima Indian Legends.* Tucson: University of Arizona Press, 1968.

Shaw, Anna Moore. *A Pima Past.* Tucson: University of Arizona Press, 1974.

Shoemaker, Nancy, ed. *Negotiators of Change: Historical Perspectives on Native American Women.* New York: Routledge, 1995.

Silko, Leslie Marmon. *Almanac of the Dead: A Novel.* New York: Simon & Schuster, 1991.

Silko, Leslie Marmon. *Ceremony.* New York: Viking Press, 1977.

Sklar, Kathryn Kish. *Catharine Beecher: A Study in Domesticity.* New Haven, CT: Yale University Press, 1973.

Sklar, Kathryn Kish. *Florence Kelley and the Nation's Work: The Rise of Women's Political Culture, 1830–1900.* New Haven, CT: Yale University Press, 1995.

Solomon, Barbara Miller. *In the Company of Educated Women: A History of Women and Higher Education in America.* New Haven, CT: Yale University Press, 1985.

Springer, Kimberly. *Living for the Revolution: Black Feminist Organizations, 1968–1980.* Durham, NC: Duke University Press, 2005.

Stansell, Christine. *American Moderns: Bohemian New York and the Creation of a New Century.* New York: Owl Books/Henry Holt & Co., 2000.

Stanton, Elizabeth Cady, Susan B. Anthony, Matilda Joslyn Gage, and Ida Husted Harper, eds. *History of Woman Suffrage.* 6 vols. New York: Fowler & Wells, 1881–1922.

Stevens, Doris. *Jailed for Freedom.* New York: Boni & Liveright, 1920.

Stivers, Camilla. *Bureau Men, Settlement Women: Constructing Public Administration in the Progressive Era.* Lawrence: University Press of Kansas, 2000.

Strane, Susan. *A Whole-Souled Woman: Prudence Crandall and the Education of Black Women.* New York: W.W. Norton & Company, 1990.

Straub, Eleanor Ferguson. "United States Government Policy towards Civilian Women during World War II." *Prologue* 4 (Winter 1973): 240–54.

Stuntz, Jean A. *Hers, His, & Theirs: Community Property Law in Spain and Early Texas.* Lubbock: Texas Tech University Press, 2005.

Tax, Meredith. *The Rising of the Women: Feminist Solidarity and Class Conflict, 1880–1917.* 1980. Reprint, Urbana: University of Illinois Press, 2001.

Taylor, Helen. *Scarlett's Women: Gone with the Wind and its Female Fans.* New Brunswick, NJ: Rutgers University Press, 1989.

Terborg-Penn, Rosalyn. *African American Women in the Struggle for the Vote, 1850–1920.* Bloomington: Indiana University Press, 1998.

Terrell, Mary Church. *A Colored Woman in a White World.* 1940. Reprint, Washington, DC: National Association of Colored Women's Clubs, 1968.

Treadwell, Mattie E. *United States Army in World War II, Special Studies: The Women's Army Corps.* Washington DC: U.S. Government Printing Office, 1954.

Tyack, David. *The One Best System: A History of American Urban Education.* Cambridge, MA: Harvard University Press, 1974.

Tyack, David, and Elizabeth Hansot, *Learning Together: A History of Coeducation in American Public Schools*. New York: Russell Sage Foundation, 1992.

Ulrich, Laurel Thatcher. *Good Wives: Image and Reality in the Lives of Women in Northern New England, 1650–1750*. New York: Vintage Books, 1980.

Valenti, Jessica. *Full Frontal Feminism: A Young Woman's Guide to Why Feminism Matters*. Emeryville, CA: Seal Press, 2007.

Van Kirk, Sylvia. *Many Tender Ties: Women in Fur-Trade Society, 1670–1870*. Norman: University of Oklahoma Press, 1983.

Van Voris, Jacqueline. *Carrie Chapman Catt*. New York: Feminist Press at the City University of New York: 1987.

Waite, Morrison. "Opinion of the Court 88 U.S. 162 Minor V. Happersett, 1875." *Cornell University Law School Supreme Court Collection*, http://www.law.cornell.edu/supct/html/historics/USSC_CR_0088_0162_ZO.html.

Walker, Rebecca, ed. *To Be Real: Telling the Truth and Changing the Face of Feminism*. New York: Anchor Books, 1995.

Ware, Susan. "American Women in the 1950s: Nonpartisan Politics and Women's Politicalization." In *Women Politics and Change*, ed. Louisa A. Tilly and Patricia Gurin, 281–99. New York: Russell Sage Foundation, 1992.

Ware, Susan. *Beyond Suffrage: Women in the New Deal*. Cambridge: Harvard University Press, 1981.

Weatherford, Doris. *The History of the American Suffragist Movement*. Santa Barbara: ABC-CLIO, 1998.

Weigand, Kate. *Red Feminism: American Communism and the Making of Women's Liberation*. Baltimore: Johns Hopkins University Press, 2001.

Weiss, Jessica. *To Have and To Hold: Marriage, the Baby Boom and Social Change*. Chicago: University of Chicago Press, 2000.

Wellman, Judith. *The Road to Seneca Falls: Elizabeth Cady Stanton and the First Woman's Rights Convention*. Urbana and Chicago: University of Illinois Press, 2004.

Wertheimer, Barbara Mayer. *We Were There: The Story of Working Women in America*. New York: Pantheon Books, 1977.

White, Deborah Gray. *Too Heavy a Load: Black Women in Defense of Themselves, 1894–1994*. New York: W. W. Norton and Company, 1999.

Wilson, Jan Doolittle. *The Women's Joint Congressional Committee and the Politics of Maternalism, 1920–1930*. Champaign: University of Illinois Press, 2007.

Winch, Julie. *Philadelphia's Black Elite: Activism, Accommodation, and the Struggle for Autonomy, 1787–1848*. Philadelphia: Temple University Press, 1988.

Wolf, Naomi. *The Beauty Myth: How Images of Beauty Are Used against Women*. New York: William Morrow, 1991.

Wollstonecraft, Mary. *A Vindication of the Rights of Woman.* Philadelphia, 1792.

Woloch, Nancy. *Women and the American Experience.* New York: McGraw Hill, 2000.

Women Union Leaders Speak. U.S. Women's Bureau Union Conference, April 18–19, 1945. Washington, DC: U.S. Department of Labor, 1945.

Woody, Thomas. *A History of Women's Education in the United States.* 2 vols. New York: Science Press, 1929.

Yee, Shirley J. *Black Women Abolitionists: A Study in Activism, 1828–1860.* Knoxville: University of Tennessee Press, 1992.

Yellin, Emily. *Our Mothers' War: American Women at Home and at the Front during World War II.* New York: Free Press, 2004.

Yellin, Jean Fagan, and John C. Van Horne, eds. *The Abolitionist Sisterhood: Women's Political Culture in Antebellum America.* Ithaca, NY: Cornell University Press, 1994.

Yezierska, Anzia. *Bread Givers.* 1925. New York: Persea Books, 2003.

Young, Alfred. *Masquerade: The Life and Times of Deborah Sampson, Continental Soldier.* New York: Knopf, 2004.

Young, Louise M. *In the Public Interest: The League of Women Voters, 1920–1970.* New York: Greenwood Press, 1989.

Zagarri, Rosemarie. *Revolutionary Backlash: Women and Politics in the Early American Republic.* Philadelphia: University of Pennsylvania Press, 2007.

Zitkala-Sa. "The School Days of an Indian Girl." *Atlantic Monthly* 85, no. 508 (February 1900): 185–94.

Electronic Resources

Web site of *Bitch: Feminist Responses to Pop Culture.* http://www.bitchmagazine.org/.

Web site of *BUST* magazine. http://www.bust.com/index.php.

Feministing Community. http://www.feministing.com/.

Library of Congress, American Memory Web site. "Votes for Women: Selections from the National American Woman Suffrage Collection, 1848–1921." Rare Books and Special Collections Division. http://www.memory.loc.gov/ammem/naw/nawshome.html.

Library of Congress, American Memory Web site. "Women of Protest: Photographs from the Records of the National Woman's Party." http://memory.loc.gov/ammem/collections/suffrage/nwp/.

Third Wave Foundation. http://www.thirdwavefoundation.org/.

Women of the West Museum Online. http://www.museumoftheamericanwest.org/explore/exhibits/suffrage.

Index